Kindra,

What a pleasure it was to connect again.

All the best,

Victor

Praise for *Hack Recruiting*

"Hack Recruiting is an essential read for anyone hiring employees or gig workers today—from employer branding to technology to recruiting processes, it offers fresh thinking based on research and years of experience. Victor Assad is a rare author who understands that strategy and metrics drive successful recruiting in a world of intense competition for talent—many kudos to Assad for *Hack Recruiting."*
--Bill Schiemann, Principal, Metrus Institute, Inc.

"It is a brilliant piece of work. A must-read for those of us in global corporations, or companies of any size really, that seek to act NOW."
—Julia Martensen, Head of HR Strategy
& Innovation at DB Schenker.

"Victor Assad uncovers longstanding empirical research from I/O psychologists on how to best match job candidates to jobs and the best of today's digital technology. He sees a world (that is emerging today) in which AI ontologies (which are identifying information and relationships about today's global and diverse workforces) will make significant improvements for matching candidates to jobs while reducing recruiting cycle times, costs and selection biases. Victor points out that HR now has the digital tools it needs to dramati-cally transform recruiting and the role of the recruiter. During these times of talent shortages, he also encourages CEOs and HR leaders to reach out to America's forgotten workers and provides helpful screening tips. HR can now build strategic talent pools, improve the employee experience, and digitally collect insightful analytics that will open up a new era of understanding on what truly drives employee performance and innovation. Armed with powerful new digital tools, analytics and measures, Victor asserts, and I would agree, HR can strategically drive business success."
—Angela Hood, Founder and CEO of ThisWay Global.

"Must read book if you are a recruiter or talent acquisition head. It goes over best practices and hacks each step of recruiting."
—Sandeep Purwar, Founder/CEO, Bevov

HACK RECRUITING

The Best of Empirical Research, Method and Process, and Digitization

VICTOR ASSAD

Archway Publishing books may be ordered through booksellers or by contacting:

Archway Publishing
1663 Liberty Drive
Bloomington, IN 47403
www.archwaypublishing.com
1 (888) 242-5904

Because of the dynamic nature of the Internet, any web addresses or links contained in this book may have changed since publication and may no longer be valid. The views expressed in this work are solely those of the author and do not necessarily reflect the views of the publisher, and the publisher hereby disclaims any responsibility for them.

Any people depicted in stock imagery provided by Getty Images are models, and such images are being used for illustrative purposes only. Certain stock imagery © Getty Images.

ISBN: 978-1-4808-7670-5 (sc)
ISBN: 978-1-4808-7671-2 (hc)
ISBN: 978-1-4808-7669-9 (e)

Library of Congress Control Number: 2019907122

Print information available on the last page.

Archway Publishing rev. date: 07/17/2019

To Lety, Marc, Karina, Marisa, and all the leaders
and human resources professionals who have the
ambition to match people with purposeful roles

CONTENTS

PREFACE

Recruiters and human resources now have the same tools available to them that have been available for years to marketing leaders: chatbots, machine learning, artificial intelligence, and soon block-chain. HR leaders can transform HR and make it more strategic, more analytical, and an important partner for driving profitable growth in companies. HR leaders can build employer brand just as effectively as marketing leaders build a company's customer brand.

HR and recruiting need to aggressively use these tools and improve our ability to recruit, motivate and retain excellent talent, drive profitable growth, and build more awareness of what makes our best employees the best!

While I have consulted, I am continually amazed by how many executives, human resources leaders, and recruiters didn't understand the excellent and empirically researched methods for recruiting and selecting the best workers. In addition, they didn't recognize that recruiting is one of the most critical, often high-volume processes in their organizations.

It is time to step into the sunshine.

The good news is that industrial/organizational psychologists have been conducting academic studies on the best methods for selecting employees for decades. The bad news is that much of their work seems to be ignored. Why? I think much of it is due to the academic nature of their writing, which many find boring. Industrial/organizational psychologists are academics, after all, and are required to publish peer-reviewed articles that review previous research, use precise language, and have something to add to the field. Empirical research requires the sophisticated use of statistics, which is both intimidating to most readers and a turnoff. Although time-consuming, academic articles provide empirically based truth, transparency, reviews by critical experts, and the opportunity for future researchers to validate today's findings.

Structured interviews significantly improve the reliability of making great hires. Yet many interviews are freewheeling discussions without much preparation.

Validated selection assessment tests based on I/O psychologists' studies improve the reliability of hiring decisions. However, because the tests take time and cost money (although the cost these days has fallen dramatically), they are underused. Another concern is adverse impact, that is, concerns that assessment tests may culturally discriminate against women and people of color. While these are legitimate concerns and certainly of interest to me, many of these studies have been continually tested to look for adverse impacts. Also, with ongoing data collection and analysis, companies and academics can collectively check if adverse impact occurs and make the necessary adjustments to assure companies are indeed selecting the best employees regardless of gender, race, age, national origin, color, religion, disability, or sexual orientation.

I have observed throughout my career that many organizations fail to recognize that recruiting is a repeatable, and in growing and large organizations, a high-volume process, just like software development, medical examinations, and manufacturing. Companies ought to use the best recruiting and selection methods that science has to offer and have well-understood, efficient processes, participants who are trained for their roles in the process, the appropriate mix of contemporary technology and human work, timelines, and measures and metrics to predict success—or to raise alarms when adjustments are urgently needed.

Still, many companies treat recruiting like an administrative burden. It doesn't have to be that way.

Now with the Internet of Things (IoT) and digital technology coming to recruiting we can incorporate great processes with digital technology and truly hack recruiting so it works with digital speed.

Investing in digital technology won't guarantee success, however. Only 16 percent of digitization efforts succeed. That is a dismally low percentage and the cause is often a culture or poorly trained workers who reject the digitization. In order to improve upon it, you first need to thoroughly vet the new technologies that are bursting on the scene like dandelions on a spring prairie to separate the wheat from the chaff. Second, you need to change your processes to smartly integrate digital technology into your work processes and work through the human/robot interface. The lesson here is to allow technology to do what it does best and keep the humans doing what they do best. The new digital processes will require change, retraining, and new rewards for the workers in the process.

The role of the recruiter is also being hacked, and all those involved with recruiting will change as robots do more of the administrative, logical, and redundant work. If companies fail to do this well, they will squander a well-intended investment.

Finally, recruiting is highly dependent on a company's employer brand, culture, and values. The employer brand should align with the company's customer brand, but it is to a different audience: job candidates and current employees.

How a company recruits speaks to how it values its human assets. Job candidates have caught on to this, and they are evaluating how your recruiting process treats them and makes them feel. Many CEOs say that their human resources are their most prized assets. For most, however, it is lip service. They really view their workers as costs to be manipulated.

CEOs who allow their organizations to treat job candidates as an expendable burden in the recruiting process will find it harder and harder to recruit the best employees; they are also the ones, I have learned, with the highest (and most costly) employee turnover.

On the other hand, CEOs who authentically value their human resources, create an employer brand, and put in place the integrated talent strategies to nurture and develop these cultures and their employees will have the upper hand with recruiting.

In today's fast-paced, competitive, continuously changing global economy, CEOs are realizing that in order to be financially successful, they need to continually transform their companies. Today's business environment is made more difficult by the tight talent economy in the United States (where there are more job openings than unemployed).

In this environment, enlightened CEOs will realize that recruiting and whom their managers hire (and develop) are the most critical decisions they will make. These CEOs will invest in recruiting as an essential process.

Recruiting won't be successful if it is treated as an isolated function. The success of recruiting—even among recruiting processes that are highly robust, with the right mix of digitization and human interfaces, well-trained hiring managers, and the best selection assessments—is highly dependent on the company's employer brand and motivation and the dedication of its current employees.

A company's employer brand, rating on Glassdoor, and level of current employees willing to recommend it to their friends as a great place to work will greatly impact your recruiting success. When an interested job candidate checks your company's ratings on Glassdoor and finds it is a 2.5 on a five-point scale, it is game over. If you don't have 33 percent of your hires from employee referrals, you are needlessly burning through your recruiting working capital and throwing money out the door.

In today's tight talent economy, it is essential that companies recruit differently. Companies need to develop strategic talent pools of passive, external job candidates. It is the recruiter's job to develop relationships with them to know when they will be ready to join their companies and with what mix of pay, benefits, and career opportunities to shape a winning job offer.

Recruiting in today's talent economy also means continually searching for new entrants to the labor force, whether they are on university campuses, transitioning out of the military, the formally incarcerated now integrating with the larger society, or immigrants.

Recruiting on university campuses today means recruiting Generation Z, the first truly digital generation, and they expect the latest in digital technology. Like college graduates of other generations, Generation Z wants to work for companies that are dedicated to a higher purpose for humanity and are ethical.

The purpose of this book is to inform readers what works and what doesn't work with recruiting and employment screening based on empirical evidence, how to set up fast-paced, high-volume processes for recruiting, how to create an employer brand and employee value proposition, and how emerging digital technology will hack recruiting, allowing you to gain the upper hand.

After reading *Hack Recruiting*, CEOs and human resources and recruiting leaders will be able to significantly improve their ability to recruit great employees and the speed and quality of their hiring, have better analytics on where to find job candidates and how long it takes to hire them with better diversity, and will possess more information on what competencies make their best employees the best.

Step into the sunshine and start hacking your recruiting.

CHAPTER 1: YOU WON'T RECOGNIZE RECRUITING IN THE 2020S

There was a lot of anxiety in the room in the Fall of 2006 when I wrote on the whiteboard "150 in 90."

I told my recruiting staff that, while they had done a great job, we needed to double our hiring rate of very specialized clinical researchers, engineers, and regulatory affairs professionals to one hundred and fifty in ninety days. Making this task more difficult was our location for Medtronic Vascular's business. It was in the city of Santa Rosa, California, sixty miles north of San Francisco, better known for incredible redwood trees, natural beauty, wineries, organic vegetables, tourism, and pot smoking than as a mecca for making a career in the medical device industry.

Now that I had caught their attention, I told my recruiting team that every Monday morning, the executive team of the business wanted an update on recruiting. This would be the next topic considered after their review of quality and reliability issues reported by the doctors who implanted our products and after the technical reviews from our innovation teams. In this weekly report, they wanted to know how many résumés we had for each job posting, the number being interviewed, the percentage of offers accepted, and when the new hires would start.

Progress with innovation and recruiting was what stood between the business's poor market and financial performance and being number one in the marketplace. The goal was to offer the best coronary drug-eluting and bare metal stents on the market, along with the ancillary products to support them.

"This is why we love recruiting," I told them. "You are part and parcel of the success or failure of the business. This is a revenue-generating business, a make-it-or-break–it, fast-growing business based on innovation. The business needs great workers now and lots of them. There is nowhere to hide, and the success of the business is on the line.

"Now," I asked, "what do you need to achieve this?"

They were an exceptional recruiting staff. They were hunters. Great recruiters are like sales reps. They are hunters and love competition. They love to win. I love to win. In recruiting you get a win with a job offer acceptance and a loss when a great job candidate goes to the competition. They were not like my staff of human resources business partners assigned to one or more of our functions. The human resources people were also a great staff; they knew the labor law and could resolve disputes, give career advice, build up people's confidence, develop leaders and teams, and help build great cultures. The business partners were more like farmers: they grew great talent and great organizations. The recruiters hunted them down and lured them in.

The recruiters were dedicated to the mission of the company: to alleviate pain, restore health, and prolong life. They believed in our current products, our executive leaders, and the men and women they hired to do the work of developing the next generation of drug-eluting stents to open arteries and either stop or prevent heart attacks. Some of them had family members who had coronary stents in their hearts. Based on internal seminars, they knew that new drug-eluting stents with better polymers and drugs could reduce the swelling of scar tissue in the interior heart vessel wall and improve the patient's chances of recovery.

The recruiters had sensible answers to my question "What do you need?" More ads on job boards, participation at more career fairs, the latest recruiting technology (which then was from LinkedIn), an increase to the employee referral bonus amount, a rise in our below-market pay in the San Francisco Bay Area, and more postings on specialty boards to avoid the hundreds of unqualified résumés Monster sent them—and to be relieved from some of the "bullshit." Bullshit was how they referred to the administrative duties that went with clunky Applicant Tracking Systems (ATS) that then were a necessary evil and the too many pointless meetings that too often were part of the trappings of corporate life. They also complained about how the ATS often required them to wait for what seemed like minutes on end showing a whirling circle symbol while the system updated their entry, or worse, lost their entry before it was recorded, requiring that it be reentered.

No one said we couldn't do it.

I worked to get them their "want list" and more.

Organizations that outsource their recruiting function have no opportunity to rise to the business challenge. They are dependent on several headhunters to find them the talent they need. Headhunters have conflicting priorities with many clients, they don't know your business strategies, and they are expensive. In today's rapidly digitizing business world, the success large recruiting firms have in searches with their large number of contacts can no longer compete with artificial intelligence's ability to find and screen candidates using the internet.

Today, if I scribbled "150 in 90" on an electronic whiteboard in a virtual meeting for recruiters spread across the country, I would receive a different want list—in part. Getting out of the wasteful meetings would still be on the list. The flourish of digital technologies means being inundated with more requests from emails, texts, chatbots (sometimes called "bots")—taking you away from your job.

In addition to posting jobs on Indeed, CareerBuilder, BioSpace, and LinkedIn, they would want to use artificial intelligence for recruiting, bots to contact entry-level and college-level candidates and determine their interest and availability, automated scheduling technology, and social media posts. They would want someone dedicated to monitoring the employer brand on social media and with the reviews being made on Glassdoor. They would still want to post ads, but on digital job boards and social media, not newspapers.

They would still want to use the learning of industrial/organizational psychologists to understand which selection methods are the best. This long-standing science shows us that a mix of cognitive assessments, structured interviews based on job family competencies, personality tests, and work sampling provide the best methods of selecting new hires who will perform well on the job. They would want to do the best they could to eliminate the biases of past or current selection processes to create a fairer world. They would still want to use career fairs in addition to digital recruiting platforms. Some tactics never seem to grow old.

The world of recruiting is currently going through a rapid transformation. Some of it will be borne out to be significant steps forward. Other new methods will prove to be false starts or poor impersonations of social science. The wise HR and recruiting leader will always want to validate any selection process used with the knowledge, skills, and competencies of their best workers. The best of the wisest leaders will always be looking at how to integrate new technologies and focus on what digital technology does best and what human recruiters and hiring managers do best. In a competitive talent market, smart recruiting organizations will need to have a great talent brand and will have to build relationships with job candidates and offer them something their current employers do not make available. In order to make improvements continually, the wisest leaders will need to stay on top of the latest technical, socioeconomic, and legal news and developments and be discerning.

Recruiting Is Being Disrupted

The $200 billion recruiting industry is changing all the time, with mergers, acquisitions, and new digital technology start-ups every month. In the hot US economy, recruiting once again is getting the attraction of CEOs, who are putting demands on their HR leaders to improve recruiting speed and the quality of hires. Employees are looking to jump ship for better opportunities. Gallup has found that 51 percent of employees are searching or keeping their eyes open for a new job.[1]

The US Bureau of Labor Statistics shows that 20 to 24 percent of Americans change jobs every year. That is 41 million Americans who are searching for jobs annually. Bersin by Deloitte estimates that the average employer spends four thousand dollars to fill an open position, which is nearly three times the amount spent on training per employee.[2] (Which raises the question, if you spent more on training, would your turnover go down, your productivity go up, and your costs go down? The answer is yes.)

Despite the increased hype about spending on professional networks, most research shows that job boards, company websites, and referrals drive more hires than other sources. The research found that in 2015, 10 percent of open positions were filled using professional networking sites—the same percentage as in 2011.[3] Traffic for mobile apps on smartphones overtook social media sites for volume in 2015. Apps for recruiting are now where it is at over the internet. Most people after experimenting with social media settle in on two or three social media sites they like, and they are picked for their personal preferences. LinkedIn, Facebook, and Instagram are the most popular.

In September 2018, the United States achieved a record low in unemployment, 3.7 percent, which was the lowest unemployment rate since 1969.[4] It also set another record. In June 2018, there were 6.7 million job openings in the United States, another record, while only 6.3 million Americans were looking for jobs.[5] There are now more job openings in the United States than unemployed. Year over year wages rose in September 2018 at 2.8 percent, which was an increase but was still low by economists' estimates for full employment.[6] Expect wages to increase, women and people of color to be tougher pay negotiators to assure they are getting a fair deal, and more employee demand for transparency.

It is time to switch from recruiting as usual strategies to full employment recruiting strategies. Posting your jobs on your career sites and job boards won't cut it. Recruiting now is about being first to those new to the workforce and offering those who are employed something better. This takes quickly finding candidates using artificial intelligence—not just posting and praying—building relationships with the qualified candidates you find, and acting with speed. It is time to incorporate the best of the new technologies to enable your company to rapidly find and recruit the new entrants to the workforce: college graduates, veterans, the formerly incarcerated, immigrants who can work legally in the United States, and the skilled passive candidates your company needs.

Now is the time to use the best employer branding your firm has to offer and the latest processes and technology for recruiting. While technology in 2018 gets most of the attention, your employer brand and the employee value proposition you offer job applicants and your employees are also vital.

Why? Because three-quarters of job applicants look up how current employees rate your company online before deciding to apply for your openings. You may dismiss what is written on Great Place To Work, Indeed, or Glassdoor about your company as the complaints of malcontents, but those reading what is written on these sites are taking it as the gospel truth, especially if your overall ratings are below 3.5.

The higher purpose for your business is its authentic values (not what you have hanging on a conference room wall), the ethics and empowering nature of your leaders, the collaboration of team members, and the transparency, innovation, and speed of your work culture. Not many employees today want to work for autocratic firms that lay off the bottom 10 percent every year like GE under Jack Welch.

There is an important intersection between a company's brand and ethics with its customers and the public at large and its employer brand. They both impact each other. If the company brand suffers due to a scandal (consider Wells Fargo, Facebook, and Uber), it will take a loss to its stock price, revenue, and profits. It will also take a hit on its ability to recruit and retain great employees.

The reverse is also true. If a company's recruiting process is so onerous and dysfunctional, with little to no feedback during the process, job applicants can become so enraged that they will take their anger out on social media against the company, or worse yet, stop making purchases from that company as a consumer and switch to a competitor.

If you believe a free breakfast, a barista bar, and free lunch a couple of times a week will distinguish you from your workforce competitors, think again. That is so 2010. As millennials age, they are now more interested in better pay, health care, retirement benefits, paid time off for paternity leave as well as vacations, and career advancement. They are tired of paying off huge debts and being broke.

Gen Z will judge you on the digital technology you use. Baby boomers, and frankly all workers, are more interested than ever about work-life balance and flexible work arrangements.

All workers want flexible work arrangements (especially couples who both work) to help eliminate long commutes and allow them to work through the stresses of their work and life integration. Technology enables it for many jobs and improves productivity, morale, and retention and lowers costs. It is not as big a deterrent to innovation and teamwork as some believe. (Many crowded, open office bays with their incessant distractions are a worse detriment to productivity and innovation.) It is time executives lose their twentieth-century attitudes about everyone being in the office.

You can't improve your recruiting and be successful in the long run if you don't also address the issues you may have with your culture that hurt your organization's employee retention. There are few secrets these days about company culture. Chances are, whatever secrets you fear being public about your business are on the internet now.

Rapid Change of Technology Will Disrupt Recruiting

Today's reliance on social media searches and job boards, even job boards such as CareerBuilder and Indeed, will change significantly due to artificial intelligence (AI), bots, blockchain, facial recognition software, video interviewing, and other transformative technologies—or the current dominant players in recruiting such as the big job boards and LinkedIn will buy up AI start-ups or invest heavily in AI to stay even with the changes. Artificial intelligence platforms will replace recruiters poking around social media and LinkedIn using slow and error-prone Boolean searches.

Clunky applicant tracking systems will still be in use for large companies to gather analytics and to complete affirmative action plans for government contractors, but ATS systems that can smartly incorporate machine learning and AI (not normal software programming disguised as AI) will enable recruiters to more easily find the talent already in their systems. ATS will integrate more text chats and machine learning to improve the communications with job applicants, keeping them engaged, and to do more of the administrative tasks. They will also generate dashboards to give updates on recruiting progress, with measures such as average days to fill and applicants per job.

As you will learn, job candidates are increasingly dropping out of the recruiting process for many companies because of the awful experiences they are having with career centers and applicant tracking systems that function poorly. Job candidates are frustrated with the lack of follow-up from the company about its interest and the status of their applications and a poor experience while interviewing. This experience can be long waits in the lobby for the hiring manager, poorly prepared interviewers, and dysfunctional company hiring processes.

The data collected by Talent Board on the candidate experience shows that more than one-third of all job seekers spend two or more hours researching a single job.[7] It often then takes them an hour to complete the job application, and more than half of the candidates who participated in the survey rated the search process as poor or mediocre. Applicant tracking systems and mediocre recruiting processes are creating a lot of pain, effort, and complexity for job seekers everywhere.

This is a critical issue. I am recommending that recruiting departments establish a relatively new metric to measure the job candidate's experience, the job candidate net promoter score. The model for it is the customer experience metric that is used in retail from hotels to Lyft to restaurants, where customers are quickly asked to rate and provide their feedback. This may be a bit overdone these days. I know I feel like I am pushed and prodded by my smartphone to complete a customer assessment, and I have grown tired of it. But it would be a new and powerful request for feedback by a company regarding its recruiting practices.

More importantly, it becomes a tool HR can use to benchmark their recruiting processes, technology, and interviewers and begin to make improvements.

Currently, only 27 percent of the two hundred companies contacted by Talent Board survey the candidate's experience, and those candidates surveyed are only the ones hired. Only 14 percent ask for candidate feedback before a hiring decision is made.[8]

This is horrible performance, and the companies that want to win the digital war for talent will start by correcting this deficiency. How you treat job candidates during the recruiting process says volumes to them on what it is like to work for you as an employee.

As a recruiter, wouldn't you like to receive 100 percent accurate and verifiable résumés and conduct instant background checks? That technology is here and is being developed for HR. It is called blockchain.

Blockchain will begin in 2019 or 2020 to disrupt human resources in the areas of recruiting, performance histories, employee background checks, I-9 verifications, and even payroll. Some technologists are predicting that it will replace the need for résumés as we think of them today and background checks. The careers of employees at other companies and their academic histories, graduation dates, degrees, and GPA may be pulled up from blockchain transactions.

To win support from executive management and the chief financial officer for investments in recruiting digitization, HR and IT executives will need to make a business case with an impressive return on investment. The proposal will need to show how increased speed, less bureaucracy and dependence on expensive third-party searches, more efficiency, the elimination of redundant employees and IT servers, and better branding will save the company money and enable the company to hire the people needed to enable financial growth. The proposal must pass whatever investment hurdle the company set to justify an investment. The promoting of great features, trends, and the marketing hype of vendors probably will not be your best selling points.

In chapter 4, I discuss a case study on the business case for investing in recruiting. Start working your plan and spreadsheets and partner closely with finance and IT. Start hacking!

A New Set of Metrics Is Needed about the Job Candidate Experience

In full employment, recruiting organizations need to put in place a new set of metrics. Time to fill openings, best résumé sources, cost per hire, one-year retention rate, and the like are no longer enough.

What is needed is a new set of metrics on the candidate experience, the **net promoter score** (NPS) for job candidates. It is an index from negative 100 to 100 that measures the satisfaction of job candidates with your recruiting process and its communications and their willingness to recommend the company's jobs to others.

NPS has submetrics, which can include the following:

- Were candidate applications acknowledged with a text or email within twenty-four hours?
- Were candidates told of the decision throughout the recruiting process, such as the recruiter's decision to move the candidate's application forward? Supervisor's decision?
- Moreover, if the candidate was rejected, did the ATS recommend other open jobs that were a good match for the candidate?

Your applicant tracking system should calculate your NPS by job family and overall. Does your ATS track these communications and convert them to measures and dashboards that also show you how many of the applicants who go to your career site complete an application and stay engaged with the process?

Many companies, such as Virgin Hotels and The Gap, have

realized that many of their job candidates are customers. If their recruiting process is so disjointed, difficult to complete, and time consuming and treats job candidates like they are doing you a favor, this disaffected job candidate will quit on your hiring process or spread bad news about you to their friends and family members and online.

If they are customers, they will select your competition next time around.

Recruiting and HR Will Have New Roles and New Partners: Artificial Intelligence and, Soon, Blockchain.

The role of recruiters will change due to AI from hunting for talent on job boards, social media, and LinkedIn to building relationships with future employees and building a strategic talent pipeline that will enable the best employer brands to fill job openings in a day. In addition, AI can now tell HR how many competing open requisitions there are in a location and the average rate of pay.

With these new data, the role of the recruiter and HR will elevate. It will go from being a job requisition order-taker to being a strategic partner on future workforce needs. HR will also have better information from AI on the leadership practices and culture your organization will need to recruit and retain the workforce going forward. HR will be able to tell the executive team, backed up by data, what are the best sources of various key talent positions, how long it takes to find and attract them, and what it will cost. HR will be able to be a more predictable and reliable source of talent and a better partner at motivating and retaining your current talent and selecting who among your employees will perform best in future leadership roles.

Due to the assistance of AI, the role of recruiters will change. It will no longer be difficult to identify the passive candidates. Excellent AI platforms can do it in seconds and screen them. The smart executives at job boards are integrating AI to find this talent and screen them. The role of the recruiter will be to contact the best of these passive candidates (using effective strategies to get their interest and a return call or text), build a relationship with them, and find out what it will take for the passive candidate to leave an already good job to join a new company during an era of full employment. Will it be more pay? Higher title? Better health care or retirement? Being allowed to work at home three days a week? Career opportunities, or more paid time off? The answer will depend on the job candidate.

The recruiter will also want to know the timing of a future move if the candidate is not ready to move now. Building a strategic talent pool with the support of AI in finding the candidates, the recruiter will need to build a relationship and follow up. The human touch will still be required for recruiting highly valued talent.

HR will need technologists and data analysts as much if not more than marketing business strategy and R&D departments to analyze and identify the talent the company needs to profitably grow. Data in HR will be used in a meaningful way, like in the movie *Moneyball,* where economist Jonah Hill tells Oakland As' GM Billy Beane that the team management can build a competitive team by using new analytics to replace traditional and intuitive scouting and hire undervalued players whose value is not understood by scouts.

Technologists working with recruiters and hiring managers will also need to maximize the process layout for recruiting and make sure that the ATS is aligned to the process and that the technology is optimized to generate text or email updates to candidates at every step in the process. The technologists will also need to maximize the transfer of data between ATS and payroll and HRIS systems to eliminate errors and human administration and intervention.

Technology is rapidly changing recruiting and HR, and that change will accelerate. HR and recruiting leaders need to stay ahead of the power curve and get used to technology doing a heavy part of traditional HR duties. The integration of digital technology and human workflows and maximizing this disruptive innovation will be the order of the day. Understanding the business model, relationship building, listening, strategic problem-solving, and providing solutions with an excellent ROI won't be achievable without understanding digital technology.

What Hasn't Changed about Recruiting

What hasn't changed with recruiting is the long-standing empirical evidence from industrial/organizational psychology on which selection procedures are the most valid and reliable for hiring great workers who will perform well on the job and get along with their teammates. The best methods are general mental aptitude tests, structured interviews, peer reviews, work sampling, and job knowledge and skill tests.

Humans have many attributes and varying levels of knowledge, skills, and abilities. Many executives I have worked with believe it is IQ that is most important for leadership. While the ability to rapidly learn information, often the written word, understand the principles of abstract thinking and mathematics, and have excellent recall and recognition is important, many extraordinarily intelligent people cannot do many roles and fail. Why? They often don't have emotional intelligence, which is the ability to understand your own and others' feelings, discern among them, and put them to use for a good purpose. Others fail because they cannot articulate a vision and draw people to it. Others fail because they are narcissistic or suffer from untreated mental illness.

Moving away from the roles of leaders, some of us are excellent at biology or chemistry but not physics or can't understand the complexity of *Hamlet* or the abstract expressions of poets.

On every job it is important to objectively understand (from data and analysis) what attributes when performed well (and that become a competency) are essential for success among your best employees in their roles. It is then important to understand how you can best objectively and accurately assess these same attributes in others who are in your pool of job candidates. Is it an assessment test on skills or personality or intelligence? Is it detailed questioning through structured interviews of the knowledge, skills, and ability to overcome adversity in previous roles? Is it job sampling? Or for unskilled roles, is it integrity and conscientiousness, which we can measure very well with validated online tests?

It is better to use a combination of these methods in an integrated way to see who truly shines among your job candidates. When used together, each selection method becomes more valuable. For example, if an assessment test on sales personality identifies that a sales representative candidate struggles with rejection and will not have the important sales attribute of resiliency, the interviewers can be more focused to follow up on resiliency in the structured interview.

However, many organizations do not use these procedures when recruiting. Almost all companies interview job candidates, but the interview isn't planned and does not have a well-thought-out list of questions and "best answers" that would indicate success on the job. Moreover, most interviewers do not know how to dig deep into a job candidate's answer to understand what they did on the job, what worked and what didn't work, and how they achieved or did not achieve success. With the number of job candidates stretching the truth on résumés and during interviews, it is only prepared and thorough interview teams, with assessments, who will figure out fact from fluff, who is the best skill fit and culture fit for their jobs, and which candidate has a track record of building relationships and overcoming obstacles to achieve success.

I have been in organizations where executives told me they could decide in five minutes if a job candidate would be a good hire or not. Sorry, but that is bullshit. That impression is usually a first impression bias, which may be based on the two hitting it off well, good looks, graduating from the same MBA program, or sadly discriminatory factors. The rest of the interview is then spent by the hiring manager looking for evidence to justify his or her intuitive first impression rather than probing work history and indicators of achievement and determination. When you hire with biased first impressions, you might as well make your hiring decision by flipping a coin and save everyone a lot of time and money.

What also hasn't changed is that recruiting is a business process, especially large volume recruiting. Just like any business process, its steps should be well thought out and articulated, have clear roles and handoffs from step to step, and have measures to judge its efficiency and success—and to alert business leaders when there is trouble ahead. The process participants should be trained for their roles and provided feedback on their performance.

Most importantly in an era of full employment, the element of speed and keeping the job applicant interested and enthused throughout the process is the key to success. The days of job applicants getting a call weeks after completing an application online are over. They should get a text or email, and for executives a call, within twenty-four hours. The shoe is now on the other foot, and you'd better adjust or you will be left in your competitors' dust.

While new exciting technology exists to improve a company's ability to identify and reach out to new passive job candidates—who already have great jobs—and to significantly improve the job candidate's experience in the recruiting process, for most positions the successful company is the one with the recruiters and hiring managers who build a great relationship with the job candidates. Even the ones who get rejected for the role. Those rejected job candidates who meet the job criteria but lost out on a close call are the first people you want to call when your next opening occurs. If you treated them with respect and dignity and have come to understand what they want for their next move and careers, they will answer your call.

The enlightened CEO needs to understand and embrace how technology and a keen understanding of the empirical evidence of industrial and personal psychology and economics will empower this new knowledge. My advice to CEOs about HR and recruiting is straightforward. CEOs have a business model; they have a brand and value proposition to take to investors and customers. They have reliable products and services that satisfy a market need. They have operations and technology that support their products and services, and they have measures in place to assess if they will meet their commitments and profitably grow the firm.

Their talent and recruiting strategies are no different. Talent strategies (or people strategies if you are in high tech in Silicon

Valley) also need an *employer* brand and *employee* value proposition. They will need an *authentic* purpose and values to share with employees, ones that are aligned to their business brand and will serve as a lasting foundation for their organizational culture and to resolve a higher-level purpose for humanity. Executives will need to provide support for and get directly involved with a reliable recruiting process that attracts, recruits, and onboards the best talent they can find. They will need the empirically proven digital technologies that are now emerging in recruiting to improve the efficiencies of their recruiting process and help them find and recruit the best talent they can find and help them decide who to hire. Finally, they will need a process that is measured all along the way—and will provide them improvement suggestions and warnings when they will not meet hiring goals and will continually assess the performance and turnover of their new hires. If they cannot achieve their hiring goals, they cannot meet their commitments to their investors and customers and grow the business profitably.

The enlightened CEO will realize that the technology I am writing about is currently being used in the CEO's strategy, business development, marketing and sales, and supply chain departments. It is past time to apply it to HR and recruiting.

The enlightened chief human resources officer will need to make friends with technology. Now, sadly, that is not the case. According to LinkedIn's Global Recruiting Trends for 2018[9], 56 percent of companies in their survey rate as very important the use of new interviewing tools, 50 percent rate the use of data as very important, and 35 percent rate the use of artificial intelligence as very important. However, only 8 percent of companies in the survey currently use AI, and only 18 percent now use data and new interviewing tools in their recruiting processes.

These are alarming statistics and may serve to confirm a stereotype that HR leaders are not only not tech savvy, but they don't want to be tech savvy. For these HR leaders, the tables of recruiting are being overturned. What chair are you sitting in, and what chair do you want to be sitting in when the dust settles? To sit in a leadership chair, you will need to be tech savvy and good at selecting and incorporating new technology. However, that won't be enough. You will also need to know how to align processes, job tasks, skills,and the rewards for your recruiters to the new technology so you can drive the best efficiencies and the highest value from the technology-human interface.

Also, that will not be enough. Because the enlightened HR leader also knows the HR leaders of today—forget the future—need to have great business acumen. They need to understand the company's business model and how it makes a buck. They need to understand not only the skills the company will need in the future but how to best integrate their workers with the processes, digital technologies, and organization structures the company needs to be effective. They also need to understand the importance of purpose, value, and culture and how to best align the workforce and its external partners to the company's purpose.

HR and recruiting leader will need to be just as savvy as marketing leaders about building brand and attracting people to the brand. While the marketing leader is building customer and investment brand, the HR leader is building employer brand. The brands must be aligned and integrated, but they are for very different audiences. The technical tools now have become the same for both leaders.

Candidate Assessment

Finally, how is the candidate assessed? I have found the best method to be a combination of structured interviews based on job competencies and a thorough discussion of a candidate's work history, roles, and achievements, with validated work skill, conscientiousness, integrity, or personality assessments. Cognitive testing and work sampling are also excellent methods.

Whatever combination you use should be integrated together. The first reason to use an integrated approach is that success on the job for most jobs is due to more than one factor. The primary factors typically boil down to cognitive ability, personality style (which in-cludes emotional intelligence), job skills for highly skilled roles like technicians, engineers, and other professions, and conscientious-ness and integrity.

For unskilled labor, structured interviews, assessments on con-scientiousness and integrity and the cognitive and motor skills to do the job, and work sampling are essential to understanding how well they will be trained on the job and get along with others and perform on the job.

The second reason is that when the assessments are admin-istered early in the process, the results can be used to clue inter-viewers on areas for additional questioning during the structured interview. For example, when I screened for medical device sales representatives, after the initial screen by HR, qualified candidates were asked to complete an online personality assessment by Berke that we validated with the performance of our twenty best sales workers.

The assessment measured key traits for successful sales workers, such as their need for utility (which is a professional word for the desire to make lots of money), being the expert, being outgoing, having a killer instinct to close the deal, persistence, and resiliency. These are a very different set of personality traits than those re-quired of engineers and managers. Based on the assessment's re-sults, we would coach the interview team to probe in areas that the assessment had identified as potential weak spots. If a candidate tested poorly on resiliency, for example, we could put extra focus on that trait during the final round of on-site structured interviews.

We used assessments from the Center for Creative Leadership and PDI Ninth House to assess the executive leadership skills of external candidates. If a candidate scored low on delegation and remaining calm during stressful circumstances, we could focus on those leadership traits during our interviews.

The importance of structured interviews has been known for forty years, yet many CEOs and human resources organizations have ignored the advice. Many Fortune 1000 organizations (but not as many as you might think) now do use empirically developed assessments to gather reliable information about the candidate's cognitive abilities, problem-solving abilities, trustworthiness, skills, and personality styles, but many smaller ones are not taking advantage of how these assessments improve their ability to hire great candidates and reduce turnover.

Long legacy assessments are tolerated less frequently these days, and many companies have pushed their assessment companies to come up with an equally reliable but shorter test—which isn't always easy to do. However, more and more assessments are now available online and can be completed in fifteen to twenty minutes, not an hour. Many also include games in the assessments.

Recruiting has always given HR credibility and, along with payroll and data onboarding, it is the primary reason CEOs in start-ups begin to use an HR service.

I have led recruiting in organizations from coast-to-coast in the United States and overseas in business units of vast Fortune 200 companies. Once recruiting is organized like a well-oiled machine and the organization gets the excellent talent it needs to execute its business strategies, HR is viewed in much higher regard.

Formerly prominent CEOs in old-line industries, such as Jack Welch and Larry Bossidy, and Silicon Valley prominent CEOs in high technology companies, such as former CEOs Steve Jobs of Apple and Eric Schmidt of Google, have emphasized the essential importance of making great hires and taking time to do it exceptionally. Former Google CHRO Laszlo Bock has underlined the importance of hiring great talent, even going so far as to say that the most critical role of leaders is to hire great talent.[10]

Still, many organizations do a poor job of it.

I remain dumbfounded by how many companies complain about a tight labor market and the difficulties of finding and hiring workers—yet they have abhorrent recruiting processes. They make candidates wait in lobbies for interviews, don't provide tours of the work campus, fail to allow them to meet future coworkers, and generally treat them like high school students. Wake up. The shoe is on the other foot.

You need to offer candidates an experience that treats them like prospective customers, complete with precise information about what your company has to offer them and their careers; details about your work environment, pay, benefits, flexible work policies, and career development; and timely updates on your decision-making. I suggest your website or social media sites also feature the work and experiences of your current employees—they are your best salespeople when it comes to recruiting.

Just as important as the candidate experience is having a recruiting process that runs smoothly and is based on performance results and measures, especially when you have a large number of openings to fill.

Organizations that are excellent at attracting, screening, hiring, and retaining great talent understand that they need first to have a comprehensive talent strategy that has the enthusiastic support of top and middle management and human resources leaders who have aligned their human resources technologies and processes to effectively attract, align, motivate, reward, and develop their great talent. These organizations attract and retain excellent industry talent at more successful levels than their industry and talent-competition peers.

When you think about it, recruiting involves just about every department in the organization and, most of all, managers. It is comprehensive. Moreover, it should run like a finely tuned Maserati or semiconductor factory. Recruiting is, after all, a repeatable process. Why wouldn't it be well designed, well managed, well measured, and move at the speed of the business, not the pace of 1990 bureaucracies?

It can.

The Essential Components for Great Recruiting

I have been involved with recruiting for over thirty years. I led several recruiting and human resources departments for several Fortune 200 business divisions, from coast-to-coast in the United States, Europe, and Asia. I have learned from these experiences, the successes and failures; from industrial/organizational psychology; from the successive technologies used in recruiting; and now from the emerging digital technologies that are available to recruiting and HR.

Every successful recruiting effort needs the following essential components of recruiting.

1. **Employer Brand.** An authentic, well-known, and alluring employer brand integrated with comprehensive talent strategy that fits the company's values, business purpose, and culture is required for recruiting in a competitive talent economy. The people you most want to hire have jobs. You must attract them to your company's higher purpose for humanity, build a strategic talent pool, build relationships with them, and offer them something better than what they currently have. You will want to recruit the best workers you can find. There is now overwhelming research that shows that companies with diverse workforces have higher financial performance, especially if the company has sophisticated clients and is high tech, fast-changing, and global.[11] Your brand ought to reach out to the best without regard to demographics. The most powerful tool you have to differentiate yourself is your employer brand.

2. **Recruiting Process.** In fast-growing and large companies, recruiting is a repeatable, high-volume process that directly impacts your brand reputation. Like manufacturing and customer service, your recruiting process must be a smooth, efficient, and measured process, with a high job candidate net promoter score.

3. **Candidate Search Strategy.** Today's job candidates want to be in charge of their job searches, and they have the digital tools to conduct a thorough job search. Most of them will seek out jobs from job boards and the company's career website. Over two-thirds of today's job candidates will look at ratings of company management, culture, and recruiting practices on such a site as Glassdoor. Only a third of job candidates like to be contacted by a recruiter. With texting apps, many job candidates, especially those for entry-level jobs and at colleges, are being inundated with texts. In an era of full employment, 40 percent of job candidates are looking for something better. What will your strategy be to differentiate yourself to either experienced and passive job candidates or those graduating from tech schools and colleges to get their attention and keen interest?

4. **Screening Candidates.** Once great candidates have been found, it is time to screen their résumés either by recruiters or by an artificial intelligence platform. It is also time for the first videoconference or phone screen. The thoroughness of an initial screen will vary by industry and level of job. What questions you ask will vary by whether you are interviewing a college graduate business major or engineering major, an experienced candidate, a manager, or an executive.

What recruiters and hiring managers also need to learn to do in the screening process is to avoid unconscious bias (or first impression bias) and discriminatory decisions. Neuroscience has taught us that it is not only the bigot or sexist (who come in all races and both genders) who discriminates; it can be all of us based on experiences in childhood or college that made a lasting impression deep in our amygdalae (the almond-shaped mass in our cerebral hemisphere that stores the emotions of our experiences and generates a fight-or-flight response). During interviewing, past experiences or lessons taught can unconsciously shape biases about the job candidate whose résumé we may read or who may be speaking in front of us. These biases need to be identified, faced, and controlled. Learn how. Also learn some great initial screening methods and questions.

5. **On-Site Interviews.** There is only one time to make a great first impression and sit face-to-face with a job candidate to assess the candidate's job skills, ability to overcome obstacles and succeed, ability to collaborate with others, and whether they will be a fit with their work team and your work culture. That job candidate will also be assessing you and if your company's purpose, culture, pay and benefits, flexible work arrangements, and career development policies and opportunities meet his or her needs. The shoe is on the other foot in an era of full employment. Well-run on-site interviews with a facility tour and time to meet potential co-workers who make the candidate feel welcome and valued are more important than ever.

6. **Recruiting Metrics.** Recruiting is an essential business process and is part of an integrated talent strategy that starts with a firm commitment that the workforce and leadership are the corporation's most valued assets. Like any major business process, it needs to have winning strategies; well-thought-out, fast-moving, and reliable processes, roles, and handoffs; up-to-date technologies that maximize efficiencies and take advantage of the latest advances with machine learning and AI; participants who are trained for their role in the process; and metrics, beginning with a job candidate net promoter score.

7. **The Gig Workforce.** Can your resource needs be met by contractors, temporary employees from agencies, or gig workers as opposed to full-time regular employees? It is worth looking into as the use of contractors and gig workers increased up to the days of full employment. Now the trend is reversing during the era of full employment in the United

States as longtime temporaries and contractors accept full-time employment offers with the preferred benefits that come with it: paid time off, health care, retirement benefits, and peace of mind. Remember, however, that if you are providing gig or contractor tools such as computers or trucks to drive, providing them office space, and controlling their hours, dictating their work like you would an employee, and if they work only for your company, you will end up with a lawsuit for coemployment.

8. **HR Geek: The Empirical Evidence for Hiring Great Employees.** Industrial/Organizational psychology has provided us with long-standing empirical evidence on how to select job candidates who will perform well on the job. General mental aptitude assessments, such as IQ tests, are one of the best predictors of job success. Great workers have more skills than intelligence. Hiring for intelligence alone won't provide you the talented workforce you need. Human beings have a wide range of aptitudes and personalities that create a fit on some jobs and not others. Assessments that have been through a rigorous validation process can help you select the best engineers, sales reps, leaders, and assemblers. There are plenty of validated assessments, which are cheaper than they used to be and will help you hire better and more loyal employees. However, some long-standing assessments are criticized for being biased against women and people of color.

9. **Background and Reference Checks.** Eighty-six percent of candidates stretch the truth on résumés or outright lie, and 30 percent of companies make a bad hire because of receiving wrong information from résumés and interviews[12]. It is very difficult to discern if someone is lying to you in an interview. Background checks, reference checks, and rigorous selection methods such as assessment tests and structured interviews are your best bets to uncover truth from fiction and to hire great employees. The Ban the Box movement

in several states and municipalities is now delaying background checks until a provisional offer is made to allow fairer consideration of the over 70 million formerly incarcerated adults in the United States.

10. **Onboarding.** Great onboarding experiences to align your new hires to the values and culture of the business, learn the unwritten rules to gain influence, learn how work gets done, and begin their career growth will help new hires accelerate their time to full productivity and enable them to find their place among their coworkers and your culture. Great onboarding drives the bottom line.

11. **HR Technology Geek.** Use the most current technology and analytics to find, attract, and screen candidates. IT is unending. Technology will source and screen faster than relationships. Current technology such as artificial intelligence for recruiting will make post and pray on Indeed and CareerBuilder and even LinkedIn searches less important or even obsolete—or these current recruiting giants will accelerate their purchases of this technology revolution.

12. **Values Fit.** Hire people who have the right values and behaviors and who can work effectively in your teams and culture. Hire people you can trust and who overcome obstacles to succeed. Don't hire everyone who will think like you, look like you, or are cut out of the same "cloth." It will kill the one thing every company needs today: innovation.

13. **Drug Testing.** I recommend you continue to test for drugs, especially in regulated industries, because drug use is rising as the use of marijuana and medical marijuana becomes legal in more and more states. While medical marijuana has real promise to alleviate pain and suffering and may provide medical cures, it still has serious side effects and impairs workers' judgments and the ability to drive a car. The rise of other controlled substances such as opiates is also alarming. However, you need to carefully stay within the laws of your state or city, not to mention the federal government.

Besides, no one wants to fly on a plane or have an implanted medical device that was assembled or tested by a stoned worker.

14. **The Impact of Laws and Regulations.** The regulations and laws in some areas such as overtime, the difference between exempt and nonexempt employees in the US, and how to determine who is a contractor and who is an employee haven't changed much. However, laws on diversity and inclusion, banning the box, and not asking for salary histories have changed dramatically. Cities and counties have gotten into the act, as have different states. Avoid costly lawsuits that will damage your brand. More importantly, salary transparency and fairness ought to increase so you can attract and retain the best talent from all walks of life.

15. **Hiring Strategies Needed for Full Employment.** There are now more job openings in the United States than unemployed people.[13] It is time to switch from normal recruiting strategies to full employment recruiting strategies. Posting your jobs on your career site and job boards won't cut it. Recruiting now is about being first to those new to the workforce and offering those who are employed something better, building relationships, and acting with speed. It is also time to learn how to recruit veterans and the 70 million formerly incarcerated adults.

How to Read This Book

Hardly anyone reads a book from cover to cover, especially a business book. You are too busy. So, after this chapter, I recommend you read chapters 2 through 9, which cover employer branding, workforce planning, recruiting process, candidate search strategies, effective screening, recruiting metrics, and the contingent workforce. I also recommend you read the last chapters, hiring during full employment (14) and call to action (15). Then if an additional topic interests you, turn to the HR Geek sections. They are on the empirical evidence for hiring great employees (chapter 10), additional important issues such as emotional intelligence and "the Big 5" (chapter 11) digital technology (chapter 12), and the impact of laws (chapter 13). In addition, the "Contents" at the front of the book provide detailed subchapter headings to allow you to easily find the desired content. The HR Geek sections are more technical and provide valuable information if you are buying an ATS system, considering an AI platform, or wondering if hiring for culture fit is really stunting your company's innovation and perpetuating the unconscious biases of its leaders, and what is legal and the personal and company fines for violating the law.

Remember that technology innovation and recruiting and HR digital technology consolidations and acquisitions are occurring monthly. Big players like Indeed, Monster, ZipRecruiter, and Microsoft, to name a few, are regularly making purchases of technology start-ups. Google and IBM are investing heavily in the space. In addition to what I have written in the technology section, you should subscribe to or assign someone in IT or HR to subscribe to websites like TechCrunch, ERE Media, SHRM (Society for Human Resource Management), or HR.com to stay on top of technology changes and how they will impact HR and the profitable growth of your company. The laws also change but a little more slowly in some areas. Also worth tracking are sociodemographic changes and the differences of how HR is practiced from region to region and nation to nation around the world.

I also have a blog that you are invited to sign up for, and it will keep you updated on changing issues.

I hope many CEOs read this book because the most critical changes in your companies start with you, your strategic vision, strategies, the technologies you choose to invest in, and your operating mechanisms. Every company is a software company and needs to transition to digitization and disruptive innovation aggressively. You can't do that without shaping a transparent, collaborative culture of innovation, building the talent strategies to support such cultures, and hiring, aligning, nurturing, rewarding, and retaining the exceptional and normal talent to grow your business profitably.

It will require an HR executive leader up to this task who has a deep understanding of the long-standing research, empirical models of industrial/organizational psychology, labor economics, labor law in the countries where you operate, and socioeconomic trends, as well as an understanding of the importance of digital technology transforming HR and how to integrate it and change people workflows to leapfrog to new efficiencies and innovations.

This transition in HR is as vital as the digitization of your products and services and of marketing, R&D, and the rest of your operations.

If you want innovation and profitable growth in *your* fast-changing, global world, which has weekly technical, political, and economic changes, it is essential.

CHAPTER 2: EMPLOYER BRANDING AND COMPREHENSIVE TALENT STRATEGIES

Employer brand is the reputation of your company. Every company has a reputation whether planned or unplanned. You can read about the employer brand of companies in newspapers and on the internet. Companies have better outcomes when they manage their employer brands.

As with a company's customer brand, the employer brand should convey the company's larger purpose for humanity, its mission and the good of its product and services, but with a different audience, the larger workforce from which the company recruits and its employees to maintain their loyalty. Employer brand also needs to convey the employer value proposition to employees and job candidates. It needs to answer the question if you work for us, what is the benefit to customers and humanity, and how will your employment with us benefit you?

Employer branding for recruiting is necessary to distinguish your company from others and to be an employer of choice in your markets.

Employee branding and recruiting should be as bold and high tech as any marketing campaign—and transparent, because your employees and potential job candidates can smell a snow job. With the internet today, there is dramatically more transparency on company hiring practices, culture, pay, and leadership practices.

With the internet of everything (IoT), employee branding and recruiting should be interactive, multi-media, and mobile, and feature not only your business purpose and culture, but also video testimonials from your employees.

The right branding and recruiting approach will depend on your business strategies, purpose, principles, and culture, and your unique business circumstances. There can be several different employer brands. I will outline a few below:

- From your employer brand, you must put together an employee value proposition. If they join this firm, how will they benefit? Will they received leading pay and benefits and an opportunity to work on innovative new products or services?
- If you are a mature start up or growing small firm, will they received good pay and benefits, but not those to compete with major firms like IBM, Microsoft Google, but the opportunity to be in a fast paced innovative culture where they can see the results of their work, get immediate feedback and become a millionaire if the company's innovations pan out?
- Does your company offer a great customer brand and reputation for developing talent with good pay and benefits, but an accelerated career development environment that puts a premium on success, fast job rotations with relocations to gain experience in different markets and businesses, and has the understanding that incumbents will move on to greener pastures in a few years?
- Will your company be a trusted provider to customers and have more stable environment with good pay and benefits and the opportunity to work from home a few days a week?

For the best several years, companies such as L'Oreal, VMWare, Dominoes, and Medtronic have used gamification to build employer brand and attract job candidates, particularly millennials, to their jobs. Learn more about how gamification used in Chapter 11: HR Geek: Technology.

Employer branding and recruiting is not a stand-alone function within human resources. It is one vertical of an integrated set of comprehensive talent management strategies to attract, align, motivate, engage, recognize, and develop the talented workforce you need to execute your organization's business strategies. The power of comprehensive talent management is having all the human resources verticals aligned horizontally to enable the business's purpose and strategies and drive bottom-line business results. When this occurs, the company can see dramatic and sustainable improvement in business results and shareholder equity.

The chart below on Talent & Organizational Capability Strategy shows how the company's vision, values, strategies and culture, external environment, workforce make-up and competencies shape its external brand. When the verticals of human resources are aligned to deliver a great employee experience and fulfill the employer brand, the results will be an aligned and motivated workforce, successful execution of business strategy, improved employee performance and innovation, and higher financial results. The processes and systems that deliver on a company's employer brand need to be managed like any important business process and be measured and monitored.

Talent & Organizational Capability Strategy

Begin Defining Your Employer Brand by Reviewing The Company's Customer and Investor Brand

Employer branding begins with your company's vision, mission, strategies and culture and the brand the company presents to its customers and investors. The easiest way for human resources and recruiting leaders to familiarize yourself with the company's customer brand is to go to your company's website and read it. What are its credos, main product, or service areas? What are the processes it uses to find and attract new customers and to please current customers, especially the ones with a complaint?

Next, read the annual report. It is loaded with great information regarding the company's mission, past products, services, new ventures, market share, and financial performance. The good, bad, and ugly of the company's performance and the risks of its investments need to be detailed there, or the company can run afoul of the law and Securities and Exchange Commission guidelines. It is a wealth of information.

Now read the recent press releases and the information posted on the investor relations page of its website. Then go to the *Wall Street Journal, Seeking Alpha, Yahoo Finance, Google Business News,* or *Bloomberg* to read what others, particularly investors, are saying about your company, its brand, its performance, and whether it is a good or not so good investment—and why.

Interview your top executives and especially the marketing, sales and investor relations leaders to learn their insights, the reactions and feedback from customers and investors, the company's competitive position with competitors and the changes they believe are needed.

Review the feedback from Job Candidates and Employees About Your Brand

Now look at the feedback from your current employees that you can obtain from your employee satisfaction or engagement surveys, sensing sessions and the results of your HR and recruiting metrics. How do your recruiting metrics compare to known standards? What jobs are the easiest and most difficult for your team to find candidates? What jobs have the highest offer rejection or ghosting rate? (Ghosting is when a job candidate doesn't show up for an interview or doesn't show up after accepting a job offer). For what reasons? Pay? Benefits, Culture? Location? Long-term opportunity?

After getting a good understanding of your company's brand to its customers, investors, the job candidates and employees, it is time to consider what employees want from a company today and then to decide how your company will compete in the labor market. And how will you market your employer brand and employee value proposition to the workforce.

What themes are there that will make for a great employer brand while continuing to support the company's customer brand? The employer brand and the company customer brand need to overlap if not be the same in their opening. The employer brand then needs to support distinguishing your company from its industry, regional, and workforce competitors. It needs to also convey your employee value proposition. Why would an employee want to work for you? Great pay, benefits, career development, and the stability of a larger company? Great early career development with increasing responsibility and accelerated promotions in exchange for long work hours and frequent moves to new businesses and geographies? The start-up attraction of work with purpose, empowerment, accountability, and chaos but the chance of becoming a millionaire in your thirties? More work/life balance with opportunities to telecommute two to three days a week?

How does the company market itself to its investors and customers?

External Factors to Consider for an Employer Brand

Before you finish your employer brand and employee value proposition and decide how your company will compete in the labor market, there are four external factors you will need to consider before deciding or updating your employer brand.

First, look at the emerging legal and regulatory hurdles in the United States and its states, counties, and cities where you have operations and sales offices and in whatever countries and cities you have operations and sales offices around the world. For example, how will California's new law on not asking for salary history impact your salary plan and its transparency? How will India's requirements for foreign companies to share technology and invest in native companies impact the skills and requirements of an Indian workforce? What will the company's response be to these changes to enable it to successfully recruit employees?

Second, closely study the emerging socioeconomic and demographic trends emerging in the United States and around the world. For example, will Generation Z demand a different work environment and experience than millennials? Are millennials moving into a new phase of their life cycle, and will they be more demanding of traditional health care and retirement benefits? Will these trends require changes in your benefit offerings in the United States and your company's global brand? The next section, "What Are Today's Job Candidates Looking For from an Employer?" will review their preferences in great detail.

Third, look at your current recruiting and HR performance metrics and feedback. Is your ability to attract employees to your job postings competitive? What is your cost per hire, and is it competitive? What is the candidate dropout rate? Are your ninety-day, annual, and overall employee turnover rates higher than industry or regional norms? If so, do you know the cause? What is your job candidate rating score? What is your net promotion score? Chapter 7, on Recruiting Metrics will provide further guidance for you.

Fourth, what are your current and former employees saying about you in employee surveys, exit interviews, and on the internet? Do you know your Glassdoor ratings? I have worked with companies who have Glassdoor ratings below 3—which isn't good at all. When I raise this issue, I am frequently told, "These are isolated malcontents who wouldn't be happy working anywhere." My response is that for a job candidate who doesn't know your company and sees your low score and these terrible comments, it looks like the truth because you have not provided a response, and no one is writing anything positive about your company.

A study conducted by Software Advice in January 2014 uncovered that 48 percent of job seekers reported they had used Glassdoor at some point of their job search, and most consulted reviews to find the best employers before they even considered applying at a company.[14] Glassdoor, in 2016, had more than 11 million employee reviews for a half million companies. It gets 30 million unique visitors a month.[15]

In a full labor market—even in ordinary times—companies need to proactively manage their social media image. If the complaints about your company have merit, they will need to be addressed and corrected. If, for example, you have harsh management that is driving away good employees or pay poorly, you will need to address these issues with real change.

Also review any employee satisfaction, engagement surveys, or exit interviews you may have recently conducted to see what issues employees have identified that could tarnish your brand, hinder your ability to recruit, or drive up turnover.

The internet has given the public more transparency than it has ever had before. Your brand strategy needs to be mindful of this and proactively manage your brand's image. More importantly, you need to create a work environment that meets the expectations of today's workforce. Companies can't fake it with slick marketing.

What Are Today's Job Applicants Looking For from an Employer?

In this section we look at contemporary and long-standing research on what attracts workers to a job site and a new job. We identify what information should be on your career site from these studies and the importance of using job boards such as Monster, Indeed, Glassdoor, or CareerBuilder over social media sites or third-party searches.

In a tight labor force, companies need to offer something more to lure workers away from a current job. In full employment, you must lure workers away from their existing job with its security despite not being perfect with something substantially more. Or you need to recruit from new entrants to the labor force, such as high school, trade school, or college graduates or immigrants. Or lure back into the workforce those who have retired or for some other reason, such as raising a family, dropped out of the workforce.

A new survey released on July 25, 2018, taken by Harris Poll for Glassdoor, identifies the crucial pieces of information job seekers look for when examining job ads. They are the following:

- Sixty-seven percent look at salaries.
- Sixty-three percent look at benefits.
- Fifty-nine percent look at worksite location.
- Forty-three percent look for commute time.
- Thirty-two percent look for employee reviews about the company.

The Harris Poll survey on behalf of Glassdoor was conducted between May 7 and 9, 2018, among 1,151 US working-age adults who were eighteen or older.[16] Of the total survey participants, 1,015 of the survey takers were employed either full- or part-time or were self-employed. The rest, 136, were unemployed and looking for work.

Looking at crucial pieces of information is one thing, but

what will make a job candidate decide to apply for a job? The Harris Poll survey also asked the respondents what would make them *more likely to apply for a job*. Here is the breakdown of responses.

- Forty-eight percent cited attractive benefits and perks such as paid time off and gym memberships as a key factor. Please note: I will show below that as millennials age and take on mortgages and family-raising responsibilities, traditional benefits such as health care, paid time off, and retirement benefits are more important to them than perks, like the free breakfast bar, which has become a hygiene factor. Hygiene factors are items that are expected and when they are not available, then workers are disappointed, but they are not the distinguishing factors to attract workers.
- Forty-seven percent cited convenient and close commutes.
- Forty-six percent cited high salaries.
- Forty-three percent cited good work-life balance.
- Forty-one percent cited work from home flexibility.
- Thirty-five percent cited great company culture. Note: I will point out below that company culture becomes important for job seekers that want to find a long-term employer and to retain employees.
- Twenty-six percent cited the company's financial performance.
- Twenty-three percent cited familiarity with the company's brand.

It is interesting to observe that pay, benefits, and commute times still top the list of the "likely to apply for a job" factors as in the first question the *crucial pieces of information employees look for.* Glassdoor's Global Head of Talent Acquisition, Julie Coucoules, said in the press release, "Job seekers crave transparency on pay, not only to make an initial judgement about whether to consider applying for a job, but also to assess if an employer holds long term potential for them. Quality candidates are typically well-researched and those that go beyond job ads and look for a richer set of background data that includes benefits and employee reviews, among other specific traits about an employer. This means that employers should make information available to job candidates proactively, or they risk missing out on quality candidates applying."[17]

Coucoules's advice should be heeded by CEOs, HR, and recruiting leaders. The company's career site and social media presence should make the company's policy on pay, available benefits, perks, and options to work from home very transparent. And as you will see with the next round of questions reported by the Harris Poll Survey for Glassdoor, transparency on pay, career development, culture, and company values are important factors for employees who are looking for longer term careers and job satisfaction.

Are job candidates looking for their next job or a company that will enable their long-term career growth? The Harris Poll Survey for Glassdoor asks another interesting line of questioning: when it comes to assessing long-term potential as an employer, what are workers and job seekers looking for? The answers change. Here are the answers.

- Forty-four percent report company *transparency* on pay and benefits.
- Thirty-nine percent report long-term career potential. That is an explanation from employers about how they can grow within the company after joining. This is more effective if employees of the company provide their own testimony on the career site, via podcast, about how their careers progressed.
- Thirty-seven percent say a company having a track record for promoting from within would signify a company has long-term potential for them as an employee.

Glassdoor notes that in a separate survey, "Does Money Buy Happiness? The Link between Salary and Employee Satisfaction,"[18] they had determined that pay and benefits do

not have a huge influence on employee long-term satisfaction. Money doesn't buy happiness. But in full employment, it will enable you to attract hard-to-find talent. Once on the job, culture and values take over. According to Glassdoor Chief Economist Dr. Andrew Chamberlain, once on the job, culture and values are the biggest drivers of employee satisfaction, followed by career opportunities and senior leadership.[19]

Glassdoor's finding confirms the long-standing research of Frederick Herzberg, who reported in the 1960s that pay is a hygiene factor.[20] That is, employees expect it. When good pay is provided, great, but it does not drive loyalty or discretionary effort. Instead, in Herzberg's model, what drives loyalty and discretionary effort are motivational factors. Motivational factors include issues such as challenging work, a sense of achievement, growth and development, recognition, and more responsibility. While people work for money and benefits and will keep their jobs for good money and benefits, it is the motivational factors that drive discretionary effort—the good things like innovation and extraordinary effort.

The overall findings by the Harris Poll Survey for Glassdoor are not alone. A survey conducted in 2017 by Fractl, a content marketing agency and growth marketing services company, shows similar findings. Fractl's survey results were published in *Harvard Business Review*.[21]

What Benefits to Offer When You Can't Compete with Google and IBM?

The Fractl survey, led by its Inbound Marketing Manager Kerry Jones, looked at the issue of attracting job candidates from a slightly different lens—the view of the employer who cannot compete with the benefits of leading employers such as Google, Apple, IBM, and other Fortune 500 employers. Google, for example, offers top-level pay, health care, and retirement savings benefits and provides three free meals a day, massages, yoga classes, laundry services, and more. What if your company cannot offer these types of perks and benefits? What do employees want? What should you do?

The Fractl survey gave two thousand US workers between the ages of eighteen and eighty-one a list of seventeen benefits and asked them how heavily they would weigh the options when deciding between a high-paying job and a lower-paying job with more perks. (Fractl did not survey about pay.) They discovered that survey respondents ranked the several benefits in this order:

- Eighty-eight percent wanted better health, dental, and vision insurance.
- Eighty-eight percent wanted more flexible hours.
- Eighty percent wanted more vacation time.
- Eighty percent wanted work-from-home options.
- Sixty-eight percent wanted unlimited time off.
- Forty-four percent wanted tuition assistance.
- Forty-two percent wanted paid maternity/paternity leave.
- Thirty-nine percent wanted free gym memberships.
- Thirty-eight percent wanted free day-care services.
- Thirty-three percent wanted free fitness/yoga classes.
- Thirty-two percent wanted free snacks.
- Thirty percent wanted free coffee.

Scoring between 26 percent and 20 percent in descending order were weekly free employee outings, on-site gym, and team bonding events.

On this list, better health, dental, and vision insurance is by far the most expensive. According to the Kaiser Family Foundation in 2018, the total average cost for health care per employee per year is $6,896. The cost for family coverage is $19,616.[22]

The bottom line is that if you cannot offer top level pay and benefits, offer more flexible hours, vacation time and work-from-home options.

Offering the ability to work from home, flextime is relatively

free, and it will raise your productivity and employee morale as well as save you money. In my own experience, when I, my HR staff, the corporate real estate office, and the local facility management organization implemented a flexible workplace program for Medtronic's two businesses based in Santa Rosa, California, it improved worker productivity and morale and lowered real estate costs. As a matter of fact, even after investing in new carpet and modular office furniture and significantly expanding the number of huddle rooms and large conference rooms with top-notch high-definition videoconferencing equipment, the whole program had a return on investment of one point five months.

Vacations, too, can be nearly free to implement if companies switch to unlimited time off vacation policies, but they also have serious consequences if not managed well. Vacation is expensive because it is a huge expense that must be accrued per employee in the company's accounting system. The price of unused annual vacation in the United States is $224 billion.[23] Unlimited time off was started by Silicon Valley companies such as Netflix and Evernote. When unlimited time off policies are used, these vacation accrual costs evaporate from the books. However, not all is roses with unlimited time off policies because many companies have found that employees take less vacation time. According to Glassdoor, only 1 percent of employers in the United States offer paid time off.[24] Kickstarter axed its unlimited time off policy because they found employees actually took less vacation time.[25] For unlimited time off to be effective, it needs to be part of the company's culture of commitment to work and work-life balance, and companies need to put in clear expectations and communications to assure no one department suddenly finds itself unable to meet its commitments because a majority of employees planned vacation at the same time.

What about Millennial Job Seekers?

Since 2015 millennials have replaced Generation X as the largest generation in the US workforce, now comprising 35

percent of the workforce. So, what do millennials want from an employer?

A recruiter complained to me recently about millennials, "I have so many millennials who do not show up for their interviews. Once they are hired, our managers have a hard time motivating them, and their turnover is high. It's not like when we were young."

"Maybe it is," I countered. I reminded her of the high turnover rate of baby boomers and Gen Xers in their twenties. I offered to introduce her to hardworking millennials among my clients. As with any generation, there are the hard workers and the not so hard workers.

My experience as an HR leader taught me that if you could keep a twenty-something employee of any generation for two years, and certainly for five, you had a long-term employee. The trick was getting over the two-year hurdle.

My point is that many of the traits pundits associate with generational differences are really traits of the human life cycle. College students will experiment with alcohol, drugs, sex, and relationships regardless of their generation. Employees in their twenties will be impatient for career advancement, want the latest technology their age allows, and be more idealistic and prone to impatience and turnover. As these employees transition to their child-rearing years, the obligations of family will modify the traits of their twenties and raise new work environment and benefit demands on their employers.

Academic research bears this out. A recent study on generational differences in work-related attitudes found that meaningful differences among generations probably do not exist, and the differences that appear to exist are probably attributable to other factors.[26] Many can be explained by the life cycle. However, each generation is shaped by factors of their times. These factors certainly include technology, economic boom, recession, war, atrocity, and other generation-shaping events, such as 9/11 and the shootings of Presidents Kennedy and Reagan.

Today, when compared to Baby Boomers and Generation X, Millennials do more job hoping, are two times more likely to believe their bosses are too demanding and are not as engaged as the two older generations. While they are willing to work hard when motivated, they prefer doing it on their time.[27] But when you compare millennials to the two older generations when they were in their twenties, millennials aren't that different.

There is a truly unique millennial trend, however, that will begin to impact their expectations about employers. Millennials have been delaying adulthood much longer than Gen Xers and baby boomers did, at least when it comes to getting married, buying a house, and having children.[28] Because of this, many employers have been able to attract millennials with inexpensive perks like bring your dog to work. Employers have shortchanged costly, long-term benefits, such as retirement, fuller and tailored health care coverage, and paid paternity leaves. But that is changing. Two juggernauts are coming.

The first is that millennials are beginning to buy their own homes, enter long-term relationships, and have children. As a result, they will want competitive pay and benefits. Several recent studies have found that millennials expect competitive pay and pay for performance as opposed to pay-for-longevity systems. A 2017 study by Glassdoor that tracked over five thousand job transfers on their platform from 2006 to 2017 showed that pay matters.[29] Employees who received a 10 percent pay increase had a 1.5 percent higher probability (which in this sample was statistically significant) that they would stay with the company for their next career move and not go to another company.

Millennials are also preferring work environments like those desired by older generations, with more work-life balance, paid family leaves for both sexes, comprehensive medical benefits, and stronger retirement benefits. This is borne out by recent surveys of millennials on benefits.[30]

All employees in a hot economy are going to want competitive pay and will leave their jobs for pay increases of 10 to 15 percent. For millennials, who have resisted the traditional habits of young adulthood such as marrying, entering long-term relationships, having children, and buying homes, are still looking for the right employer and where they will fit in. They have expectations to change employers, but as they transition into owning homes and raising children, they will prefer to settle in with a stable employer.

Maturing millennials are looking for an employer that offers them career growth in a company that has a higher purpose for humanity, offers subsidized health care, a 401(k) with an employer match, time off with pay, paid leaves, and two-month sabbaticals after five years. For millennials, the top nonpay benefit is flextime and working from home. They also prefer companies that have flatter organization structures, drive innovation, have leaders who provide frequent feedback and will coach, ongoing training, team-oriented cultures, diverse and global workforces, and the latest digital technology.[31]

Note that millennials are not looking for more perks such as the coffee bar and free breakfast. While they have come to expect these perks, they won't attract a millennial worker to a job. They now want grown up benefits.

The second of the two looming juggernauts is Generation Z, which is hitting the labor market now as they graduate from high school and college. I will discuss Generation Z next.

Generation Z Is Here, and They Are Different from Millennials.

Generation Z are individuals born in the late 1990s and early 2000s, and they number nearly 73 million, about 25 percent of the workforce.[32] They are very different from millennials in many ways. They grew up during the Great Recession and have watched millennials struggle with college debt and have a tough time finding a job during the recession. They are the first generation that grew up dedicated and addicted to electronic devices, social media, and YouTube. They want knowledge and solutions on the internet and your company website more than millennials do.

They are all about financial security and independence, and they are socially awkward. They might text you about something even when they are standing right in front of you. They are willing, according to surveys, to work hard and longer hours than millennials. They are also the most ethnically diverse generation in US history, with nearly half of them being Hispanic, black, Asian, or of other ethnic backgrounds.[33] They are fast workers but will expect companies to have all the information they need on an easy-to-navigate company website.

In an article for the *Wall Street Journal*, Janet Adamy writes of Gen Z, "Its members are more eager to get rich than the past three generations but are less interested in owning their own businesses, according to surveys. As teenagers many postponed risk-taking rites of passage such as sex, drinking and getting driver's licenses. Now they are eschewing student debt, having seen prior generations drive it to records, and trying to forge careers that can withstand economic crisis."[34]

Gen Z is literally sober. Data from a Michigan survey and federal statistics, cited in the *Wall Street Journal* article, show they were less likely to have tried alcohol, gotten their drivers' licenses, or had sex or gone out regularly without their parents than teens of the previous two or three generations.

They grew up trusting adults, and Gen Z employees want managers who will step in to help them handle uncomfortable situations like conflicts with coworkers and provide granular feedback, according to Mr. Tulgan, a management consultant, cited in the *Wall Street Journal* article.

Gen Z is reporting higher levels of anxiety and depression as teens and young adults than previous generations. About one in eight college freshmen felt depressed frequently in 2016, the highest level since UCLA began tracking it more than three decades ago. Smartphones, according to Janet Adamy, may be partly to blame. Much of Gen Z's socializing takes place via text messages and social media platforms—a shift that has eroded natural interactions and allowed bullying to play out in front of wider audiences.[35, 36]

As he told Janet Adamy of the *Wall Street Journal*, when Mr. Tulgan's company surveyed thousands of Gen Z members about what mattered most to them at work, they wanted a "safe environment." He is advising clients to create small work teams, so managers have time to nurture them.

Gen Z is also changing how companies recruit on college campuses. Intuit changed its recruiting practices by moving its job postings to Slack, a messaging platform, so that Gen Z workers who pay less attention to email won't overlook their jobs. [37]

There is still a forming consensus among research on Generation Z. But according to David and Jonah Stillman (Jonah is a Gen Z member) in their book *Gen Z @ Work: How the Next Generation Is Transforming the Workplace*, there are seven traits of Generation Z that differ from those of millennials.[38]

1. **Virtual. All generations since the industrial revolution have been influenced by the dominant technology of their age. For Gen Z, it is what the Stillmans call phigital, where the real world and the digital world overlap.** Virtual is simply part of their reality. They want to work for companies with high digital sophistication. (Other researchers draw a different conclusion: that despite Gen Z's digital sophistication, they want a more traditional approach to personal development and more face-to-face meetings than millennials.[39] Strong training and coaching programs will help retain them.)

2. **Hypercustom.** Due to social media, which they have known from an early age, Gen Z members have always worked hard to customize their own brand. This creates an expectation that their employers will have an intimate understanding of their behaviors and desires, from job titles to career paths. Gen Z wants to write their own job description, more so than millennials. They judge employers by their social media.

3. **Realistic.** Growing up in the aftermath of 9/11 and the Great Recession has created a much more pragmatic cohort than millennials when it comes to planning and preparing for the future. They want more stability than millennials and to only work for a few employers during their careers.

4. **FOMO.** Gen Z suffers from an intense fear of missing out on anything. They will stay on top of all trends competitively and worry that they aren't moving ahead fast enough and in the right direction. (Frankly, I am not sure this is any different from earlier generations in their twenties.)

5. **Weconomists.** Gen Z has only known a shared economy, from ride sharing to Airbnb. They look for sharing work environments. Gen Z wants to break down internal silos at work to leverage the collective in new, convenient, and cost-effective ways. Like other generations in their twenties, they look for partners in their employers to fix the wrongs in the world and be a positive impact on society.

6. **DIY.** They are do-it-yourselfers. They grew up watching YouTube videos that explain how to do everything. On top of that, they have been taught by their Gen X parents to be fiercely independent, rather than follow traditional paths.

7. **Driven.** Their Gen X parents, the Great Recession, and the ever-present fast pace of change have taught Gen Z that there are winners and losers. They roll up their sleeves, work hard, and compete. Companies will love the work hard trait but may struggle to convince Gen Z to be empathetic and collaborative. It may be hard to fit Gen Z into a collaborative, innovative culture.

You will need to shape your business to attract and retain Gen Z workers. This will include reshaping your training to be more like a YouTube training video.

Just as it was a mistake to believe that Generation X were going to be a chip off the old block of baby boomers, it is wrong to believe that Generation Z will be the same as millennials. So far, they are proving to be more interested in security and secure jobs over entrepreneurism, fearful of debt, more willing to work hard than millennials, more tech savvy, trusting of adults, and faster learners, but also more anxious and socially awkward.

Companies will need to prioritize their internal employee

websites and career pages and start using collaboration software like Slack on college campuses. They will also need to launch training programs that look and feel like YouTube videos, and be available to coach and mentor the more timid Generation Z employees.

Back to my original theme in the millennial section of this book: much of what pundits attribute to generational differences may be more the result of where one is in their life cycle, as well as the impact of significant world events. But as millennials finally roll into traditional adult lifestyles and Gen Z emerges from college campuses, employers had better be prepared to offer the benefits and work environments desired by four generations—and keep those baby boomers engaged long past their mid fifties to counter the US and European labor shortage.

Men and Women Job Seekers Have Different Preferences

While working at Medtronic, the head of human resources for the cardiac rhythm management business, often called pacemakers, commissioned an exit interview study of employees who left that business of Medtronic. One of the main findings of the study that I recall were the distinct differences in reasons why men and women left the company. The men left, largely, for bigger roles in their career progression and for more pay. The women left, largely, due to not feeling a good working relationship with their manager and not feeling the potential for mentoring and career growth. Women also left more often because of family issues. This is not to say that women weren't concerned about earning higher pay; it just didn't top their list on this survey.

That was twenty years ago. Today, pay equity is a much more prominent issue among women that companies need to address. Often a bellwether on workforce regulation, the State of California in 2017 passed a law making it illegal to ask job applicants their pay histories, in an attempt to have pay decisions be based on skill and market factors and not historical pay discrimination against women.

California is not alone, as thirteen states and eleven localities have adopted laws and regulations prohibiting employers from requesting salary information from job applicants.[40]

The "Me Too" movement is now a movement for change. It began after the *New York Times* published an expose on Harvey Weinstein[41], and was propelled to a national credo for justice when actor Alyssa Milano used the "Me Too" term (first coined by Tanya Burke over a decade ago) to urge other women to come forward with their stories of sexual harassment on social media.

Let's look at today's research on the preferences of women and men job seekers and then the issue of sexual harassment.

The 2018 Harris Poll Survey for Glassdoor[42] found the following the preferences between men and women job seekers.

- **Working from home**. Forty-nine percent of women indicated that the option to work from home would make them more likely to apply for a job. Only 35 percent of men would be enticed by a company that offered the flexibility to work from home.
- **Searching on job sites for research on employers**. The survey found that 63 percent of women were more likely than men (45 percent) to say they would look to job search sites when doing research on a potential employer. However, the report added an additional perspective. On Glassdoor's platform, 51 percent of its monthly 57 million users are women, and 49 percent are men. Contrary to the survey findings, men and women search Glassdoor in equal percentages.
- **Assessing long-term potential as an employer**. Forty-eight percent of female workers/job seekers reported company transparency on pay and benefits as important information for assessing long-term potential at a company, compared to only 40 percent for men. Similarly, 44 percent of women reported that a company's explanation on how they could grow their careers after joining would make them

think the company offered long-term potential, compared to only 34 percent of men who reported the same.

The Fractl survey published in the *Harvard Business Review* also noticed gender differences with regard to benefits.[43] Most notably, women were more likely to prefer health care benefits and family benefits like paid parental leave and free day care services. Women also preferred more flexible hours, work from home options, and unlimited vacation. Parental leave and free day care were highly valued by female employees. Men were more likely than women to value team-bonding events, retreats, and free food. Both genders valued fitness-related perks, albeit different types. Women were more likely to prefer free fitness and yoga classes, while men were more likely to prefer an on-site gym and free gym memberships.

In order to attract and retain women, companies must be transparent and equitable with pay practices. Companies need to become comfortable posting or giving out their salary ranges when asked, and align their pay decisions to match the knowledge, skills and abilities of the job candidate regardless of pay. Women must also feel that they have a good relationship with their bosses and are being developed for career advancement.

As we have seen from these two recent surveys, women also prefer flexible work and work-from-home options more than men and paid parental leave, free day care, and different perks than men, such as yoga classes.

The problem of harassment and discrimination at work is dramatic.

According to a CNBC survey of eight hundred adults in December 2017, 27 percent of women and 10 percent of men reported being sexually harassed at work. Among the women, baby boomers reported the highest percentage, 39 percent, of being harassed at work. According to CNBC, 74 percent of Americans believe their company takes sexual harassment seriously. Be sure your company does as well.

Shockingly, a study by a research organization called Stop Street Harassment of 2009 adults in January 2018 found that a much larger percentage of adults have experienced sexual harassment in their private lives, work lives, or on the internet. Stop Street Harassment's survey found that 81 percent of women and 43 percent of men had experienced some form of sexual harassment during their lifetime at work or in their private lives. Their survey, unlike others, included cybersexual behavior. A lesser percentage of women, 38 percent, said they experienced sexual harassment at work (matching the CNC survey above). Sadly, 27 percent of women and 7 percent of men experienced sexual assault. Again, these numbers are alarming and speak to executives taking sexual harassment at work seriously and the need to take measures to prevent it.

In addition to transparency on pay and career development Women--and people of color--job applicants will be looking for signs that a company has a sizable number of women in its work-force and in management and executive roles before deciding to join a company.

Long-Standing Research on What Attracts and Retains Employees

Long-standing research. In addition to the recent studies I have cited, long-standing research conducted in the 1960s showed a similar pattern. Job seekers expected to receive competitive pay, and benefits factors and working conditions that attracted a worker to a job were not the same factors that motivated extraordinary effort and innovation.

Frederick Herzberg[44] discovered in the 1960s that employees have two different categories of needs that are independent from each other and affect behavior in different ways. The categories are hygiene factors, which relate to the work environment, and motivators, which relate to the job. Herzberg's hygiene and motivational factors are shown below.

Herzberg Hygiene and Motivational Factors[45]

Herzberg Hygiene (Maintenance) Factors	Herzberg Motivators The Job Itself
• The Environment • Policies and administration • Supervision • Working conditions • Interpersonal relationships • Money, status, and security	• Challenging work • Achievement • Growth and development • Recognition and accomplishment • Increased responsibility

The critically important conclusion from his research was that hygiene factors produced no growth in worker output capacity. Employees expected good hygiene factors, and when hygiene factors were below industry standards, they became dissatisfied and demotivated.

Motivators, on the other hand, can drive employees to higher job satisfaction and increased performance and output. Incidentally, Herzberg's hygiene factors align with Maslow's physiological, safety, and belonging/love needs, and Herzberg's motivators align with Maslow's esteem and self-actualization needs.

It is worth noting that other studies have found that Herzberg's model has staying power nearly fifty years after Herzberg's original findings. In the scholarly work by the Oxford Brookes Business School "Does Herzberg's Motivation Theory Have Staying Power?" the authors reported that Herzberg's two-factor analysis still had utility. After completing a survey of thirty-two hundred people, they found that the factors associated with intrinsic satisfaction played a more important part to motivate workers than money.[46]

Let's sum it up.

When job seekers first begin to look for work during this time of full employment, they will look for employers that offer competitive pay and benefits, especially health care and 401(k)s with a match. They will want an employer that allows them close proximity to their homes to avoid long commutes.

If the employer offers what is listed above, what can tip a job seeker's hand to decide to apply is if the company also allows flexible work arrangements and some perks like gym memberships. Flexible work arrangements are wanted by 50 to 78 percent of US workers, depending on what study you look at. It is a big driver.

When you break the workforce down by generations and gender, other features rise to the top to attract job candidates. Women will prefer transparency on pay and career development and paid medical and family leaves for both genders, work from home options and more paid time off.

Millennials today aren't as attracted to perks like in the past and want competitive pay and mature benefits such as subsidized health care, 401(k)s, tuition reimbursement, paid time off, sabbaticals, work from home options. They prefer purposed-based, innovative, team-based organizations with flat organization structure and, the latest technology.

Generation Z is the first truly digital generation. They will expect the latest digital technology at work. It is best to recruit them from colleges using texts and sharing platforms. They want good pay and benefits and financial security. While they will work hard, they will require more coaching on teamwork and face-to-face socialization skills. As all young people, they prefer ethical companies.

Finally, it is always good to remember that job seekers expect "maintenance factors" from their employers. These include a safe working environment, competitive pay and benefits in the industry, supportive and fair managers, and fair policies. The distinguishing motivational factors are how employees feel recognized and rewarded at work, their sense of achievement and growth, and the pride they have in their work. Be sure to highlight these motivational factors on your career site through the authentic stories and voices of your employees.

CHAPTER 3: EMPLOYER BRAND CASE STUDIES

What is important about an employer brand is to tell your story, not use a stylized script. Authenticity matters. As much as you can, let your employees speak to your brand and the fantastic work they are doing, which fulfills your higher purpose for humanity.

Some may believe that it is easy for a Johnson & Johnson, Google, or NASA to speak to its brand, but it isn't for most companies that aren't curing illness, being darlings of Silicon Valley, or reaching for the stars.

But you can.

Consider the example of Recology, the garbage collection company in the San Francisco Bay Area. They pick up trash and process recyclables every day in the Bay Area. Like anyone else in the Bay Area, they are finding the recruiting and retention of employees competitive. Yet they have an employer brand.

A World without Waste

Their vision is a world without waste. They have made a world without waste—and remember they collect and process garbage every day—their purpose in an environmentally and sustainability sensitive world.

On their website (www.Recology.com) is information and stories on the technologies they use to sort and recycle waste, how to capture gas from landfills, its partnership with Google and the city of Mountain View to increase recycling, and how they are working with farmers to return nutrients to the soil. Moreover, the company is 100 percent employee owned.

I attended a business mixer at Recology in San Francisco. Their food and wine were terrific. At the end of the mixer, the Recology executives on hand discussed their purpose with us—"A World Without Waste"—and then gave us a shocker that also demonstrated how seriously they take their purpose. *They told us the wine was made from reclaimed water.* Ugh! The sound of that can turn your stomach, but I must say as a wine lover and member of two Sonoma County wine clubs, it was pretty good.

Your employer brand competes in a larger market than your market brand. Your employer brand competes with whomever you compete with for employees and for retaining your current employees. While that may include your market competitors, it will be broader than your competitors. For example, in hiring IT workers, your competition will most likely be any employer who also is hiring IT workers either in your geographical region or nationally—not just your market competitors.

An uplifting employer brand, with a higher purpose, will serve you well in this competition.

Whatever you select as a strategy to compete for your company's employer brand, you should have a framework to measure it on an ongoing basis, with a dashboard and submeasures for each dashboard measure that will predict when the brand is going from green to red. The measures should also provide a return on investment for the workforce and the work of human resources. (They are related but separate.)

Microsoft's Revised Employer Brand

In the days of Bill Gates, the company's brand was "putting a PC on every desk in every home around the world." The brand was very clear and easily measured. Everyone at Microsoft could relate to it and the revolution of personal computers over minicomputers and

IBM software versus the competing Apple computers. Today it has been changed to "to empower every individual and every organization on the planet to achieve more." Today's brand is about purpose. It translates to an employer brand that is "to be the one who empowers millions"—which is a simple derivative of the Microsoft company brand.

Microsoft has a second employer brand tagline: "Come as you are, do what you like." It helps them emphasize inclusion and encourage employees to join projects that interest them.

According to Microsoft Consumer Marketing Director Paul Davies, Microsoft has a measurement framework for the employer brand, and one of the key measures is employee referrals. Their brand is also on every employee's badge to constantly be present. They review what is written by employees on Glassdoor about them as another way to gauge the pulse of employees, but they have learned that it is easy for unhappy employees to voice their concerns on Glassdoor, and so they take it with a grain of salt.[47]

To go along with its brand, Microsoft is highly rated for its pay and benefits by employees on Indeed and Glassdoor. In 2015, Microsoft was one of several high-tech companies that announced five or more months of paid leave for new parents (not just women—which is critical for further assisting the careers of women). Others included Netflix, Amazon, and Facebook. They were followed in 2016 by Twitter, Etsy, and American Express. If you are going to be in high tech, you need to provide the pay and benefits and informal, self-starting, and hard-charging workforce expected in that industry.

Medtronic's Brand in Santa Rosa, California

Let's discuss Medtronic and its iconic corporate brand and how I was able to use it to improve our strategic business unit brand in Santa Rosa, California. However, it required a lot of work and collaboration with our marketing, engineering, and legal teams.

At Medtronic Vascular in Santa Rosa, we had the great advantage of the corporate Medtronic brand, which was created by the company founder, Earl Bakken, during a financial crisis in 1961. In 1957, Medtronic came out with the first pacemaker to meet the need of hospital patients who went into cardiac arrest when their pacemakers lost power during violent thunderstorms and tornados that blew down power lines, cutting power off to the hospitals and their patients.

Despite this lifesaving invention, Medtronic in 1961 ran into a problem common with rapidly expanding start-ups: cash flow. Earl Bakken's board of directors told him that they could help him raise money from investors, but they would need a detailed business and financial plan to show them. Instead, he gave them the Medtronic mission, written on a half page of paper. It remains largely unchanged today.

Medtronic's mission is to "contribute to human welfare by the use of medical technology to alleviate pain, restore health, and prolong life." (You can see all six tenets of the Medtronic Mission in the box at the right.)

During my tenure at Medtronic, forty-five years after the writing of the mission, it still stirred passion among employees. New grads and experienced workers were eager to join the company to create new pacemakers, coronary stents, brain scanning technology, artificial pancreases, and a whole host of other medical devices and biomedical inventions.

In the 1960s Medtronic was a classic

Medtronic Mission

1. **To contribute to human welfare** by application of biomedical engineering in the research, design, manufacture, and sale of instruments or appliances that **alleviate pain, restore health, and extend life.**

2. **To direct our growth in the areas of biomedical engineering where we display maximum strength and ability;** to gather people and facilities that tend to augment these areas; to continuously build on these areas through education and knowledge assimilation; to avoid participation in areas where we cannot make unique and worthy contributions.

3. **To strive without reserve for the greatest possible reliability and quality in our products**; to be the unsurpassed standard of comparison and to be recognized as a company of dedication, honesty, integrity, and service.

4. **To make a fair profit** on current operations to meet our obligations, sustain our growth, and reach our goals.

5. **To recognize the personal worth of employees** by providing an employment framework that allows personal satisfaction in work accomplished, security, advancement opportunity, and means to share in the company's success.

6. **To maintain good citizenship as a company.**

American start-up. It was begun by Earl Bakken in a garage; after years of hard work and building relationships with customers, it flourished with a major invention. If you had joined the company in the sixties and seventies, your stock values would have skyrocketed. In the 1990s, its mission and value were rejuvenated by CEO Bill George, who set about making many successful acquisitions to spark Medtronic's revenue and stock growth. (Bill George would later go on to fame and fortune as a Harvard professor and author of *True North*.)

The problem in Santa Rosa, and more widely in the San Francisco Bay Area, was that no one knew about Medtronic and its mission. For my colleagues in Minneapolis and other places like Memphis, where Medtronic was a bigger employer and had longer roots, this was not a problem.

This hit home to me one night when returning from the airport I had to take a cab to my home. The cabdriver asked me where I worked. I told him Medtronic off Fountain Grove Parkway. He said, "Never heard of it." That amazed me since we were among the top handful of private employers in the area.

The response I received while attending professional associations in the area was frequently the same. "I never heard of Medtronics." People unfamiliar with Medtronic would often mistakenly add an "s" to the word Medtronic, as if it was the word "electronics."

Making matters worse, for the people who did know about us, we did not have a good reputation in Santa Rosa. We had just laid off half the workforce due to the injunction and obsolescence of our number-one selling stent. On top of that, the previous management team had a reputation for being demanding and cruel and for not properly staffing the business for the work needed. In effect, we were thought of as a medical device sweatshop.

We had to change this and build up our brand and awareness in the area.

The advantage we had was Medtronic's corporate mission. But when you went to Medtronic's corporate website in those days, you would see the products and innovations going on in Minneapolis, not in Santa Rosa. We had to figure out how to make it relevant to Medtronic Vascular and exciting to the Bay Area workforce, the college campuses where we recruited, and our own employees, who had legitimate concerns about workloads and leadership style.

I turned to Vascular marketing to the list of exciting new products and services in R&D to learn what was exciting about them. I also developed a list of employees to feature in ads that we placed in newspapers (newspaper ads were still relevant then) and on job boards and social media. The featured employees talked about the exciting work they were doing on various products and why they liked working for the company. We made sure to emphasize female and diverse employees to be able to attract the best and the brightest among all sectors of the labor force. I also had our legal team review our ad copy to make sure we did not violate laws on marketing products that were not approved by the FDA in the United States but were for sale in other countries.

Our ads also featured our health care, life insurance, and 401(k) benefits and our flexible workplace program, which allowed employees in certain job classifications that did most of their work on their computers and most of their communications by phone or videoconference to work at home three to four days a week.

The flexible workplace program was particularly helpful since most of the talent we needed did not live in Santa Rosa. To meet our staffing goals, we had to recruit talent from the San Francisco Bay Area, easily an hour's drive each way. In many cases, we hired employees in flexible work-friendly job classifications from faraway places such as Des Moines, Iowa, Dallas, Texas, and Philadelphia, Pennsylvania, and never relocated them to Santa Rosa. (We flew them in to Santa Rosa for their first two weeks to go through new hire orientations and to build relationships with their managers, teams, and internal clients, and then we typically flew them back every six weeks for key face-to-face meetings.)

Our brand had one other problem. We were on a national pay scale, which underpaid in the San Francisco Bay Area by an average of 9 percent and up to 21 percent for some critical job classifications.

Changing this was very difficult, as the corporation (and its highly paid compensation consultants) believed strongly in national pay scales.

For the folks in Minneapolis, their local pay scales matched the national pay scale, so it was not a problem. After nearly a year of lobbying from the Santa Rosa HR and business team, the corporation agreed to work with us to put in place a San Francisco Bay Area pay scale by job families. The local business team was given an estimate of the costs and the costs of bringing the current employees up to the new regional scales and approved my proposal in five minutes. They understand they were not going to get the talent they needed without paying competitive pay in the region.

Now armed with a brand that highlighted Medtronic's inspiring mission, made relevant by the innovative projects in Santa Rosa, highlighting the exciting work experiences of our employees, offering competitive pay and benefits, and providing flexible workplace options for certain job classifications, we were able to make significant headway with recruiting.

How Will Your Employer Brand Compete? What is the Employee Value Proposition?

Above we reviewed what job seekers are looking for today and even broke it down into segments such as millennials, women, and Generation Z. I have also advised that you conduct a competitive analysis to see how your company stacks up against your labor force competitors. With this information, you will need to decide on a strategy that will give your company the best advantage you can have in the labor force and retain your current workforce. You cannot be number one in all factors, and you may have to face agonizing decisions on how to compete.

There are eight factors that your employer brand can compete on with your regional and industry competition. You will not be able to compete on all these factors. You and the

executive team will have to make some strategic decisions here that will include tradeoffs. Let's review these factors.

1. **Pay.**

We saw in Chapter 2 that pay in this tight talent economy is often the No. 1 item job seekers look at to determine where to apply. Frederick Herzberg defined as a maintenance factor back in the 1960s. That is, job seekers expect competitive pay in their industry and region, and if they don't find an expected maintenance factor in the work environment, they move on to another company. This is especially true in a tight labor market

You may still get candidates at submarket pay, but they will be either inexperienced candidates requiring training, poorer performing candidates, or employees who are willing to trade competitive pay for other forms of equity such as part-time work or the ability to work from home full-time.

The importance of pay varies among employees depending on the availability of skilled labor. During an economic recession, the importance of pay to attract and retain workers goes down. Factors such as job security become more important. For example, during economic recessions, employees will often prioritize finding an employer who will offer more job security than their current employer over pay and other factors. The opposite is true during a tight labor market. Then pay rises as a selection factor as employees look to gain pay increases that they did not receive during tough times.

In addition to competitive pay, what is important to women, people of color, and the young is transparency about pay. They want to see pay ranges posted on job postings, and they want to have enough information available to them to make judgments that they are being paid fairly.

When looking at pay, you need to look at pay for your industry and your region. Pay can be very different from Tampa to Chicago, New York, Houston, and San Francisco. You need to pay market competitive pay for your location. If you are going to lure a high-talent employee away from his or her current employer, you will need to offer them a 10 to 15 percent pay increase to be successful.

If you cannot offer competitive pay, I suggest you look at offering a gain sharing, profit sharing, or group incentive program where additional pay is granted to workers based on individual (such as with sales), group, or company-wide goals that are achieved that also correlate with improved financial performance. Another popular alternative would be flexible work arrangements.

2. **Benefits.**

As we saw in Chapter 2, benefits if often the second item job seekers look for. Benefits, like pay, are a maintenance factor. If you don't offer competitive benefits, especially during full employment when you are recruiting employees from another company, you will lose out recruiting the best job candidates. Occasionally you will find candidates who are not interested in benefits because they get medical benefits from their spouse or another source. If they are technical experts, they may instead demand a higher pay level for their services either as employees, contractors, or gig workers. But for others, you need to offer benefits at competitive levels in your industry and region.

Still, maturing millennials are making a difference on the competitiveness of the health care package. An eye-popping 96 percent of millennials say they would take a job based on the comprehensive health care package offered, all other factors being equal.[48]

Benefits are not just medical, vision, and dental. They include a 401(k) with a competitive match, paid time off for vacation, paid sick time, and paid time off for both men and women for births and to care for sick family members. Offering paid time off for births to both men and women improves women's probabilities of advancing their careers as quickly as men.

Millennials have seen tough times during the Great Recession. They face repayment of their college student debt (which on average is at higher debt levels than for their parents when at the ages of millennials), and they strongly doubt that social security or traditional pension plans will be there for them during their retirement. Many millennials are looking for tuition reimbursement benefits to continue their education and help pay off their tuition debt. More than half of millennials want to invest in retirement savings, and they seek a generous employer match.[49]

If you are not offering competitive retirement options, you need to rethink your priorities.

3. **Purpose and Interesting Work.**
While purpose and meaningful work falls below pay and benefits, it can top the list for many millennials and Generation Z and for job candidates of all generations that are looking for an employer for the long haul. If you want workers who will be aligned to your higher purpose for society and have a strong commitment to your innovation and customers, you need to pay attention to purpose and interesting work (and culture).

Over forty years ago, Studs Terkel wrote in his book *Working*, "Work is about a search for daily meaning as well as daily bread." Long-standing research published in the *Harvard Business Review* in 1973 has shown that interesting work and job satisfaction (which are typical, such as a sense of achievement, recognition, autonomy, responsibility, and growth) are critical factors in attracting employees (and for that matter retaining employees).[50] Younger, highly skilled, and high potential workers will especially want autonomy.

It is true today as it was then. New research from *Fortune's 2016 Best Companies to Work for* list shows that an employee's belief that "My work has special meaning: this is not 'just a job'" tops the list of distinguishing factors associated with the desire to stay, followed by the belief that "I make a difference here" and "When I look at what we accomplish, I feel a sense of pride."[51] This finding is particularly insightful because the companies that top *Fortune's* list are known for their outstanding pay and benefits, strong employee development programs, fun work cultures, and perks. Those outstanding pay and benefits didn't top the list (although they are important as maintenance factors). The motivation factors topped the list. And they include being able to make a difference, pride, and feeling a sense of accomplishment.

Among millennials, 60 percent cite "a sense of purpose" as part of the reason they work for their current employer.[52] Purpose, not happiness, is the best intrinsic motivator. A sense of purpose drives discretionary effort, greater productivity, and increased innovation, which add to the bottom line. Talent-minded CEOs are well advised to align their company's mission to a larger socially conscious purpose.

According to a recent survey of five thousand workers by Korn Ferry, 33 percent of employees who changed jobs last year did it because of boredom with their current jobs.[53] If you are in a STEMM (Science, Technology, Engineering, Math, and Medical) industry, it is all about providing interesting work that stirs the emotions and life purpose of employees. Among service and manufacturing industries, the necessary pay and benefits packages will need to be competitive in these industries. These workforces seek employment stability, especially with workers who have families to feed.[54]

What are your company's mission and purpose to improve humanity, and how do they distinguish you from your competition? Is the purpose of your company to find life on a distant planet? Discover a cure for cancer? Create a world free of waste? Do you want to write the next algorithm software that will change how people collaborate with each other around the world? What is the interesting work you do, and how do you align it to a larger purpose to benefit humanity?

Whatever it is, let the external labor forces know and attract them to you.

4. **Career Development.**

Are you offering a job or a career? As we learned in Chapter 2, the job candidates who prefer a longer-term relationship with a new company view career development and opportunities for growth as important. Once a new hire joins your company, pay and benefits as a priority falls to the background and it is the work itself, relationships with the boss and peers, culture, and career development that take offer as an important determinate for loyalty and retention.

If the intent of your employer brand and employee value proposition is to provide long-term careers, how will you distinguish your career development on your employer brand marketing materials and on your career center? Most young workers of any generation, not just millennials, want an employer to develop their careers. They want continual feedback from their managers, and more than training, they want on-time digital learning sources and coaches to coincide with their on-the-job real learning opportunities.

A 2017 study by Glassdoor, which tracked over five thousand job transfers on their platform from 2006 to 2017, showed that employees who did not have a career move in the past ten months were more open to recruiter calls.[55] Career development is much more than just outlining promotional steps or a career ladder at a company. It also includes identifying how their careers can grow with transfers to other departments or business units, interesting parts of the world, or opportunities to work with new technology or innovation. It means on-time access to digitally available learning materials and video training, as well as timely classroom training, coaching and mentoring, and interesting work to enable them to learn on the job.

5. **Work Culture.**
    Work culture can top the list of attractive qualities for an employer among job candidates that want a longer-term relationship with an employer. Once on the job, culture, purpose, relationships, and career development are critical for retaining employees.

One of the most attracting features of *Fortune's Best Companies to Work for* list is an exciting and fun work culture that fits employee values.[56] Nearly a quarter of employees who changed jobs last year did it because the culture of their former company did not fit their values. Employees looking to make a change will search for signs of collaboration from testimonials on your career center and from what they read about your company on Glassdoor. Glassdoor's previously mentioned 2017 study found that raising a company's overall rating on Glassdoor by one star (on their five-star scale) was associated with a 5 percent higher chance that employees would stay for their next role. Their study found statistically significant links between two measures of workplace culture: higher career opportunities ratings and higher culture and values ratings. The Glassdoor authors concluded:

> In each case, raising a company's Glassdoor rating on these two dimensions by one star (out of five) was associated with a five-percentage-point higher chance that workers would stay for their next role. It appears that employees who see clear career paths for themselves and who feel committed to a company with a positive value system are statistically less likely to leave for their next role.[57]

Glassdoor's findings are not new. Research from the 1970s found that employees stay at a job because the work is interesting, as noted above, and because of the match between the employees' values and the company's work environment.[58] In addition, the same study found that some external factors drove up retention, such as the proximity to good local schools, safe neighborhoods, and other family amenities. What the study found was that if job dissatisfaction rose due to a drop in interesting work or the alignment of the company's work environment and the employees' values, turnover could rise quickly.

In addition, companies with highly collaborative and innovative cultures many times have flatter organizational structures. They are more agile, diverse, and global and have the team-based cultures that millennials find particularly attractive.

Companies that decide to compete on culture need to take it seriously. I am not talking about adding Ping-Pong tables, free breakfast bars, and Blue Bottle baristas to your workplace. I am talking about very purposeful, collaborative, and adaptive cultures that change frequently and are aligned to the business's strategies. We are talking about cultures where innovation is a strategic imperative set by the CEO. Where competitive information is shared through-out the organization. Where culture is valued. Where there are well-known processes to propose innovative ideas, build on them, prototype, gather data, talk to experts in and outside of the company, and quickly commercialize the best innovative ideas.

If you take it seriously, it will be a magnet for top talent.

6. **Flexible Work.**

Chapter 2 showed us that avoiding long commutes and having the opportunity to work from home a few days a week is a huge draw to many workers. If you cannot offer leading pay and benefits, this is an option you should consider seriously. Well thought out flexible workplace arrangements will also increase productivity, morale, retention and reduce your costs.

Today's workplace technology enables, by my research, 45 percent of the workforce to work from home or at a customer or supplier site three to five days a week. According to the US Census Bureau, US employees spend twenty-five point four minutes traveling each way to work. It can be one and a half hours each way in US cities like Atlanta, Chicago, Los Angeles, New York, and San Francisco. Outside of the United States, Moscow, San Paulo, Brazil, Bogota, Columbia, and London have the worst commute times. Workers want relief from commuting and will jump at opportunities to work productively from home three days a week.

About 80 to 90 percent of the workforce want to be telecommuters.[59] More than 75 percent of millennials say that flexible work hours make them more productive. In addition, 43 percent of millennials say they would switch jobs for more flexibility. This is a frequent finding of many studies and should not be ignored by talent-minded CEOs and CHROs. As a matter of fact, flexible work hours are highly popular with any generation, for men as well as women. While flexible work arrangements are frequently thought of as a benefit for women and millennials, research shows that the average telecommuter is forty-nine years old, a college graduate, who works for a company with one hundred or more employees and earns $58,000 a year.[60] In some studies, women have indicated they would take a cut in pay for flexible work arrangements. I am not advocating that women receive less pay than men for similar work and performance, but this study indicates how important flexible work arrangements are for women.

Your company should put into place flexible workplace arrangements that allow employees who do most of their work from their computers or most of their communications digitally to build relationships with your value chain or customers to work from home or a customer site two to four days a week. In addition, if your company cannot offer the competitive pay and benefits of some of your labor force competitors, flexible work arrangements should top the list of an equity to offer in place of competitive pay and benefits.

I have implemented a flexible workplace environment that resulted in higher employee productivity and morale, as well as reduced company costs, on average about 20 percent. Despite their popularity, flexible work environments have received strong pushback from corporate America. Former Yahoo CEO Marissa Mayer famously ordered Yahoo telecommuters to the office to better connect them with the company's culture and strategies and to be more innovative. Many of them eventually left the company. IBM CEO Ginni Rometty called in Big Blue's teleworkers on the very day IBM's internal blog on the subject highlighted Big Blue's productivity and financial improvements from telecommuting.[61]

Silicon Valley's high-tech giants such as Google and Facebook have never endorsed flexible work environments and believe in having everyone on campus as much as possible to improve innovation.

A flexible work environment won't be a competitive employer brand offering for every employer. But when it is, it will significantly improve your company's ability to attract and retain talent.

7. **Ethics.**

If your brand is damaged by a public scandal, your ability to recruit and retain employees will be seriously diminished.

Most workers want to work for ethical companies and feel proud about the product or services their companies provide to their customers. A company's image becomes a big part of the employee's own self-image and identity. Ethics seem to be falling among many US and global brands such as Wells Fargo, Samsung, Uber, Fox News, Weinstein Company, Volkswagen, United Airlines, Turing Pharmaceuticals AG, and Theranos. Even some Silicon Valley companies that had reputable brands, such as Google and Facebook, have seen their brands tarnished and stock values fall after news broke on how they either sold or gave away troves of user data, won't disclose how the information is used and repeated massive data breaches.

In the past three years, we have had many more examples of companies with bad behavior, leading to a fall in their financial performance

- Volkswagen—Its profits fell 20 percent after its diesel emissions scandal.[62]
- Uber—After several bad headlines and scandals for Uber, Lyft gained riders after a half-million Uber riders deleted the Uber app, and Uber's market cap fell $10 billion.[63]
- Wells Fargo—After its false accounts opening scandal, its new accounts dropped 31 percent.[64]
- Theranos—Its value fell from $9 billion to $100 million after its blood-testing scandal.[65]
- The Weinstein Company—After seventy women in the #MeToo movement accused film producer and co-owner Harvey Weinstein of sexual misconduct including rape, the company lost its influence and filed for bankruptcy.[66]

The message is clear. Once you violate the public's trust, it will hurt your top and bottom lines and your ability to attract and retain talent.

There is a strong body of evidence that supports that employees prefer working for employers with strong ethical behavior. These days, ethical behavior includes being champions of environmental sustainability.

Consider the following:

- The World at Work published the results of its survey of eight hundred full-time workers about ethical behavior. They found that 94 percent of respondents said it was either "critical" or "important" that they work for an ethical company. Further, 82 percent of respondents said they would prefer to be paid less and work for a company with ethical business practices than receive higher pay at a company with questionable ethics.[67]
- PwC reports in *Why Millennials Matter* that over half of millennials were attracted to companies with values that matched their own, and 56 percent would leave or consider leaving an employer that didn't have the values they expected.[68]
- A survey of more than two thousand people by Global Tolerance in the United Kingdom found that 42 percent of the workforce wanted to work for organizations that had a positive impact on the world. The same survey found that millennials led this sentiment, with 62 percent of millennials wanting to work for a company that had a positive impact.[69]
- The Network for Business Sustainability found that twelve peer-reviewed studies showed that job seekers were attracted to organizations with sustainability practices. Why?
  - It builds a sense of pride among workers (key for employee engagement).
  - Second, employees believe if a company cares about the environment, it will also care about them.
  - Third, sustainability connects the organization's values with job seekers' values.[70]

In the current US economy of 4.1 percent unemployment and a tight labor market, employers need to remember that one of the keys for successful recruiting and employee retention is their expressed values and behavior. Employees, potential employees, and consumers are watching.

8. External Environment.

The external environment is also important. For many office and factory workers, this can include a safe neighborhood, the commute time, the availability of free parking, and an exciting lunch scene. For higher educated and scientific workers, homes in neighborhoods with great school districts may be essential to attract and retain them.[71] In my experience, I have witnessed office and engineering workers leave a company for employers that offered neighborhoods with better schools. Younger workers may want to live in exciting urban areas.

Human resources and the executive team will need to decide on which of these factors they will compete in the labor market during a time of full employment. While it is important to consider all eight factors, you will need to really lead with no more than four factors.

Once that decision is made, as with any business strategy, it is important to put in place a lean and scalable process for recruiting that includes predictive measures and metrics of final success—and to measure how recruiting is contributing to the bottom line: profitable growth. A great recruiting plan integrated with comprehensive talent strategies will enable a company to hire better candidates faster than the competition. It will enable effective onboarding and shorten the time to full productivity. It will accelerate the new hire's ability to fit in with their new team and work culture and to feel a valued member of the team. It will reduce short- and long-term turnover. That saves real money and enables profitable growth.

CHAPTER 4: THE WORKFORCE PLAN

Having a workforce plan is critical for effective branding and recruiting. Frankly, they are also easy to do, as you shall see.

After establishing your employer brand, it is time to understand how your company's business strategies will impact whom you need to recruit, their necessary knowledge, skills, and competencies, and when and where to recruit them.

Read your company's business strategies carefully to understand where the company is growing or restructuring and changing around the world. Consider these questions:

- What new technologies will the company need to implement?
- What new regions of the world will the company operate?
- Where might the company be retrenching or restructuring its operations?

After understanding the changes the company anticipates, get answers to these questions so you can create an accurate and relevant recruiting plan.

1. Are there new knowledge, skills, and competencies the business will require from its future workforce?
2. Where do you go to identify, attract, and recruit the workers with these new skills and competencies? For example, do you need to develop relationships with new universities or other new sources for talent? Recruiting on new specialty job boards?

3. Based on what has been identified, can you develop an accurate candidate profile and job description to provide clarity for the recruiters and hiring managers?

4. Do you need to create new structured interviews and find new validated assessments to help you select great candidates who will succeed at your company?

5. Will the HR team working with management need to develop new career development paths and new amenities for the new professions you will add to your workforce?

6. How will your career website need to change to attract the new talent you need?

7. Will your work culture welcome these new skill sets or reject them? If your current culture may reject them, what steps need to be taken to be sure you can retain your new workers? For example, at Honeywell Space Systems, we needed to attract new software engineers to complement the work of our electromechanical engineers. They are very different workers, however, with different skill sets, academic backgrounds, and preferences for work culture. Software engineers often preferred different work hours (usually working in the evening) and weren't early birds. We had to change our work environment to accommodate them while not tipping the apple cart over on the electromechanical engineers.

8. What work environment will these new workers require, and how does it change the environment you currently offer?

9. How many job requisitions will need to be filled in the next twelve months? Calculating job requisitions is always a function of knowing your turnover by job family and level and of the new positions required to meet business growth. If you have a multiregional business in the United States, multiple businesses (in your home country), and operations across the globe, you will need to develop plans for each business and region.

10. What percentage of the talent you need to add should be regular employees or part of the contingent or gig workforce? There can

be beneficial tradeoffs here, but companies need to be mindful of the costs and legal issues associated with contingent workers.

Once this review is completed, I create a quarter by quarter workforce plan using whatever software the business people use, Excel, PowerPoint, or Word. In it, I highlight the open positions (regular, temporary, or contingent workers) by job family, level and department that has been approved by Finance, using their schedule for opening these positions. What I add to it is the 12-month turnover average for each department in the organization, such as marketing, R&D, and so forth. I then get it approved by Finance, each of the department heads and the business head.

The beauty of this is that we are all aligned. During the year, HR opens the requisitions on schedule as called out in the plan, unless there has been a significant change in revenues, business disruption, or some catastrophe. It streamlines the bureaucracy to open requisitions. I also provide monthly and quarterly updates to the organization to see that the workforce plan stays align with the business and finance plans throughout the year.

Later, what I learned to add to these plans is lead times for the hard to fill positions, based on our recruiting analytics. In medical devices, these were technical, clinical research and regulatory affairs roles which always required more time to find qualified candidates.

This workforce plan was global and listed the regions of the world and significant countries such as China, Ireland, Italy, and Japan.

These plans were never difficult to do. What is essential for their success are their transparency with the business team and the alignment with Finance and the business heads.

The use of machine learning and artificial intelligence technology embedded in applicant tracking systems will further improve the analytics for these plans.

After completing a workforce plan, you will need a recruiting budget. I have put the recruiting budget section in Chapter 5: The Recruiting Process. Why? Because streamlining and leaning out the recruiting process to make it work at digital speed is essential to eliminating wasteful costs and delays in recruiting. These costs savings enable you to better staff recruiting and invest in necessary training and technology.

Chapter 5: The Recruiting Process

Recruiting must be viewed as a highly reliable, repeatable process, like a smooth-running manufacturing line or dynamic marketing branding, customer identification and attraction process with an engaging customer relation management software. Today's recruiting process, like marketing, can use the latest chatbots, machine learning and Artificial Intelligence technologies to make the whole process of recruiting as effective and efficient as possible and to raise the employer brand of the company—just as these technologies are used by marketing. Blockchain technologies are not far behind, and will revolutionize how HR will validate the academic degrees, credentials, and work histories of job applicants in seconds, not days or weeks as required of today's background check systems.

I identify in a Recruiting and Selection Process Flow chart a linear process for a big company with high volume recruiting. It covers workforce planning, search planning, sourcing and screening, phone or Webex screening interviews, onsite interviews, decision making, and offer generation. The chart also identifies roles in the process for recruiters, hiring managers, interviewing teams, and human resources administrators to make the process work smoothly. It also provides timelines, which will vary depending on the industry. Digital technology will further improve the process.

Let's look closer at the process. Note that this process is set up to go for forty-five days from opening a job requisition to getting an acceptance on an offer. The process also calls for a seven-day period to conduct a strategic workforce intake meeting and a strategic candidate search strategy. If these meetings are used for high-volume jobs, after the strategy is set, these meetings do not need to be held every time a job is posted.

Recruiting & Selection Process Flow
Track metrics throughout and adapt as necessary

Workforce Planning	Search Planning	Source & Screen	Phone/WebEx Screens & Tests	On-site Interview	Decision	Job Offer
Hires by quarter plan	With Manager: • Set budget • Strategy • Digital strategy	ATS Screen • Algorithm • All applicants apply on line below VP level	Recruiter • Why interested • Verify resume • Successes/failures • Culture/team fit • Pay range fit	• Greet candidate • Use scheduler • No more than 5 interviews • One day	• Group decision and manager has a veto • Document reason • Decide within 1 day of last interview	• Pay to competency level and experience • Check internal and diversity equity
Profiles • Key goals • Tasks • Key stakeholder attributes • KSAs & experience	Active Candidates • Career site • Job boards • Career fairs	Recruiter Screen • KSAs • Culture/team fit • Diversity • Candidate social media	Manager • Similar questions • Technical competency	• Manager & other key stakeholders • Structured Interviews (divide question among interviewers)		• Approvals • H R makes offer • Manager calls to cajole or congratulate
Sourcing • Regular employee • Contingent • Supplier • Talent platform	Passive Candidates • Artificial intelligence • Social networks • Candidate bank • Professional networks • Referrals Post!	• Check sources • Top 5 from hiring manager • Half-page summaries on top candidates • Code in ATS & communicate	Test your candidates before the interview Code in ATS and communicate with candidates	• Work sampling • Tour • Lunch with peers • Each interviewer completes a one-page assessment. • Code in ATS & communicate	• Code in ATS and communicate with candidates	• Begin payroll and cultural onboarding • Code in ATS and communicate with all finalists
-5 work days	-2 days	+ 10 days	+ 5 days	+ 10 days	+ 3 days	+ 2 day

As with any dynamic and fast moving, agile process, everyone involved with recruiting must understand their role in the process, how to use the technology, be trained on it, and perform their roles well. Recruiting should use the latest helpful methods and technology to improve your recruiting outcomes—just like in manufacturing. It must be scalable. Recruiting brings value to the organization by quickly attracting the qualified candidates the company needs to grow. The faster the recruiting of these valuable human assets, the quicker the company can reach its financial goals.

Many of my colleagues in human resources have not understood the importance of having lean processes in human resources that use helpful technologies and predictive measures and metrics. It often bored them as their interest was first in finding and attracting talent to the organization and trying to improve the organization's ability to conduct structured interviews.

Do you believe you will be successful in improving your recruiting efforts by hiring more recruiters or throwing money at more third-party search firms? If you do, think again. Without clear roles, clarity, lean processes, and a commitment to a talent management mindset, throwing money at third-party search firms won't solve your problem. In my experience, it only makes it worse.

Recruiting Budget with an ROI

What is your recruiting budget? They are usually never large enough, so you need to make wise decisions with the resources you have. The good news is that employer branding and recruiting has a strong return on investment (ROI). I have never been denied a recruiting budget by executive management when I have shown the cost savings from recruiting process improvements, the reduction in first-year and overall turnover (which generates huge savings), and the reduction in use of third-party searches (which again provides huge savings and usually improves candidate quality).

I gathered from finance the total cost of their current recruiting processes:

   ◆ The cost every department spent on third-party searches and the percentage of hires that were from their third-party searches.
   ◆ The cost of current ads and recruiting trips by human resources and line departments.
   ◆ The cost of the current staff.
   ◆ The turnover rate of new hires and the cost of turnover.

What I added to this was whatever recruiting resources were needed to recruit and hire the needed number of candidates by the client departments' due dates. In every instance, I was able to show on a one-page budget the current cost of recruiting by open job requisition and the lower cost by improving our capability to internally source and reduce third-party search costs and the cost of turnover by hiring better candidates. In effect, it showed that internal recruiting could hire faster, better, and cheaper. The budget was also scalable, as it was based on the number of positions to be hired by quarter. If the requisitions expanded, I built in triggers that said,

"Here are the number of additional recruiters, sourcers, or administrators I will need to bring on temporarily to meet the demand."

How did I do this? I thought strategically about the business and how I could lower the cost per hire but improve the quality of hire while shortening the time to hire. Nearly all businesses want to lean out their business processes to accelerate their ability to deliver products and services to their customers, lower working capital, and improve revenue and operating profits. The same holds true for human resources processes such as recruiting.

What I look for is what steps of the process are inefficient and how to reduce them and what will improve the process and the end goal, which is usually to efficiently scale the process. In the chart below, I have identified typical costs to reduce with recruiting and typical areas to invest in that will improve the process, accelerate the time to hire, improve the quality of candidates, and improve the company's financial outcomes.

Drive Recruiting ROI

Costs to Reduce
- 3rd party search
- Lost productivity
- Management inattention
- Candidate withdrawal rate
- Job offer rejection rate
- New hire quits within one year

Areas to Investment
- Internal recruiters
- Project coordinator
- Talent management mindset
- Employee referrals
- Social media, networks, mobile devices
- Job boards/ads
- Career fairs
- Branding
- Digital technology

When people look at this chart, they are often surprised to see items such as lost productivity and management inattention and turnover. They shouldn't be. An improved recruiting process will address these inefficiencies in the recruiting process and improve the company's return on investment. In times of full employment, this is especially true. Quality candidates will receive multiple requests to be interviewed and job offers. The company with a compelling purpose, culture, and opportunity to hire and that moves quickly will get the candidate.

Similarly, I include areas to invest in, especially for high-volume recruiting. If you are reducing your dependence on expensive third-party searches, you will need to hire competent internal recruiters. If your interviewing process is disrupted by poor scheduling techniques and inefficient travel arrangements, you will need to add schedulers or technology such as Calendly to schedule individual interviews or Acuity to schedule a group of interviews.

Many may be surprised to learn that I have consistently experienced that hiring managers or others scheduled to interview candidates can be the worst link in the process by not looking at résumés within forty-eight hours or by canceling interviews at the last minute or making candidates wait in the lobby. This makes a terrible impression and costs the company time and money. Keeping a tight process with hiring managers showing up for interviews can substantially improve your process. Providing interviewing training and learning to narrow your search for job candidates to successful sources, including employee referrals and new technologies such as artificial intelligence, which combs the internet looking for the talent you need, can significantly shorten the time it takes to find qualified candidates.

New applicant tracking systems are becoming more user friendly and more efficient when the technology is mapped to your recruiting process. In addition, some applicant tracking systems, such as iCIMS, incorporate text recruiting (they purchased TextRecruit) to have ongoing messaging with candidates to improve the transparency of the recruiting process and keep candidates engaged.

Once I reviewed the data I collected from sources such as finance, examining line department budgets, and checking the company's recruiting and turnover metrics, I put a budget together that always will cut out inefficiencies or costly methods and invest in improvements. Let's look at two case studies.

Recruiting Budget Case Studies

In the first case study (see the chart below), which was with a research and manufacturing site, the company had outsourced its administration and manufacturing recruiting to a third party, which found candidates and then hired them on a six-month temporary contract. The employer could then convert the temporary worker to regular employment. Technical and managerial talent was recruited by the human resources business partners, who also did employee relations, harassment investigations, and leadership and team development. (Yes, they were busy.)

In gathering the data and looking at what inefficiencies to cut and where to invest while lowering the cost per hire and improving the quality and speed of hiring, I could give the business a return on investment. What I quickly learned in this case was that at least 50 percent of the hires made by the third-party search firm were from the company's own employees. Yes, employee referrals.

I told senior management we could do that on our own and save a lot of money even after hiring a recruiter to manage the process. To augment the employee referrals, the third-party search firm also said it had kiosks at shopping malls and our positions open on its website to hire the additional needed workers. However, the days for requisitions open was sixty-three days in a time of 5.5 percent unemployment—which is not full employment. Management complained that the long time to hire entry-level workers was a "barrier to their growth." We could do better.

What I proposed was to terminate our contract with the third-party search firm and hire our own recruiter for manufacturing and office work with a modest posting budget and administer a manufacturing test battery to replace the test battery the third-party search firm used. I promised them that after this investment, we could cut their hiring time and costs per hire by one-third. We achieved it. The plan worked so well, they later agreed to hire a second recruiter to focus on technical recruiting.

Case Study 1: Drive Recruiting ROI

Situation
- R&D and manufacturing site
- Circumstances
  - Outsourced office & manufacturing sourcing
  - Multi-source recruiting
  - Skill test
  - 50% employee referral rate
- Results
  - Management complaints
  - "Barrier to growth"
  - 63 day cycle time

Resolution
- Proposal to insource
- Investment:
  - 1 recruiter
  - Cut cycle time by 1/3
  - Cut costs per hire by ½
  - General aptitude skill test
  - Referral fee & 10k ad budget
- Results
  - Management praise
  - "Enabler of growth"
  - Cut cycle time to 35 days
  - Exceeded cost saving goals

The second case study is more complex. It was for a business that had lost over half its revenue and profits after losing a copyright lawsuit to a competitor and having another competitor launch an improved product. This business lost 50 percent of its market share in one quarter. It would lose or lay off half its workforce.

It was a turnaround and badly needed to recruit new workers across the board to get the company back in the game with newer products than the competitor that disrupted it. The business needed to hire engineers, assemblers, technicians, quality assurance people, clinical trial people, regulatory affairs people, salespeople, and leaders.

The business had an understaffed recruiting team that only focused on hiring engineers. Everyone else depended on their overworked human resources generalists and third-party searchers. Some of the third-party search companies placed the VPs in their roles in this company. That meant that they had strong relationships with the VPs and would mightily resist a diminished role for third-party search.

Although the company had a good applicant tracking system for the time (it would be outdated by today's standards), its previous recruiting team oddly did not use it. It took over 120 days to fill positions on average, except for manufacturing, with an unemployment rate of 6 percent—not full employment.

Turnover was at about 20 percent on average. Some employees were so frustrated with the understaffed conditions and demanding managers that they literally walked into their HR generalists' office, threw their badges at them, announced, "I f*****g quit," and walked out with a box of their possessions.

Although recruiting was a huge priority to turn the business around, the management team thought the word "process" was a dirty word.

I reviewed the business plan for the year, which had preliminary numbers of additional hires by function to ramp up its staffing to meet the business goals. My intuition told me the number of hires was dramatically underestimated, but the business believed that was all it could afford.

After gathering data on the costs of third-party search by each functional department, looking at the number of job applicants by opening, and identifying the best job boards and career fairs to attend to find these candidates, I proposed a budget that would add competent recruiters to replace the third-party search, except for VP search. This alone would significantly improve the cost per hire and reduce the time to find and hire qualified candidates. Because I believed the number of hires was grossly underestimated, I had top management agree to a ratio of job openings per recruiter, so it would be scalable. In order to be compliant with US and California regulations, we would mandate use of the applicant tracking system and generate our first affirmative action plan in years. I also proposed process improvements to recruiting, such as deadlines for HR recruiters and managers, such as for managers to review applicant résumés in seventy-two hours. Please see the case study 2 chart below.

Case Study 2: Drive Recruiting ROI

Situation
- Large division of Fortune 200 company
- Third party search used over 50%
- Little use of ATS
- Hiring cycle time of >120 days
- High turnover
- Fast recruiting of qualified candidates was critical for business model
- "Process" was a dirty word

Resolution
- Proposal
  - Aggressive social networking/recruiting model
  - Hire one recruiters per 100 requisitions
  - Hire project coordinator to manage ATS
  - Strict adherence to ATS & DOL protocols
  - Use third party search only for VPs
  - Applied lean sigma to recruiting process
  - Trained managers
  - Cut costs per hire by 25%
  - Cut cycle time by 50%
- Results:
  - Hired >650 in 18 months
  - Exceeded goals including recruiting ROI
  - Earned respect for H R

I proposed a recruiting budget using an Excel spreadsheet that looked like the chart below. Please note that I proposed changes in recruiting staff and processes and was clear on what inefficiencies I would improve. I calculated the change in costs per hire, which showed a reduction of 50 percent. The savings projected by reducing turnover was $2.5 million annually. My proposal was accepted in five minutes.

Case Study 2: ROI Detail
Double the hiring and reduce costs and turnover!

Current Situation 120 hires	Cost	Next FY Budget (240 planned hires)		Cost
3rd party search at 40% (48)	1,200,000	3rd party search at 10% (24)		600,000
Staff of 2	150,000	Staff of 4		400,000
Employee referrals (10% at $500/award)	12,000	Employee referral (30% at $1.5 award)		108,000
Branding, social media and networks	0	H R managed branding, social media & networks		10,000
Job boards	15,000	H R managed Job boards		10,000
		Scheduler (process improvement)		50,000
		TA&S change management/training		2,000
Total	1,377,000	Total	(-14.3%)	1,180,000
Cost per hire	11,475	Cost per hire	(-57%)	4,917
Turnover (20%/annual) .50 of salary	10M	Reduce Turnover (15%/annual) .50 of salary		7.5M

Later we would further improve our ability to recruit by implementing a regional job and compensation structure and a plan for flexible work arrangements that allowed 25 percent of the office and

IT workers to work from home three to four days a week. It significantly reduced our office footprint. After investments in videoconference rooms, huddle rooms, and new office furniture, it provided a return on investment in less than two months.

Roles in the Recruiting Process

I also divided out the recruiting duties to various roles to accommodate all the very important aspects of recruiting, play to employee strengths, and control costs. The five main roles were the recruiting manager, recruiter, sourcer, recruiting project coordinator, and scheduler. In small organizations, it is usually only the recruiter. Technology in 2019 has a major role to play in these traditional roles.

For the recruiter, technology can sort through the résumés using machine learning to bring to the top of the list the best candidates based on the candidate profile and job description. Technology should also seamlessly input résumés from job boards like Indeed and put them into your applicant tracking system. However, I have spoken with recruiting managers who have had to hire project coordinators or assign recruiters to manually do these uploads and downloads, even when they are using recently released ATS platforms. Why? Because the ATS's technology was too clunky and slow or because the ATS processes were not aligned with the company's processes or organization structure and coding.

Today's texting technology can also keep job candidates up to date on where their application is in the process. This is important as most candidates rate the application process poorly for failing to keep them up to date on their standing in the process after they receive an initial confirmation of their application. Technology can also conduct initial interviews of basic questions for the job using texting software and even digital interviews that were previously recorded with a recruiter or conducted by a robot. The recruiter can then review the answers from each candidate the next day. Some of these technologies I have not yet found to be reliable, but using technology to find, sort through résumés, and maintain communications with candidates should be on the list of upgrades for every recruiting department, provided it gives your company an ROI.

Recruiting Manager Role. The recruiting manager's role is to champion and lead the process, engage management, secure the budget, and work with marketing and IT to not only shape the employer brand but to use the latest IT and social networking technologies to promote the brand. The manager is within the budget and aligned to the business strategies; plans the recruiting calendar, which recruiting events to attend, and campus recruiting; and decides how to invest in recruiting tools such as job boards, social networks, social media, telephone sources, and employee referrals. I believe the manager should recruit the leadership roles and the key technical roles. Like any leader, the recruiting manager needs to align her team to the purpose and strategies for the organization; provide clarity for roles, goals, information flows, and decision rights; and manage, engage, and develop her workforce.

Recruiter's Role. Many large companies misunderstand the role of the recruiter, confusing it with a human resources generalist. That is a big mistake. Recruiters are hunters. Recruiters have the heart of salespeople and are competitive. They are digitally savvy and can close the deal. Human resources generalists are farmers, by and large. They are interested in developing individuals, teams, and organizations; resolving conflicts; and keeping the company true to its culture, principles, and the law. You need both hunters and farmers. Leave the recruiting to the hunters.

If you ask a recruiter to find you a Lebanese goat herder in Montana, they ought to be able to figure it out. Recruiters need to identify the required knowledge, skills, abilities, and competencies to perform a job and the degrees, certifications, and experiences that predict success. Good recruiters will also know that the worst form of screening is an unstructured interview and will champion an organization's data collection to further the KSA and competencies and to explore if there are any selection tests that will improve the predictability of the hiring process.

Recruiters also need to be competent in social media, social networks, which job boards and recruiting conferences will provide their company the best ROI, and how to put it all together. Finally, in person, through LinkedIn messages, texts, or by phone, they need to be able to engage the passive candidate and pique their interests, draw them in, keep them engaged during the interviews, and seal the deal.

Recruiters also need to keep the hiring manager and the interview team engaged, making sure they are prepared for their interviews, follow the process, and complete their evaluations. Some days that is the more challenging task. Finally, recruiters also need to complete the administrative tasks assigned to them for résumé and candidate tracking and evaluation scoring, or the company will not be able to prove itself an affirmative action recruiter and equal opportunity employer. However, do not allow your recruiters to fall into an administrator's mind-set. If the administrative tasks of your applicant tracking system become too burdensome (and I have seen many that are), assign many maintenance tasks to project coordinators and keep your recruiters hunting.

Recruiters ought to screen the final five to ten candidates down to a final list of three by detailed phone and/or Webex screens, where they are checking for the following:

- Why the candidate is interested in the company and that they know the company's mission and major products or services; the information can be accessed on Yahoo Finance.
- Probing questions that verify that what is on the résumé is accurate regarding years of experience and competencies.
- Probing questions to learn why the candidate moved from his or her last three jobs, and the major successes and disappointments on each job.

- ◆ Screen preferences in supervisory style and culture to match the work team and company culture.
- ◆ Finally, present the company's culture, pay range, and benefits and check to see that the candidate is interested in a referral for a supervisor screen.

Sourcer's Role. For high-volume recruiting when you are needing to recruit passive candidates, it is good to use sourcers. They may be entry-level recruiters or recruiters who enjoy finding, contacting, and luring candidates to openings as opposed to presenting the candidates to the management team and closing the deal. Sourcers ought to build up a database of passive candidates and check in with them at critical points in their career, which they have learned about during the interview. This may be at the end of a project when they are looking for another challenge or key junctures in their careers when they may be interested in a career move. Sourcers need great skill sets for mining social networks and functional networks and cold-calling or emailing candidates. Sourcers can start their databases by getting names of five or ten great candidates to have from hiring managers in their area of expertise. Without sourcers, recruiters need to do this role, particularly in tight labor markets. With high volume, specializing in sourcers can have a high return on investment.

However, artificial intelligence platforms designed for recruiting, such as ThisWay Global, Ideal, and Entelo, are very capable now of replacing the sourcer's role in finding qualified job candidates and in some cases even predicting if a candidate is ready to leave a company with algorithms that I believe still need to be tested. With today's technology, sourcers can do much of the computer interface with AI, and text recruiting can reach out to entry-level job candidates who apply on the company's career site or are identified by artificial intelligence platforms. However, for experienced job candidates, leaders, and executives, it is best for a sourcer or recruiter to contact them. The sourcer's role may change and will need someone who is good at striking up conversation, piquing a job candidate's interest, and building relationships—like a great sales rep.

Recruiting Project Coordinator's Role. Their role is first to keep the data in the applicant tracking system (ATS) up-to-date and accurate. Secondly, they are to manage the communications to many of the rejected job candidates by triggering text or email communications from the ATS system (with the recruiter managing the communications with job candidates who move forward in the process). Third, they control the interface between the ATS and the payroll system. Managing this interface is critical so that new hires do not have delays in receiving their pay and in assuring the data are accurate. They work in the background and make sure the administrative details are kept accurate and current.

The role of the recruiting project coordinator will be significantly reduced as Artificial Intelligence is upgraded into ATS software and can manage many of these repetitive tasks at digital speed.

Key Roles in Recruiting

Recruiter	Hiring Manager	Interviewing Team**
• Hunter	• Recognizes TA is No. 1 Job	• Recognizes TA is No. 1 Job
• Company ambassador	• Active	• Active
• Build relationships using social media & email/text	• Company ambassador	• Company ambassador
• Initial screen for competencies, effectiveness and match to company culture and pay structure	• Responds with urgency	• Responds with urgency
	• Builds relationship	• Builds relationship
	• Screens recruiters list with deep technical screen	• Screens recruiters list and deep technical screen, as assigned
• Includes phone screens	• Major decision maker—veto	• Major decision makers
• Technologist*	• Certified to interview	• Certified to interview
• Trained for role	• Trained for role	• Trained for role

*In large volume use a H R project coordinator for many non-decision ATS coding and administration, and payroll onboarding. The adm. work will be automated.
**In larger organizations H R Generalist can join interview team

Human Resources Business Partner's (HRBP) Role. Whether this role is at the vice president level for a large division of a global corporation or is a sole human resources business partner for a fast-paced five-hundred-person company, the role is to align recruiting to the strategic talent acquisition needs of the business and to align management to its role in recruiting. The HRBP needs to align recruiting to the needs of the business—its purpose, principles, and strategies—and very specifically to the number of positions the human capital plan predicts either through growth or attrition and the knowledge, skills, abilities, and competencies of each job family. Recruiters will recruit better when they know the scope of requisitions to fill, the timing, and the business climate. This understanding should not be shallow or superficial but substantive, so the recruiter can engage passive candidates with passion and authority in her or his voice. The HRBP should be a member of the interview team. The HRBP should hold at least quarterly meetings with recruiting to review progress, measure success, encourage what is working, discourage what is not working, and see what obstacles he or she can remove.

Hiring Manager's Role. As said earlier, recruiting is the number-one priority of everyone in management, and the future success of the business depends on the speed and quality of the recruiting. At the end of the process, the hiring manager and the work team should believe they have hired the best candidate possible and used a smooth and fast-moving process.

I recommend to all hiring managers that they keep a list of the top ten candidates they would love to have working for them based on their knowledge of their industry and to share it with HR. Together they can woo these candidates over time using social media and reaching out to them when the company has openings that are great matches for the next step in their careers. This tactic is especially helpful in tight labor markets.

However, managers should not have sole decision-making on who joins their team. That should be shared with human resources and a qualified group of interviewers on the interview team and the director to whom they report. Why? The best strategies don't just hire an employee for this one role but for several roles, so that new employees will have a successful career with the company.

Like any member of the interview team, the hiring manager needs to be trained in the ethics, legal issues, and interview techniques of interviewing, and they should be evaluated on their interviewing either through candidate feedback or through expert observation. A major role of hiring managers is to join in with the recruiting process. First, they should be on the lookout for great talent wherever they are and recruit! Second is to actively engage in the recruiting process: approve requisitions on time, cooperate with the writing of job descriptions, be available for interviews, show up on time, take an active interest in candidates, follow the techniques for structured interviews, and complete evaluations. Recruiting cannot be successful without the engagement of hiring managers.

Recruiters hate it when hiring managers wait two weeks before reviewing résumés they have sent them or take a month to decide which of the three candidates interviewed will be offered the job. These delays disrupt the process, making it inefficient for everyone, and disillusion the candidates. In a tight market, the candidates will lose interest and go with another employer. When managers delayed the process like this, I would put their requisitions on hold and reassign the recruiters to work with other managers who were eager to engage in the process.

I recommend that managers hold telephone or Webex screens with a focus on the current challenges of the role and a review of the candidate's resume and how they overcame obstacles in the candidate's previous roles. If such a prescreen is done, the managers will be free to do more detailed probing when the candidate comes into the office for a face-to-face interview.

Interview Team's Role. In addition to the hiring manager and the human resources business partner, it is critical to have other interested and competent interviewers evaluate the final candidates. The interview team should be no more than four. Research shows that with more than four well-prepared team members, the company doesn't learn any more about the candidate and annoys the candidate.[72] The interview team should have members who are either technically competent in the candidate's field or have a major stake in the candidate's contributions and success. Break the structured interview into different questions assigned to the interview team members depending on their expertise so you play to interviewer strengths and make the process more interesting to the candidate. Nothing is more boring and shows a lack of planning than to have each interviewer ask the same set of questions.

Scheduler's Role. Like with the interview team, this is a role usually performed by a department administrator or secretary. While scheduling technology can do much of this role, a person still has an important role to play in greeting and hosting job candidates and making a great first impression. Conventionally, the scheduler arranges the interviews, calendars everyone's schedule, checks for confirmation, prepares the interview agenda (at the direction of the recruiter), and mails out the schedule, directions, and any prereads to the candidate and to the interviewers. The scheduler also sends reminders out the day before. The scheduler also reserves conference rooms, arranges videoconferences if necessary, and makes meal arrangements.

The scheduler or the recruiter should greet the candidate upon arrival. (I like to have the recruiter be the last person to meet with the candidate to answer any remaining questions, clarify issues on the company's culture, strategic direction, onboarding, and benefits, and most importantly, check on the candidate's continuing interest.) The scheduler's role is time consuming, but it is very important—too important for making a great impression to be left as the last-minute task on the recruiter's or hiring manager's mind. This role has proven to be so important to recruiting and such a time-saver for departments and human resources that I have had functional departments contribute resources to human resources budgets to hire and direct schedulers.

Technology can simplify this role. Some of the newer ATS systems have a scheduling function. Some use Calendly, which can schedule one-on-one interviews. Acuity is a scheduling platform that can schedule groups of interviews. I recommend companies incorporate this technology to reduce the time required of schedulers. However, someone should be accountable to see that the job candidate has a great experience when they come in to the facility for a half-day or day of interviews. In addition, this software may not be able to reserve the conference rooms needed, set up tours, and provide the human touch candidates like during an interview, especially candidates who are applying for senior management and technical roles.

I will now review how to create excellent job descriptions, so we know what we are looking for and how to attract impressive job candidates, and then how to conduct strategic workforce intake meetings, as called out in the process flow above. In the next three chapters, we will cover candidate search strategies, screening candidates, and recruiting process metrics.

Job Descriptions: First Think of Them as Marketing Tools

Many job descriptions are written to accurately describe the major and minor duties of the job and the knowledge, skills, and abilities of qualified candidates, and include the legal and regulatory requirements of the governing country and municipality. This is well and good but is not enough for today's talent scarcity. In the first paragraph of your job description, you need to market your company's employer brand, beginning with the higher-level purpose for humanity, the cool work your employees do, and any employer awards you have won.

Unless you have a worldwide brand like Adecco, Apple, Daimler, Google, or Johnson & Johnson, for many job seekers, your job description may be the first time they learn about your company. Make a great first impression.

The test for effective marketing and making a great first impression is for the job candidates to quickly know what your company is about and how it is distinguished in your industry. Most of all, you want to draw job candidates who would be a great fit for your company to you. Don't be dull and don't write the trendy stuff everyone else writes. Be authentic.

In addition to conveying your employer brand, the other key ingredients for a job description are to describe how the role fits into the company's mission, what the incumbent will need to achieve over the course of the year, the required knowledge, degrees, skills, and abilities, major and minor job duties (which the EEOC wants to see in the United States), and the working conditions. Be as efficient as possible in the writing and don't bore job seekers. I have seen many job descriptions that repeat the same information (which are rehashed job requirements and duties) throughout the job description. Only say it once and keep the document as brief as possible.

For example, I had to recruit a director of physician training for a new start-up business. The job description for the role began with Medtronic's mission and how this new business for Medtronic was going to provide a solution for an unmet need in cardiovascular treatment, that is, reducing high blood pressure for those patients who were not responsive to the pharmaceutical treatments.

It then outlined what the candidate had to achieve in the first year. It included the main objectives to achieve in that year, such as:

1. recruit a new staff.
2. develop contacts and build relationships among the community of physician customers.
3. establish medical training for this new therapy to be delivered to the physicians and medical staff who would participate in the business's clinical trials, and to new staff members for the business.

The goal was to explain what the individual had to do to be successful on the job.

Here is an example of how it may appear in your job description in two paragraphs:

> The director of physician training is to establish a new physician training program for the physicians on our FDA-sanctioned US clinical trial for our new renal denervation therapy to reduce drug-resistant and uncontrollable high blood pressure. This includes

establishing smart measures and milestones for success and open feedback. The incumbent will be a part of developing the latest innovation by "Company" and bring a lifesaving and health-restoring therapy to thousands of patients in the United States and around the world whose high blood pressure is not effectively treated by existing therapies.

"Company" is the largest medical device company in the world, and every second, a patient around the world receives a "Company" device to alleviate pain, restore health, or prolong life.

The nuance is important. It is very different to recruit a leader who will lead an already existing team with established procedures and training in a large company such as Medtronic, IBM, or Honeywell than it is to hire someone who will start from scratch. The latter requires someone who has the entrepreneurial spirit to establish such an organization, not just inherit what someone else set up before him. Not everyone with experience in a major corporation with established procedures will have the initiative, courage, and persuasion skills to create something new.

At this level, I also put in title of the individual the incumbent will report to, collaborate with, and need to establish relationships with inside and external to the organization. Look at this example:

This position reports to the general manager of renal denervation and is a member of her executive staff. The incumbent will need to develop excellent working relationships and be able to influence members of the executive team and the leaders of physician education and clinical trial management at "Company" corporate, and build trusting relationships with field clinical representatives, key opinion leading physicians in the community and with our

clinical trial sites, and marketing and sales representatives in the United States, Europe, Asia, and around
the world. The incumbent will recruit and lead a staff
of five during the first year.

Critical for this role are recruiting and leadership skills in an entrepreneurial environment that involves the ability to multitask and
at first to do the work of yet-to-be hired staff. In order to be successful, however, the incumbent will need to quickly delegate work and
decision-making after staff is hired and to then focus more time and
energy on the more strategic requirements of the position. Consider
this example:

The incumbent will need to achieve the following
leadership objectives in the first year of operations:

1. Recruit a global, energetic, and committed physician train-
    ing staff aligned to the business's strategies and with the
    successful track record, competencies, and skills to achieve
    its goals and to provide ongoing feedback and innovation.
2. Establish operational norms for a global staff that will fa-
    cilitate staff alignment, speedy digital and face-to-face in-
    formation flows, constant communications, collaboration,
    teamwork, decision rights, and high effectiveness. This in-
    cludes regular staff meetings and the smart use of digital
    and videoconferencing technologies to enable teamwork
    and timely execution.
3. Build relationships with a diverse and global staff to assure
    their alignment, understanding, and motivation. This in-
    cludes being able to provide timely performance and devel-
    opment feedback, regular one-on-one meetings, and strong
    delegation, empowerment, and performance management
    skills.

Knowledge Skills and Abilities. Certainly the job description will need to also cover items that are critical to set objective standards for selection, as is often required by the US Department of Labor and its agencies to help prevent unfair hiring lawsuits. This includes the duties and responsibilities and the knowledge, skills, and abilities required to perform well on the job, including the degree or certification requirements and requisite experience. The EEOC has provided guidance that employers provide major and minor duties for the job to help distinguish what is truly important and what might allow for an ADA accommodation. Here is an example for this role; these are the major requirements:

1. Excellent understanding of scientific knowledge regarding cardiovascular disease, high blood pressure, the sympathetic nervous system, and the current treatment protocols.
2. Excellent written and verbal communications skills using medical and scientific terms. This includes active and passive listening and great persuasion skills.
3. Strong proficiency with scientific adult learning and surgical procedures and safety; and an understanding of how highly intelligent and educated opinion-leading physicians and nurses learn and adapt new practices and treatments.
4. Strong leadership skills to recruit, align, and lead a staff of diverse and competent professionals in a global environment in the biotech industry.
5. Understanding of the laws and regulations, scientific requirements, and ethics of the biotech industry.
6. Benchmark, analyze, make recommendations, and establish the physicians' education program, including the latest means of digitally delivered training.
7. Propose and manage the physician education budget within organizational guidelines and with quarterly reviews.
8. Develop and implement all physician education policies and procedures, including those for education standards, physician standards, security, purchasing, and service provision.

9. Negotiate and administer vendor, outsourcer, and consultant contracts and service agreements.
10. Strong ethical values and a lifetime dedication to improving the welfare of humanity by bringing forward safe, reliable, and ethical innovations to improve the lives of our patients and the reputations of our doctor and health management system clients.
11. Proficient computer skills in the Microsoft Office suite, EduTracker, LMS, and various education-related applications

Education and Years of Experience. Currently there is lot of debate on the value of degrees. There are many pundits who are critical of academic credentialization. They like to point to key entrepreneurs such as Bill Gates, who dropped out of Harvard to start Microsoft. Or they point to the competencies required of great software engineers and software code writers, and that a college degree is not a predictor of success for these professions. In this case, I agree with them.

I agree that a BS or MA degree is not always a predictor of success in some professions, but it depends highly on the job and the industry. For example, while recruiting software engineers beginning in the 1990s (and up to today) for the aerospace business, my recruiting team and the R&D leaders discovered that what mattered most in hiring software engineers or code writers were certain competencies for language and logic not necessarily a degree in computer science or mathematics. We used a specific software language for the severe element of space, with its high quality and reliability requirements.

We discovered that the competencies that predicted software engineering and software code writing success were the same human competencies that predict great acumen with languages, mathematics (which is a language of symbols), and music reading and composition, not an electronic engineer's degree as we first thought. These skills typically included abstract thinking, logic, recognizing patterns, curiosity, and a love to solve problems. Like learning a language or music, it takes dedication and the willingness to endure repetition.

The point is not to justify or denigrate academic degrees. The point is to understand the importance of specific competencies that drive success on the job by job family (or profession). With software engineers and code writers, the above competencies were more predictive than degrees.

Conversely, when we went to hire system engineers, hiring degreed engineers who could also understand all parts of the code, system performance, integration of systems, and the emergence of new codes and technologies were strong predictors of success. Computer science degrees taught these competencies and were better predictors of job success.

Let's switch professions and look at the knowledge, skills, and abilities of accountants. If you are going to hire an accountant in the United States, you will want to hire someone who understands the FASB and general ledger accounting. The knowledge for this skill set often comes from a bachelor of science degree in accounting and finance, usually with different specialties such as international accounting or cost accountant. Often certifications can be added to refine their skill, such as a Certified Public Accountant (CPA). Will you want someone with solid experience working in a publicly traded company or a private company? Nonprofit? They have different processes and requirements. Does finance in your company use SAP or Oracle or a different enterprise software? You will prefer someone who knows the software your company uses. In large companies, accountants may specialize in areas such as manufacturing, sales and marketing, or general ledger, and again, previous experience and competencies with these areas of focus on the position of the general ledger may be important. Who will the accountant be working with? Do they have good experience building relationships and solving problems with past clients, or will they be pure number crunchers?

Many companies put a premium on specific universities. It is a fact that some universities typically score higher than others on assessments of number-one areas of academic focus such as MBAs. Harvard, Wharton, Kellogg, Duke, Stanford, and University of California at Berkeley often lead the list for MBAs, and there are others in various ratings. But are the candidates of these leading universities worth the extra pay and perks they can demand on the market? Are they worth the expectations of accelerated career paths? When I worked for Honeywell and Medtronic, the answer was usually a resounding yes in the minds of the executives—who often came from these schools and helped us recruit at their alma maters. These companies spent lots of money for access to these candidates and to interview them on campus. Usually executives had to make guest appearances at classes and give lectures as part of the recruiting/corporate relationship.

Some companies are beginning to challenge this. Google executives, for example, have said that they followed this common wisdom of recruiting at top universities as they began their rapid hiring in the early 2000s. But based on their own workforce analytics, they moved to other criteria, such as a careful definition of job competencies based on collecting and analyzing their workforce data.[73]

With over twenty-seven years working with clients, Bill Schiemann, CEO of the Metrus Group Inc., has observed that companies can recruit great leaders, MBAs, engineers, and professionals from the best regional schools and earn a higher return on investment from these local hires. Why? In an interview with me in December, 2018, Bill said "The top students from the regional schools stay longer at these companies than the students from the highly regarded national schools, often due to their family and cultural ties in the regional area." Besides Bill continued to explain, the graduates from regional schools were less frequently recruited than graduates from the top national schools and less expensive. Finally, organizations such as Johnson & Johnson, other multinational corporations, and marketing and legal firms have learned that the graduates from the top national schools wanted more autonomy in their roles and faster career moves, which may not be met in many organizations. For all these reasons, Bill recommends that companies reconsider the type of school they are recruiting from in terms of expectations of the candidates, longevity of candidates, expense, and fit.

I have learned to begin with job competencies and then to identify the universities that have degrees with the knowledge, skills, and competencies you need in the various professions you hire for. For example, when needing to hire clinical researchers, my staffing team discovered that the same highly ranked national MBA schools usually did not specialize in this profession. The team researched and identified other schools, such as UCLA, San Diego State University, Johns Hopkins, and Texas A&M.

Another key area for screening is employment history. It can be desirable to hire candidates from companies that have great competence and processes in the desired field. This means not just targeting a candidate by simply the number of years they have in biomedical, software, or mechanical engineering experience and whatever certification is necessary, but with specific experience from a company that has similar strategies to those you may have or is known for excellent training programs.

Also review the career progression of candidates. Are they moving between jobs frequently without any sign of career progression or without moves caused by family considerations? If so, this can be a warning sign of someone who struggles to hold a job or can't get along with coworkers.

The importance of degrees will also be very important by industry and the standards of the governing professions and laws and regulations by country and national trade associations or industry codes. My experience is that in industries that have high levels of government regulations and require extraordinarily high standards of quality and reliability, such as pharmaceuticals, biomedical, and aerospace, to name a few, have higher requirements for credentialization. This is due to the importance of workers in the industry understanding the major theories and dynamics that shape the industry, such as chemistry, biology, and epidemiology in pharmaceuticals and aeronautics and physics in aerospace.

In the software industry, these criteria are not so rigid except in highly specialized environments such as aerospace and biotech. In the software industry, the concepts of agile teams and the Agile Manifesto, with its bold thinking, team scrums, involvement of the end user, development as you go, and soft launches, are very important. It doesn't work as simply when you are researching and testing a cure for cancer, working out how to keep a plane in flight, designing and manufacturing computer chips, or improving a cardiac pacemaker.

Regarding years of experience, empirical research shows that when someone has more than five years on the job, it has a diminishing return on job competence—although ongoing training and coaching help. When a new technology and methodology occurs that substantially changes the role, it is effectively a new job.

Education is a complement to experience as it teaches the models, theories, procedures, laws, and regulations of a profession, how problems have been overcome, and how the achievement was achieved. As discussed above, education in many professions is the starting point.

Recruiters look for combinations and tradeoffs of education and experience in roles. For example, in the mechanical engineering career family, a normal progression from the entry level title of "Associate Engineer" for a college graduate may be for two years of experience to be considered for a promotion to the title of "engineer" and four years to be considered for a promotion to the tile of "senior engineer." But having a Master's Degree may count for two years of experience, accelerating consideration for promotions. Graduating from a top engineering school, such as MIT, may mean two additional years of experience credit. All promotions should be based on performance not just experience and education level formulas.

Note, the US EEOC has given guidance to companies to be specific on years of experience and not to give ranges, such as two to six years. They are trying to drive down the years of required experience in an effort to improve the recruiting of protected classes.

Let's get back to our job description example for the director of physician training and specifically for education and experience together:

Education and Experience.

Ideally the incumbent will hold a master of arts in medical sciences, such as epidemiology, nursing or physician assistant, or other life sciences. A bachelor of science degree in medical sciences with four or more years of professional experience will also be considered.

The US EEOC does not require that companies have job descriptions but encourages it. Through the EEOC, government provides guidance to employers to list major responsibilities and minor responsibilities, including office or work environments and any physical job requirements, as a way to minimize unnecessary work obstacles to the disabled or that might pose an adverse impact in the selection of protected classes.

The EEOC has provided guidance that job descriptions, properly prepared, can support the goal of eradicating unlawful employment discrimination. Racial requirements are never lawful in job descriptions and should not be used under any circumstances. Job requirements based on an employee's gender, national origin, religion, or age can be used in very limited circumstances. Job requirements based on these protected characteristics are lawful only when an employer can demonstrate that they are bona fide occupational qualifications ("BFOQs") reasonably necessary to the normal operation of a business.[74]

Let's look at three examples where job description requirements were found to be either discriminating by the US courts or were not. In the first one, the employer was faulted for enforcing a height and weight standard that discriminated against women. In the second, the EEOC backed down from forcing a restaurant chain whose image was scantily clad women serving alcohol and food from hiring men servers. In the third example, a retail company wrongly refused to hire a Muslim woman who wore a hijab due to her religion in violation of their "Look Policy" and didn't ask for an accommodation to wear the hijab.

The first example is the famous 1977 discrimination claim in Alabama known as *Dothard v. Rawlinson,* where a female prison guard was rejected because she failed to meet the minimum 120-pound weight requirement and five foot two-inch height requirement of an Alabama statute. An appellate court ruled in the woman's favor on the basis of national statistics as to the comparative height and weight of men and women, indicating that Alabama's statutory standards would exclude over 4 percent of the female population but less than 1 percent of the male population. The court found that, with respect to such standards, the appellee had made a prima facie case of unlawful sex discrimination.

On the other hand, the restaurant chain Hooters in 1996 successfully overcame an EEOC claim of discrimination when a male was denied a job as a server because it would not fit the image of Hooters' restaurants and sports bar, where scantily clad female servers in tank tops and hot shorts serve up beer, wings, and burgers. The EEOC decided it could not pursue the case due to a limit of resources. It also received extensive calls and mail from Hooters patrons after the company launched a promotional campaign calling for the EEOC to back down.[75]

The third example is when Abercrombie & Fitch lost a discrimination case brought by the EEOC to the US Supreme Court. The US Supreme Court ruled eight to one, in a decision written by Justice Antonin Scalia, that an employer may not refuse to hire an applicant if the employer is motivated by avoiding the need to accommodate a religious practice. Such behavior, the court said, violated the prohibition on religious discrimination contained in Title VII of the Civil Rights Act of 1964.

The case arose when a teenager who wore a hijab headscarf as part of her Muslim faith, applied for a job at Abercrombie & Fitch in her hometown of Tulsa. She was denied a job for failing to conform to the company's "Look Policy," which Abercrombie & Fitch claimed banned head coverings. Before the Supreme Court ruling, an earlier court of appeals ruling held that Abercrombie & Fitch was not on sufficient notice by the teenager of her religious practice because, despite correctly "assuming" that she wore a headscarf because of her religion, Abercrombie did not receive explicit, verbal notice of a conflict between the "Look Policy" and her religious practice from the teenager. Abercrombie & Fitch, however, never disclosed the "no head coverings" rule in the "Look Policy" to the teenager.[76]

As you write these parts of the job description, be mindful of US laws and court cases in general. Below is how the work environment, physical demands, position type/expected hours of work, and travel sections are written. Under the ADA, a reasonable accommodation is assistance or changes to a position or workplace that will enable an employee to do his or her job despite having a disability. Under the ADA, employers are required to provide reasonable accommodations to qualified employees with disabilities, unless doing so would pose an undue hardship.[77]

These items are minor requirements and are the first place to look for an area to allow accommodations under the ADA.

Work Environment

This job operates in a professional office environment. This role routinely uses standard office equipment such as laptops, iPhones, smartphones, phones, photocopiers, filing cabinets, and fax machines. Business casual dress is appropriate most of the time except for special meetings with customers, investors, and government officials.

Physical Demands (This is required by the US American with Disabilities Act)

The physical demands described here are representative of those that must be met by an employee to successfully perform the essential functions of this job. While performing the duties of this job, the employee is regularly required to talk or hear. The employee frequently is required to stand; walk; use hands to finger, handle, or feel; and reach with hands and arms.

Position Type/Expected Hours of Work

This is a full-time position, exempt, and days of work are Monday through Friday during normal working hours.

Travel

Expect 50 percent travel in total in the United States and frequent international travel.

Job descriptions should also include disclaimers like the following: "Nothing in this job description restricts management's right to assign or reassign duties and responsibilities to this job at any time." Or "This job description is subject to change at any time."

Remember, job descriptions are as much about marketing your employer brand as accurately conveying the key goals and required knowledge, skills, and abilities of the job in a manner that does not discriminate against protected classes.

If you want more information on the guidance from the EEOC on avoiding discriminatory language or language that violates the ADA, I encourage you to go directly to the EEOC website or the website of an HR organization, such as SHRM, or consult with your labor attorney.

Strategic Workforce Intake Meeting

For each job posting, it is important to first have a strategic work force intake meeting, as called out in my Recruiting and Selection Process Flow above. At this meeting, the recruiter learns from the department VP hiring, human resource business partner, and hiring managers, the annual operating plan-approved number of hires that are planned for the department's positions for the year and their timing. These numbers should also include the number of openings that are expected from the department's current rolling twelve-month turnover rate.

If the company has several locations, whether domestic or global, the recruiter will also want to get clarity on where the locations will be housed and whether workers will be able to work remotely for the roles. The recruiter will want to update any changes in required tasks, knowledge, skills, and abilities in the job description and the candidate profile. They should also clarify if there are any changes in sources to recruit, such as from companies or universities that have known experts in the field.

The company's recruiting and workforce plan, as described in Chapter 4, The Workforce Plan will be a guide to this process. However, this meeting is to get clarity between the business function and its recruiting team. Once the recruiting numbers are understood, the work should turn to the candidate search strategy.

In addition, get clarity on whether the roles are going to be for regular employees, temporary employees, or contingent or gig workers; the sourcing of the contingent workforce; and finally, any suppliers specializing in this work. It is important to keep in mind the legal issues with temporary and contingent workers, which are explained in Chapter 13: HR Legal Geek.

CHAPTER 6: CANDIDATE SEARCH STRATEGY

Where will the recruiter search for the candidates? Research shows that about 50 percent of job seekers search for jobs on job boards such as Indeed, Glassdoor, CareerBuilder, and Monster and specific specialty boards such as Dice (for STEMM (Science, Technical, Engineering, Mathematics, and Medical) roles). About one-third of job seekers find jobs on the company's career web page, especially if the company has a strong employer brand.

About 45 percent get a reference for a job opening from a friend. This knowledge is a good reminder to check to see that the company's referral bonuses are motivational. If the positions being recruited for are particularly rare, hard to find, or needed in great numbers, be sure your referral fee will motivate referrals.

Only about 20 percent of job seekers look for jobs on social media. It is good to have recruiters advertise their openings on social media, but it is not a great source for job candidates. Now it is about apps and text recruiting. More on that in Chapter 12, HR Geek: Technology.

I have had great success purchasing banner ads on job boards when I have a high volume of openings for a specific field or for an R&D or commercial launch ramp-up when large numbers of hires are required.

In addition to the above active ways to search for candidates and wait for a response, there are also aggressive tactics to get the attention of passive candidates. Let's explore these options.

Other sources of candidates to consider are professional associations, professional networks such as LinkedIn, and professional or technical conferences. I have found that technical or professional conferences are particularly good for recruiting experienced and successful job candidates.

Will your recruiters or sourcers use direct calling of candidates from lists of candidates you have gathered from either artificial intelligence or past recruiting efforts? About one-third of candidates are open to direct recruiting calls. This strategy, however, requires persistence and follow-up calls at certain key career events for each candidate (such as the end of a project or after a review period), much like any sales strategy.

Where Do Job Seekers Look for Jobs?

Below I have reported on the best research I have found, from Harris Polls, on where job seekers look for work. It is important for recruiting teams to stay up on this research to know how wisely to spend their recruiting budgets for their locations and industries.

Where do you find the workers that you need? Postings of job openings on digital job boards such as Monster, Indeed, and CareerBuilder? College campus recruiting? Professional associations? Technical conferences?

According to the Harris Poll taken for Glassdoor in July 2018,[78] most job seekers want to be in control when it comes to managing their job searches. Let's look at the results of the Harris Poll survey.

- Fifty-one percent preferred looking for a relevant new job opportunity at an online job site such as Glassdoor, Indeed, and so on.
- Forty-five percent preferred to hear about a job opportunity from a friend.
- Thirty-five percent preferred visiting company websites.
- Thirty-four percent preferred a recruiter or hiring manager to proactively call them.

- ◆ Twenty percent preferred to find a new job via social media.
- ◆ Nineteen percent preferred to become aware of a job through a staffing agency.

According to Julie Coucoules, Glassdoor's Global Head of Talent Acquisition, "Job seekers are taking control of their own destiny by harnessing the power of information to find the right job and employer for them. Today, job seekers are more informed than ever. For employers, by helping prospective talent find and access the information they want, you'll be helping your recruiting efforts by attracting quality and informed candidates who often translate to top performing employees who stay longer too."[79]

Jobvite, which sells applicant tracking systems, text recruiting, videoscreening, and social recruiting capabilities, has begun publishing recruiting benchmark reports. The 2018 Jobvite Recruiting Benchmark Report[80] shows the sources of job candidates. Like the Harris Survey for Glassdoor, Jobvite found that 51 percent of job candidates came from job boards and 36 percent applied through the company's website (independent of job boards).

Sourcing Candidates

Once you have the budget and sourcing strategies understood and agreed to, it is time to get recruiting.

The first step is for the recruiter to place the job posting on the company's website and on all appropriate job boards. It is time to search for passive job candidates, especially during times of full employment. Turn on your company's artificial intelligence platform to identify qualified job candidates in the area of your search using your carefully developed job description. I also recommend standard passive recruiting methods such as asking each manager in this filed for their top-ten list of outsiders to recruit and former applicants for the same role. Then the recruiter, or a sourcer if there is one, should start contacting these passive job candidates. The goal here is not just find candidates ready for a job move now, but to build a strategic talent pool for future openings. With all of the interested job candidates you want to set up a searchable data base that includes their criteria for a career move and timing.

The US government Equal Employment Opportunity Commission has given guidance to companies that are obligated to have an affirmative action plan requiring them to publicly post all positions below the vice president level and to post them on the Department of Labor's website. It is very important to post all your jobs for another reason: powerful analytics. You want to collect and track the data from start to finish in your recruiting process, from best recruiting sources, time to fill, and a host of other measures. Posting all your jobs is necessary to gather these data. With the ATSs available today, if they are set up to follow your processes, they can collect the data and most of the analytics for you.

For entry and midlevel positions, I urge companies to use text recruiting software such as TextRecruit or AllyO to contact passive candidates to see if they are interested. Research shows that only about one-third of job candidates like to be called about job openings. We know that millennials and Generation Z are text friendly and are more open to texts than the older generations. Give it a try and track your results. You can learn more about these platforms and others in Chapter 12: HR Geek: Technology.

Now move on to the active job candidates, who are always your best bet for entry and midlevel positions. If your applicant tracking system has a built-in texting capability to continually update job candidates, be sure it is being used. First, use your ATS texting capability to acknowledge the receipt of a résumé, and then have it set to update job candidates as their applications move through the process, whether that is to be selected for a phone screen and on-site interview, to take an assessment, or not to be selected. If your ATS doesn't have texting capability, you can purchase this service from texting platforms such as AllyO and Olivia. Update candidates all along the way, including when there is bad news to deliver. Bad news on the final round of interviews should also be given by the recruiter to build up goodwill with the rejected candidate. This candidate may be your number-one candidate the next time the job is open. By giving this feedback in a transparent way, you will be improving the candidate experience and raising your net promoter score.

I have a complete discussion on selection of ATSs, what to screen for, and ratings in chapter 12, HR Geek: Technology.

CHAPTER 7: SCREENING

For decades industrial and organizational psychology has provided us the best methods to screen job candidates for a variety of jobs. I/O psychologists used academically accepted empirical evidence with rigid experimental designs with control and experimental groups and statistical analysis. While some of their recommendations have raised questions about gender and race bias, there are ways to mitigate these effects.

The problem is most companies and executives ignore their recommendations. HR and recruiting leaders, who should be experts in these areas, too often are not. Too often they do not persist in educating their line leaders about the return on investment by hiring better workers and improving retention by using these methods.

The use of machine learning and artificial intelligence platforms is beginning to uncover new correlations between skill traits and behavior and high performance and can help reduce unconscious bias. However, the enlightened human resources executive needs to discern unjustified bold claims, usually from digital technology start-ups that understand software programming but do not understand I/O psychology and do not publish the results of their data or empirical evidence.

Based on empirical evidence (which I cover in detail in chapter 10), the most reliable and predicable methods for selecting great employees are the following:

1. Work Sampling (which are hands-on simulations of part of or the most important skill requirements for the job and can be used to select the best among experienced workers). An example of this is to have an assembler read the typical instructions at a work site and partially build a product to speed and quality standards for novices.

2. General Mental Aptitude Tests (GMATs). These are IQ tests or tests like the General Aptitude Test Battery. Intelligence alone, however, is usually not a reliable measure of who will be a great worker.

3. Structured Interviews, which are preplanned questions based on the knowledge and skills needed for great performance on the job. These are much stronger than unstructured interviews.

4. Peer Rating. Ratings from the job candidate's peers, which is a good screen for internal job candidates if the recruiter can see the ratings. Obviously, it is tough to get peer ratings from external candidates.

5. Job Knowledge Tests. These are tests on the critical knowledge or ability to conduct key functions of a job. Examples of these include typing tests for secretaries or tests of a candidate's competence in Word, Excel, PowerPoint, or Google Sheets, or tests of a software engineer's ability to write code.

Companies can best increase their ability to hire excellent candidates by using a combination of the best screening methods. Based on empirical research, the use of a general mental aptitude test with a structured interview improves the ability to hire great candidates. A general mental aptitude test with a personality test that measures integrity and consciousness or by using work sampling improves the ability to hire great job candidates. Next in line to be used with GMATs are the following: job knowledge tests, work sampling, job tryouts (which usually include a ninety-day probation period), peer ratings (which you almost never see when hiring an external candidate), a training and experience behavioral consistency model (which today is more commonly called job competency model), and reference checks.

My advice is that for every job family, the recruiting team and hiring managers need an agreed-to strategy for screening candidates. I nearly always encourage the use of a structured interview based on job-specific competencies that were developed by examining what competencies make your best workers the best employees, combined with an applicable assessment, such as a Microsoft Office Suite test for administrators, a general mental aptitude test for assemblers, a software writing trial or applicable software test assessment for software engineers, or a personality test for sales reps. Whatever test you use needs to be validated for its reliability and predictability and to be sure it does not discriminate based on age, race, or gender.

The most powerful reason I encourage the use of structured interviews, assessment tests, and job trials is to avoid the biggest mistake that most interviewers make: first impression bias.

First Impressions and Unconscious Bias

Studies have shown that poorly prepared interviewers, who conduct interviews without first looking at the required skills, experiences, and knowledge, and then prepare questions to elicit answers that will help them understand if the job candidate has those competencies, do a poor job of making good hires.

Their unconscious bias has gotten in the way. Because of neuroscience we know scientifically (not just allegorically) that it is not only the bigot and sexist who makes stereotypes about people. We all do. The bigot and sexist are usually making a *conscious decision* to discriminate or harass based on a strongly believed stereotype. Unconscious bias is an attitude or stereotype that affects an individual's understanding, behavior, and decision-making *without the individual consciously realizing it most of the time*. Scientists have observed it using magnetic resonance imaging (MRI) technology. *Psychology Today* recognizes unconscious bias as real and measurable. It is demonstrated by all of us, despite our most altruistic and equitable intentions.[81]

There is a scientifically developed test for it, the Harvard Implicit Association Test (IAT). The IAT measures attitudes and beliefs that people may be unwilling to, or are unaware of and not able to, report. More than 6 million people have taken the IAT since 1998. Its purpose is to create awareness of unconscious bias and then enable the person to better manage their implicit biases.[82] Awareness is one of the first steps to combat unconscious bias. Training is also effective.

There is a bias center in the brain's amygdala, an almond-shaped set of neurons deep in the temporal lobe of the brain. The amygdala is the "emotional" center of the brain that reacts to fear, threats, and other emotions. The frontal cortex of the brain is also involved in forming impressions about groups of people and in measuring empathy.

Unconscious biases have been observed and measured for over a hundred years. Frankly, we didn't need neuroscience to prove they exist. Now that we have scientific evidence of them and that nearly all of us have one or more impressions that make for an unconscious bias—including while making hiring or other managerial decisions—it makes good sense to me that we call it out, train people to be more aware of their biases, and use interviewing techniques that reduce unconscious bias.

First impressions based on appearance, facial expressions, and dress are not the only bias in interviews. Research has shown that physical attractiveness, gender, and scholastic standing impact hiring manager decisions, particularly when they complement the information on the résumé.[83] What you have heard is true. Being tall, attractive, thin, and blond increases a candidate's chances of being hired, even if the candidate is not well suited for the role. As you will see, evidence also supports that in many professions, being male and white also helps with first impressions.

One of the best ways to counter first impressions and unconscious biases is by using structured interviews and

objective and validated assessments, job knowledge tests, or job sampling. Structured interviews have preset interview questions based on the objectively developed job competencies where the interviewer is looking for the right answers. They also dig deeply into the candidate's work experience to truly understand what they accomplished and under what circumstances. Each interview can go for an hour and a half. Unstructured interviews are when there is poor preparation or questions are asked that have no direct bearing on the job or job-related success, such as when Google used to ask brainteasers of their engineering candidates.

Research dating back sixty-five years ago showed that first impressions in the initial four minutes of an interview play a dominant role in shaping an interviewer's decision, establishing a bias that colors **all subsequent** interviewer-interviewee interaction.[84] In many ways, the interview is a search for negative information, and just one unfavorable impression was followed by a rejection decision 90 percent of the time.[85] First impressions are influenced considerably by nonverbal cues, such as greater direct eye contact, smiling, attentive posture, smaller interpersonal distance, and a direct body orientation.[86] A more recent study found that first impression judgments are made **in the first ten seconds**, and the hiring manager spends the rest of the interview trying to confirm the first impression.[87]

It is certainly wise in an interview to judge a candidate's socialization skills, including the same nonverbal skills, such as eye contact, smiling, attentive posture, and so on that are important in making a great first impression, just as long as you don't make the mistake of spending the rest of the interview trying to confirm or prove your first impression. When decisions are made based on first impressions, it renders the interview virtually useless. (Note that a job candidate's ability to make a great first impression can be a job-related and important competency in customer-facing roles, but it must be remembered it is one of several competencies in building relationships, and the interviewer still must resist the first-impression trap).

Since first impressions can be so misleading in determining who to hire, some academic researchers have begun to worry about the effect of rapport building, or friendly ice-breaking chitchat, at the beginning of the interview.[88] To me, that is a bit extreme. It may lead to creating a negative opinion of the company among the interviewees, and especially among those fresh out of college and in their twenties—today's millennials and Generation Z. In fact, one academic study found that allowing for rapport building positively impacted mock-interview ratings and actual job offer acceptance.[89] But because of the impact of first impressions, I do support limiting the amount of time spent on rapport building to avoid first impressions being made or to prevent the interviews from overly indulging in rapport building.

Unstructured interviews are terrible for making hiring decisions. Research shows that they are not much better than a coin toss in selecting good candidates. When unstructured interviews are used, many hiring managers go from their "gut" and first impressions to decide. If your organization will not take the time to create job-specific structured interviews, get a flat coin and flip it. You will be saving people a lot of time.

If you or your company is interviewing and is not using a structured interview, you have a recipe for disaster. You should begin immediately to put in place structured interviews. I will show you how I have developed structured interviews in Chapter 10: HR Geek: Empirical Evidence for Hiring Excellent Employees, and in the section, "Job Family Competency Case Study to Improve Selection. In Chapter 10 I will also discuss validated assessments tests.

Gender Bias in Hiring

Women have made progress in the workplace, but only up to a certain level. Women now graduate from college in record numbers and at higher numbers than men and are moving up the career ladder and do better but not equal to men at earning equal pay for equal work. Women still, however, face discrimination with hiring and a glass ceiling.

Research shows that we tend to hire people who look like us. So male bankers tend to hire more males, and female teachers tend to hire more women.[90] Male and female stereotypes are still prevalent in today's workforce despite the progress made by women.[91] The stereotypes tend to hurt women more than men. I have come upon teams made up of women who have told me pointedly that they would never hire a man to join the team because they would have to change how they run their meetings and interact with each other. Gender bias cuts both ways, but women are still at the overall disadvantage. In addition, women in the labor market are becoming bifurcated.

Excellent research by British economist Alison Wolf in her book *The XX Factor* demonstrate that women are increasingly divided between an elite group of intelligent, hard-driving women who graduate from the best universities, get great jobs in corporate industry or government, and in many ways begin to act like men, have spouses who take care of the kids, or have two-career families with live-in nannies.[92] These women have the means to overcome the burdens of child-rearing that women at lower-income levels face, and they have figured out how to compete and get ahead in male-dominated corporate America. The other segment of women struggle on the lower end of the economic ladder and are faced with the challenges of day care and balancing the time crunch of two wage earner families or being single moms.

Let's look at the numbers. Overall, the percentage of women in the US workforce has risen from 39 percent in 1965 to a peak of 60 percent in 1999 and is at 55 percent in 2018. Prime working age women (ages 25-34), however, are surging back into the hot talent economy in 2018. Their participation rate is 77 percent.[93] The percentage of male workforce participation rate has fallen to 69 percent, down from a peak of 80 percent in 1970.[94]

Women today outnumber men in college graduation. In 2013, 37 percent of women ages twenty-five to twenty-nine had at least bachelor's degrees, compared to 30 percent of men in the same age range. The same trend continues for master's degrees. In 2012,

women earned 60 percent of all master's degrees (up from 46 percent in 1977) and 51 percent of all doctorates (up from 21 percent in
1977). In 2013, women earned 36 percent of MBAs.[95]

**Despite their progress in earning college degrees and
higher participation rates in the workforce, the pay for women,
although making progress, still trails that of men.** In 2012, the
median hourly earnings for female workers sixteen and older were
84 percent of men's earnings. However, the gap is smaller among
younger workers, ages twenty-five to thirty-four, where women
make 93 percent of what men make. In 1980, by comparison, the
median hourly earnings for young women were 67 percent of what
young men were paid, and for all employed women, the pay was 64
percent of what men were making.

**However, a study released on November 28, 2018, by the
Institute for Women's Policy Research (IWPR), found the gender gap is worse than previously reported. It concludes that
women earn forty-nine cents to every dollar men make.** IWPR
said earlier studies left out part-time workers and people who have
taken time off from work, which is more common for women than
men. When this was considered and taking a longer-term view, they
learned the actual experience of women, who over a fifteen-year period are more likely to shoulder the demands of childcare than men.
More than four of ten women stepped back from the workforce for
at least a year—twice the rate of men. The study further found that
women's progress has slowed in the last fifteen years relative to the
preceding thirty years in the study.[96]

IWPR points to research that has shown that policies such as
paid family and medical leave and affordable childcare can increase
women's labor force participation and encourage men to share more
of the unpaid time spent on child, sick person, and retiree care. IWPR
is an affiliate with the Program on Gender Analysis in Economics at
American University in Washington DC.

I would add to IWPR's findings that women for the same reasons cited by IWPR also earn less retirement pay than men. The
National Institute on Retirement Security has found that for women

sixty-five and older, their income is 25 percent lower than that of men. Consequently, women were 80 percent more likely than men to be impoverished at age sixty-five and older, while women ages seventy-five to seventy-nine were three times more likely to fall below the poverty level as compared to their male counterparts.[97]

For all the reasons above, women want transparency in the workplace on pay, benefits, careers, and the rules for getting ahead.

Researchers have found that gender stereotypes can be overcome by using structured interviews and one-on-one interviews.[98] In addition, researchers have found that gender and race biases can be significantly reduced by using blind evaluations (when names and gender references are "blinded" from the résumé) and when evaluations are made on a group of candidates together rather than on individual candidates one by one. Having the hiring decision made as an option among the candidates rather than a series of individual choices reduces gender stereotypes.[99] Other researchers have found that when female or racially diverse candidates make up half of the interview pool, the odds of the female or racially diverse candidate being selected went up dramatically. Why? The hiring managers upon seeing more than one female or diverse candidate did not see the hiring of a woman, black, Hispanic, or Asian as so out of the norm. It felt less like change.

As you will see in Chapter 12: HR Geek: Technology, Artificial Intelligence platforms offer another tool to overcome gender and racial stereotypes by cloaking names and other information that betray a person's gender or race requiring the AI or recruiter to make decisions only on their knowledge, skills, abilities, education and experience.

Hiring Bias against Blacks

An *American Economic Review* study in 2004 found that job seekers with résumés that had so-called white-sounding names received 50 percent more callbacks for interviews. Names such as Jamal or Lakisha or others that are perceived as black-sounding names received fewer callbacks. That racial gap is uniform across occupation, industry, and employer size.[100]

A study conducted by the business school at Rutgers University in New Jersey found that the race of the hiring manager, was a contributing factor to racial disparity in the workplace.[101] The researchers found that hiring managers tended to go to their own networks for candidates, and if blacks were not in those networks, they would not be considered. When you consider the wisdom promulgated by career coaches that 70 percent (the real number is more like 55 percent but still high) of all jobs are found from your personal networks of friends or on social networking platforms such as LinkedIn and Facebook, being excluded from this inclusion is a huge hurdle. In my own career coaching, I am always telling people in job searches to "utilize your networks"!

Hiring Bias against Hispanics

Hispanics account for nearly 17 percent of the US population and will account for nearly 60 percent of the population growth in the United States over the next forty years; however, Hispanics represent less than 1 percent of the top executive positions in our largest corporations.[102]

The National Hispanic Corporate Council, whose members include some of the United States' biggest corporations report that Hispanics rise to middle management positions faster than others but remain there longer. Why is this? The council reports that while there are variations in the cultures of many Hispanic and Latino country cultures, there appear to be in the United States common cultural qualities that hinder Hispanics rising to the top of the corporate culture. Here they are.

1. **Power distance, meaning the tendency to accept and respect distances between hierarchical levels.** Most

Hispanic cultures score high on this attribute. Individuals raised in those countries may be reluctant to disagree with their supervisors or to speak up in meetings full of higher-status individuals. This may be acceptable rising to the ranks of middle management, but most US corporations looking for executive talent may view such talent as too passive for executive roles. The council advises that this can be overcome with self-awareness training.

2. **Personal connections.** People get ahead in part from their personal connections. Given the small number of Hispanics in corporate leadership, those Hispanics in middle management positions are at a disadvantage. This can be overcome by learning new networking skills and by reaching out to new social networks.[103]

How do you counteract first impressions, unconscious bias, and discrimination in hiring? The research shows the answer is straightforward. Use one-on-one structured interviews based on job competencies. Blind the résumés to names or gender and race and color references. Use validated assessments and job sampling or work tests. Awareness building and training also help.

Ban on Salary History Questions

There is a growing trend among states and cities to ban employers from asking job applicants questions about their current pay and salary histories in the interview process. The purpose is to make a dent in the pay inequity between men and women and whites and people of color. Rather than asking job candidates what they are currently making and their salary histories (which was done as a measure of successful career progression), I suggest employers share the pay range for the position and ask the job candidate if they are still interested in the role. To learn more about bans on salary history questions, go to Chapter 13: HR Legal Geek.

Résumé Review and Phone or Text Screens

Recruiters should take a close look at the résumés of the job candidates who make it to the top of their lists, often with the assistance of automated screening either by Boolean search or artificial intelligence. Too many recruiters only give the résumé a cursory look, which is not detailed enough. Even the top résumés that were screened by AI should be carefully reviewed by the recruiter.

I believe it is important to screen the résumé for the following issues:

- **Do they have the requisite college degrees or technical training, and did they do well in school?** I first look at their education, their degree, school, and GPA, and if they have the required certifications for a job, which are frequently required for technical roles. The higher the GPA the better, and the higher the school is on the lists of "the best" business schools, or engineering schools the better.
- **Signs of Good Character.** I also look to see if the job candidate worked during college, had internships, or did volunteer work for charities. Working during college speaks to work ethic and determination and builds real-world experience for careers. Charity work speaks to values and character. For trades, I would look for successful participation in apprenticeships.
- **Have they been successful on the job with notable achievements?** Have they written their résumés to show what they achieved as opposed to just what they did? During the interview you will want to ask them specifically how they made those achievements, what worked and what didn't, and what was their role.
- **Have they worked for companies in your industry (or in the profession you are hiring for), especially companies that are industry leaders?** How relevant is the work

experience? Are they doing the same type of work you are hiring for from a well-regarded competitor? Does their work experience align with the circumstances of your business?

◆ **Does their career history show a forward progression? Some companies don't like to hire job-hoppers, employees who change jobs every one or two years.** Frankly, that is not always bad if it shows career progress or the employee had a great reason to move on, such as an overbearing or micromanaging boss or due to a reduction in force or the career move of a spouse or partner. In some industries such as software, it is a good sign to job-hop because some employers in software like employees who have varied technical and work environment experience. If you have concerns you want to ask the candidate about, bring it up in the screening interview.

◆ **If they wrote a cover letter or added one to your ATS, is it concise? Does it make note of one of your company's successes and make you want to read their résumé? Or is it uninspiring?**

If you are hiring for a start-up business or a new business venture for a large corporation or a new region, you will be better off hiring a leader who has had experience hiring a new team and shaping team culture, norms, and operating mechanisms than someone who has always inherited a team and never had to build one from scratch.

It is also timely to raise the issue of blinding the résumé to guard against illegal discrimination and the tendency people have to default to unconscious biases and to hire people who look like them, as was discussed in previous sections. If your organization has underutilized representation by gender or race in any of your job categories, you should seriously consider blinded résumés in those job categories.

Is the candidate overqualified? The long-standing concern here is that an overqualified candidate will leave your company when the job they are more qualified for comes along. It is good to see if job candidates are overqualified in the best interest of assuring a great job match and a new hire who is excited about his or her new role. There are concerns, however, that "overqualifications" is a code word for age discrimination and the bias that the job candidate may have outdated skills or be too stubborn to fit in. If you explain the job and expectations well, you can screen for this. In an era of full employment, smart companies will turn to baby boomers who have the skills they need and are not interested in the job level or pay they previously had. In this case, look for employees who have kept their skills up and can work with diverse teams. People over the age of fifty-five are now the hottest demographic to recruit during this time of talent scarcity.

Google your selected candidates before the screening interview. Early in the screening process is the time to look up candidates by first Googling them to see what they post and if they are involved in unlawful activity. Then check social media to see what they post. Are they posting blogs related to their profession? If so, you may want to compliment them about their post or publication and even ask them about it—or the response that they received from it. Are they posting anything that would violate your company's norms of behavior and values? If so, they may be a candidate to pass over. The purpose of this screen is not to find pictures of their childhood or embarrassing moments during spring break.

I recommend videoconferencing interviews over phone screens because you can see the candidate's expressions while they answer questions. In addition to their tone of voice and their vocabulary, you can check for their enthusiasm and if they give any visual signs of struggling to answer a question, especially questions about why they want to leave their current employer, their least favorite supervisor, or their weaknesses.

Phone screening for professional candidates to introduce your company and the job to the candidate. I begin by giving the title and a description of the role, location, its duties, and the business circumstances, such as is it a start-up environment, the launching of a new product, or a replacement position, and the primary goals to be achieved. I also recommend you share the company's mission and purpose and describe its culture. For the first screen of professions that require a technical or four-year college degree, I am checking to see that the individual understands the role, why they are interested in the role and company, and why they believe they are qualified for the role. I check to see if they are a fit for the company's culture and that our salary range matches their expectations.

Finally, I check to see if they are interested and their availability. The screening interview will take about thirty minutes.

Screening Questions for Positions Requiring a College Degree

1. Why are you interested in this position?
2. Why do you want to work for [Your Company]?
3. How did you find out about this position?
4. Why do you want to leave your current employer?
5. Tell me about your current company—its products and services, size, and your role.
6. What is the name and contact information for your manager?
7. If it is a supervisor role, I ask: How many people directly report to you? Indirectly report to you? Are they all in your building, or are they geographically dispersed? What are their titles? Did you hire any of them?
8. Why do you believe you are qualified for this role? Ask them to put their qualifications in perspective with the work experience on their résumé.
9. I then turn to key technical questions to ask them based on the job. For example, if it is an administrative job, I ask them to describe for me their competence with Excel, PowerPoint, or Google Sheets—whatever software is used on the job. If it is for a software engineer, I would ask them to describe for me their competence in the languages used on the job and their experience with Agile software development.
10. What is your greatest strength?
11. What is your greatest weakness?

12. Which company was your most favorite employer and why?
13. Which company was your least favorite employer and why?
14. Who was your favorite supervisor and why?
15. Who was your least favorite supervisor and why?
16. I then tell them the pay range for the role and check to see if they are interested in the role. In an increasing number of states that are concerned about the trend of women and people of color to be paid lower wages than Caucasians and men while being equally qualified, it is illegal to ask candidates for their salary history. Recruiters can, however, share your salary range for the job and ask them if it meets their expectations. Transparency is helpful because research shows that women and people of color like organizations that are transparent about pay.
17. If they are interested in the role, in order to be compliant with Ban the Box legislation, which is in twenty-nine states and 159 municipalities, I tell the clients that we conduct reference checks and background checks on all candidates. Once that is disclosed to the candidate, I ask them when they could begin working for the company.

I close by telling them that I will get back to them by phone, email, or text (whatever is your company's protocol) on our decision on who to move forward for an on-site interview within two weeks. For entry-level roles it is usually within three days. In an era of full employment, it is imperative to meet your deadlines, or you will lose the candidate.

I put these questions into a Word document set up so that I can write their answers during the interview. I also tell the candidate that I will be recording notes by typing while interviewing them and ask them if they have any concerns about me taking notes. No one has ever said no, and I believe they appreciate being asked. No matter their answers, I will take notes during the interview.

Have a half-page summary for the hiring manager. I have always encouraged recruiters to prepare a half-page summary of the job candidate's experience to be accompanied by the résumé, which the hiring manager can access online through the ATS or by attachment. The summary would include the candidate's degrees, GPA, and university or whatever certificates are looked for, and a brief description of his or her previous experience, including previous employers and titles, and their preferences in leadership and work culture. Ideally, I like giving the hiring manager and the interviewing team five top candidates to interview.

If you are screening for entry-level positions requiring a high school degree and little to no experience, I have a different and shorter set of screening questions.

1. Why are you interested in this role?
2. Who is your current employer?
3. How long have you worked for them?
4. Why do you want to leave your current employer?
5. Do you have experience as a (your job title and environment, such as "warehouse forklift driving outdoors in an extreme environment" or "in call center sales")?
6. Have you worked in our industry?
7. When can you begin to work for us if we offer you a job?

Some companies recruiting for entry-level work skip the phone or text screen and invite job candidates in for a group interview, where one or two interviewers interview up to ten candidates. While this is effective for telling candidates about the company, its purpose and culture, and working conditions and then see if they are interested, there is no empirical evidence I could find to support this method. Hiring managers I have spoken to like to see who responds first and best to their answers. Not all great employees are extroverts. I have found that companies that use this method have a higher turnover rate or no-show rate after job offers are extended. When they switched to phone screens in one-on-one interviews, their hiring numbers and retention improved.

How you treat employees during the interview process signals to them how you will treat them as an employee. If it feels like a cattle call, you probably will not make a great first impression.

Use of Preemployment Assessment Tests

The use of validated preemployment assessment tests with structured interviews substantially improves the reliability of hiring great candidates and avoiding illegal discrimination, so it is a smart tactic for hiring.

In fact, there is growing empirical evidence that suggests that companies should conduct an assessment before doing the on-site interview. In many cases, I have found that to be the smartest thing to do so I knew the job candidates had the necessary skills to do the job before they went into the interview with the hiring managers.

There are assessment tests available to measure a candidate's general mental aptitudes, such as reading comprehension, writing skills, and spatial relationships. I have used general mental aptitude tests successfully to select factory workers. I have used job skill tests to successfully select project coordinators, project managers, administrative assistants, and electronic technicians. There are many validated assessments that will help select software writers and several other technical professions.

There are also very good assessments to determine if salespeople have the personality characteristics for sales, which I have used to improve the quality, retention, and diversity of salespeople.

Research published in the *Harvard Business Review* has found that many industries, such as call centers, retailers, and security firms, can reduce costs and make better hiring decisions by using validated and inexpensive web-based psychometric tests as the first screening step after the résumé. They weed out the least suitable candidates, leaving a better candidate pool for the most expensive parts of the recruiting process.[104]

Assessments these days are generally available online and take less than twenty minutes. Be sure to use an assessment that has been validated to predict job success without adversely selecting out job candidates based on gender and protected classes.

I cover in great detail the research of industrial/organizational psychologists on preemployment assessment tests and the scientific research behind them. If you are interested in using an assessment test, please see chapter 10, HR Geek: The Empirical Evidence for Hiring Great Employees. I also provide online resources to help you select preemployment assessment tests to add to your selection methodology and the questions you should ask of vendors.

On-Site Interviews

After the phone or videoconference screen has occurred, the on-site interview is an opportunity to achieve four important goals. First, welcome the job candidate and make them feel very special. Second, share with the job candidate your open role, its goals, and the business situation. Third, provide an overview of your work culture, the purpose of your organization, its meaningful work, and your physical work environment. Fourth, closely assess the candidate with a series of structured interviews and whatever assessment or job sampling you may have decided to use and have validated. The interviews themselves ought to be structured interviews.

It is important to remember that you are recruiting and wooing the job candidate as much as you are carefully selecting who among these job candidates will be the best fit for your job.

Welcome! As candidates arrive, they should be welcomed by someone who is trained in the role and understands the importance of putting the candidate at ease. This is really like customer relations. In the process I laid out in earlier chapters, this is the role of the scheduler. It can also be done by the recruiter or the hiring manager, but in my experience their busy schedules lead to time conflicts and candidates waiting to be greeted—not a good first impression.

Days before their arrival, the job candidate should receive a schedule of their day, including who they will be interviewing

with, the individual's title, and the interview's location.
Interviewers need to be on time! And come prepared having read
the résumé and understanding their role, the competencies they are
to check out, their questions, and the preferred answers.

**Thoroughly explain the job, desired outcomes, and the
business situation.** While I have already recommended that a thorough explanation of the job duties, business situation, and company
culture be described during the phone screen, I also recommend it
during the on-site interview. The reason to do it twice is to assure
the job candidate has a good understanding of the role, situation,
and your culture and that there is no misunderstanding.

The candidate will also be looking to see that you are being
consistent with how the job is described in the phone screen and
with the on-site interview and that you are being transparent. Your
transparency will also display to the job candidate an important
norm of your culture in action, not words. Be sure to give time to
answer any of the candidate's questions. Transparency is important.
Misleading a candidate on the role may lead to a misunderstanding
and a bad hire that will result in turnover.

**Thoroughly explain your work culture and organizational
purpose.** As we have seen from the research, job candidates who
are looking for a long-term fit for themselves and their careers with a
company are going to want to know about the company's corporate
culture, its larger purpose for humanity, and its mission. They are
also going to want to learn about opportunities for learning, career
development, and advancement in your company. Be prepared to
speak to the training, mentoring, or coaching your organization
provides new hires and newly promoted employees.

**To this end, I encourage companies to also arrange for the
job candidates to have coffee or lunch with current employees,
without management present.** At lunch, employees can share with
the job candidate their experiences working for your company, its
training and advancement opportunities, and what they like about
working for your company. Allowing job candidates to meet with
employees allows the job candidate to get authentic information

on what it is like to work for your company, its principles, how work gets things done, and opportunities for learning and career advancement. This will go a long way to conveying transparency and building trust between your organization and the job candidates.

Work in a tour of the facility during the course of the day that allows you to showcase what you are most proud of, whether it is an awesome office design, great cafeteria, incredible research labs for the scientists or engineers you are recruiting, or "honor walls," which feature the outstanding achievements, patents, publications, and awards of your workforce.

On-site interviewing questions using a structured interview. When many people hear the term "structured interview," they think of behavioral interviewing. I don't mean that. Behavioral interviewing is an approach that began in the 1990s when interviewers asked questions such as, "Tell me about a time when you had to…" Behavioral interviewing uses the STAR approach, which stands for Situation, Task, Action, and Result. For example, with decision-making, an interviewer might ask, "Tell me about the most difficult decision you have had to make on this job." And then ask follow-up questions of the job candidate about the **situation** for the decision, the **task** to be achieved, the **action** taken to make a good decision, and finally the **result** of the decision. I liked the thoroughness of the STAR approach. STAR wasn't the problem.

The problem was that too many job candidates learned to come in with canned answers to the questions. It often felt too stifling. My biggest objection to behavioral interviewing was that it was too indirect, as if the candidate never sent you a résumé. Rather than the indirect behavioral interviewing technique of "Tell me about a time…," why not bring up a job on the individual's résumé and ask them to tell you about the jobs that are closest to the job you have open? What were the goals for the job? The business situation? How were the goals achieved? What went well? What didn't? What was the outcome? And if they had to do it over again, what would they do differently? As you do this following the applicable roles on the job candidate's résumé, I suggest you borrow the STAR approach to understand the **situation**, the **tasks** or goals to be achieved, the **actions** taken, and the **results**. You keep asking questions when the candidate is evasive or does not provide you specifics to get to a result and understand what worked and what didn't work.

There is a place for behavioral interviewing after a thorough review of the résumé. After you have gone through the résumé in detail, I do believe, however, that there is a place for behavioral interviewing and its format of "Tell me about a time…" to gather information about the individual's ethics and values, the work cultures they prefer, and their adaptability. These are individual attributes that aren't on a résumé.

There are validated assessments that are excellent at measuring integrity and consciousness, but if your company doesn't use assessments, then you need to ask questions about individual values, collaborative and assertive behaviors, preferred work cultures, and leadership style preferences, or you will never learn about them. If you don't assess for ethics, values, and culture fit, you may make a hire who is not well suited for your culture or may behave badly at work. This is where behavioral interviewing is helpful, and if you are thorough in using the STAR model, the answers to these questions are harder to fake. More on the specific questions to ask about ethics, values, and culture fit later in this chapter.

Therefore, I recommend you ask questions in these broad work areas.

1. **Begin with their work history**. Understand what job the candidate has achieved in their previous roles. Most interviewers and unfortunately many recruiters only give a cursory review of the résumé; that is a huge mistake. The résumé should be carefully reviewed, and interviews should use very detailed and probing questions to understand what type of work the candidate has done, what they achieved, and its impact on their employer. Ask the job candidate specifically what goals and outcomes they had to achieve on each job, their role, how they were achieved, who supported

them, and if the goals were achieved. This will require two interviews of an hour and a half each. While I am not a big fan of large panel interviews, this is a good opportunity to have two interviewers interview each candidate over a two-hour period if it is necessary to save time. But mostly, I recommend one-on-one interviews.

2. **Understand if they have the technical and professional skills to be successful on the job.** This will require at least one in-depth interview for an hour and a half by one of your technical experts. These questions are very specific about using a specific skill or tool on the job and their respective competency, such as software code for software engineering or their ability on an enterprise software platform for finance or supply chain.

   There are good, valid,and reliable assessments for specific technical skills such as for administrative roles, accountants, project managers, software, electrical, and mechanical engineering to name a few. But if your company isn't using assessments for technical skills, make sure you have one or two technical experts interview the job candidates using the same structured interview.

3. **Understand if they have the team and collaboration behaviors for the role to collaborate, adapt, or challenge the status quo** by raising their hand and saying, "There is a better way, and here is how I propose we try it out." This is about an hour-long separate assessment.

4. **Understand if they have the values for your organization and if they have had any prior behaviors that would disqualify them to be an employee in your organization.** This is about an hour-long separate assessment.

Structured interviews are at their best when the organization has objectively reviewed and identified the education, training, developmental experience, skills, and abilities that make their best employees in this role the best employees. This is known as job competency development. It is discussed at length in chapter 10: HR Geek: The Empirical Evidence for Hiring Great Employees.

Research shows that if more than four people interview a candidate, the company generally is not learning anything new about the job candidate, and it begins to become a waste of time.[105] This may vary for extraordinarily complex technical roles or for an executive, where perhaps more experts, members of the executive staff, or board members are needed to assure that a great decision is being made. Or if you are hiring someone for a global role, it may be necessary to involve functional experts or others from corporate outside of the specific region of the world to asses that the candidate has the values, technical skills, and culture fit required for the corporation at large.

I recommend that the on-site interview questioning be divided up among the interviewers. Ideally,

- two interviewers will probe the job candidate on their work history and achievement success;
- one or two interviewers will deal with the technical job competencies; and
- one or two will check for appropriate teamwork and collaboration behaviors, ethics, and culture fit. These questions can be a stand-alone interview with one or two interviewers or can be inserted in either the work history and résumé review interviews or the technical job skills interviews (but don't repeat them at every interview).

In this way, the candidate is not getting bored by answering the same questions from each interviewer, and the company has conducted the planning to make sure they are gathering the information they need to make a great choice among their candidates. Each interviewer should have written out on a digital form the questions they will ask, the types of answers they are looking for, and room for notes and important follow-up questions to ask. At the end of each interview or by the end of the day, each interviewer should complete their forms to document the interviews, the answers, and their impressions of each job candidate.

At the end of the interview cycle when all the job candidates have been interviewed, the interviewers should meet to provide their assessment of each candidate and to make a group decision on what candidate they would like to hire. Or if they should keep looking. Why not meet at the end of the day after each day of interviewing rather than wait until the end? Research has shown that when all job candidates are reviewed together, there is less discrimination against job candidates based on demographic characteristics.

I don't recommend that hiring managers be given the sole decision. It should be a group decision by interviewers trained for their roles in interviewing and in general what the company is looking for among new hires. Candidates should not be hired for one job. Instead, assure that the job candidate hired is a good fit for the department and company and has the potential for a long-term career at the company. I recommend the supervisor be given a veto on the job candidate.

In summary, I recommend you have two interviewers go through a generic set of questions that are very detailed reviews of the candidate's work history and résumé. Then, one or two people interview the candidate for technical competence. Finally, have an interview on the candidate's work values, teamwork and collaboration behaviors, and culture fit.

Below is a generic detailed work experience and résumé set of questions.

Generic Detailed Work Experience and Résumé Review Questions

1. What is the name and contact information for your manager? (Asking this question with every intention of contacting the job candidate's current managers after an offer has been extended makes a big difference in the quality and

honesty of answers the job candidate will give you. Tell the candidate that you will not contact their current manager until a job offer has been extended.)

2. What was your specific role on this project?
3. What were the goals you were to achieve and for what outcome?
4. What went well? Why? Keep asking the question "What else went well?" until there are no more answers from the candidate.
5. What didn't go well? Why? What obstacles did you have to overcome? How did you overcome them? What were the results? Keep asking these questions until there are no more answers from the candidate and you have all the results. From these questions you are seeking to understand if this individual is able to overcome obstacles with problem-solving, teamwork, taking initiative, and figuring out ways to achieve great results. Or is the person someone who throws up their hand and quits or complains? On any project, there are obstacles and hurdles to success. You are looking to hire those job candidates who overcome obstacles to achieve success.
6. Why do you want to leave this company?
7. Repeat questions 2 through 6 for the next two roles at this company.
8. Repeat questions 2 through 6 for the two previous companies the job candidate worked for. With previous companies focus on the roles that the job candidate had that are most applicable to your company's role.
9. What are your greatest strengths?
10. What are the most significant awards you have won?
11. What is your greatest weakness? Many people struggle to answer this question. We all have weaknesses and skills and behaviors to improve upon. You are looking for the candidate's level of self-awareness and emotional intelligence about their weaknesses, and what they are doing to overcome them. If they can't answer the question or flip the

questions by trying to impress you by saying, "My fault is I am too hard a worker," it is a bad sign.

12. What is your highest level of education and in what subject? From what university? What was your GPA? (You cannot ask when the candidate graduated from high school or college as it is a trigger of age discrimination.) I prefer to ask questions based on what is on the résumé like this: "I see from your résumé that your highest level of education is an MBA from UC Berkeley and your GPA was 3.9. Do I have it right?" If there is something not right from the résumé, they can correct it.

13. Tell me about your last performance appraisal. If your company has ratings, what was your rating? What did it say about you accomplishing your goals? What development did it say you needed? An alternative to this question is to ask: If I asked your manager to tell me about your strengths and development areas, what would your manager tell me? Because you have the manager's name and contact information, you are likely to get a more honest answer. (Don't contact a current manager or company without the candidate's permission.)

14. If I asked your peers to tell me about your strengths and development areas, what would they tell me? (This can elicit a different response than what managers would say.)

15. What are you looking for in your next job?

Next are structured interview questions for the profession's technical job requirements. They should be asked by an expert in your company and be based on the objective knowledge, skills, and abilities to perform well on the job. Below I have examples for engineering in general, software engineering, bioengineering, and mechanical engineering.

General Engineering Questions

1. Ask the work history and résumé questions 1 through 6 to start the interview.
2. Pick one of the jobs you reviewed with the job candidate in the asking of questions 1 through 6 and ask, "On this job, tell me how you went about organizing and preparing your work."
3. Describe the most challenging technical report you have written.
4. Describe for me a prototype you have been involved with and the design of experiment protocols you used. Was it a success or failure? What did you learn? What did you do next?
5. Describe for me how you go about writing code, from requirements to delivery.
6. Have you used the Agile design methodology? Tell me about it.
7. What checks and balances do you use to make sure you do not make mistakes?
8. How have you engaged outside resources to gain knowledge you and your team did not have?
9. Have you been involved in cost reduction projects? What was the outcome?
10. Do you have any patents? Tell me about them.
11. What do you do to stay current with the latest technology?

Software Engineering Questions

1. What programming languages have you used in the past three years? What are your top two programming languages?
2. How much are you coding on a daily basis? If you do not code on a daily basis, what is typical in your role?
3. What's the most important thing to look for or check when reviewing another team member's code?
4. If needed, how would you go about designing scalable applications? Walk us through your process.

Collaboration, Adaptability, Juggling Tasks, and Assertiveness Questions

Finally, the company should screen for key competencies that are important for the success of your work culture—competencies such as collaboration, adaptability, emotional intelligence, juggling tasks, ethics, and assertiveness. These questions are typical behavioral interviewing questions because these competencies often aren't discussed on résumé, so you have to tease these issues out of the candidate. I recommend using the behavioral interviewing STAR approach, which stands for Situation, Task, Action, and Result. So for each question you ask, you want to hear from the job candidate the situation, the task or issue at hand, the action the candidate decided to take, and what was the result or outcome.

1. Tell me about a time when you and a boss had a conflict and what you did to resolve it.
2. Tell me about a conflict you had with a client and what you did to resolve the conflict. What was the outcome?
3. Tell me about a time that a better idea occurred to you, but you knew it would be received with resistance. Did you raise the idea? How? What was your plan for mitigating the resistance? How was your idea received? What was the outcome?
4. Describe a situation in which you had to learn a new process, technology, or idea at work that was a major departure from the old way of doing things. How did you adjust? What was the outcome?
5. Tell me about the biggest change you have had to deal with during one of your previous jobs. How did you adapt to that change? What was the outcome?
6. What role do you often play on a team? The team leader? Facilitator or peacemaker? Technical expert? Or the person with the big idea? Please give me a real-life example.
7. What training have you received for team processes or communication style processes? What did you learn?

8. Tell me about a time when you were extremely frustrated with too much to do and too little time to complete it all on time. How did you prioritize your work? What plans did you make? Did you ask anyone for help? What was the outcome?
9. Tell me about a project you had to organize and plan. How did you organize it and schedule the tasks? Involve others? What was the outcome?
10. What do you want to be doing in two years? Why? Five years? Why?

Culture, Values, and Behaviors Questions

1. Tell me about a time when one of your previous companies was about to do something that you believed was detrimental to customers or workers and a violation of their ethics code. What did you do about it?
2. When were you most excited or tuned in at work? What happened and what were you working on? What was the outcome?
3. Who has been your best manager and why? Please give me an example of what you are speaking about. (With this question and question 4, you are looking for the type of leadership style the candidate prefers. Does it match your leaders?)
4. Who has been your worst manager and why? Please give me an example of what you are speaking about.
5. What has been your favorite place to work and why? (With this and the next question, you are looking for the candidate's preferred work culture. Some job candidates may like more autocratic or stable work environments; others may thrive on constantly changing, innovative cultures. Does it match yours?)
6. What has been your least favorite place to work and why?

Job Competency Questions for Leadership Roles

Leadership is a fundamentally different role than that of the individual contributor. The role of leaders is to first align their teams to their role within the organization and who they receive work from, their value-added work, and the requirements of the internal teams that receive their work or the customers. Work in the global digital area is fast paced and constantly changing, and most work teams have members from different backgrounds and cultures, which requires more effort to be clear about goals and expectations and to build trust and teamwork. Leaders, especially in large organizations, must be continually interpreting new strategies, information, and goals to their teams. Most importantly, they must also be clear on what previous goals or strategies are no longer urgent or are to be stopped.

Leaders need to establish clear communications and operating norms for when the team meets, work hours, shares data, collaborates, and makes decisions. The more clarity the better. Leaders also need to be competent on the use of digital collaboration platforms and videoconferencing.

Leaders need to be extraordinary at listening and giving performance and developmental feedback. Employees do best when leaders support them and help them overcome obstacles at work, not micromanage their work.

Leaders certainly need to hold employees accountable to their commitments and make sure the team provides the organization value-added contributions.

However, the most important aspect of a leader's job is to build trust among his or her employees and among the team and who the team interacts with. Empirical evidence from several studies has determined that trust, even more than intelligence, professional competence, extroversion, assertiveness, meaningfulness of work, and clarity on operating norms and goals, is vital for team success.[106] Leaders who cannot establish relationships with their team members and build trust will not be the most effective leaders.

The functional job questions for leadership should be for these traits, assuming these are the traits your organization wants in a leader. I hope that is the case.

First-Level Manager Job Competency Questions

Leadership is very different from being an individual contributor. Those promoted into leadership need to perform as a leader, and you need to assess their performance as a leader—not as an individual contributor. For leaders, the technical questions are as much about the role and art of leadership as they are about the functional competence of their discipline such as finance, engineering, or marketing.

If your leadership role includes doing some individual contributor work, as a so-called "working leader," then you may have to augment these leadership questions with technical questions for their discipline or questions on the outcomes of their projects. Below are questions to ask first-level leaders going through the résumé and reviewing their work history.

1. How many people directly report to you? Indirectly report to you? Are they all in your building, or are they geographically dispersed? What are their titles? How many of your direct hires did you hire?
2. For this job (the best fit job on the job candidate's résumé), please describe for me the operating norms you established for your team. That is to say, the time and frequency of staff meetings, one-on-ones, and use of share sites and collaboration software? How did it work out?
3. Were all your team members colocated with you? If some team members worked from home or different offices, what did you do to bridge the geographical difference and maintain close relationships with them? What were the outcomes? Do you use collaboration software or videoconferencing technology? This question is critical if your organization has

geographically dispersed teams or global teams and uses videoconferencing and digital communication platforms such as Slack.

4. Tell me how you go about setting goals with your team, how they are given feedback and measured, and how you go about updating the goals.
5. How do you go about screening and hiring new members of the team?
6. Please describe for me a typical one-on-one between you and your employees.
7. What skill or behavior training have you provided to your team in the past year? Why did you feel it was necessary? What was their reaction? What was the outcome?
8. Have you ever had to put one of your employees on a performance improvement plan or terminate an employee? If yes, please tell me how you went about that, the situation, the issue with their performance, and the coaching or training they may have needed. How many of the employees improved as opposed to being fired? What were the outcomes?
9. How many of your employees have been promoted during your tenure and what you did to develop them? (This question is about how good this manager is at developing employees for promotions. A manager good at developing his or her employees will have a long answer to this question.)
10. What are the top three achievements of your team on the _____ role?
11. Tell me about your best coaching success with a direct report. What were the employee's development goals and the outcome?
12. What is the biggest failure of one of your team? What did you learn from it?
13. If I asked your team members to describe you as a leader, what would they tell me?
14. What would your boss tell me about you as an employee and as a leader? Your strengths? Your development areas?

(Or you could ask for a copy of their last two job performance appraisals.)
15. What do you do to stay competent in your field (engineering, marketing, sales as an example)?

VP or Department Head Interview Guide

The role of VPs and department heads is very different from the roles of the first-level leaders and so is the questioning. With each leadership passage, such as individual contributor to a manager or from a manager to a leader of managers or up to a functional department head, leaders need to stop doing their previous role and begin doing the new role, which is very different. Often the great job and outcomes they achieved in the previous role, such as an entry-level manager leading a team of individual contributors, need to end. And they need to learn new skills required at the higher level.

For example, first-level managers are expected to be great at starting and leading teams, including who to hire for the team, and for setting goals and giving development and performance feedback. Department heads and VPs need to be more focused on external factors such as the needs of customers, the top-line performance of the business, new technologies and methodologies for the department, putting in place operating mechanisms and measures to predict and measure department success, intervening to raise questions when predictive measures or sensing sessions with employees identify problems, putting in place talent management practices to align, motivate, develop, recognize, and reward department members, identifying the next generation of leaders and technical experts and developing them, building relationships with other executive team members, and competing for scarce resources for the department so it can accomplish the mission.

VPs will not be successful on their jobs if they cling to the role of the first-level manager or continually try to micromanage a problem themselves.

I start VPs and department head interviews by telling them the situation the business and department are facing, and after answering their questions, I ask them what they think of the situation and what strategies they would put in place. (The best job candidates at this level will have already used their best resources to get this information before the interview.) As they talk rather free form, I am evaluating how they would go about learning the organization's culture, building relationships, and gaining influence. How would they create a shared vision and lay out goals over the first thirty days, ninety days, one hundred eighty days, and for the first and second years? What measures would they establish? How would they assess their new staff, the current technologies used, and their resources? How would they solve problems? I would be looking for very specific descriptions and not glittering generalities.

I then would turn to their résumé and ask, for a job implementing a global physician education program as an example, which included developing the curriculum and training and flawlessly making it available to clients, I would ask the job candidate to use their résumé as a guide and walk me through their steps for establishing such a program.

Below are twenty-one questions I recommend for interviewing executives. They are divided among three categories.

1. **Questions regarding interest and strategy in the open executive position**
2. **Detailed work history and review**
3. **Questions on leadership style, conflict resolution, and ethics**

In addition, I do recommend a fourth category, which may be a technical area or an area of expertise that the firm requires at this level but does not have currently. It may be a competence in digitization, a specific strategy such as growth in East Asia, an emerging technical area or business opportunity. Whatever it is, a team should be established to identify the area and flesh out a competent set of questions for a structured interview to ascertain which of the candidates has the right knowledge, skills, abilities, and experience to shape, launch, and successfully execute a strategy in this area.

As with other interviews, I recommend the first questioning topics above be divided up among the interviewing team to prevent boredom and to allow for more than one opinion on the subject area. Questions that begin with "Describe for me" or "Have you ever" are questions that have a behavioral interviewing feel to them. As mentioned above with behavioral interviewing, it is important with these questions to use the **STAR** method. So for each of these questions, be sure to ask about the **situation** the job candidate is explaining, the **task** to be implemented, the **action** taken, and the **results** achieved.

Questions regarding interest and strategy in the open executive position

1. Why are you attracted to our company and this role?
2. What are your career goals and how does this move help you achieve your goals?
3. What are your strengths and how do they apply to this role?
4. What do you see as the top strategic initiatives for this role?
5. In this role, what do you believe would be important to achieve in the first thirty, ninety, and one hundred eighty days, and the first and second years?
6. Describe for me the strategic planning process you have used in your previous roles. What was your role in the process?

Detailed work history and résumé review

7. Let's turn to your résumé and your previous role. You had several impressive achievements. What were the top three challenges you had to overcome? What were the results?

8. What resources and assets did you have that helped make the program a success? What additional assets and resources did you have to secure?

9. What digital technology do you use to achieve your goals?

10. What did you learn from this experience? Or, in retrospect what would you have done differently? What were the results? Did they meet the goals? How were you rewarded for this achievement?

11. What operating norms do you put in place for your staff?

12. Do you do anything different to accommodate geographically remote staff?

13. How diverse is the composition of your current staff?

14. What percentage of your current staff have you hired?

Questions on leadership style, conflict resolution, and ethics

15. How would you describe your leadership style?

16. If I asked your current staff to describe your leadership style, what would they tell me?

17. If I asked your last three bosses to describe your performance, the good, the bad, and the ugly, what would they tell me?

18. Tell me about your development areas and what you are doing to improve them.

19. Have you ever had an internal complaint or charge filed against you for harassment, discrimination, or any ethics violations?

20. Tell me about a time when you had to stand up for a value you strongly believe in when you saw an organization about to violate that value.

21. Tell me about a time when you and another executive had a conflict and how it was resolved.

University Recruiting and Interviewing

During a time of full employment, universities offer a valued and increasingly rare asset: new entrants to the labor market who are trained in the models and techniques of their disciplines and the latest technologies.

The long-standing advice for university recruiting today is similar to what it was twenty years ago, with emerging digital technologies to be relevant to today's college graduates, Generation Z.

What has been working for several years is the following:

1. Begin identifying the best students and wooing them when they are sophomores with internships, constant contact, and advice.
2. Use members of management who graduated from your targeted universities to build and maintain relationships with the staff and key professors.
3. Sponsor school events such as engineering design contests.
4. Give money or donate equipment to the school.
5. Assign a member of HR or an executive to manage the relationship with the university and to act as a program manager.
6. Have alumni do the interviewing with an HR recruiter with them.
7. Make job offers early in the fall of their senior year.
8. Track measures, metrics, and results and adjust as needed.

All this effort is to build relationships with faculty who will inform you about who they believe are the students with the most potential for your company.

University recruiting is the time for fun. Today it is also the time for using new digital technologies that Generation Z has grown up using. Generation Z are the first truly digital natives, and they should not be expected to be clones of millennials. For example, they are all about making money, not getting into debt, being successful in their careers, and learning how to do things by watching

YouTube videos. (They will want to watch YouTube videos or videos on your career site to learn about your company, its cool work, and career opportunities, especially from the voice of your employees.) They are less prone than millennials to create a start-up and more comfortable working with adults. They are showing signs of being socially awkward and will need more coaching on collaboration and teamwork. To learn more about Generation Z, please see chapter 2, Employer Branding and Comprehensive Talent Strategies and the section on Generation Z.

With today's digital expectations of Generation Z, you also need to engage with them online on social media they use, like Instagram and Facebook, the university's version of Slack, and YouTube. Also find out from the college what apps are used by the students. You need to start early in their collegiate careers and keep up with them on how they are doing in their classes and with their internships (if you haven't offered one) as well as understanding their career and personal interests.

Potential at this level is not measured by intelligence or grades alone. It includes looking at leadership skills, community service projects, how well they collaborated with other students on team projects, and student organizations they led such as being class president or leading the school newspaper. Also if they worked during school to pay tuition and housing. It is a time commitment, and that is why I believe it is best to target your effort to the schools that can and will provide you the best students for the salaries and benefits your company can afford.

Start by having some fun. I remember being interviewed in graduate school by a Hewlett-Packard executive who, upon learning I had a degree in English, asked me to identify my favorite American novel. My answer was *Moby Dick*. To which he responded by saying, "Call me Ishmael," and asking me who was my favorite character in the book. It was a fun exchange. The point is to begin with a fun exchange that gets the student smiling before digging into the structured interview questions.

I will make one other point before getting to the interview

questions while on the college campus or on-site. In chapter 4, The Recruiting Process, I make the case that there is growing research that shows that most companies can get just as good candidates from major universities in their regions, such as the University of Michigan, University of Minnesota, or Georgia Tech, as they can from the top nationally rated schools such as Ivy League schools, Duke, or Notre Dame. Why? Because these students from the top regional schools are well trained, are usually less expensive, are not as demanding in their career expectations, stay longer, and are easier to work with than students from the more highly regarded schools. In addition, they want to stay close to their families in their home states.

As you consider where to recruit, consider this emerging trend. This is not to say Harvard and other top national schools do not produce great students or Stanford doesn't produce great high-tech entrepreneurs. They are great schools. The point is most companies have great options with their top regional schools.

Below are common questions I ask while going through a student's résumé.

1.   Why did you choose this school?
2.   Why did you choose your major? Was there another major you considered?
3.   What is your GPA in your major? Overall?
4.   What was your favorite class? Why?
5.   What was your least favorite class? Why?
6.   What extracurricular activities were you involved in?
7.   Which ones did you like best? Like least?
8.   Have you worked while going to college? Where? Why?
9.   Tell me about your various college internships. What were the goals? What was your role? What were the obstacles? What did you achieve? Were the goals achieved? Why or why not?
10. What was **your** biggest success in the internship?

11. What was **your** biggest failure? What did you learn from it?
12. What did you like best and least in the internship?

(Repeat questions 9 through 12 for each internship.)

13. What do you want in your first job after college?
14. What do you want to be doing in five years?
15. What companies do you most admire? Why?
16. What companies do you least admire? Why?
17. What questions do you have for me?

Graduate School and MBA Candidates

Most graduate students have worked professionally between their graduation from college and attending graduate school. This is especially true of MBAs. I have found MBA students are intense and very driven, especially the ones from the Ivy League schools and other top MBA schools such as Duke and Stanford and the top regional MBA schools around the country (and in Europe, the Middle East, and Asia).

They have already had great experiences working and good career progressions. They want to join a company that will give them great opportunities, with challenging leaders who will continue to develop them and their careers. They want to work for companies with inspiring and innovative CEOs and that are using the latest technologies and methodologies, including digital collaboration software. While they won't be as eager to relocate as baby boomers and Generation X were, they will be interested in global assignments. The women from these schools are also hard-charging like the men. They prefer organizations that provide paid leaves and transparency on pay and career progressions and mentors. They and graduate students of color also look for organizations that have women and people of color in executive roles.

The competition to attract, recruit, and retain these students is fierce. As with university recruiting, you need to identify the best of these students based on your talent needs and begin wooing them early in their MBA careers. Also follow the other advice I gave in the university recruiting section above.

For graduate school candidates, I use a combination of questions from the leadership interview and the college interview. I begin by looking at their résumés, graduate studies, and work experience before graduate school and determine what I want to learn more about them. Then I zero in on their graduate school studies and achievements, including internships.

A common set of interview questions I use for graduate school students are listed below.

1. Why did you decide to go to graduate school?
2. Why did you pick *this school*?
3. I see that you worked at (Business on Their Résumé of Interest) before attending graduate school. Please tell me about your role there, beginning with who you worked for and what you were supposed to achieve.
4. Tell me about your objectives and your level of success.
5. What was your biggest achievement there and why?
6. How did you accomplish it?
7. What was your biggest failure there and why? What did you learn?
8. What did you like most about working there?
9. What did you like least about working there?

(Repeat questions 3 through 9 for each job of interest before the student went to MBA or graduate school.)

10. Now to graduate school. What is your GPA in your major? Your overall GPA?
11. What has been your favorite class and why?

12. What has been your least favorite class and why?
13. Tell me about your graduate school internships on your résumé.
14. What did you work on and what were its goals?
15. What did you achieve?
16. What was your biggest success on the internship?
17. What was your biggest failure? What did you learn from it?
18. What did you like best and least on the internship?
19. (Repeat questions 13 through 18 for each internship.)What do you want your first job out of graduate school to be?
20. What do you want to be doing in five years?
21. What companies do you most admire? Why?
22. What companies do you least admire? Why?
23. What are your strengths?
24. What are your development areas?
25. What questions do you have for me?

Questions Job Candidates Will Ask You

In today's fierce recruiting environment, you should expect to be asked penetrating questions about your company, its culture, and the career development employees may expect. If you are not asked questions by a candidate, it would be a red flag for me about their interest in your company and their drive. You should build in time during each interview for candidates to ask questions and for the interviewers to thoughtfully respond to them. Interviewers should be instructed that if they don't know the answer to a question, to tell the employee that they will investigate it and get back to the candidate within twenty-four hours.

Be prepared for the followig questions.

1. Tell me about *your* career advancement at your company.
2. What do you like most about your culture? What do you like least about your culture?

3. Has this company ever asked you to do something that violated your ethics or values? If yes, what happened?
4. When is the last time your company had a reduction in force?
5. How will I know in ninety days and one hundred eighty days that I am successful?
6. What is the most important norm I should know about the company's culture to be successful?
7. Tell me about your favorite boss and what made him or her your favorite boss.
8. What qualities do you look for in one of your direct reports?
9. Do you have any reservations about hiring me?
10. May I expect an offer today?
11. When will you decide on filling this position?
12. Will you call me about your decision? If not, who will call me?

If a job candidate didn't ask you questions, I would be worried about it. People who ask questions and take a genuine interest in your business and the success of their teams and supervisors are who I want on my team. Having people who question and a company work environment that welcomes questions is the mark of an open, transparent, and innovative company.

CHAPTER 8: RECRUITING METRICS

Every business process needs metrics and measures to track its progress, to warn the process owners about obstacles and concerns, and to assure its success. Recruiting is no different. The top-level metrics should be displayed on a dashboard. Each top-level measure should have submeasures that will serve as an alert that a problem is occurring and needs immediate attention to assure success. The measures should also provide the data to calculate a return on investment for recruiting and onboarding.

It is time to use a new metric, the job candidate net promoter score, to keep track of the job candidate experience. It measures the engagement job seekers have with the company's brand and the overall satisfaction of job candidates with the hiring and onboarding process. If this job candidate net promoter score sounds like a metric transferred from the marketing department, it is.

In marketing, the net promoter score is an index from negative 100 to 100 that measures the willingness of customers to recommend a company's products or services to others. It is a measure of customers' satisfaction and loyalty. It also comes from the employee engagement industry. For example, I have administered surveys that asked employees how likely they were to recommend their company to a friend or colleague as a place to work. I used the answer to this question as the bellwether metric on how engaged employees were with the company. If they can't recommend the company to their friends and family, you have a problem.

The job candidate net promoter score should be the top metric of your recruiting effort.

According to the Talent Board, more than one-third of all job seekers spend two or more hours researching a single job. It often then takes them an hour to complete the job application, and more than half of the candidates who participated in the survey rated the search process as poor or mediocre. Currently only 27 percent of the two hundred companies surveyed by the Talent Board ask about the job candidate's experience. Usually the job candidates being surveyed are the ones who were hired. They will have a bi-ased answer so they do not disappoint their new employer. Only 14 percent of companies in the Talent Board survey asked for candidate feedback before a hiring decision was made.[107] The latter is a better measure of job candidate satisfaction with the recruiting process. Even better, I believe, is asking all the job candidates about their experience, with detailed questions about each step in the process about a week after a hiring decision is made. You will get a better response after all job candidates have been told how far they made it in the hiring process and if nonselected job candidates have been given suggestions for other roles.

Your goal is to have everyone who was told they were not quali-fied for the role or were qualified but were not selected feel so good about the process and its timely communications that they will give you good feedback and recommend your open jobs to their friends.

For most of these top level measures and their sub-measures, today's applicant tracking systems and chatbots that have machine learning or artificial intelligence can make tracking the measures easy.

Top-Level and Submeasures

With measures, I recommend breaking the measures into top-level measures that are frequently discussed among the recruiting and HR team and with hiring teams and executives. Each top-level measure should have submetrics that predict if you will reach the goal of the top-level metric. Top-level metrics can stand on their own, meaning that they are a key metric that is an excellent measure of overall success and near-time deviations are indications of problems. Or the top-level metric can be an index of the submetrics. Even when a top-level metric is a stand-alone metric, it is wise to track lower-level metrics to quickly identify recruiting issues before they impact business results.

For example, if the tracking of résumés to postings or the time it takes hiring managers to review résumés shows that you are not getting the number of job candidates needed or that management is taking too long to review résumés, this is a warning that the process is slowing down and the company may not hire to meet its revenue growth deadlines. Sometimes the submeasures are elements of a top measure, such as with cost of recruiting.

When automated software is programmed to track the metrics, it makes the process smooth and pain free.

Here are my five top-level metrics with their sublevel measures. The goal for each metric will depend on the company's industry and region. For example, you can hire administrative staff, assemblers, and call-center workers faster than engineers and vice presidents. You can hire workers in professions with abundant availability faster than workers in professions with scarce skill sets.

Recruiting Cycle Time (sometimes called job days open) and Its Submeasures

Recruiting cycle time is the time from posting the job to getting an acceptance of an offer from the selected job candidate. Today's applicant tracking systems can track these metrics and generate reports (eliminating the need of keeping separate Excel spreadsheets) if you map your ATS to do so. Otherwise, you can track it using Excel or Google Sheets spreadsheets. Recruiting cycle time is a stand-alone metric. Its submeasures to predict if the recruiting process will hit its goal are:

1. Best recruiting sources for job candidates by job family
2. Percentage of new hires hired by employee referral
3. Recruiter review time
4. Hiring manager review time
5. Phone screens completed of selected job applicants in one week
6. On-site interviews completed within two weeks of identifying selected job candidates
7. Job offers made within twenty-four hours of selecting finalists
8. Job offer acceptance rate at 95 percent of offers
9. Background check cycle time

Brand Attraction to Candidate Hire Ratio and Its Submeasures

Brand attraction to candidate hire ratio is the ratio of the number of candidates who visit your career site to hires. It first measures your success in getting job candidates to look at your website. It also provides measures of the success of your employer brand, as well as the success of your social media, job board postings, and texting and calling from a passive job candidate list from artificial intelligence. Finally, it measures the ratio of hires from the job candidates who visit your site and then apply for a job. If your applicant tracking process is mapped to capture this data and to calculate the ratio, it will not be hard to track.

This ratio will help you understand, when compared to benchmarks, if your brand is attracting job candidates and if, after visiting your career site and learning about your company's purpose, meaningful work, pay, benefits, work culture, and opportunities for career growth, they decide to apply for open positions. Information learned from this metric should be carefully reviewed by the head of human resources, as well as the recruiting and the HR analytics teams.

Here are submeasures to go along with the brand attraction to candidate hire ratio.

1. Visitors to the career center who applied
2. Applicants to open requisitions
3. Applicants to interviews
4. Interviews to offers
5. Offers accepted

Every metric needs to have benchmarks. Jobvite and SilkRoad provide some good benchmarks. While the information below is good, the best benchmarks are the ones most applicable for your industry and region and the workforce you target for recruiting. Below is a table I put together from data gathered on brand attraction from Jobvite and SilkRoad. The data are good data on national benchmarks for brand attraction metrics.

Benchmarks for Brand Attraction and
Candidate Hire Ratio Submeasures

Metric	Jobvite US Metric 2017[108]	SilkRoad 2018[109]
Visitors to the Career Center Who Applied	12%	
Average Applicants to Open Requisitions	36	
Applicants to Interviews	12%	3.4%
Interviews to Offers	28%	20%
Offers Accepted	91%	
Average Time to Hire (or Time to Fill) in Days	38	28
Source to Hire		129:1

Is the reject rate of your offers less than 10 percent? If not, this is a big warning sign that you either do not have competitive pay or benefits or you have a stifling culture or a bad interviewing process that is driving candidates away.

Applications and Hiring Percentages
from Various Recruiting Sources

Source	Application %	Hire %
Career site	36%	30%
Job boards	51%	20%
Employee referrals	3%	13%*
Recruiter sourced	2%	15%*
Third-party agency sourced	1%	4%
Internal transfers	1%	8%
Email and/ or custom campaigns	>1%	>1%
Social media shares	0%	>1%

*Note: the SilkRoad Survey found a much higher employee referral application rate of 33 percent and employee referral hiring rate of 54 percent. Also, the SilkRoad Survey found a higher number of hires from internal recruiter-sourced candidates.

My own experience is that if your company is not at a 33 percent referral rate, you have a lot of room for improvement. The employee referral number will be higher for less skilled positions than for professional and managerial positions. The easiest way to improve your employee referral rate is to offer higher rewards for referrals (with a criterion that new hires stay longer than three months at least). A higher percentage of hires from employee referrals often lowers the company's costs of other recruiting sources, leading to an improved ROI for recruiting.

How many employees report on employee engagement or employee satisfaction surveys that they recommend the company to friends and family as a great place to work? While this is a standard employee engagement measure for human resources and the business, it is also an important measure for recruiting to understand how many employees will enthusiastically recommend your job openings to their friends and family. If this falls below 80 percent, it is a warning sign for the effectiveness of your recruiting efforts, your company's culture, and the overall engagement of your workforce. It should go without saying that employee referrals are an inexpensive and usually high-quality source for recruiting.

Job Candidate Net Promoter Score and Its Submeasures

The job candidate net promoter score measures the engagement job seekers have with the company's brand and the overall satisfaction of job candidates with the hiring and onboarding process. It is an index from negative 100 to 100 that measures the satisfaction of the job candidates with your recruiting process and its communications and their willingness to recommend the company's jobs to others. Its submeasures are:

1. Percentage of job applicants sent acknowledgment text or email instantly.
2. Percentage of job candidates advised by text message or email of other openings in the company within twenty-four hours of nonselected decision.
3. Percentage of job candidates told of phone screen decisions within twenty-four hours of completed phone screens.

4. Percentage of job interviewed job candidates informed of the hiring decision within twenty-four hours of selected candidates' acceptance.
5. Percentage of job candidates' satisfaction with the recruiting process one week after the hiring decision was made.
6. Percentage of hires satisfaction with the recruiting and onboarding process 90 days after hire.

The new applicant tracking systems, such as iCIMS, and new chatbots, such as AllyO, enable these metrics and their machine learning will automatically track them. The use of an applicant tracking system that is set up to follow this process and has the technology to send text messages or emails will enable the process and save the company the cost of much of its administrative staff. These systems have demonstrated that with their automated efficiencies, they can significantly improve job candidate net promoter scores. Here technology is an enabler to significantly improve the job candidate experience, so much so that even rejected job candidates will speak highly of the process.

Why is the job candidate net promoter score important? Virgin Media first learned of the revenue-damaging impact of rejected candidates when it began to survey rejected candidates. The company discovered that 18 percent of their rejected candidates were customers. Worse yet, 6 percent of the roughly seventy-five hundred candidates surveyed were so angry with the poor recruitment experience, they switched to a Virgin competitor. They estimated that this was a £4.4 million loss of revenue.[110]

A 2016 study by LinkedIn uncovered that the cost of a bad reputation for a company with ten thousand employees could be as high as $7.6 million in additional wages, and employers who failed to invest in their reputation could be paying up to an additional $4,723 in costs for each employee hired. These are staggering numbers.[111] The LinkedIn study also provided estimates of the cost of a bad reputation in other countries, such as the United Kingdom at $5.9 million, Germany at $8.2 million, and France at $5.6 million.

Let's be clear, rejected candidates can not only hurt your employer brand, they can hurt your customer brand and cost your company revenue and profits.

Costs per Hire

Costs per hire is measured by the money spent on job postings, ads, the cost of the recruiting department and its technology (divided by hires), and any third-party agency fees whether spent by human resources or the hiring manager's department. Its submeasures are the costs of hires, some of which can be tracked monthly while others are tracked quarterly depending on the norms of your financial system.

These costs of hires occur in human resources or the hiring manager departments.

1. Job posting costs
2. Ads cost
3. Cost of the recruiters and the recruiting administrative staff, including their fully burdened costs for benefits and floor space
4. Third-party agency fees
5. Subscription or service fees for applicant tracking systems, tech recruiting systems, and any other technology
6. Subscription fees for LinkedIn or other recruiting search fees

New Hire Turnover Rate

The new hire turnover rate is the turnover of new hires in an acceptable time span for your industry. For biotech, I used one year. In call centers, for example, it may be better to use six months from hire. It doesn't have any stellar submeasures except for breaking down turnover by region and organizational function, such as research and development and marketing. You may discover that if new hire turnover spikes overall, it may the sales department or some other department that is the cause and that it is not a company-wide problem. I recommend you track a rolling twelve-month average for turnover and track the month-to-month changes to watch for trends.

The purpose of tracking new hire turnover is to see what the cause of its spikes is when it rises, and to identify what are the causes when it lowers. Hopefully, drops in turnover are due to improvements in finding job candidates who are better qualified, are a better fit for their teams and managers, and are happy working for your company after their onboarding. Nonetheless, it is good to know what change you made that led to the progress, or whether it was caused by an external factor such as a downturn in the regional economy or employees putting off resignations to wait for the year-end bonus check.

Turnover is a top-line metric that the whole human resources department should use, as it also is a great measure of confidence in the business leaders and the company's strategies and how well employees like working for management in the company and its individual departments and how well they like other factors such as benefits, pay, and so on.

Do more than 90 percent of your employees plan to continue working for the company in twelve months (based on results from your employee engagement or employee satisfaction survey)? This threshold is the benchmark for excellence in company culture and employee commitment to the company's mission, their work teams, and their leaders. Although it is a broader measure than employer branding and recruitment, if you fall below this threshold and by how much, it can signal a significant morale issue emerging, which may show up as increased turnover or on social media such as Glassdoor in the form of poor former employee reviews.

Is turnover higher than the industry or location average in any of your sites, including global sites? Do one or more functions have significantly more turnover than others? Turnover cost is heavily dependent on industry, location, skill, and experience of the employee. Cost-of-turnover studies suggest that the cost can be 16 to 20 percent of annual salary in retail, 50 percent for skilled medical professions, 100 percent for the most experienced skilled employees, and 213 percent for an executive.[112]

The point is to know your external benchmarks so you know where you stand. Turnover is very expensive. I have found turnover costs are often 50 percent of annual salaries in high technology and medical and engineering industries, which have highly skilled employees and high technology/high-touch customers, particularly when you include the recruiting costs, lost productivity, and novice errors. (It's much higher when you include relocation costs for specialty and executive roles.)

Differences in internal turnover between functional departments is also very telling. I include internal turnover in the talent management plan, with quarterly updates on annual rolling averages. Functions that have higher turnover than the other departments and higher than their functional norms are a sign of either intense external competition for talent or internal strife or bad management. It is a key indicator and requires more investigation to determine the cause and build support to correct it. In my experience, it is often an indication of poor management or poor pay.

What are the top reasons employees leave your company? If you are not collecting these data, you are working on assumptions or the hallway buzz. This workforce analysis is critical for improving recruiting and employee engagement success (and ultimately the performance of the business). Based on his research (from the Saratoga Institute data), Leigh Branham learned that 89 percent of managers believe that employees leave for money, but that in fact, 88 percent of employees leave for reasons other than money.[113] His research found that employees disengage before they resign and move on, but alert managers can listen and see the signs of disengagement and intervene to prevent good employees from leaving.

Note, in today's tight talent economy, pay and benefits are leading causes for turnover. Their influence on turnover subsides in average economies or during a recession. The importance of culture, leadership, career opportunity and team relationships should not be discounted, even in a tight talent economy.

Data from the Saratoga Institute shows that while 95 percent of human resources departments claim to collect exit interview data, only 32 percent of these departments share the data with management and only 30 percent follow up with action. So if it is largely not about pay, why do employees leave? Based on his research and root cause analysis, Leigh presents the following seven reasons.

1. The job or workplace not living up to expectations
2. The mismatch between job and person
3. Too little coaching and feedback
4. Too few growth and advancement opportunities
5. Feeling devalued and unrecognized
6. Stress from overwork and work-life imbalance
7. Loss of trust and confidence in senior leaders

The first two items on the list have a lot to do with the recruiting and selection process. Recruiters need to have access to this information and adjust their recruiting and selection processes based on the information.

Chapter 9: The Contingent Workforce or Gig Economy

The use of contingent workers is not new, and it is on the rise in the United States and around the world. It is also fraught with legal issues and pitfalls.

A 2015 report by the General Accounting Office found that 31 percent of the US workforce is made up of contingent workers. The definition includes independent contractors and self-employed workers, agency temps, direct-hire temps, on-call workers, day laborers, contract company workers, and part-time workers.[114]

However, a separate study found a much smaller number of contingent workers in the United States. A 2015 survey conducted in part for the RAND American Life Panel by Lawrence Katz of Harvard and Alan Krueger of Princeton University found that 15.8 percent of the US workforce in 2015 were alternative workers, up from 10.1 percent in 2005. In 2015, only 0.5 percent of workers were using online intermediaries such as Uber, Lyft, or Task Rabbit to find work. The study found that about twice as many workers selling goods or services directly to customers reported finding customers through offline intermediaries than through online intermediaries. For this study, alternative workers were defined as temporary help agency workers, on-call workers, contract workers, and independent contractors or freelancers. The percentage of workers hired out through contract companies showed the sharpest rise, increasing from 0.6 percent in 2005 to 3.1 percent in 2015.[115]

Upwork's 2017 study (based on a survey of six thousand US

workers) estimates that 57.3 million Americans are freelancing (36 percent of the US workforce) and this population contributes approximately $1.4 trillion annually to the economy, an increase of almost 30 percent over last year. Their study also found that 47 percent of millennial workers freelance, more than any other generation. Their results also show a progression of fewer moonlighters and part-time freelancers and more full-time freelancing. The study finds that a majority of these workers believe the Affordable Care Act has helped them and depend on it for medical benefits. The study reports that freelancers like the freedom and flexibility of freelancing, being their own boss, and the ability to earn extra money. They lament the lack of income predictability, the difficulty in finding work, and the absence of benefits.[116]

The Upwork study predicts that freelancers will be the majority of the US workforce by 2027, based on the growth rates of the past year. The study also reports that freelancers prefer dropping the term "gig economy" for "freelance economy" or "on-demand economy."

So while the 2017 Department of Labor data finds that baby boomers are increasing their numbers of independent contractors in the hot US economy, the Upwork survey finds that millennials are leading the way in using apps to find work.

The finding that millennials are leading the way in using apps to find work doesn't surprise me. However, I find the Upwork study's findings and its predictions a bit overblown, especially when academic and government studies find a significantly lower number of contract workers. Without improvements on issues such as affordable medical care and retirement benefits (especially for millennials, who are moving into their family-rearing years), my prediction is that the gig economy will hit a wall and not become a majority of the workforce. Unlike the academic and government studies, Upwork's study is short on disclosing its methodology. Since Upwork is the leading technology platform for contracting online, it feels a little self-serving.

Throwing a wrench into the evidence on the growth of

contingent workers and the gig economy is a 2017 study by the US Department of Labor. The percentage of Americans working in alternative work arrangements—such as independent contractors, on-call workers, and those who contract through a third party—has shrunk 0.6 percent since 2005. According to a US Labor Department report, the total of people working in such alternative arrangements now is 10.1 percent.

According to the survey, this change appears to be due to the drop of independent contractors in the workforce, who were at 7.4 percent of those working in 2005 and now are at 6.9 percent. The independent contractors are presumed to be taking full-time work in the hot US economy. The 2017 report was based on a survey of more than sixty thousand households.[117]

On the surface, this report appears to dim the dramatic predictions of the growth of the gig economy. Upwork, the largest online platform for gig workers, predicted this year that freelancers will become a majority of the US workforce in a decade.[118]

However, the Labor Department's survey appears to have limited its count of gig workers based on how they asked the questions. The survey asked if the respondents worked on a job where they "obtain customers on their own to provide a product or service." The wording of this question could have excluded workers at Lyft and TaskRabbit, who depend on these platforms to find customers. Today's definition of gig workers should include anyone with or without full- or part-time work who uses an app to find full- or part-time work, whether or not they are directly finding customers on the app. This would include workers who use Lyft or TaskRabbit to augment other full- or part-time work.

Bloomberg quoted Karen Kosanovich, a Labor Department economist, who said the survey was "designed to replicate what we have done in the past," adding that any constraints on the data are the same as in the prior reports.[119] The problem with maintaining this historical definition is that mobile apps on cell phones have proliferated since 2005, as have work apps like Upwork for gig workers.

There are two other interesting story lines here. According to the

Labor Department survey, US workers age fifty-five and older have a bigger share of the independent contractor workforce in 2017 than in 2005, with more than a third of 2017 workers age fifty-five or older being independent contractors. This age group constitutes about only 25 percent of the traditional workforce. Second, more than half of contingent workers (temps, on-call workers, and independent contractors) would have preferred a permanent job.[120]

I know all of this is a bit confusing with various results, definitions, and methodologies for counting the number of gig workers and their future. The growth of gig workers using technology platforms or traditional methods to find work is growing and offers freedoms and conveniences over the regimen of working for a large corporation or the chaos of a start-up. Platforms like Upwork also are building an ecosystem where gig workers receive feedback on their work and ratings, like Lyft drivers or apartments on Airbnb. Employers on Upwork also receive ratings, and contractors can see the range of hourly rates from competing bids for a job. It is a convenient alternative for some workers, usually the more highly skilled.

In short, I don't believe Upwork's predictions will come true, and as traditional employers improve pay and benefits to compete in this tight labor economy, many gig workers will join the world of full-time workers. Still, you should consider how gig workers can meet some of your workforce needs.

Case Study on the Use of Temporary and Contract Workers

In 1999 I shaped the contingent workforce policies for Honeywell Inc. Aerospace's business due to an eight-year lawsuit by long-term contingent workers for Microsoft, who were not granted Microsoft stock options and bonuses despite working exclusively for Microsoft for several years. At that time, Honeywell Inc., like many other large companies, had 25 to 35 percent of its workforce comprised of contingent workers who were either independent contractors, who often possessed a unique technical skill, or temporary engineers and technicians who worked at Honeywell through a third-party vendor such as Manpower.

Microsoft's contingent workforce won the eight-year class action lawsuit in 2000, and Microsoft was required to pay them $97 million.[121] At Honeywell Inc., we were delighted to have put in our new contingent workforce policy and to avoid the legal issues and bad publicity.

Honeywell Inc.'s strategy was to attract key workers for one to two years during periods of business cycles' growth to support innovation projects while avoiding long-term commitments and the benefit costs to workers such as health care, paid time off, and retirement and 401(k) benefits. However, workers with the specialized skills could command a significantly higher level of pay as independent contractors than less skilled workers who came to the company through a temporary agency. This, of course, was before the age of gig worker platforms such as Upwork.

The strategy worked well with manufacturing, administrative, and some engineering jobs where labor was not in short supply. However, in some highly skilled specialty professions, contractors could demand a higher wage than employees even with benefits thrown in, and not work as employees, maintaining their independence and earning higher pay.

The workforces of Honeywell, and other companies at the time, were told that contingent workers were a buffer to their employment and would be laid off first before employees in the event of a downturn. That was acceptable for a while, but as more independent contractors with specialty skills were hired, they became the priority to be retained talent during the downturn. The promise to full-time employees was broken.

Today, many companies use contingent workers, with contingent workers being as high as 50 percent of the workforce for a host of strategies. Some companies add surge workers during temporary upswings in customer demand. Others prefer to outsource certain specialties to experts rather than incur the long-term costs of having that expertise in-house.

Labor Laws Are Still a Major Obstacle to the Gig Economy

The laws governing alternative work from 1999 (when I put Honeywell Inc. 's contingent workforce policy in place) to now have not changed much. Then and now, federal law has a multiple-point checklist to determine who is or who is not a regular employee. Basically, if a worker reports to a place of work, their work is controlled by company managers and policies, is paid hourly, and they use company equipment, such as computers, and they don't work for others doing the same type of work, they should be considered an employee, especially if the worker is at the company for a year or more.

With the growing concern about the loss of real wages and benefits among American workers, I predict these laws will get stronger. Uber and Lyft have learned the hard way, from lawsuits or settlements, that even contractors, temps, and gig workers have rights, especially when they are used in circumstances that define them as regular workers under the law.

Some advocate that these laws should be changed. Maybe, but the larger issue is the loss of real wages and benefits of the US worker. Labor shortages are forcing companies to raise wages and benefits as companies compete for too few workers in the surging US economy. But if the wages don't meet expectations, workers have other employment choices, can sue companies when their rights are violated, or can vote in lawmakers who will better protect their interests. All these scenarios are bad ones for employers.

As in all areas of labor law, in addition to federal law, employers must look at the laws of the states, counties, and cities where they are located or where they do business. On May 1, 2018, the California Supreme Court adopted a new legal standard that will make it much more difficult for businesses to classify workers as independent contractors, drastically changing the legal landscape across the Golden State. The misclassification of workers can result in significant legal exposure concerning wage and hour compliance and fines.

Although the court case was about the trucking industry, this case will impact office, engineering, and manufacturing workers. If your company uses contractors in California, you will need to carefully examine how this new standard may change your policies and practices with contractors and who you classify as employees.

Specifically, the court adopted a new standard for determining whether a company "employs" or is the "employer" for purposes of California wage orders.

Under the new "ABC" test, a worker is considered an employee under the wage orders unless the hiring entity establishes all three of these prongs:

1. The worker is free from the control and direction of the company in connection with the performance of the work, both under the contract for the performance of such work and in fact.
2. The worker performs work that is outside the usual course of the hiring entity's business. (One example of a worker performing work outside of a business's normal work is a plumber doing repairs for a retail business.)
3. The worker is customarily engaged in an independently established trade, occupation, or business of the same nature as the work performed for the hiring entity.

This decision not only expands the definition of "employee" under the California wage orders; it also imposes an *affirmative burden on companies to prove that independent contractors are properly classified.*

Because of the decision, all California businesses with independent contractors will need to conduct a thorough evaluation of their contractors to determine whether they are properly classified.

In order for you to learn more about the California Supreme Court's new legal standard, I have provided you an excellent article

"California Supreme Court Adopts Broad New Misclassification Test" by Ashton Riley of Fisher Phillips that was published May 2, 2018, on SHRM.[122]

The happiness of contingent workers varies widely. Independent contractors and self-employed workers are happy with their contingent employment. Eighty-five percent say they are content with their employment type, and 57 percent of independent contractors report being "very satisfied" with their jobs, compared with only 45 percent of regular full-time workers. In sharp contrast, 50 percent of agency temps and on-call contingent workers want a different employment type.[123]

Over the last two years, we have seen headlines about two companies that employ drivers and, according to the courts or regulators, violated laws on contingent workers and the definition of technical platforms. FedEx disclosed a $228 million settlement for not classifying its twenty-three hundred delivery drivers in California as employees, after losing in a federal appeals court in Oakland, California. The court ruled that FedEx drivers aren't independent contractors because FedEx controls how drivers do their jobs, including schedules, appearance, and equipment requirements.[124]

In July 2015, the California Labor Commission ruled that an Uber driver in San Francisco is an employee of the ride-hauling app company and not an independent contractor, as Uber claimed. The ruling requires Uber to pay the driver $4,152 to cover reimbursable business expenses. Uber claimed it is a neutral technology platform, enabling drivers and passengers to transact business. But the commission found that Uber was "involved in every aspect of the operation."[125]

There is long-standing guidance regarding what defines independent contractors versus employees in the United States. (European countries also have their own laws on this matter.) Independent contractors perform services for companies under an express or implied agreement. Being an independent contractor means not being subject to an employer's financial, behavioral, or type of relationship controls regarding the method and means by which services are performed. If a company provides all or most of the tools required for the job, gives detailed work direction, and determines schedules, an independent contractor begins to look like an employee.

You can learn more about the legal issues of hiring the contingent workforce from your attorney, The US and State Departments of Labor, and from the Society of Human Resources Management.

Technology Platforms Can Be a Great Source of Talent!

Technical platforms organize free agents, matching them with clients, and offer new ways to get work done. They allow companies to access key talent for less cost than traditional firms in engineering, marketing, legal, and other highly skilled professions. Technical platforms are growing and can pose a real threat to established companies. Currently Upwork is the largest global talent platform, but there are others that specialize with different professions of workers.

For example, the advertising platform Tongal does not employ any of the creative talent it uses to make ads. Instead, Tongal's technical talent platform connects advertisers to free agents who make ads at low prices that blue chip advertising firms can't match. Tongal also provides a system for organizing work. It crowdsources ideas and videos via a contest where the top few ideas win the initial contest and get paid. After a series of other contests, an ultimate winner is selected to produce the ad for the client. Tongal has clients' rate freelancers for quality and reliability.

As companies plot their talent management strategies, they should carefully plan for the use of contingent workers and talent platforms as a way to complement their regular workforce. This strategy gives them access to additional talent that may provide a competitive advantage. Companies need to be mindful, however, of protecting their competitive value and intellectual property. They also need to be careful not to violate current employment laws. Doing so can cost them dearly and tarnish their reputation.

The smart use of alternative workers should be part of your talent strategies.

Should you use temps, contractors, and gig workers? It all depends on your values, purpose, business model, strategies, and how much legal risk you want to take on. Every talent strategy begins with aligning the company's workforce to its purpose and values and to efficiently execute its business strategies. Every company needs to have an employer brand and a value proposition for the labor force. All talent strategies should include the smart use of contractors, temps, and gig workers to augment their regular workforce—as long as they don't run afoul of the law or attract lawsuits, fines, and the loss of good faith that goes with bad publicity.

There are many great scenarios for the use of alternative workers to augment your regular workforce, as in the Honeywell Inc. strategy I outlined above. Another scenario is that in this tight labor market, when open jobs outnumber the unemployed, contractors and gig workers may be an excellent source of talent to augment your traditional workforce or for specialties you don't need to have available full-time.

As companies plot their talent management strategies, they should carefully plan for the use of contingent workers and talent platforms to complement their regular workforce. This strategy gives them access to additional talent that may provide a competitive advantage. Companies need to be mindful, however, of protecting their competitive value and intellectual property. They also need to be careful not to violate current employment laws. Doing so can cost them dearly and tarnish their reputation.

You can ignore the debate over the number of alternative workers and the future of the gig economy. The important questions are "What is your talent strategy?" and "How do you attract a workforce and align your workforce to the values and purpose of your company?"

Why Not Create Your Own Contingent Worker Platform?

That is precisely what a leading global freight forwarder has done. The enterprise's warehousing business unit was looking at the costs and fees for traditional temporary labor agencies as well as contracting with workers on platforms such as Upwork and thought, why not create our own, building up a ready "casual" workforce that we can depend on for either seasonal work, part-time work, or surges in workforce demand.

"We observed that at some of our warehouses around the world, we had colleges located nearby and thought many of those students would like seasonal work over the summer to make extra cash working flexible, part-time during our busiest times of the year," said the company executive who is heading their Global HR Innovation department and asked not to be identified. "So we created our own platform that enables us to tap into a pool of available workers 24-7."

The executive explained that in addition to reducing the fees the company pays for temporary labor, as well as the cost for overtime of their permanent staff, they wanted to build relationships with casual workers near their facilities and offer them work that fits their needs. The community employment centers have welcomed this approach, which also allows tapping into "nontraditional" warehouse workers, such as students or stay-at-home parents.

The company is trying to find creative ways to overcome the labor shortage in the United States and other countries, especially for short-notice workers. They observed that some workers cannot work ten-to-twelve-hour shifts, but they can work a six-hour shift. Other workers wanted different workday and hourly work schedules. The company wanted to offer them the flexibility they needed for their roles that also fit the company's needs.

The externally built platform is a beautiful and easy-to-navigate site, where casual workers can register and apply for jobs after completing the application process. It enables the enterprise to more rapidly onboard their casual workers. Onboarding is easier when you already have employed the worker, have already screened them, and have their personal information and documentation to prove they can legally work in the United States. The casual worker's hours are limited to no more than a set number of hours a week to meet statutory requirements for benefits. The minimum number of hours required is one four-hour shift.

The platform is currently in its pilot stage with three warehouses that are in close proximity in the Midwest, where the labor shortage is extremely high. As of the printing of this book, other entities of the company, such as China and Australia, have already expressed great interest, and a global rollout of the platform is in the planning stages.

Chapter 10: HR Geek: The Empirical Evidence for Hiring Excellent Employees

When I entered graduate school for a master's degree in human resources and industrial relations at the University of Minnesota in the 1980s, my faculty advisor, Dr. George Seltzer, told me the best predictor of future performance is past performance. If you want more electronic engineers, hire electronic engineers with a degree and experience and give them a trial period on the job. In the research, this is known as the job tryout procedure.

After years of implementing performance management systems, I know that not all electronic engineers (or assemblers, managers, or sales reps, for example) provide companies with the same level of economic output or have the same teamwork behaviors or are all the same in their potential to be leaders in management.

Human beings have different aptitudes, abilities, and skills and different sets of values and norms for behavior. So how do you determine, before you make the hiring decision, which job candidates will be the best performers for your company?

Should you use tests to assess which job candidate has the best knowledge, skills, and abilities to be a great performer in your various job families? Should you use IQ tests? Personality assessments? Behavioral interviewing? Structured interviews based on job competencies? Job trials as Professor Seltzer suggested? Or just flip a coin and save everyone a lot of time and heartache?

The Research from Industrial/Organizational Psychologists Provides Reliable Answers

To answer these questions, a whole field of psychology has arisen known as industrial/organizational psychology. It is the scientific study of human behavior in organizations and the workplace and how to use scientifically developed tests (or assessments) to predict who will be high-performing employees at work. IO psychologists also scientifically measure which knowledge, skills, and abilities people have and need to be successful in various professions and how to measure performance and other key abilities at work such as creativity.

When creating an assessment, IO psychologists and other scientific researchers are concerned about having an assessment that has criterion validity and does not have a bias against people based on demographic factors such as age, race, or gender. The best way to establish criterion validity is to perform a long-term validity study, known as predictive validity, by administering employment tests to job applicants and then seeing if the test scores correlate (and in fact predict) future good job performance. Predictive validity studies take a long time to complete and require large aggregate sample sizes to produce meaningful statistical analysis.

The relationship between test performance and a business metric in a criterion correlation can be quantified by a correlation coefficient (ranging from -1.0 to +1.0), which can be used to demonstrate how strongly correlated two variables are depending on how close the number is to -1.0 or +1.0. The more correlated the two variables are, the higher the predictive validity of the test.

Because determining predictive validity can take a long time, many employers prefer to use concurrent validity to measure criterion correlation; it can be done much faster and at less cost. Concurrent validation is done by administering tests to existing employees and comparing the results to performance. For example, I have correlated a sales personality test to a sample of an existing sales force to see if high test scores correlated with our best performers. The good news is that it did. With this information we could be confident that the test would predict good performance. We also tracked the test results of all test applicants to determine if there was any adverse impact by demographic factors such as race and gender. I have done the same for leadership tests and for general aptitude skills required for entry-level factor jobs.

Another form of validity that is preferred because of its low cost is called valid generalization. According to Criteriacorp.com, IO psychologists have concluded that validity evidence can be generalized across a wide range of positions for certain kinds of employment tests, particularly cognitive aptitude tests. By generalizing the validity of tests across many position types, companies of all sizes can be more confident that the preemployment tests they are using are valid for the positions they are testing for within their organizations.[126]

What is not acceptable is to use "prima facie" or "armchair" validity, which is using a test that you think is valid without gathering data.

Using validated assessment tests is legal in the United States and can help you select better workers—but not if the tests are bias and lead to discriminatory hiring decisions.

The EEOC has put out guidance that "the use of tests and other selection procedures can be a very effective means of determining which applicants or employees are most qualified for a particular job." However, the EEOC has warned that the "use of these tools can violate the federal anti-discrimination laws if an employer intentionally uses them to discriminate based on race, color, sex, national origin, religion, disability, or age (40 or older). Use of tests and other selection procedures can also violate the federal anti-discrimination laws if they disproportionately exclude people in a particular group by race, sex, or another covered basis, unless the employer can justify the test or procedure under the law."[127]

Many fear that employment assessment tests adversely impact people based on demographic factors and we might not know it or haven't taken the time to prove it. The advocates of AI believe that their technology will find better correlations between the knowledge, skills, and abilities to perform best on jobs without having adverse impact, but it is too early to tell. Many who are making this claim have not provided the public with their data to verify their claims. And employers can be sued it they use data that have not been validated and are found to cause adverse impact.

The answer to the question *How do I determine who will perform best on this job?* is critical because many companies hire from a list of job candidates based on who they know or which candidate makes the best first impression from looks, dress, a charming smile, or by hitting it off with areas of common interests. Who you know and first impressions are the least reliable ways to make hiring decisions.

Others go a totally different direction and want to make hiring decisions based solely on intelligence. Hiring for intelligence is strongly correlated with success on the job. Depending on the study, intelligence accounts for about 25 percent of the validity for predicting good job performance, as I will review shortly.

There is a limit and diminishing return with hiring for intelligence, though. First, intelligence, or IQ, is not the only criterion for many jobs, especially for leadership roles and roles involving relationship building and customer service. With these jobs, emotional intelligence is a critical factor. In addition, people have different acumens. Some are strong in mathematics and logic. Others in writing and storytelling. Some are emotionally cold like *Star Trek*'s Spock. Others are empathic like *Star Trek*'s Dr. McCoy. Others, like *Star Trek*'s Captain Kirk, take in various and contradictory inputs and make courageous and creative decisions, then implement them efectively.

The most intelligent people in the world (I am referring to people gifted with an IQ above 140), by and large, are not very employable for a whole host of reasons. In Malcolm Gladwell's book *Outliers*,[128] for example, he describes Christopher Langan, who claims to have an IQ of 195. (Average IQ is 100, and genius is in the 140 to 145 range, which is .0025 of the population or 1 in 400.) Although he published the "Cognitive-Theoretic Model of the Universe," because of Langan's use of convoluted language and lack of mentors in rural Montana, Gladwell argues that Langan did not reach his potential. In addition to mentoring, as we shall see, other skills such as empathy, self-discipline, and initiative are strong predictors of success.

Many who want to hire the smartest people select students with the highest GPA from the best universities, such as Ivy League universities (Harvard, Yale, Cornell, Penn State, Columbia, Brown, and so on), Stanford, Duke, Northwestern, or the University of California at Berkeley. While GPA is a good substitute for an IQ test, this is also not a great way to make a hiring decision, even though many of the Fortune 500 make their hiring decisions competing for this talent from the top 20 MBA schools. Studies show that companies can hire just as good workers from among the best at good regional schools, as I've discussed above. In addition, most MBA students have a work history from before or during their graduate studies. Pry into that work history. It will tell you volumes about them as workers and their potential to succeed.

Let's look at the research. As we do, we will review the correlation coefficients to identify from meta analyses which methods and tests are best at predicting job success.

The science around selection dates to almost one hundred years ago. In 1920 Edward Thorndike published a paper entitled "The Constant Error in Psychological Ratings."[129] He coined the term "halo effect." He studied selection procedures for US soldiers. He found that soldiers who had great physiques were also rated highly by their military leaders for intelligence and other qualities. Upon further testing, he concluded that there was no correlation between physique and intelligence or the other qualities. Military management was incorrectly generalizing physique onto other qualities. It is what we now call an unconscious bias.

In 1988, a meta-analysis by Frank L. Schmidt and John E. Hunter, titled "The Validity and Utility of Selection Methods in Personnel Psychology: Practical and Theoretical Implications of 85 Years of Research Findings," looked at eighty-five years of research on employment selection.[130] They reviewed the validity of nineteen selection procedures for predicting job performance and training performance. Schmidt and Hunter also reviewed the validity of paired combinations of general mental ability (GMA) tests and eighteen other selection procedures. A meta-analysis is a combination of separate empirical research studies to create a larger database and more powerful conclusions about a topic—in this case, understanding which selection methods provide the best predictors for hiring great workers. The academic term for best predictors is predictive validity.

Rank Order of Best and Worst Hiring Methods

Based on the meta-analysis study published in 1988 by Schmidt and Hunter,[131] the most valid methods for determining which job candidates will succeed on a job are the following in rank order based on the best validity score.

- Work Sample Test (which is a hands-on simulation of part or all of the job). It can be used to select the best among *experienced* workers).
- General Mental Aptitude Test (which includes IQ tests and other tests of general mental ability, special relationships, and reading, writing, and mathematics needed on the job). They work if they are validated for the job family and do not adversely exclude otherwise qualified job candidates based on demographic factors.
- Structured Interviews (which are planned and go into detailed fact gathering on the person's work history and look for matches to the required job competencies and teamwork skills and alignment to the company's purpose, values, and culture).
- Peer Ratings, which have high reliability compared to other methods, but they are hard to get during an interview process with external job candidates.

- Job Knowledge Test (for example, assessment tests for Microsoft office and project management skills for project coordinators or software coding for software engineers).
- Training and Education Behavioral Consistency Method (this is hiring people whose training, education, skills, and previous experiences align with the job). It requires a structured interview or assessments to discern who is or is not a job fit.
- Job Tryout Procedure (usually a thirty- to ninety-day period for unskilled workers) works best with heavy doses of training and coaching).
- Assessment Centers are rated low for most jobs and much better for leadership and sales roles.
- Unstructured Interviews, which are not much better than a coin toss.

The worst predictors for determining which job candidates will succeed on a job are the following (from the worst to less bad—you don't want to use methods on this list).

- Age, which is the only factor with a negative correlation—old or young, it isn't a predictor.
- Graphology (handwriting analysis) is almost as bad as age.
- Interests. Many start-ups and call centers love to select for interests, but if you don't also select for job skills, collaboration skills, conscientiousness, and integrity, you are depending on luck.
- Years of Education. A bachelor's, and to a lesser extent a master's, degree are essential for many professions, such as finance, human resources, science fields, and many engineering and medical and leadership disciplines because of the need to learn the theories, models, body of knowledge, legal framework, professional skills, and strategic thinking skills required and as an indicator of perseverance. But higher years of education does not correlate well with job success.

- Training and Education Point Method (typical civil service methodology to earn points for job hiring preference or to get a promotion) is objective and can hold guard against political cronyism.
- Job experience measured by years. The problem with job experience is that there is no correlation with performance after five years on a job.
- Biographical measures (which include life experiences and gender, age, race, color, and so on), which are outlawed in the United States and other countries as screening criteria.

Using Combinations of Most Reliable Hiring Methods Leads to Best Results

The most insightful learning from Schmidt and Hunter's meta-analysis is that using combinations of hiring methods provides the most reliable and predictive hiring results. Below is their summary of combinations of hiring methods for experienced and inexperienced job candidates.

> Of the combinations of predictors examined, two stand out as being both practical to use for most hiring and as having high composite validity: the combination of a GMA test and an integrity test (composite validity of .65); and the combination of a GMA test and a structured interview (composite validity of .63). Both combinations can be used with applicants with no previous experience on the job (entry-level applications), as well as with experienced applicants. Both combinations predict performance in job training programs quite well (.67 and .59, respectively), as well as performance on the job. And both combinations are less expensive to use than many other combinations. Hence, both are excellent choices. However, there might be reasons why an employer might choose to use one of the other combinations with high, but slightly lower,

validity. Some examples are combinations that include conscientiousness test, work sample tests, a job knowledge test, and the behavioral consistency method.[132]

The top methods combined with the general measurement aptitude tests to predict who will perform best on the job, in rank order, are as follows.

- Integrity Tests
- Structured Employment Interviews
- Work Sample Tests
- Conscientiousness Tests
- Job Knowledge Tests
- Job Tryout Procedure
- Peer Ratings
- Training and Experience Behavioral Consistency Model
- Reference Checks

The job categories for this analysis included blue-collar jobs and up to midlevel white-collar jobs. In addition to being excellent selectors of job performance, GMAs, integrity, conscientiousness tests, and structured employment interviews are excellent predictors of who will learn the most from job training.

Below is a table I created from Schmidt and Hunter's academic paper[133] that shows the validity of each individual selection method and the multiple (or combined validity) with the GMATs .

Method	Validity	Multiple Validity with GMA Tests	Validity Gain with Pairing	% Increase in Validity
General Mental Aptitude Tests (GMATs) Test	.51			
Work Sample Test	.54	.63	.12	24%
Integrity Test	.41	.65	.14	27%

Conscientiousness Test	.31	.60	.09	18%
Structured Employment Interview	.51	.63	.12	24%
Unstructured Employment Interview	.38	.55	.04	8%
Job Knowledge Test	.48	.58	.07	14%
Job Tryout Procedure	.44	.58	.07	14%
Peer Ratings	.49	.58	.07	14%
T&E Behavioral Consistency Method	.45	.58	.07	14%
Reference Checks	.26	.57	.06	12%
Job Experience measured in years	.18	.54	.03	6%
Biographical Data Measures	.35	.52	.01	2%
Assessment Centers	.37	.53	.02	4%
T&E Point Method	.11	.52	.01	2%
Years of Experience	.10	.52	.01	2%
Interests	.10	.52	.01	2%
Graphology (Handwriting Analysis)	.02	.51	.0	0%
Age	-.01	.51	.0	0%

Now we will look at each of the most valid methods for selecting workers based on the Schmidt and Hunter study and other research since then.

Work Sample Tests

The most well-known conclusion from this research is that for hiring employees with previous experience on the job, the most valid predictor of future job performance and learning is a work sampling.[134] Work sampling is simple and straightforward. The recruiting and hiring manager set up one or more workstations to let the job candidate do key parts of the job and compare their results with the results of good employees.

I have used work sampling with manufacturing and technician roles with great success. Let me review two examples. In the hiring of assemblers, a team of assembler managers took a basic work instruction and electronic schematic and the parts necessary to make this build and gave the work to job candidates to complete it. Each job candidate was given an overview by an assembler group leader, and they could ask questions of the group leader if they were confused. (Actually, asking questions was viewed favorably for the test). Their build was reviewed for quality and the percentage of the build that was completed within a time limit. Those who scored above a threshold were then invited to participate in a structured interview.

Another example was for marketing professionals to prepare and make a twenty-minute presentation and to field questions. Each candidate who had passed the résumé and telephone screen was asked during their on-site interview to make a presentation to the interviewing team and other experts based on material that was on a share site that they had been given access to. They were also given the presentation template to use. With this work sample, we were able to judge their ability to use medical terms on par with physicians, make a presentation, project confidence, and field questions. It was an effective tool.General Mental Ability Tests and IQ

General mental ability tests (GMATs) measure the cognitive functioning that works across several different mental domains such as science, mathematics, word knowledge, paragraphs, numeric, coding, special relationships, and problem-solving to name a few. It was first proposed by Francis Galton, an English geneticist and relative to Darwin, in 1888. It can be called by other names such as "g," IQ, and simply intelligence.

GMATs are one of the highest predictive measures for job candidate success on the job. Schmidt and Hunter, in their study published in 1984, found that GMATs predict about .25 of job success. In their meta-analysis, however, the predictability increases substantially, with .51 predictability of job success. The difference appears to be based on the competency level of the job. The higher the job sophistication and complexity, the higher the predictability of GMATs for job success and learning in training.

Other recent academic studies have also found that GMATs

were predictors of job success based on the complexity of the job. Studies conducted in the 1990s and 2000s have made the empirical case for GMATs being the single best predictor of performance. The predictability varies by occupation. Meta-analytic studies conducted in the United States report predictive validity between GMATs and job performance with coefficients ranging from a low of around .25 for manual labor jobs, .31 for refinery workers, .50 to .60 for white-collar workers, to .73 for computer programmers. The more complex the job the higher the predictability of GMATs for job performance and training success. Meta-analytic studies from the European Community report a similar range and an overall operational validity of .62 (higher than the Schmidt and Hunter study).[135]

A 2007 meta-analysis on the validity of general mental ability and specific cognitive abilities for predicting job performance and training success in the United Kingdom found that GMATs and specific ability tests are valid predictors of both job performance and training success.[136] This study looked at results for different occupations such as clerical, engineer, professional, driver, operator, manager, and sales and by specific ability test, such as verbal, numerical, perceptual, and spatial. The meta-analysis found that occupation families that had greater job complexity had higher validities for GMATs and job performance and job success.

Schmidt and Hunter reported that GMATs when used for screening for relatively inexperienced job candidates with tests for conscientiousness and personal integrity and with structured employment interviews based on the competencies required for the job significantly improved the predictability of success and learning in training. For experienced workers, structured interviews, job knowledge, and work sample tests when used with GMATs improved the selection of successful job candidates.

These more recent studies, like Schmidt and Hunter, found that the validity of GMATs increases when they are used with other selection methods, especially in selecting inexperienced candidates. These studies found that when screening inexperienced candidates, GMATs used in combination with integrity tests achieved a composite validity of .63. Used with a conscientious test, they achieved a composite validity of .60. However, when screening experienced candidates, a combination of cognitive ability and work sample testing achieved a composite validity of .63.[137]

Other research on GMATs found that as a stand-alone tool, they were less predictable but are still helpful. It gets back to the complexity of the job. GMATs are a predictive measure for employees without previous experience, but GMATs can only make about 25 percent of the predictive correlation.[138] As with the above cited research, GMATs, when used to predict job success with inexperienced workers, had higher predictability of job success when used with tests for conscientiousness and personal integrity and with structured employment interviews based on the required job competencies. For experienced workers, job knowledge and work sample tests were better at predicting job success.

Schmidt and Hunter were not the only researchers who found limits of predictability for GMATs. McClellen found that GMATs and academic grades alone were a poor predictor of job and career success. He found that a specific set of competencies distinguished the high performers from the average performers. Those competencies were empathy, self-discipline, and initiative. More importantly, McClellen advised that to truly understand how to distinguish star performers, one had to look at their current star performers and find the competencies that made them successful.[139] Note that job competencies are also referred to in the academic literature as "Training and Experience Behavioral Consistency Model." I have a section dedicated to that below—as it is critical for increasing the selection of great performers.

New research beginning in the 1990s on emotional intelligence has shown that it is a better predictor of success for executives, leaders, sales and customer service workers than intelligence alone. In addition, it is a very important measure for succession planning. I will cover Peter Salovey and John Mayer's definition of emotional intelligence, and Daniel Goleman's framework of emotional intelligence in Chapter 11: HR Geek: Additional Important Issues.

GMATs, or IQ, should be thought of as a minimum threshold level for many professions; their other attributes are more predictive for high potential employees and for those who go into management, lead program teams, and take customer-facing positions. There is also the criticism that GMATs have a cultural bias that tends to have females and people of color score less than Caucasians and some Asian nationalities and Ashkenazi Jews (who actually score higher than Caucasians).[140] One resolution to diminish potential adverse impact with GMATs I learned early in my career working with The General Aptitude Battery is to normalize test results by gender and race/ethnicity.

An individual's general mental ability is rather constant over time but is positively affected by education level, family income, and self-esteem. It is also negatively impacted by weeks of unemployment.

GMA tests are valid and reliable for all ethnic groups tested. Because of the different ethnic scores among the test results, some observers have suggested that GMA tests may have culture biases or that companies should use ethnic-based scores when testing and making selection decisions.[141] Different ethnic groups score differently on GMATs. For example, East Asians (ethnic Chinese, Japanese, Korean, Taiwanese, Hong Kongese, and Singaporeans) score higher (especially with math) than whites, who score higher than Latinos, who score higher than African Americans, who score higher than Sub-Saharan Africans. Ashkenazi Jews (from central Europe) score the best overall, about a half a standard deviation higher than whites. Men score higher on the visual-spatial intelligence and math sections than women, while women score higher on verbal intelligence. Overall, men and women generally have equivalent scores.

However, an abundance of empirical evidence for this culturally sensitive and politically explosive issue has determined that the statistical differences by ethnic groups are most likely valid.[142]

These data don't mean that there are no Ashkenazi Jews or East Asians with low IQs or no blacks with high IQs. They don't mean that there are no Central Americans who are smarter than Ashkenazi

Jews. About 20 percent of African Americans score higher than the average white score.

I can add the story of an African American I hired who was a member of the "4H" club. He was not involved in the "4H" club you see at state fairs. He has never milked a cow or raised a horse. He earned his 4H club designation among his professional peers by receiving four degrees from Harvard University. They are a BS in chemistry, an MS in chemistry, a master's in public policy, and just for kicks, he also earned a Harvard medical degree. He earned his BS in chemistry while also being the starting tailback for the Harvard varsity football team. He now works as a vice president of clinical research at a leading global biotech firm.

Judging people's IQ, character, attributes, and abilities by skin color, ethnicity, national origin, or religion is the definition of racism. Judging people by gender is the definition of sexism. Judging people by their sexual orientation is the definition of homophobia. Judging people by their place of national origin is the definition of xenophobia. Everyone is to be judged by his or her own character and abilities as an individual. This is a founding premise of the US Declaration of Independence and an unshakable principle of the US democracy, society, and economy. However, it is a principle that has needed to be repeatedly defended and revisited in our nation's history.

When I look at the differences in test scores, I draw a conclusion that education and cultures that value education are the great equalizers in raising IQ scores.

Various GMA tests include the General Aptitude Test Battery (GATB), Wonderlic Personnel Test, Armed Services Vocational Aptitude Battery (ASVAB), and various "IQ" tests such as WAIS-IV and Stanford-Binet tests.

I used the GATB to test factory workers for Honeywell Inc. in Research Triangle Park in combination with a structured interview, work sampling, and facility tour with great success. I did use ethnic-based scoring, meaning I selected the best scoring whites based on the white mean score and the best scoring African

Americans from the African American mean score. The test improved the quality and retention of all of our workers. Please note, the workforce in this facility was 50 percent white and 50 percent black and had 85 percent full utilization on its affirmative action plan, meaning it was a very diverse workforce with excellent affirmative action plan "utilization" to use the EEOC's term.

While mental ability tests are a close second to work sampling, the advantage of general mental ability tests is that they can be used for nearly all jobs, whether entry-level or advanced jobs, and the job applicant does not have to have experience. They also have the highest validity and lowest cost to use.

GMATs and specific aptitude tests are used across many countries, but generally less in the US than in Canada and Europe. Approximately 16 percent of companies in the United States administer GMA tests, and 42 percent use aptitude tests. In Canada, 43 percent of companies administer aptitude tests. In Europe the use of GMATs varies by country, with Germany at 6 percent, Italy at 20 percent, United Kingdom at 70 percent, and Finland at 74 percent. In Europe, the use of aptitude tests varies by country as well, with Germany at the low end at 8 percent and Spain on the high end at 72 percent.[143]

With their success, why aren't they used more? It is for many reasons. Some organizational cultures don't like the idea of GMATs as opposed to the belief in individualism and letting new hires show their stuff on the job, come sink or swim. Other companies are concerned about the legal challenges that may come if their hiring practices are disparate against protected classes (which may have little to do with GMATs but all to do with other biases in selection). For others, the cost may be a concern, although they tend to be cheap. Another factor may be the use of more digital technology in recruiting and an emphasis on too much speed, which cuts out the use of GMATs.

Nonetheless, they are useful and predictive over most other selection methods, especially when used with other selection methods, and watching for any adverse impact on protected classes from the tests.

There are many vendors today that provide validated assessment tests. I have had success using Berke for sales workers and sales leaders. I have had great success with leadership and executive assessments as well using the Hogan, which is widely used and validated, and leadership and executive assessment tests and two-day assessment centers from the Center for Creative Leadership and PDI Ninth House.

You can learn more about validated assessments by going to Capterra's website for preemployment testing software at https://www.capterra.com/pre-employment-testing-software/. The assessments are ranked by users, and you can see the number of reviews.

Another website with helpful data is Digital HR Tech. at https://www.digitalhrtech.com/top-pre-employment-assessment-tools/. They provide general information about each preemployment assessment, what is unique about the test, a summary of who uses the assessment test, and pricing information.

Assessments these days are generally available online and take less than twenty minutes. Be sure to use an assessment that has been validated to predict job success without adversely selecting out job candidates based on gender and protected classes. Don't take the claim on the website; ask to see the data, an academic paper, or a white paper. Research the tests online to look for ratings and any information concerning legal activity. Compare costs among vendors and also speak with current clients to get their feedback. Then benchmark the assessment by having a good sample size of your current employees in the job family take the assessment. This will help you determine what test score results should be set as your criteria that the candidate has the general mental abilities, job skills, or personality to qualify for the next step in the process.

Structured Interviews

A structured interview is a quantitative approach to interviewing based on the knowledge, skills, abilities, and competencies to perform on the job and in the company's culture.[144] With structured interviews, the company creates a set of questions to ask each candidate to determine if they have the education, experience, technical skills, social skills, and emotional intelligence to do well on the job. The structured interview is also set up to see if the job candidate has a record of success and how they achieved their success. Structured interviews dig deep and don't hover over the surface.

Another reason to use detailed structured interviews and background checks is that it is a reliable way to determine if the job candidate is telling half-truths or lies. The number of job applicants lying on their résumés and in job interviews is increasing, and it is very difficult to catch someone lying in an interview, even among those trained to watch body language and tone of voice to determine if job applicants are lying. For more on this, please read the section on "How to Tell If a Job Candidate Is Lying to You" in Chapter 11: HR Geek, Additional Important Issues.

Empirical studies conducted in the 1980s and 1990s have shown the strength of structured interviews over unstructured interviews. See Hunter and Schmidt[145] and another meta-analysis by McDaniel, Whetzel, Schmidt, and Maurer.[146] Structured interviews have higher reliability and predictability than unstructured interviews in selecting candidates who will perform better on the job. A more recent meta-analysis on structured interviewing, conducted in 2014, arrived at the same conclusion of the earlier studies. The 2014 study reports that "Twelve meta-analyses have been conducted on this topic, and they have consistently found strong evidence for the superiority of structured interviews compared to unstructured interviews."[147]

Schmidt and Hunter's 1988 meta-analysis found that structured interviews were the third best selection method, with a validity factor of .51. It rises to .63 when used with a GMAT.[148]

Unstructured interviews have no or very little fixed format, fixed set of questions to be answered, or fixed procedure for scoring applicant answers, and in many cases, different job candidates will be asked different questions. Unstructured interviews have a validity factor of .38 based on Schmidt and Hunter.

A British academic meta-analysis on structured vs. unstructured interviews by Willi Wiesner and Steven Cronshaw in 1988 found that the structured interview was a very valid and reliable assessment method. It was nearly twice as valid as unstructured interviews. The meta-analysis also found that structured interviews are more valid when they are based on job analysis.[149]

Research has also shown that when using phone interviewing and video interviewing, with the ability to view facial expressions, make eye contact, hear the change in voice intonation, and see body gestures is not available or reduced, these types of interviews benefit more when there is a structured interview. Why? Because more care is used by the interviewer with asking questions and accurately listening to and understanding the answer.[150]

Structured interviews are usually established by first having an up-to-date job description of the job or role that identifies the knowledge, skills, and abilities required on the job and a profile of the ideal candidate. Interviewing managers or the job incumbent is helpful in gathering these data.

Even if you don't have this information, I recommend that you launch an effort with the hiring managers of a job family to identify the knowledge, education, skills, aptitudes, mentoring, coaching, and on-the job experiences that molded your best employees. In detail, I look for the following:

- What education, certifications, or training do your best workers have?
- What developmental experiences were critical for their development before you hired them?
- What industries or previous employers provided the best hires?

- ◆ Which of your own training programs, mentors, and coaches have had the best success and why?
- ◆ What on-the-job experiences provided the best development?

It is also helpful to check on the academic literature to see if there are relevant studies on the most successful job competencies for your job families. Many academic studies have identified the characteristics and competencies of good sales representatives in various industries and of mechanical, biomedical, software, and electrical engineers. In addition, some Silicon Valley high-tech firms with people operations workforce analytics groups also publish their findings. Google, for example, posts the research results from their People Analytics department on what makes for the best engineering manager or team manager on their website re:Work, https://rework.withgoogle.com/.

After all these data are gathered, train the interviewers on how to ask questions and carefully listen to the responses, watching the candidate's body language and verbal intonations. The interviewers should take copious notes. Structured interviews may also be called research-based interviews or standardized interviews.

You may be thinking, "This sounds like work!" It is work. Some pundits have criticized structured interviews as being boring and old-fashioned. The interviewing process can be made livelier with great questions and a dynamic interviewer. These are not reasons to lower your ability to spot great talent. Structured interviews will improve your ability to rapidly hire great candidates, save you costs per hire, reduce your turnover, and enable you to not be deceived. It is work worth doing.

Structured interviews are more likely to be successfully defended in court than unstructured interviews. A study of 158 cases in US Federal Court involving hiring discrimination from 1978 to 1997 showed that unstructured interview processes were challenged in court more than any other selection tool. Remarkably, the structured interview survived 100 percent of the legal challenges mounted against it, while the unstructured interview survived only 59 percent of challenges.[151] Structured interviews based on job competencies with trained interviewers and work sample methods can reduce rater bias and improve the predictability of selection.

Structured interviews are not as effective with inexperienced candidates such as college graduates.[152] There, measures of intelligence and the ability to learn and apply new information, solve problems, and work in teams, and the strength of their technical competencies are more predictive. Structured interviews can be made more predictive with inexperienced candidates when the interviewing team looks for achievement factors such as leading teams and taking initiative in college or for assemblers having a good time and attendance and grades in high school and being a member of student activities.

Group Interviews

Group interviews (sometimes called panel interviews) are when two to five interviewers interview one candidate. Although, they are widely used in interviewing, research on the use of group interviews is mixed. Companies use group interviews for a few very good reasons. They can save time for the interviewers and the job candidates. Group interviews allow more than one person the opportunity to listen and observe the job candidate's answer to a question, and they allow for interviewers to process information from the same source.

Some companies like to see how a job candidate performs under the higher stress of the group interview pressure cooker. Some believe the panel interviews reduce unconscious bias, but again, the research is not conclusive. Group interviews with the use of standardized questions and multiple ratings increase the validity of structured interviews.[153] As with individual interviews, well-trained interviewers make more accurate, consistent predictions about candidates' performance than do untrained interviewers.[154]

Peer Rating or 360 Reviews

Peer ratings are evaluations of performance or potential made by coworkers, and the scores are averaged across all the worker inputs. Beginning in the 1990s, companies and the US military have used peer ratings for development and performance management and in job interviews. The concern with peer ratings is that they can be influenced by friendship and social popularity. Another concern is that peers or clusters of peers may secretly agree in advance to give each other high peer ratings. I have unfortunately seen this in a peer rewards program, where peers took turns rewarding each other in the program. According to Schmidt and Hunter, the academic research doesn't support such concerns with selection. [155]

Job Knowledge Tests

Job knowledge tests are used to assess workers who are experienced on a job. I have used them to test the competency of administrators using the Microsoft Office suite, such as Word, Excel, and PowerPoint. They can be used to assess a software engineer's ability to write code or an electric technician's ability to read a schematic or their understanding of Ohm's law. They can also be used to assess someone's carpentry, welding, or plumbing skills. These tests can be purchased commercially. They cannot be used like a GMAT to predict which untrained workers will be good on a job.

Training and Experience Behavioral Consistency Model or Job Competency Model

"To truly understand how to distinguish star performers, look at your current star performers and find the competencies that make them successful." —David C. McClelland

David C McClelland's research in the 1970s and 1980s showed that star performers have unique competencies that go beyond their

IQ, education, training, and experience. McClelland proposed that while stars had to have high IQ and the required education, training and experience, they had set of specific competencies including empathy, self-discipline, and initiative which set the stars apart from the average performers.[156] The unique qualities of the stars allow them to excel and overcome obstacles. To find out what makes your stars successful, companies have to discover the competencies that make them successful. Daniel Goleman credits McClelland's research for being a guiding force for emotional intelligence.[157]

The training and experience behavioral consistency model is known outside of the academic literature as the job competency model. The first step is to determine what education, experience, job competencies, or other attributes or indicators best separate the top job performers, the stars, from the low performers. This information can be gathered by looking at the work histories, training, education, and past employers of the company's top performers by job families, such as software engineers, marketing professionals, or sales representatives. This is known as competency identification. That is, what are the skills, knowledge, and abilities that the top performers have? It is also good to interview supervisors and the top employees to get their opinions so that you find the softer skill sets, such as empathy, ambition, and unique traits that set the stars apart from the others.

There are promising artificial intelligence tools that are currently being used to find job candidates on the internet who have the competencies employers need. With the addition of performance data, these AI tools over time should be able to identify the competencies by job families that make up the best performers.

After the competencies are identified and described, they can be weighted for importance and used to evaluate job candidates.

This technique is not limited to experienced candidates. The T&E behavioral consistency model can be used to identify candidates who have transferable skills in one job family to another. For inexperienced candidates, the method can be used to identify competencies that show potential in a field or at least entry-level experience, such as mechanical engineering interns who, upon graduating from college, are looking for entry-level work.

The research to identify the competencies takes time, and for that reason, some companies shun doing it. I have found that the time is worth it.

I have used the training and experience behavioral consistency model, or job competencies, extensively to identify the right mix of IQ, soft-skills, knowledge, skills, abilities, and experiences from best performers to help identify which job candidates to hire in the future. I will describe one case study below.

Job Family Competency Case Study to Improve Selection Procedures

In 2011, Medtronic Coronary needed to hire about a hundred new US sales workers to support the release of its newest drug-eluting stent, Endeavor. The goal was to go from third in market share to number one.

Sales leadership and human resources worked together to identify the job competencies of our best sales representatives and how those competencies would need to change to reflect the dramatically changing world of medical device sales.

In the 1990s, Medtronic's philosophy of hiring medical device sales workers was to hire experienced sales representatives who worked for its competition or who worked for hospital supply companies that had great sales training programs, such as Cardinal Health and Merck. Another area to look for talent were the most successful sales representatives of small medical device start-ups.

Medtronic also had data that showed that college graduates who had played varsity sports would make great sales representatives. The former varsity athletes thrived on taking risks, and when they failed, they were resilient and would try again enthusiastically. Much like the starting quarterback who misses his receiver on a long pass play trying it again on the next set of downs.

They also looked for talent who were personable and physically attractive. When I began my role there, I commented to my boss that these sales workers were some of the most fun people to go to happy hour with, and they all looked like Barbies and Kens.

Medtronic preferred to not recruit sales workers from the pharmaceutical industry, believing that their typical sales model was not sufficient enough for medical device sales and built bad habits. The prevailing view was that pharmaceutical sales representatives were on a "milk run," building relationships with doctors by dropping off free samples of their latest drugs with smartly written brochures and that the sale was "too easy." As you shall see, we discovered a huge talent pool from among pharmaceutical sales that was previously misunderstood and untapped.

The model for the sales workers in the 1980s, 1990s, and early 2000s was that they were largely on their own in a sink-or-swim, competitive sales environment. They had to build relationships with the doctors in their territory and figure out ways to build sales or open new accounts. If they didn't after a year, they would be replaced. Medtronic had great data on which hospitals conducted intravenous cardiovascular procedures down to the various product levels. The sales reps had to learn the characteristics of their products and which stents to recommend depending on the level of the disease state of the patient and the size of the patient's coronary artery blockage.

However, after 2010, four powerful trends were overtaking the medical device, biotech, and pharmaceutical marketplace that would change the requirements of medical device sales representatives.

The first was concerns about collusion between sales workers and physicians. Iowa Senator Chuck Grassley held hearings on sales practices in these industries and shady sales tactics such as taking doctors out to strip clubs, too many cozy golf outings, and even kickbacks.[158] The outcome of all this was to create the AdvaMed Code of Ethics on Interactions with Health Care Professionals. My business had a very good track record for ethical sales practices. Medtronic's CEO at the time, Art Collins, led AdvaMed and was a chief architect of the AdvaMed ethics code. He rightly insisted that

Medtronic implement the code and strictly adhere to it. We then needed to be sure we were hiring sales reps who had the values to comply with the AdvaMed code.

The second was consolidation in the industry—the buying up of doctors' offices and stand-alone hospitals by large health care providers or by regional or national hospital chains. This power shift to large chains over medical device companies gave rise to stronger supply chain departments that required more cost competition among medical device suppliers. Medtronic and other medical device and pharmaceutical organizations countered by setting up national sales organizations to build relationships with and negotiate terms with these national chains. Once the national deals were in place, the regional sales rep would go in to activate the national contracts, sell product, and begin supplying the local hospitals.

Third was the raised interest in superior scientific medical evidence for efficacy and safety. Companies and their sales forces found themselves arguing and making claims of superiority based on minuscule differences from the results of double–blind, nine-month clinical trials with two-year follow-up. Frankly, every company that had a stent approved by the FDA provided a reliable, effective, and safe stent. What was left to argue about with the clinical trial evidence was how safe, how reliable, and how long-lasting. Nonetheless, the sales reps had to learn how to distinguish their products based on this scientific evidence while scrubbing their hands with the physician for thirty seconds prepping for a procedure.

Fourth, the advantages of the Medtronic mission could no longer be conveyed by personal discussion and PowerPoint discussions. The expectations and the technology had changed. Now sales pitches and product information were being conveyed by podcasts that were on the sales representatives' iPhone or iPad, complete with animated illustrations. Contemporary sales representatives had to be comfortable using digital technology.

These changes required that future sales reps have the values to comply with the Medtronic mission and AdvaMed and understand how seriously the company believed in AdvaMed standards.

Second, they needed to be able to work within the structure of national or regional contracts and be good team players—not lone wolves like their predecessors. Third, they needed to be able to understand the basic research and science behind coronary heart disease and articulate in scientific terms the superiority of our coronary stents, balloons, and delivery systems. And most importantly, they had to be able to do that in an elevator pitch in thirty seconds or while scrubbing with a doctor over a sink just before an intravenous procedure and be comfortable showing a twenty-second podcast using their iPhone or iPad.

Job Analysis

With this understanding of how the sales role would change, we set about understanding what competencies enabled our best sales representatives to perform so well.

We looked at our current performance data that was put together using sales performance, sales commission earnings, performance appraisals, and 360-degree feedback assessments. We identified our top ten percent.

We then went and looked at the following factors:

1. What was common about their university experience?
2. What was common about their professional experience before Medtronic hired them?
3. In addition to sales and commission earnings, what was unique about their performance?

We also interviewed their managers, customers, and the Medtronic employees in marketing and supply chain that they worked with.

Here is the profile of our best that emerged.

1. **They all had college degrees, and most of them played on varsity sports in college**. This is not surprising as

Medtronic used these criteria to screen those who the company would interview for sales representative positions.

2. **Regarding their work experience prior to coming to Medtronic, what we learned surprised us. These top sales representatives did not come from our competitors. Instead, they tended to come from smaller medical device start-ups where they had to show initiative, self-discipline, relationship building skills with new prospects, and resiliency to succeed. They also came from pharmaceutical companies when the sales representative sold to hospitals, not to the doctor's office, or from outside of the medical device industry altogether.** This was fascinating as the company would pay not only long sales guarantees to sales reps from our competitors but would also give them lavish signing bonuses. These sales reps had a disadvantage, however, that showed up in our performance data. Due to noncompete clauses in their employment contracts with Medtronic competitors (outside of California and a few other states), they could not sell the same products to the same customers. This often meant they were selling coronary products to new customers. And like any other sales representative, even the most inexperienced, they would then have to build relationships with their new clients and learn Medtronic's product lines and cultures. That took time, and their previous very successful experience did not provide many shortcuts for them.

3. **They tended to have won distinguishing sales honors from their previous employers such as sales representative of the year, rookie of the year, or President's Club.**

4. **They worked hard at building strong relationships with individuals in their customer organizations.** This included not only the doctors but also the individuals who ran the catheter labs and the supply chain organizations. They went out of their way to make their lives easier, even

volunteering to help them with tasks that were not part of their jobs, such as inventory counts.

5. **They worked hard at building relationships with the Medtronic customer service call center representatives, contracting representatives, and supply chain representatives.** They did this for many purposes. They wanted to understand how to make their jobs easier by doing what were usually small administrative tasks (which sales reps often deplore). They wanted to be on good terms with this group so that if they needed to call in a favor to advance the cause of a client, accelerate a delivery, or win a contract, they had the emotional capital to do so. These representatives would often speak to how nice these top-performing sales reps were and that they did not yell at them, like other sales reps sometimes would when things went wrong. When they called about a problem, they were in learning and problem-solving mode and would often end the conversation by thanking them for their time and offering assistance.

We also looked at those sales reps who were not top performers, trying to understand if there was a false predictor of sales rep success. The first thing that jumped out at us was that MBAs didn't last long. We did not hire many, but the few that we did hire didn't last long in the role. As one sales VP told me, "They are too smart for this role. Although it pays well, they get bored with the sales routine. It takes the building of relationships, which takes time, constant follow-up, and the tedium with finding the right contract mix to please the customer and our own financial goals. And getting your nerve back up the next day after having a door slammed in your face."

This effort also improved the diversity of our sales force. By disproving the bias against pharmaceutical sales reps who sold to hospitals and lessening our dependence on hiring competitive sales reps, our recruiting of females, blacks, and East Indians rose dramatically. The pharmaceutical industry, ahead of us, had made great gains with diversity recruiting. We benefited from their progress and offered these pharmaceutical sales reps a great career progression to higher-paying sales roles.

We also set goals for sales managers to identify great diversity sales reps they saw in the hospital catheter labs. Our sales managers knew who the good sales reps were. We simply set goals for them to bring in candidates whom we could call and ask if they were interested in a role at Medtronic.

Case Study 3: Improving Selection of Sales Employees

Current Situation	Plan: Double U.S. sales force, improve diversity and performance
• Relationship sale	• Switched to clinical and economic value sale
• 40% third party search	• Reduced to 10% third party search
• Inconsistent job competencies	• Implemented one set of job competencies
• Outdated candidate profile	• Updated candidate profile
• Bachelor degree & clinicians	• Bachelor degree with emphasis on business and scientific degrees
• Varsity sports experience	• Varsity sports experience
• Award winners from medial device companies	• Award winners from companies with great sales training programs--not restricted to medical device sales
• No pharmaceutical sales experience	• Accepted in-hospital pharmaceutical sales experience
• $1000 employee referral fee	• Raised employee referral to $3,000 per hire
• No assessments used	• Implemented validated personality assessment
• Unstructured interviews	• Implemented structured interview, trained interviewers
• Used diversity recruiters	• Assigned each hiring manager diversity recruiting goals

I have used job competency development in many job families such as program directors, various engineering disciplines, accountants, recruiters, and too many more to mention. It usually uncovers improvements in what skills, experiences, and attributes to look for in future job candidates, and it often improves diversity.

Integrity Tests

Integrity tests are used to determine which employees will have less of a probability for exhibiting unproductive behaviors on the job such as drinking or drugs, fighting, stealing, sabotaging equipment, and other undesirable behaviors. However, integrity tests have no correlation with ability. They also do not correlate with GMATs, which makes them a great complement to GMATs.

Integrity tests are commercially available. Some of these commercially available tests also measure other Big Five aptitudes such as conscientiousness and components of agreeableness and emotional stability.

Job Tryout Procedure

The job tryout procedure was the recommendation of my University of Minnesota professor George Seltzer. It works, but it can be improved upon. This is an ideal way to assess the skills of entry-level employees who have no previous experience on a job. Typically, such applicants are hired with minimal screening and are trained for the job, and their performance is watched to see how they meet predetermined standards of performance.

Many call centers that hire operators in phone sales or customer service roles use this method. The best ones, I have seen supplement with new hire's first 90 days with training, coaching and mentors. Also, manufacturing has used job tryout procedures in hiring. Used by itself, it is very costly, as often one-third of the new hires are terminated for failing to meet the key job standards. Often supervisors do not like terminating marginal performers, which means middle management needs to track and review the performance of workers to assure that supervisors are appropriately managing performance.

The hire-and-fire churn of employees is expensive. Any analysis of turnover will quickly show this. I recommend using another test that has a valid predictor of job success with the job tryout procedure, especially structured interviews, GMATs, or integrity and consciousness tests.

Assessment Centers

Assessment centers have been in use for over sixty years. They have substantial validity but only moderate incremental validity over GMAT or intelligence. According to Schmidt and Hunter, assessment centers had .37 validity and only improved combined validity over the individual score of GMATs by .02, from .51 to .53.[159] The reason assessment centers don't add much to GMATs is because they correlate highly with intelligence.

To be successful, assessment centers simulate individuals who need to learn rapidly and effectively to use new information to make decisions in the management simulation at the assessment center. Over the last twenty years, they have grown increasingly adept at assessing leadership style and the ability of leaders to empathize with, influence, and motivate others. Increasingly they are used for assessing job candidates for executive roles, and they are good predictors for who is ready for promotions in management, advancement, and salary progression. The reason for this is the assessment center gives the assessors a chance to see the candidates in roles different from their current jobs. They have also been used by police forces to simulate physically challenging and leadership situations to screen candidates.

However, assessment centers are expensive and can cost $10,000 or more per assessed individual. While this might be affordable for Fortune 1000 companies to assess executive hires and their high-potential managers for higher roles (and to provide them timely feedback), smaller companies can't afford this price.

A 2007 meta-analysis found a similar correlation between assessment center validity and supervisor ratings of performance.[160] A009 meta-analysis found that assessment centers provide a viable alternative and supplement to other selection methods and that when constructed well are fair and legally defensible.[161]

I have found that if the assessment center is good at discerning emotional intelligence or a leader's ability to listen, influence, and motivate others, it is exceptionally helpful in predicting success of managerial candidates at executive levels. For example, I have had great success using the Center for Creative Leadership to assess promotional capability to leaders and to also provide valid development feedback to leaders.

A business unit leader at Honeywell Inc. whom I supported credited an assessment center for providing him the single most effective development feedback that made him a successful business unit general manager. He was already intelligent, a talented engineer, and an R&D project director. As a former F-4 fighter pilot in Vietnam with the US Air Force, he was courageous and great at successfully completing missions. But his interpersonal style was too cold and domineering. He came to conclusions faster than others due to his intelligence and he was usually right, but in the process, he turned people off.

The assessment center (which was the Center for Creative Leadership) gave him feedback that if he only spent five minutes warming up to people before starting the meeting agenda and say something kind or complimentary to whomever he was speaking with, and most importantly smile, he would become much more successful.

He took the feedback to heart and implemented this simple change in all his one-on-ones and group meetings. It worked. His staff loved working for him. My HR staff, which was mostly women, loved working with him because in addition to getting his feedback, which was extraordinarily insightful, they came from those meetings feeling good about themselves.

With assessment centers, I have learned they can be very effective for selecting executives if the assessment simulations were a good fit for your culture and roles. It is important to assess the center on these criteria. For example, if you are selecting an innovation *program director* as opposed to a functional director or VP, you will be measuring for the wrong mix of skills.

Program directors have broad accountability but no one reporting to him or her and must lead by influence, collaboration, and teamwork. Functional directors or VPs, on the other hand, have direct reports, set the vision, deploy goals, track operating mechanisms and measures, and provide performance feedback, rewards, and pay raises. They have direct influence. While I recommend all leaders be great at listening, persuasion, and motivation, the functional leader has more levers to exert his or her will than the program director. They are different roles.

Conscientiousness Measures

Conscientiousness is one of the Big Five personality tests, which I will discuss more. According to Schmidt and Hunter's meta-analysis[162], it is the only major personality trait of the Big Five that consistently leads to success (with integrity coming in second among the Big Five). A person scoring high in conscientiousness usually has a high level of self-discipline. They tend to follow plans and persevere, are punctual, orderly, organized, dutiful, reliable, and responsible. As children, they tend to get better grades in school and college. As adults, they commit fewer crimes, earn higher salaries, have higher job satisfaction, stay married longer, have fewer stokes, lower blood pressure, and lower incidence of Alzheimer's disease, and live longer.

What is not to like with conscientiousness tests and the workers who score highly on them? They are not people who act on impulses or spontaneity and tend to be cautious. Individuals who score high on conscientiousness tests can be compulsive perfectionists and workaholics. If your goal is to improve your innovation, you will want to mix employees who are mavericks or who approach problems differently among your highly conscientious employees to provide new thinking and problem-solving. However, the mix of personalities may lead to conflict. Conscientiousness tests run the risk of weeding out the mavericks. So while conscientiousness tests are great for jobs that require discipline, they are not the sole measure to use to hire people for innovation roles.

Conscientiousness tests are available commercially and can be administered online in less than twenty minutes for low costs. Some of these tests also measure integrity. As with integrity tests, conscientiousness has no correlation with ability.

Biographical Data Measures for Specific Jobs like Sales and Leadership

Biographical data measures have questions about life

experiences such as childhood, high school, hobbies, participation in sports, and the discipline habits of parents. Biographical data measures are tough to put together because the researchers must correlate the life experience to a job competency, job performance, and performance in a training program. Finding these correlations are tough to do and requires rigorous statistical analysis. However, once they are achieved, these commercially available tests are easy to administer and can predict job success in specific areas such as sales and leadership and traits like absenteeism and turnover.

Each company that uses a biographical data measure must validate its effectiveness to predict job competencies and performance by testing the measure on a subset of its target workforce to see if the test correlates with the known performance of the individuals tested. Any biographical data measures that use gender, race, age, marital status, sexual orientation, and others run into violating discrimination laws in the United States and other countries.

Based on Schmidt and Hunter's meta-analysis,[163] biographical data measures have .37 validity. However, when combined with GMATs, they only lead to a 2 percent improvement in validity. This is because for the ones analyzed in the meta-analysis, they correlated highly with intelligence. Some of the commercially available tests do measure general mental ability as well as other traits that lead to specific job performance success.

Reference Checks

In Schmidt and Hunter's famous 1988 meta-analysis on eighteen talent selection points, reference checks have only a .27 validity for predicting future job performance.[164] But when combined with general mental ability tests, the score rose to .57, which is almost as high as you get. Reference checks really are about confirming the information you gathered and making sure you have not yet learned or overlooked a key bit of information. Even the authors writing in 1988 believed that their reference check validity was not valid due to the legal environment.

Despite this trend, I have found reference checks helpful in verifying what candidates worked on and how they performed.

Reference checks are usually conducted by calling the references the job candidate provided to the employer with his or her résumé or on-the-job application. I have noticed a trend of some, usually large, companies discontinuing reference checks, that is, calling the references provided by candidates to learn more about their strengths and development areas and if the managers would hire the candidate back. Some companies have stopped this believing that today's legal environment in the United States prevents anyone from giving honest feedback for fear of being sued for slander. Companies want to avoid being sued for defamation of character, slander, or libel so many companies have a policy that they do not check references, even if they are good for the inevitable case when they don't provide a good reference for a poor performer or for someone who was fired.

After a job candidate has given me a list of references for past jobs, including the supervisors and their contact information, and the permission to call these candidates (which is good to collect in online job applications), I recommend the recruiter or hiring manager call the references.

The questions I like to use in a reference check are the following:

1. What is your relationship with the candidate?
2. How long have you known the candidate?
3. What are the candidate's strengths?
4. What are the candidate's areas for improvement?
5. How well did the candidate do in meeting commitments?
6. How well did the candidate collaborate and work with others?
7. How well did the candidate perform under stressful conditions?
8. Would you look forward to working with the candidate again?

I have found that what is not said and how it is said is just as important as what is said in response to my questions. Some references will say to you, "My company won't let me make a reference." That may be the truth. When I hear that, I ask, "Please tell me this, would you work with NAME again?" or "Would you hire NAME again?" Often that answer, whether a yes or a no or a more elaborate answer, is very telling.

According to a 2018 CareerBuilder study, percent of companies go to social media sites, such as Facebook, to conduct reference checks.[165] This is up from 11 percent in 2006. In addition, 66 percent of companies are using search engines, such as Google or Bing, to research candidates, primarily looking for a social media presence, for a reason not to hire a candidate, or to see what others are writing about the candidate. Of those that conduct social media research, 57 percent found content on a social networking site that caused them not to hire a candidate. On the other hand, 37 percent said they found background information that supported the candidate's professional qualifications and to hire the candidate.[166]

Of those who decided not to hire a candidate in the 2018 CareerBuilder study[167] based on their social media profiles, the reasons included:

- Forty percent posted inappropriate pictures, videos, or information.
- Thirty-six percent posted information about themselves using drugs or drinking.
- Thirty-one percent had made discriminatory comments about race, gender, or religion.
- Thirty percent were linked to criminal behavior.
- Twenty-five percent badmouthed their previous company.
- Twenty-seven percent lied about their qualifications.
- Twenty-five percent bad-mouthed their previous company.
- Twenty-two found the job candidate's screen name was unprofessional.

- ◆ Twenty- percent shared confidential information about a previous employer.
- ◆ Sixteen percent lied about an absence.

The CareerBuilder study was conducted by the Harris Poll from April 4 and May 1, 2018. The Harris Poll had a sample of 1,012 hiring and human resources managers from the private sector across many industries and company sizes. It had a sampling error of +/- 2.01 percent.

Using social media sites to do reference checking is a bad idea for many reasons. One reason is that there is no reliable data that these social media reference checks provide information that determine if someone will be a good or terrible employee. Second, you will be learning information that you should not be learning due to legal issues. This includes family status, religion, and birthdates, from which you can determine age. In some states you are not to inquire about legal convictions prior to making a conditional job offer. While you might be checking for behavior that confirms if a job candidate fits your values, such as they have not written awful racist or sexist articles, the fact that you have learned information you should legally not be learning means that you have opened the company up to charges that you have made a biased decision in not hiring someone.

What Works the Least? Age, Graphology, Years of Education, Interest, and Job Experience after Five Years on the Job

Age, graphology (handwriting analysis), years of education (although there is a strong correlation between education and ability, at .55—but then it has a low correlation for predicting job success), interest, and job experience after five years on the job have the lowest correlations predicting job success, according to Schmidt and Hunter's meta-analysis.[168]

Age is rarely used as a basis for hiring. First, it is not a legal measure for job selection in the United States and many other countries. Second, age is about as totally unrelated to job performance and the ability to learn on the job as any measure can be.

Job experience measured by years and after five years on the job, has very little predictive value for determining who will do well on a job. It is only .18. Yet it is often one of the most used criteria in a job description because it is a number. Leaders believe in numbers even when they are nearly useless.

The problem with job experience is that there is little correlation with performance and competencies such as teamwork. Researchers have found that when experience on the job does not exceed five years, the correlation between amount of job experience and job performance is much better, at .33. But after five years of experience, job experience has no impact on job performance. Apparently, up to five years, workers are acquiring additional job knowledge and skills that improve job performance, but it flattens out at five years on the same job. When job performance is measured by supervisor ratings, the correlation gets higher. When job performance is measured in coordination with using a work sample test, the validity rises higher, to .47.

The lesson here is to not use job experience ALONE as a measure of success when the experience on the same or a similar job is more than five years, unless the candidate has had new experiences, training, certifications, and achievements they can claim as their own. It is good to also use other selection methods, such as structured interviews, work sample tests, and supervisor reviews to further assess the candidate.

The Training and Experience Point Method is widely used in government hiring and promotions and often in union factory jobs. These systems award points for various credentials, such as months of experience on the job, relevant training, or schooling. Unfortunately, these systems usually do not assess past achievements, accomplishments, or job performance. They are relatively easy to construct and administer and are inexpensive, but they have low job performance predictability.

Years of Education will predict the success of job candidates to learn on the job and their abilities but have a low correlation with job performance. Years of education is a good measure of ability, but to get a sense of past achievements, accomplishments, job performance, and an individual's fit to your values and organizational culture, other screening methods are required, such as structured interviews or assessments.

Interests. A lot of pundits and CEOs today like to assess an individual's interests to determine the ability and motivation to learn on the job and job success. The strong feeling is that if a job candidate shows strong interest and motivation in the job interview, they will be great on the job. Unfortunately, interest is not a valid predictor of job success. Interest and motivation can be easily faked. Interests are a good predictor of job and career preference but a poor measure of mental ability, job competencies, ability to overcome obstacles, and achieve and traits such as integrity and conscientiousness.

Graphology is the analysis of handwriting. Its advocates say they can predict personality traits through the analysis of handwriting. However, it has one of the lowest correlations of job success, at .02, just above age.

CHAPTER 11: HR GEEK:
ADDITIONAL IMPORTANT ISSUES

There are many other issues that are important to understand about recruiting which don't fit into traditional industrial organizational psychology studies, except for the "Big Five," which I will explain below. As I explore these issues, I will consult the empirical evidence. These important issues include topics such as:

* how do you know if a candidate is lying to you?
* the importance of background checks,
* whether to do drug testing,
* the importance of cultural employee onboarding especially if you want to keep new hire turnover low,
* the Big Five which is based on research from industrial organizational psychologists and has led to the use of conscientiousness tests
* emotional intelligence and its importance in selecting leaders, sales and customer service workers,
* whether hiring for culture fit is valid or does it lead to a bias and stilts your innovation?
* old fashion job fairs which are still effective. Ask Amazon.

You are encouraged to read the whole chapter, but if you are busy (of course you are) pick the section that has the most importance for you or use this chapter as a reference tool.

How to Tell If a Job Candidate Is Lying to You

More job candidates are stretching the truth on their resumes or in interviews. In this section, I will point out research that shows, despite the common wisdom, it is hard to catch someone lying during an interview or if they have stretched the truth on a resume. The use structured job interviews and background checks is a reliable way to determine if a candidate's story during an interview is really the truth.

An OfficeTeam 2017 survey found that 46 percent of workers said they knew someone who lied on a résumé —a twenty-five-point increase from its 2011 survey.[169] HireRight's 2017 Employment Screening Benchmark Report (which surveyed nearly four thousand HR professionals) stated that 85 percent of employers caught applicants lying on their résumés or applications, up from 66 percent five years earlier.[170]

Many job candidates also lie during interviews. And some are very good at it. Can you determine when a job candidate is telling the truth? Are you better at identifying false statements than artificial intelligence?

I believe that candidates are telling me the truth when they give me straightforward answers, maintain eye contact, provide significant detail, are easy to follow, speak in the first person, and do not use platitudes. Now there is research that backs this up in part. Candidates that use more "I" or "we" statements, past-tense verbs, more positive language, did better in the interviews because they appeared to have better problem-solving skills, self-control and more positive attitudes. However, it may have as much to do with the job candidates that were more articulate and self-confident than those who did not exhibit these qualities.

In 2017, Leadership IQ surveyed 1,427 professionals, who were asked to write answers to fifteen open-ended interview questions as though they were applying for a job.[171] Then a panel of hiring managers and HR executives graded the answers to identify whether the applicant would likely be a great hire, a poor hire, or somewhere in between.

Leadership IQ discovered that high-rated applicants used very different words than poorly rated ones. For example, high performers

- used 21 percent more "I" language statements—such as "I," "me," or "my,"—than low performers.
- used 65 percent more "we" language—such as "we," "us," and "our."
- used 38 percent more past-tense verbs. They typically tell simple, fact-focused stories that avoid distraction and detail.
- had answers that contained 28 percent more words that described positive emotions, such as "happy," "thrilled," and "excited."
- had answers that were 23 percent longer than low-performer answers. They had more and better experience and attitudes, and they gave more detailed answers.

Leadership IQ learned that interview answers rated poorly by hiring managers contained very different words than interview answers rated highly. For example, bad interview answers

- used the word "you" 392 percent more than good interview answers, and "they" 90 percent more.
- contained 104 percent more present-tense verbs, 40 percent more adverbs such as "really" and "very," 92 percent more negative emotions, and 103 percent more absolutes such as "always," "absolutely," and "unquestionably."

In summary, if candidates are afraid to talk about themselves and their past experiences, it conveys the impression that they do not have the necessary experiences to perform well on the job. When candidates use negative words, it can indicate a lack of self-control and an inability to positively resolve problems that arise. Absolutes can convey a lack of intellectual flexibility, the need to show off, or insecurity.

One caution about Leadership IQ's study: it does not link interviewing performance to job performance.

What we do know from academic research is that structured interviews significantly improve interviewers' ability to hire strong job performers because these interviews dig into past performance and skills. In addition, empirically developed and validated assessment tests also have strong correlation to performance on the job..[172]

Lazlo Bock, the former chief human resources officer at Google, studied Google's hiring practices and learned that there was *no correlation* between Google's interviews and job performance. It turns out Google during its early start-up years was enamored with hypothetical problem-solving questions such as brainteasers. They didn't work. Bock convinced Google's executives to stop the brainteasers and introduced structured interviews and interviewer training to improve Google's results.[173]

I strongly recommend using structured interviews and assessment tests.

How about reading body language? Can you determine if a candidate is lying to you if they suddenly look at the floor or dart their eyes to the right? Or change their tone of voice?

I believe candidates who look me in the eye when we speak, generally speak in level tones, and aren't fidgety while answering questions are telling me the truth. We all may look up or to the left when trying to recall details, and it doesn't mean the job candidate is lying. (Do you remember a teacher telling you in grade school that the answer is not on the ceiling? Well, in fact, it isn't written there, but raising your eyes slows down your brain waves to enable you to remember the answer to the question you have just been asked.) Candidates who have good posture and sit up straight somehow seem more interested and professional to me.

Research by the Economic and Social Research Council[174] indicates that visual cues can be deceiving even to police officers who are trained in spotting dishonest behavior. While these visual cues may indicate lying, they are not 100 percent reliable. However, speech-related cues were more reliable.

One way I have learned to help with this is to ask a candidate about their strengths. They are happy to tell you. Then ask them to tell you about their weaknesses. This question is always tougher to answer and is often nerve-racking as most people feel vulnerable about their weaknesses, especially during a job interview. Watch how their facial expressions, body language, and speech-related cues change between the two questions. It will serve as a guide to you during the rest of the interview to alert you if a candidate is stressed out about a question or potentially hiding the truth.

For example, with the weakness question, does the candidate pause their speech, change their tone of voice, or avoid eye contact? Does the candidate start to blink their eyes when before they didn't? Do you observe other behaviors you did not see before, such as moving of feet or wrapping them around the legs of the chair? Does the job candidate look away or turn his or her head away as if they are looking for something? Watch for the behavior displayed in the weakness question and see if it comes up in other questions. If it does, probe more.

Remember, it can be hard to determine if someone is lying based on visual cues and even speech-related cues. That is why it is important to follow up on answers that you may doubt, especially after you have had time to further research the candidate's academic and work history. It also reiterates the importance of doing background and reference checks.

Does face recognition technology work better at identifying a job candidate who is lying?

Face recognition technology is taking the security industry by storm. It is being deployed to identify criminals and potential terrorists. Apple now uses it to replace the four-digit security code on its phones. The retail industry is using it to identify high-volume customers and to alert the shop clerk about their preferences.

Can it help recruiters hire better job candidates, hire for better culture fit, or tell if someone is lying?

HireVue uses artificial intelligence to compare the facial expressions, word use, tone of voice, vocabularies, and body movements with your best workers.[175] It then draws conclusions about candidates based on all these factors, not just by the résumé and what the candidate says. HireVue maintains on its website that it doesn't want to replace recruiters; its aim is to make the job interview process more efficient and improve the job candidate experience. The company says that its customers can remove steps like résumé reviews, phone screens, and traditional assessments from their recruiting processes.

The MIT Medical Laboratory has looked at early analysis of artificial intelligence making judgments from facial expressions, word use, tone of language, vocabulary, and body language. Their conclusion is that when the individual is a white male, AI can be accurate. But the darker the skin of the individual, the more errors rise, up to nearly 35 percent for images of darker-skinned women.[176]

It appears AI, when it is used to make judgments on facial expressions, tone of voice, and body language, is only as accurate as the data used to train it. If the database is predominately white or male, it will be more accurate with white people and males.

Can you or AI determine if a job candidate is lying? Trained interviewers using structured interviewing techniques who watch for speech-related as well as verbal cues and then probe with more questions will do better. Assessment tests and thorough background and reference checks help verify the veracity of candidate claims. AI technology as it develops and looks to control existing biases will prove helpful. Stay tuned.

Background Checks Are Vital to Do

According to a 2017 survey by HR.com and the National Association of Professional Background Screeners, 96 percent of US companies conduct at least one type of background screening.[177]

In the United States, background checks cannot be conducted until the offer is made, and they can take three days to two weeks depending on the number of municipalities lived in by the candidate and longer for overseas background checks.

CareerBuilder research in 2017 found that 18 percent of employers have made a bad hire because they didn't conduct a background check. Making a mistake in the hiring process can be quite costly, whether it is your internal process mistake or the mistake of your background check vendor. The study shows that the average cost of a bad hire is $17,000. The study discovered that nearly 30 percent of employers made a bad hire because they received bad information about the candidate. It pays to have a reliable and thorough background check vendor. In addition, 15 percent have been forced into litigation for not hiring someone because of what was found in a background check.[178]

According to a survey by HireRight, 86 percent of employers have uncovered lies or misrepresentations on résumés or job applications. Seventy-two percent said background screening uncovered issues they would not have otherwise found.[179] It is good to verify education, past employment, titles, pay, and criminal records (following federal and state laws). I have found candidates who have misrepresented all the above, did not report criminal convictions, and even had falsified social security numbers. With the increase in security data breaches of personal information, it has become easier for people to even steal social security numbers. It is good to verify all of this so you do not make a wrongful hire.

I have a story to tell you that brings home the importance of background checks and emphasizes you can't be too thorough. I received a call from the IT department head, and she asked me, as the head of HR, to conduct a background check on one of her employees. The IT employee was a very good worker and very personable. However, another employee came to the department head to say that he had been overheard talking about how easy it was to falsify an identity and get a stolen social security number. He, in fact, had used a stolen security number to avoid our company from learning about his troubled past.

After looking at his résumé, application, reference, and

background check results from when we hired him, I called him in, and with security standing discreetly outside my office, I put the question straight to him. He was stunned and then said to me that he had not. I told him that although he had worked here for months, we had no choice but to terminate him for falsifying his application. He very quietly and quickly, with a discreet security and supervisor escort, gathered his things and left the building. We, of course, turned off his access to our servers and systems.

Here is the kicker. Later that afternoon, his live-in girlfriend, who also worked at the company, called me and asked why we fired him. I told her I could not tell her that as it was a proprietary matter. (Legally, I did not want the company to be sued for defamation of character.) She persisted and explained that she lived with him. I asked her if she was sure she knew who he was and all about his history and life. She got the hint and moved out that night.

According to the HR.com and National Association of Professional Background Screeners survey, 95 percent of US companies conduct background checks.[180] The number-one reason to conduct background checks is workforce safety, cited by 89 percent of survey respondents. Safety is followed by improving the quality of hires at 52 percent, protecting the company's reputation at 45 percent, and complying with laws and regulations at 44 percent. According to the survey, companies screen for the following factors:

- Database/national criminal searches (93 percent)
- County/statewide criminal searches (97 percent)
- Fingerprint-based criminal searches (78 percent)
- Social Security number trace (87 percent)
- Credit/financial (87 percent)
- Education verification (75 percent)
- Motor vehicle driving records (68 percent)
- Drug and alcohol testing (82 percent)
- Sex offender registry (80 percent)
- Professional license verification (76 percent)
- International checks (83 percent)

Most companies (86 percent) conduct background checks after the job interview, according to the survey, and 55 percent conduct a background check after a conditional offer is made.[181] This is probably due to the growing Ban the Box movement in the United States. Please see "Ban the Box" in Chapter 12: HR Legal Geek: the Impact of Laws and Regulations.

It is important to do reference checks and to conduct formal background checks. It is equally important that hiring decisions are made based on accurate information. Employers should only engage credit reporting agencies that follow best practices. Employers need to determine in advance the convictions that the company considers relevant for specific jobs and the time period for which they are considered relevant. When selecting a background check vendor, be sure the vendor is accredited by the National Association of Professional Background Screeners. Also test their process. Have a few employees (as volunteers) go through the process and see how it works, how employee friendly it is, and how long it takes. Background checks should be done within seventy-two hours (for domestic background checks).

Provide these guidelines to the reporting agency with instructions to report only convictions that meet the criteria. Alternatively, companies can handle the report screening in-house using a consistent process to evaluate relevant convictions.

According to the American Civil Liberties Union, it is also important to ask the following questions of all the National Association of Professional Background Screeners' accredited vendors you are considering in selecting a credit reporting agency.

- Do you verify all information with the original criminal justice source?
- Do you require the full name and at least one other identifier to match before reporting a criminal record?
- Do you require all identifiers in your possession to match?
- Do you report all charges from a single incident as a single entry?

- ◆ Do you remove expunged or dismissed dispositions?
- ◆ Do you provide regularly updated information on the disposition of relevant cases?[182]

Drug Testing

Early one morning in 2003, a manager of a manufacturing facility brought me a baggie containing a powdery substance that looked like cocaine, found by the main entrance of one of our facilities. I presented it to our facility nurse and asked her to have the sheriff's department do a chemical analysis of the substance during the morning. I was stunned when it turned out to be methamphetamines. They are an illegal substance and are a very dangerous stimulant that speeds up the functioning of the brain and produces a quick, powerful, short-lived high. Methamphetamines are produced as pills, powder, and chunky crystals called "ice." Some users believe they focus attention and help them delay sleep. Prolonged use or overdoses can produce a fever, confusion, rapid heart rate, brain damage, memory loss, weight loss, and death.

After working out the logistics with the nurse and legal team, I had a surprise drug test the next day for everyone in that building, as allowed under our policies. The surprise for me was that twenty-two members of the workforce in that facility tested positive for illegal substances. Two of the twenty-two were positive for meth. This was alarming. By all accounts this was otherwise a productive, loyal workforce, but twenty-two of them (14 percent) were working while on illegal substances (or at least with traces in their urine). All tests were reviewed by a medical review officer to determine if there was a legal justification for the positive drug tests. The workers were required to go to counseling, comply with the recommended treatment, and submit to ongoing surprise drug testing.

Two of the employees chose to resign (according to what they told me) to keep using their drug of choice rather than complying with this regimen. One worker explained to me that while she loved her job, coworkers, and the mission of the company, she regularly used pot to alleviate the pain associated with glaucoma. She deeply resented my (and the company's) intrusion into her decisions made about her personal health. While her demeanor was calm, she was very angry. My heart went out to her. I thanked her for her candor and complimented her work record. She was an excellent worker. I told her that it was never my intention to jeopardize her job or to stop what might be an effective use of marijuana to alleviate pain, but I needed to assure our clients (hospitals and doctors) and end users (patients) that our products were made by dedicated employees in a frame of mind to concentrate on their work and do a high–quality, reliable job.

Illegal drug use in the United States, as of 2013, was 9.4 percent for those twelve years old or older (up from 8.3 percent in 2002). That is 24.6 million Americans. While cocaine and methamphetamines use has declined, the use of marijuana has increased. (As you will see below, positive drug tests for cocaine have increased.) The highest users of illegal drugs are the age group of eighteen to twenty-five-year-olds, at 22.6 percent.[183] More than half of the new illicit drug users begin with marijuana. The next most common are prescription pain relievers, followed by inhalants (which is most common among younger teens).

The World Health Organization's survey of legal and illegal drug use in seventeen countries showed that the United States had the highest level of illegal drug use in the world. The United States had the highest rates of marijuana use at 42 percent, compared to the next highest country, New Zealand, with 41.9 percent, and the United States had the highest cocaine use at 16 percent versus 4 percent for New Zealand.[184]

In 2017, according to the US National Institute on Drug Abuse, more than seventy-two thousand US citizens died of drug overdoses. The sharpest increase occurred among the nearly thirty thousand deaths related to fentanyl and fentanyl analogs, which include synthetic opioids.[185] Women make up most of the deaths, and their overdose rate increased at more than 400 percent from 1999 to 2010, compared to 231 percent among men.

That is a lot of illegal and LEGAL drug use. Do you want your office and manufacturing workers working while stoned, suffering from memory loss, poor concentration, or worse, hallucinating?

The federal government promoted drug screening in the 1980s and 1990s, but there are no comprehensive federal laws that require drug screens, except in some industries such as transportation, where preemployment, for cause, after–accident, and random drug screening are required in some job classifications.

According to HireRight's 2013 Employee Screening Benchmark Report, 78 percent of responding employers conduct drug testing on some portion of their workforce. This number rises to 98 percent of the transportation industry, where it is required. Seventy-one percent also drug test current employees, usually due to reasonable suspicion or after a work-related accident. Only about 12 percent of companies have a medical marijuana policy.[186]

However, the website Statistic Brain reports that only 56 percent of US employers require preemployment drug testing, and 29 percent conduct random drug screening of employees. The average cost of a drug test is forty dollars. The average cost of treating an employee with a drug addiction is seven thousand dollars. The percentage of all work-related accidents that are drug- or alcohol-related is 65 percent. Statistic Brain's research was conducted on April 2, 2017.[187]

Federal law requires US companies to administer a drug screen for job applicants only after they have accepted a job offer. According to Quest Diagnostics, a medical lab research company, 4.2 percent of the urine tests analyzed in 2016 were positive. This is an increase from the 2 percent positive urine tests in 2012 and the highest rate since 2004. The increase in positive drug tests conducted among employees, while small, continues to increase.[188]

Positive tests for cocaine are also on the increase, increasing 12 percent in 2016. The Quest study found that, for the first time since recreational marijuana use was legalized in Colorado and Washington, failed tests in those states outpaced the national average. Positive tests increased in Colorado by 11 percent and Washington by 9 percent.[189]

What about alcohol? Alcohol abuse can be very destructive, but it is very difficult to detect because of how quickly its traces dissipate in urine. I do not recommend preemployment alcohol testing because it is considered medical testing under the Americans with Disabilities Act (ADA) and if used must meet criteria for being job-related and business-necessary.

What about legalized medical marijuana? Marijuana use, including medical marijuana use (which does appear to have real benefits for pain relief and possibly to be an alternative to highly addictive opiates and also negative affects such as mental impairment when high and an increase in lung disease) is still illegal under federal law.

In 2009, the Obama administration stated it would not prosecute medical marijuana users in states where it has been authorized. In 2018, the Trump administration announced that it was rescinding the Obama administration guidance (sending the recreational and medical marijuana industry into a tizzy).

Over half the states and the District of Columbia allow medical marijuana. However, lawsuits brought by employees charging unfair dismissal for using medical marijuana have all been dismissed to date. Some of these laws have antidiscrimination language that consider medical marijuana users as being disabled. Alaska, California, Colorado, Oregon, Washington, and the District of Columbia have passed recreational marijuana use, but three of these allow employers to prohibit marijuana use in the workplace.[190]

Employers will need to watch over the next few years to see if the courts begin to strengthen the rights of medical marijuana users.

In June 2015, the Colorado Supreme Court ruled that a worker's use of state-licensed medical marijuana off-duty and off the employer's premises during nonworking hours can be a cause for dismissal, upholding the decisions of two lower courts. The bottom line is that "if employers want to test for marijuana, they will be free to act on positive use results," according to Steve Bell, a labor and employment partner at the international law firm Dorsey and Whitney in its Denver office.[191] "There is no exception for marijuana use for medicinal purposes, or for marijuana use conducted in accordance with state law," the court wrote.[192] However, in 2019, we will probably see an expansion of employee-friendly laws or restrictions on drug testing.

Is drug testing a waste of time and money? Michael Frone in his book *Alcohol and Illicit Drug Use in the Workplace* says that there isn't any proof that drug tests reduce drug use. With more than half of Americans saying they have used marijuana, casual or medical marijuana users may choose not to work for companies that have preemployment drug screens. That is a lot of workers. He also states that employers know that drug testing doesn't mean anything. Anyone who smokes pot will just stop for a few days before their drug screen. It is an empty ritual that nobody wants to be the first to give up."[193]

I recommend drug testing of new hires and for cause, especially if you are in an industry where it is legally required or where the public confidence in your products and services would be jeopardized by sloppy work or accidents, such as biotech, pharmaceuticals, health care, aerospace, manufacturing, security, and transportation. Besides, no one wants to ride on a train or airplane where the pilot is impaired or have a pacemaker produced in a factory that has rampant drug use.

If you do implement or continue your drug testing policy, you should have a written policy, and in some states, it is a requirement to have a written policy and follow the National Institute of Drug Abuse (NIDA) procedures. You also need to know your local city and state laws and watch what happens with recreational and medical marijuana.

Employee Onboarding and Verification of Identity and Eligibility to Work in the United States

Employers need to verify the identity of their paid new hires and that they are legally eligible to work in the United States. (Every country has its own process for doing this.) In addition, employers need to have employees fill out W-4s to identify their US tax withholding and to collect contact information for their new hires such as their address, phone number, and personal email and usually to enroll in medical benefits, 401(k) or other retirement benefits, and to designate beneficiaries. A good applicant tracking system should enable this sign-up, including electronic links to the company's medical benefit providers. Many companies ask exempt employees to sign up before their start date to save time on their first day of work. Remember that nonexempt employees are to be paid (in the United States) to complete these forms, so it is best in their case to wait until the first day of work.

The process to verify the eligibility to work in the United States is the I-9 form, which was required of US employers by the Immigration Reform and Control Act of 1986. The instructions for completing the form are on the form and are easy to follow, including the documents required to identify the employees' identity and eligibility to work in the United States. Acceptable identification forms are on "List B." They must be accompanied by a document from "List C" that proves the employee is eligible to work in the United States.

Forms on "List B" include a driver's license or ID card issued by a US state or outlying possession of the United States that contains a photograph and information such as name, date of birth, gender, height, eye color, and address. While driver's licenses are most used, there are eleven other acceptable forms on "List B." Forms from "List C" must accompany forms from "List B." "List C" forms include items like the following: a US Social Security card (as long as it doesn't say "NOT VALID FOR EMPLOYMENT" or have words with other work restrictions) or birth certificate.

Documents on "List A" can be used to verify both identity and employment eligibility. "List A" includes documents such as an unexpired US passport or US passport card, permanent resident card (often called a "green card"), or unexpired temporary resident card.

The federal government began the E-Verify program, which is voluntary to speed up the verification of a worker's legal right to work in the United States. It is a web-based system that allows enrolled employers to confirm the eligibility of their employees to work in the United States by electronically matching information provided by employees on the Form I-9 against records available to the Social Security Administration and the Department of Homeland Security.

Employers with federal contracts or subcontracts that contain the Federal Acquisition Regulation (FAR) E-Verify clause are required to enroll in E-Verify as a condition of federal contracting. Employers may also be required to participate in E-Verify if their states have legislation mandating the use of E-Verify, such as a condition of business licensing. Finally, in some instances, employers may be required to participate in E-Verify as a result of a legal ruling.

Employers can learn more and sign up for E-Verify at https://www.e-verify.gov/.

Ten Steps for Awesome Cultural Onboarding and Higher Productivity

Do you want to have faster time-to-full productivity for your new hires? Improved retention? Higher employee engagement? Have your new hires be your best new hire referral source?

Who doesn't? So, what is your company doing to have an awesome onboarding program?

The Aberdeen Group, in a 2009 study, found that companies with effective onboarding programs had higher success rates for new hire assimilation: 62 percent had faster time-to-productivity, and 54 percent reported higher employee engagement. [194] I have found that onboarding programs that follow the steps below also reduce new hire turnover and raise the employee referral rate from new hires.

Onboarding is no longer only about enrolling in payroll and benefits, reading the company's policies, learning how to log into the company's computer systems, and receiving a company-branded coffee cup. These are the basics, and technology, such as interactive onboarding systems, videos, and even bots, can make the cumbersome processes easier.

Some companies have gone overboard with onboarding technology, using it exclusively to send out benefits, policy, and compliance and company information, as well as conduct enrollments. Many of these companies have eliminated face-to-face events. For me, this is a mistake, because using technology alone is too sterile.

Onboarding is as much about the heart as it is about the head. The heart is about finding purpose and building relationships. Successful onboarding programs also use the gap between "I accept" and the first day of work to build commitment to the company's purpose and brand.

Here are ten steps you need to take to have an awesome onboarding program that will improve employee engagement, accelerate the time-to-full-productivity for new hires, and reduce costly turnover. They address the head *and* the heart!

1. **Think of onboarding as a ninety-day process to help new hires find their emotional place in the business and improve their productivity.** Onboarding is no longer only about the first day, which many companies have parsed out over the first month so that new hires no longer feel hooked up to a fire hose.

   As a matter of fact, some organizations, such as eBay, have eliminated the first-day orientation altogether. They have replaced it by disseminating information about the company's mission, brand, benefits, and policies before a new employee even starts! They also hold a series of webinars, training, and events that build emotional ties to the company.

I am still a fan of a *short* first day or first week. This time should be used for meetings to provide new hires the basics of getting started, learning the basics, tours of the facility, and product and service demonstrations. I also love eBay's innovative approach!

2. **Learn the major obstacles experienced by your past new hires and help your current new employees overcome them.** Collect data from your previous new hires about their experiences. It is easy to do with a short survey or focus group. Ask them what they liked and didn't like, and what they would change about the onboarding process. I have found that most employees want training or a coach to help them learn how to use the company's systems and software, how internal processes really work, and how work gets done. Managers can help with this training, but often a peer coach is better because a new hire feels more comfortable asking a peer for help.

    Providing one or more peer coaches is essential. For example, in a marketing department I worked with, the main complaint from new hires was about mastering an online, convoluted approval process for new marketing materials to assure they did not violate ethical and legal standards. We overcame this obstacle by providing a written how-to guide, as well as a peer coach, who provided an initial training and was available for follow-up questions. As a result, the complaints of new marketing hires fell dramatically, and their time-to-full-productivity was cut in half. Incidentally, we financially rewarded the coaches, who also had day jobs. It provided a great return on investment.

3. **Proactively schedule time for new hires to meet their stakeholders**. It is essential for new hires to build relationships with the individuals they will be supporting. Have new hires learn firsthand from their stakeholders their likes and don't likes.

4. **Build community and address the heart.** New hire lunches with each other and their bosses are always appreciated. Invite new hires to join your affinity groups or sports teams. Why not use social media to **create online social networks for new hires on Twitter**? LinkedIn creates networks for new hires to exchange experiences, share tips, and build relationships on, you guessed it, LinkedIn. Millennials love it!

5. **Be clear about the role of managers in new hire orientation and hold them accountable**. New hires want a relationship primarily with their managers, not human resources. This relationship is critically important and, all too often, is not executed well by managers. Work with managers to develop their specific roles, tasks, and a time schedule for completing new hire orientation. At a minimum, this includes explaining the team's goals, the new hire's goals, where they will work, the operating norms for work, such as meeting schedules, and communication norms. Managers should introduce new hires to their new team members.

   Above all, have the managers build relationships—addressing the heart—with every new hire by learning the traits of their favorite and least favorite past bosses and work environments. Learn and answer their questions about the job and learn about their career aspirations.

6. **Have executive leaders speak to groups of new hires about the company's purpose, opportunities in the marketplace, and strategies to achieve its goals. This addresses the heart and the head.** It makes a great first impression when new hires hear from top executives and feel

their commitment about the company's strategies. Many orientations tell "creation stories" and provide history—all good when done well. These stories can build a lasting impression of important company values—but you also want to use this opportunity to get new hires excited about the *company's future success.*

I recommend that you include customers and product demonstrations in these meetings, which can be achieved through videos. For a medical device company I worked with, we provided a live feed of medical procedures that were performed using our products. The doctors described the procedures, the performance of our products, and their benefits to the patient. These sessions were standing room only (even when they were available online to employees at their desks) and created a strong commitment to the company's purpose and strategies.

7. **Provide firsthand testimonials about how your current executives rose in their careers.** One way I have done this is by inviting executives to tell their career stories to a group of new hires, offer career advice, and answer their questions. We did this through a face-to-face breakfast, which was broadcast to remote new hires by videoconference. The breakfasts were always well attended.

8. **Use technology to provide reminders to new hires**. Someday it might be Siri or Alexa providing friendly voice reminders to new hires to complete benefits enrollment or attend necessary job trainings. In the meantime, use whatever technology you must to generate reminders.

9. **Create a flawless process.** I am always amazed whenever companies have new hires start before their computers or online authorizations are set up. This does not create a good first impression! You need to build a flawless process between HR, IT, marketing, your benefit providers, and HR

systems so that new employees aren't frustrated on the first day. When new hires see that the company has their act together in getting them off to a good start, it builds their commitment to the company's goals.

10. **If you have multiple locations, use videoconferencing and virtual meetings to involve remote employees in the onboarding.** Frankly, it is not difficult or costly with today's technology.

Personality Tests and the Big Five

Personality is the set of emotional qualities and ways of speaking and behaving that distinguish us and set us apart from each other. These qualities are measured as traits by industrial/organizational psychologists. A common model of these traits developed by I/O psychologists is the "Big Five Model," which captures the basic dimensions in personality and their variation. The Big Five are:

1. Neuroticism/emotional stability: tendency to easily become angry, anxious, and depressed
2. Extroversion: high energy, positive emotions, assertiveness, sociability, talkativeness
3. Openness to experience: curious, adventuresome, appreciative of art and a variety of experiences
4. Agreeableness: tendency to being compassionate and cooperative rather than suspicious and antagonistic
5. Conscientiousness: tendency to be organized, dependable, dutiful, achieving, self-disciplined

These traits are measured along a continuum, and some of them have a strong correlation with job performance. We have already learned from Schmidt and Hunter that conscientiousness is a valid predictor of job performance. But what of the others? Agreeableness can be great for collaboration and teamwork, but some studies have shown that too much agreeableness at the expense of dominance and initiative (these two qualities are found in the Big Five trait of extroversion) can give the perception of weakness, particularly in newly forming groups.[195] Other research has suggested that those high in agreeableness (especially men) are not as successful making money.[196] Openness is linked to innovation.[197] Research has suggested that individuals who are considered leaders typically exhibit lower amounts of neurotic traits, maintain higher levels of openness (envisioning success), balanced levels of conscientiousness (well-organized), and balanced levels of extraversion (outgoing but not excessive).[198] Further studies have linked professional burnout to too much neuroticism and extraversion.[199]

Personality tests as a predictor for job success have had mixed results and mixed support from academic researchers, however, leading to debates about their effectiveness.[200] Some researchers are supportive, while others say that their predictability is unreliable. Most recently, there is a growing concern that the test taker can fake their answers to gain higher scores.

I believe the wisest guidance comes from Robert Guion and Richard F. Gottier, who wrote:

> There is no generalizable evidence that personality measures can be recommended as good or practical tools for employee selection...The best that can be said is that in *some* situations, for *some* purposes, *some* personality measures can offer helpful predictions. But there is nothing in this summary to indicate in advance which measure should be used in which situation or for which purposes. In short, it must be concluded (as always) that the validity of any personality measure must be specifically and competently determined for the specific situation in which it is to be used and for the specific purpose or criterion within that situation... It seems clear that the only acceptable reason for using personality measures as instruments of decision is found only after doing considerable research with the

measure in the specific situation and for the specific purpose for which it is to be used.[201]

With this guidance in mind about using personality tests for a specific purpose, I have successfully used a personality test to identify sales worker candidates who had personality attributes aligned with our best sales workers. This test from Berke, along with an improved candidate selection profile and structured interview, significantly improved our success rate at hiring sales workers. Note that before we used the test, we validated its content against our top twenty salespeople to calibrate test score thresholds. The test was used not in a strict pass/fail capacity with a rigid or highly set hurdle but as part of an overall assessment. However, candidates who bombed out on the test did not proceed to final interviews.

Selection: Personality Tests

- As a predictor of job success, mixed results
- Growing concern they can be faked and with adverse selection
- Costs and concerns with validation
- In many circumstances, they can be very predictive—when validated

• Frank L. Schmidt and John E. Hunter. (1988) "The Validity and Utility of selection Methods in Personnel Psychology: Practical and Theoretical Implications of 85 Years of Research Findings." Psychological Bulletin, Vol 124, No. 2, 276-274. Copyright 1998 by the American Psychological Association, Inc. 0033-2909/98/.
• Robert M. Guion and Richard F. Gottier, (1965) "Validity of Personality Measures in Personnel Selection", 18 Personnel Psychology 135, 159-160

I have also successfully used leadership assessments to provide feedback to new leaders and also leaders at the executive level. Highly reliable leadership assessments include the Hogan, the California Psychological Inventory, and the assessments by the Center for Creative Leadership.

The Hogan Personality Inventory (HPI) has proven to be an effective predictor of job performance for many different jobs, such as management, customer service, hospital administrators, and police officers. I have personally found HPI to be an excellent tool for coaching managers on leadership style.

When writing about personality tests, I am not speaking about assessments or tests that are presented with a four-quadrant break-out, such as DISC or the Strengths Deployment Inventory (SDI). (SDI used to have four quadrants and now has a triangle of three personality inventories, each with their own range.) These are great assessments to use to help improve teamwork and to help leaders and team members understand their preferred communication and work style and how their styles interact with other team members. I have used them with teams to help them understand how to work with each other more effectively and how to resolve conflicts more productively. However, they are not validated to use in selection and should not be used in selection.

Emotional Intelligence

In 1990, Peter Salovey and John Mayer proposed a new intelligence, emotional intelligence, which is "The ability to monitor one's own and others' feelings and emotions, to discriminate among them, and to use this information to guide one's thinking and actions."[202] Emotional intelligence is defined as having three main branches:

1. Appraisal and expression of emotion
2. Regulation of expression
3. Utilization of emotion

Peter Salovey and John Mayer explain that there is nothing wrong with having negative emotions; after all, it is part of being human. What is critically important, however, is the component of personal growth and using all emotions intelligently.

Our understanding of emotional intelligence leaped forward with the publishing of *Working with Emotional Intelligence* by Daniel Goleman.[203] After an exhaustive survey of the empirical research and packing the book with case histories, Goleman asserted that the higher a person's position, the more emotional intelligence mattered. It is what distinguishes star

performers from the average performer and is critical for successful leadership. He also assertsed that it can be learned.

The Emotional Competence Framework by Daniel Goleman

Personal Competence: These competencies describe how we manage ourselves.

Self-Awareness: Knowing one's internal states, preferences, resources, and intuitions.

- Emotional awareness: Recognizing one's emotions and their effects.
- Accurate self-assessment: Knowing one's strengths and limits
- Self-confidence: A strong sense of one's self-wroth and capabilities

Self-Regulation: Managing one's internal states, impulses, and resources

- Self-control: Keeping disruptive emotions and impulses in check
- Trustworthiness: Maintaining standards of honesty and integrity
- Conscientiousness: Taking responsibility for personal performance
- Adaptability: Flexibility in handling change
- Innovation: Being comfortable with novel ideas, approaches, and new information

Motivation: Emotional tendencies that guide or facilitate reaching goals

- Achievement drive: Striving to improve or meet a standard of excellence
- Commitment: Aligning with the goals of the group or organization
- Initiative: Readiness to act on opportunities
- Optimism: Persistence in pursuing goals despite obstacles and setbacks

Social Competence: These competencies determine how we handle relationships

Empathy: Awareness of others' feelings, needs and concerns

- Understanding others: Sensing other's feelings and perspectives, and taking an active interest in their concerns
- Developing others: Sensing others' development needs and bolstering their abilities
- Service orientation: Anticipating, recognizing, and meeting customers' needs
- Leveraging diversity: Cultivating opportunities through different kinds of people
- Political awareness: Reading a group's emotional currents and power relationships

Social Skills: Adeptness at inducing desirable responses in others

- Influence: Wielding effective tactics for persuasion
- Communication: Listening openly and sending convincing messages
- Conflict management: Negotiating and resolving disagreements
- Leadership: Inspiring and guiding individuals and groups
- Change catalyst: Initiating or managing change
- Building Bonds: Nurturing instrumental relationships
- Collaboration and cooperation: Working with others toward shared goals
- Team Capabilities: Creating group synergy in pursuing collective goals

Daniel Goleman (1998) *Working with Emotional Intelligence,* pp 26 and 27, Bantam Books, New York.

Goleman provided the framework for emotional intelligence that I have included on the previous page.

In many professions, emotional intelligence adds to GMA tests, or IQ, to identify those who will rise in management or with customer-facing positions. It is not a replacement for people with low IQ.

Other researchers have found that emotional intelligence has predictive validity for leadership roles and professions that involve negotiation, building trust, and working with stress.[204] One study conducted by Ruth Jacobs and Wei Chen even found that people with the highest emotional intelligence were more likely to succeed in a position than those who were strongest in IQ or relevant previous experience.[205] Ruth Jacobs and Wei Chen spoke to hundreds of top executives at fifteen global companies including IBM, PepsiCo, and Volvo. They found that statistically the difference between those regarded as star performers (top 5%) and average performers was primarily attributable to higher ratings attained by the stars on these soft skill parameters. In fact for senior leadership positions 90% of the difference between the stars and average employees was attributable to difference in ratings on emotional competencies such as influence, team leadership, political awareness, self-confidence and achievement drives. Only 10% was due to any cognitive or technical skills (mainly strategic thinking). Job retention is also linked to emotional intelligence.

There are assessments for emotional intelligence. I have personally found them helpful for coaching managers. Many companies shy away from emotional intelligence assessments due to the cost and legal risk of using them, and like any tool, they need to be validated for the role.

So how do you select for emotional intelligence if you are not going to test for it?

The answer is to create a structured interview that includes emotional intelligence questions. Following are some sample questions that can help determine if the interviewee understands themselves, their emotions, and how to effectively use them.

1. Please tell me about your development areas and what you are doing to improve them.
2. What was the biggest failure of your career, and what did you learn from it?
3. Tell me about a time you had a conflict with a peer and what you did to resolve it.
4. Tell me about a time when you received criticism from a boss, peer, or client and how it made you feel. How did you handle it? What was the outcome?

While you listen for the answers to these questions, be sure to listen for the emotions from the job candidate and not just the rational list of development areas, their learning, and the description of how they handled criticism. Listen for their tone of voice and watch their eye contact and body motions. Do they seem angry or hurt about the incidents? Or have they incorporated the feedback, learned, and moved on?

People who are low on emotional intelligence will have a hard time discussing their faults. They may be defensive and blame others for the criticism. They may even struggle to answer the questions or give you boilerplate answers like, "I am too much of a driver and want to succeed at all costs." Or "I am too much of a perfectionist when it comes to work." Or "I have a low tolerance for failure."

You don't want boilerplate answers or vague answers that do not have detail. Someone who is high in emotional intelligence will be thoughtful about their answers and will take the time to articulate a detailed answer and tell you about the outcome and how it made them, and others feel. They will talk about improving relationships.

While EI will improve your ability to select the best candidates for leadership roles, great selection processes should include other selection procedures, such as structured interviews based on job competencies and job knowledge, and work sampling, to further improve probability of success.

Hiring for Cultural Fit

Does hiring for "cultural fit" really work? Or is hiring for "fit" the lazy way to hire? Even worse, does it lead to discrimination in hiring decisions? Does the hiring of people like your company's current executives, current technical leaders, or people like you, with similar academic, university, and work experiences, limit the new thinking your company needs to be innovative?

Hiring for "cultural fit" began in the 1980s with companies such as Southwest Airlines. Southwest decided to hire staff who would be good team players and cabin crews willing to have fun with passengers. Today, other companies, such as Zappos and Google, proclaim the benefits of hiring for cultural fit.

I have worked for three companies: Honeywell Inc., Honeywell LLC (Honeywell after Allied Signal purchased the Minneapolis-based Honeywell Inc. in 2001 and kept the Honeywell name but significantly changed the culture and strategies), and Medtronic, where hiring for "cultural fit" was an important consideration, although each company had dramatically different cultures. Honeywell Inc. emphasized highly skilled employees who would lead technological innovation in their various business sectors, were collaborative, and had strong Midwestern values of trust and respect. Honeywell LLC emphasized a hard-driving, shareholder equity culture in the 1990s style of a conglomerate—what businesses to sell and what businesses to buy. Medtronic emphasized a collaborative, relationship-based culture (sometimes overly political) dedicated to Medtronic's mission statement to "contribute to human welfare by the application of biomedical engineering to alleviate pain, restore health, and extend life."

Does hiring for cultural fit work? Does it lead to discrimination? Does it have other unintended effects such as group think and a lack of innovation?

Most certainly, hiring for cultural fit works well when done well. Culture is the glue that holds organizations together, and empirical research demonstrates this.[206] Cultural fit is a key trait to look for when recruiting, developing, rewarding, and promoting talent. The potential downside of hiring for cultural fit is that it may create homogeneous workforces that are unable to recognize new trends. Employees may get used to the tried and true and fail to innovate. Empirical research shows that diverse workforces lead to higher levels of innovation and financial performance when organizations are high-tech, knowledge-based, highly complex, global, or operate in multicultural markets.[207]

Many recent articles have surmised that hiring for cultural fit may lead to discriminatory practices. All too often, hiring for fit is done poorly. Companies often hire candidates from academic institutions, other companies, or with common experience sets that match those of the executive staff. Although there is much empirical evidence that has pointed out discriminatory hiring practices,[208] I have not found any empirical studies or meta-analysis linking hiring for cultural fit to discrimination. (If you know of such a study, please let me know.)

Katherine Klein, vice dean of the Wharton Social Impact Initiative, says that cultural fit is "an incredibly vague term, often based on gut instinct. The biggest problem is that while we invoke cultural fit as a reason to hire someone, it is far more common to use it to not hire someone."[209]

Lauren A. Rivera wrote an article for the *New York Times* about her direct experience as a recruiter in a top investment bank and her research after interviewing 120 hiring decision makers. She observed that, while résumés influenced who made it into the interviews, the interviewers' perceptions about cultural fit strongly influenced who received job offers. "Critically, though, for these gatekeepers, fit was not about a match with organizational values. It was about personal fit. In these time-and-team-intensive jobs, professionals at all levels of seniority reported wanting to hire people with whom they enjoyed hanging out and could foresee developing close relationships. Fit was different from the ability to get along with clients. Fundamentally, it was about interviewers' personal enjoyment and fun. To judge fit, interviewers commonly relied on chemistry."[210]

How to successfully hire for cultural fit

When hiring for cultural fit, make sure you have clear organizational values and good structured-interview questions to use as a guide. It's important that you not allow interviewers to hire based on their own personality fit or common experience fit. It takes analytics to correctly identify the values of your organization, not what the last CEO plastered on every conference room wall.

Here's a test to make sure your "cultural fit" hiring drives value and is not discriminatory.

1. **Do you use structured interviews?** Are your interviews based on the organization's values and the role and attributes of the job in question? Do not allow hiring managers to hire based on a first impression or an unstructured, twenty-minute interview. For cultural fit, ask questions that will elicit responses from the candidates on their preferred work culture. Questions such as:
    a. What was your favorite work environment and why?
    a. What was your worst work environment and why?
    b. Who was your best boss? What made this person the best?
    c. Who was your worst boss? What made this person the worst?
    d. Why do you want to work here?
    e. What has been your greatest career achievement and why?
    f. What has been your biggest career failure and why? What did you learn from it?
2. **Do you use objective, validated measures of required attributes for every job opening, such as job knowledge or work sampling?** Empirical research shows that validated measures improve selection success.[211]

3. **Do you measure the results of your job candidate screening, including its impact on diversity?** Any organization that is serious about hiring and keeping top talent should use analytics in its hiring process. If you don't, you are using "Middle Ages" hiring practices. I am not talking about measures like days open per job requisition, new hire turnover in one year, or the cost of recruiting. These are all good but very basic. Instead, I am talking about the sources of your best hires and the attributes of successful candidates after two years of job performance. Every time I have worked with an organization to implement recruiting analytics, it has uncovered previously unknown best sources of top talent and candidate attributes. Recruiting analytics also usually improved the diversity of the workforce.

4. **Do you require more than the hiring manager's decision?** Whom you hire is one of the most important decisions a company can make. Branding, recruiting, and hiring are expensive. I recommend that you use trained hiring teams to make this important decision—not just the hiring manager.

5. **Are your recruiters screening out candidates due to ethnically sounding last names or other discriminatory practices?** Check the résumés that are received versus the candidates interviewed to find out.

Why Is Amazon Holding Job Fairs?

There are no Amazon chatbots, virtual reality, or artificial intelligence recruiting screens. Amazon is using old-fashioned, face-to-face job fairs! What gives?

They work! And Amazon is not alone in turning to older, but reliable, recruiting methods in this tight labor market. Across the pond in Sweden, high-technology company Ericsson recently held a full-day "Swarm Stockholm" to recruit R&D engineers. During the "Swarm," the company sent out ninety interns to hit the streets and talk to people about career opportunities at Ericsson. The company reported that it engaged with more than five hundred people and raised the awareness of thousands more in just one day.

While I have not used a swarm, I have a lot of experience planning and executing job fairs across the United States. I have used job fairs to attract engineers, as well as other high-demand employees, such as financial analysts, clinical researchers, and regulatory affairs workers. I've had great success: attracting up to four hundred interested candidates at a single fair, with a hire rate of 10 to 20 percent. The fairs provided a good return on recruiting investment.

An additional benefit of job fairs is that they help get your recruiting and screening procedures in order. Successful recruiting fairs depend on a fast-moving, interesting, and fun process. If you don't have your recruiting and screening honed to run smoothly, candidates will lose interest and walk out the door!

Here are my suggestions for holding a successful recruiting fair.

Get a great site with a bright, cheerful atrium to greet candidates and conduct initial, face-to-face screens. You'll also need an interior auditorium with small side conference rooms for in-depth interviews. It is best if you hold your fair at your main office, but an offsite location will do.

Do fantastic outreach. Now is the time to crank up the social media and reach out to all your passive candidates. Also, use media ads on radio, job boards, and social media to get the word out to your target audience. Pick up the phone and call passive candidates. Consider billboards in front of the offices of your workforce competitors or companies having layoffs. Reach out to outplacement firms.

Provide exciting information about your brand. Link your company's purpose with your future employees' passion. In your atrium greeting space, provide easy-to-read (or video display) summaries of your organization's purpose, work culture, exciting work projects, work environment, and benefits. Play upbeat music.

Do a quick recruiting screen. You need to immediately welcome your candidates and conduct a quick, structured recruiting screen in less than fifteen minutes. Have enough personnel available to keep lines to a minimum. For those who fail the quick screen, offer them a snack or some "gift" for coming, so they feel good about the process. Then send them on their way.

Provide product demonstrations. Invite those candidates who pass the initial screen to come into the auditorium to meet with managers in their field and discuss the projects they could work on. Also, provide product or service demonstrations.

Hold structured interviews. After getting candidates excited about the company's future, have your managers conduct structured interviews in side conference rooms to determine if candidates have the technical skills, competencies, successful track record, and teamwork and collaboration skills to join your team. It's okay if these interviews go on for an hour. However, to handle the volume, you'll need to have a cadre of management interviewers. If your company uses selection tests, now is the time to administer them, but make sure you have enough tablets available to prevent delays.

Based on the outcome of the structured interviews, you can make offers on the spot, pending background and reference checks and drug tests. Or you can invite these candidates back for one more round of interviews at your offices, but for no more than a half day. You must keep the process quick-moving and focused.

Chapter 12: HR Geek: Technology

When HR and recruiters used to speak about technology, it meant an applicant tracking system or posting jobs on digital job boards as opposed to social media. However, powerful digitization technologies are now finding their way to recruiting and will dramatically change the landscape. HR now has the same technologies that have been used by marketing departments to find, attract, build relationship with and establish strategic data bases on customers.

It is now time to use these new technologies for employer branding and recruiting. Let's use them and truly hack recruiting to significantly improve our ability to search and find candidates quickly and automate administrative tasks, measures, and metrics!

Today's applicant tracking systems make it easy for job candidates to apply for company jobs and allow for tracking of critical information and metrics in the recruiting process. In addition, the best of them allow for instantaneous communications with job candidates on their status in the recruiting process.

With these technologies, job candidate net promotor scores can be in the 90s!

But that is just the beginning. Companies can significantly reduce the cost of interviewing by using pre-recorded, videoconferencing screening interviews and chatbots to begin initial screening questions, especially for entry-level positions and positions in retail and call centers. The use of artificial intelligence is enabling recruiters to find active and passive job candidates quickly. AI is changing the roles of recruiters and is enabling companies to improve their understanding of what competencies make their best employees the best—and how to discover these competencies among their hundreds of job candidates.

Facial recognition technology is also making its way to recruiting, but it comes with the risk of screening out the wrong job candidates or of discriminating against otherwise qualified candidates based on gender, race, or age. This technology is still evolving. Any assessment test to screen out candidates must be statistically validated or it runs the risk of making bad or discriminatory decisions.

Blockchain will in the years ahead be used in recruiting and will significantly change how recruiters verify the degrees, certifications, and previous employment of job candidates nearly instantaneously.

However, human resources leaders, recruiters, and their IT partners will need to be very discerning when purchasing new technologies to truly understand which ones provide real value and which ones are more marketing fluff than substance. Or in the words of Silicon Valley technologists, which new technologies are a "hammer looking for a nail." Recruiting needs reliable technologies built with an understanding of recruiting, the laws governing recruiting, its processes, and the empirical evidence of industrial/organizational psychology.

Finally, the integration of new digital technologies will mean understanding what computers and robots can do more effectively than human beings and when human beings provide better value.

More than 80 percent of digital integrations fail because the culture rejects the technology and the digitization project did not involve the workers impacted in determining the process, properly train them, and emotionally prepare them for their new role.

If you want to be successful implementing new technology, it is all about the relationship.

The technologies are here, are already transforming recruiting, and are being continually improved. Now is the time to hack recruiting!

Applicant Tracking Systems Are Becoming Candidate Management Systems

HR departments of midsize companies and above or with high-volume recruiting really can't survive without an applicant tracking system (ATS). For the uninitiated, applicant tracking systems are software platforms that enable a company to post their job openings on the career site of their web page and then keep track of every applicant's résumé by job posting all the way through the hiring process, documenting decisions and the reasons for the decisions, and generating timely communications to the job applicants.

They are a godsend to recruiters who, in the absence of an applicant tracking system, were often using Excel spreadsheets to track applicants by job postings and doing much of the filing on their own. In addition, the good ones also provide the tracking that is required for affirmative action plans.

The good ATS requires all job applicants to complete an application form, attach a résumé or connect to a LinkedIn profile, and answer employment questions. They also collect voluntary self-identification data on race/ethnicity, gender, disability status, and protected veteran status, which is kept confidential from the hiring managers and recruiters and is used later for completing group analysis with an affirmative action plan.

Today most job seekers go to a job site such as Indeed, Glassdoor,or ZipRecruiter or a company career page using a smartphone or tablet, so ATSs that interact with your career page need to be app friendly.

However, ATSs are only as good as the time HR and its IT support put in to mapping the ATS to your hiring process. If that mapping is done poorly—which it often is—the ATS can be a train wreck. The first ATS systems from large enterprise software companies were also rather clunky and hard to use. In addition, many systems, even some of the best ones on the market today, do not seamlessly let you transfer data on your new hires to the payroll system. The data include the personal data like address and contact information, meaning the job candidate, recruiter, or an HR tech must reenter the data.

Because most applicant tracking systems are old, rudimentary, and clunky, they make the job candidate experience miserable. It is difficult for job applicants to search for jobs that are the right fit and for companies to match applicants to their jobs.

Their original design also did a poor job of keeping the job applicant informed of his or her status in the decision-making process—except for sending a text or email that the application had been completed and the company would contact the applicant if it was interested. In a period of low unemployment, that is not enough dedication to the job candidate experience, and the company will lose applicants who will take offers from companies that treat them better and move faster.

The result is that applying for a job, which is already nerve-racking, is made complicated by clunky ATSs. According to Deloitte, the average open position received more than 150 résumés, more than 45 percent of the candidates never heard anything back from the company, and a startling 83 percent of candidates rated their job search experience as poor.[212] According to the Talent Board, more than 33 percent of all job seekers spend two or more hours researching a single job, and it often takes them an hour to complete a job application.[213]

The new ATSs are rapidly evolving. Now the new ones have the capability to become job candidate management systems, like marketing customer management systems. The best of them have interactive features with candidates that enable the company to instantaneously and continuously communicate with their job applicants, giving them updates on their status in the application and interviewing process. Some of these systems also have the machine learning capability to recommend other jobs to candidates who were rejected for the jobs they applied for. Even more impressive, some ATSs can recommend job applicants join the company's social networking communities to learn more about the company and stay up-to-date on its latest news.

However, for many job applicants today, the job application process on an ATS generally stinks because they are clunky, especially the older ATSs, which were developed as a "bolt on" to an enterprise software system that's real value to the company was for financial or supply chain management.

Many job applicants have complained to me even in the year 2018 that it takes them one to two hours to complete a job application on an ATS, even when they are uploading their résumés or LinkedIn profiles. Often applicants still must answer many questions, some that the résumé already addressed. And the ATS butchers their beautifully formatted résumés by taking out the paragraph divides so the paragraphs run together and changing the margin formatting. The butchering is so bad, many job candidates must reformat their résumés in the ATS. Or they will hit a wrong key, usually by misunderstanding an instruction, or get timed out when they are interrupted and then must start over. If it is too much of a bother, the candidate, especially the good ones in a tight labor market, will simply move on to a company with a sane ATS.

According to a study conducted by Potentialpark that included thirty-seven thousand responses from a wide range of industries, half of the US job candidates who participated in the study said they quit an online application. Half![214] That is a 6 percent increase compared to 2017. Here are the top frustrations for US candidates according to the data from the 2018 Potentialpark study.

1. **Fifty-six percent were concerned or unclear about what would happen with their application.**
2. **Forty-five percent were concerned about not knowing how long the application takes before deciding to apply.** The authors advised that if you can't share the way you process applications, give some idea of what the candidate can expect. There is no need for secrecy.
3. **Closely related, thirty-five percent concluded the application took too long and quit the application.**

4. **Thirty percent found that there were too many irrele-vant questions.** Results from the study showed it was not uncommon for employers among Fortune 500 companies to ask candidates to fill out their work history after they had already chosen to apply through LinkedIn or CV parsing. Duplicate questions can cause candidates to lose focus on completing their application. If you have many other questions that are not duplicate, don't hesitate to briefly explain to candidates why the question is relevant in the process. Remember: transparency!

5. **Twenty-five percent were concerned about not knowing which documents would be needed.**

6. **Twenty-five percent quit because of technical problems with the application.**

Many legacy and new ATSs unfortunately do not automatically track and store decisions and reasons for decisions during the application process, requiring recruiters or hiring managers to upload a lot of information manually. Ideally, the ATS will also allow you to generate reports or, better yet, download the information into your Affirmative Action Plan (AAP). Fantastic ATSs have dashboards that track progress in real time or at least quarterly.

ATSs will also collect information from applicants on criminal convictions, which has become a controversial topic during a period when companies are realizing that one-third of all adult Americans have a criminal record and there are, in May 2019, more open jobs than unemployed US citizens. Is it time to look at criminals who have not served time for violent offenses and burglary? California and other states have also "banned the box," meaning they have made it illegal to ask applicants about their criminal records until after a conditional job offer is made, much like a background check or drug test.

One of the features I like most in current ATSs is the ability to automate job opening workflow, such as approval or rejection of job requisitions and updating of applicant records. When companies spend the time to set up accurate workflows with decision-making, communications, scheduling, and offer generations, it can make for a very slick process. Unfortunately, many companies do not take the time to map out their processes in the ATS. This lost opportunity means that the newly purchased ATS system is now clunky and hard to figure out a use for. If you are purchasing technology to streamline your processes and keep great records, take the time or pay an expert to set it up for you correctly.

These systems also generate reports that greatly simplify the gathering and analyzing of data required to generate an affirmative action plan or an EEO-1 report. They also can identify for you your best sources of candidates by job family. Do you attract more engineers from employee referrals, LinkedIn, Facebook, Indeed, CareerBuilder, EngineeringJobs.net, Engineer.net, or iHireEngineering? A good ATS will track and report your best recruiting sources.

ATSs also allow companies to set up a career site on their company web page where they can post their open job positions. The career sites are a wonderful opportunity for companies to build a compelling employer brand and to promote their employee value proposition—why a job candidate should select your company over another. Companies should take advantage of this capability to list the best aspects of their products, innovation, and culture and describe the benefits, career advancement opportunities, and other amenities they offer to the company workers. The best of these sites also have videos that feature employees talking about why they like working at the company, the "awesome" work they are doing, and their own career journeys. The ATS platforms also allow recruiters to post their job openings on whatever job postings (such as Indeed, CareerBuilder, Google for Jobs, Dice, and so on) they have contracted with to attract job candidates.

In addition, the good ATS also allows you to eliminate unqualified job seekers from the selection process using skills-based and/or behavior-based questions customized to a specific job opening.

Increasingly, the distinguishing feature for ATSs is their ability to improve the job candidate experience through timely feedback and suggestions. This is especially true for young job applicants who grew up on Facebook and Instagram. They want a "thumbs-up" world that has timely suggestions, tutorials, and positive reinforcement like they have become used to on Facebook and their video games. In addition, they want to check out potential new employers on social media such as Facebook. They want to do more than read about a company's mission on Facebook; they want to interact with a company representative or a contact they know or an employee on Facebook or other social media before they decide about applying for a job.

The best ATS can manage email recruiting campaigns and stay in contact with job applicants throughout the recruiting process. This enables companies to create better relationships with job applicants and even to suggest other job openings if a job applicant is rejected. This is important because in today's tight job market, no company can afford to lose interested job applicants.

While ATSs can cut down on the recruiter's workload, it is wrong to assume that they will on their own select the ideal candidate for you. Recruiters still need to view the top candidates to see that they fit the qualifications of their job postings and to look for themselves at the top résumés to look for information that might help them decide who to bring in for an interview.

Many job applicants today will apply for a job through their handheld device. So it is important to have a smooth and streamlined approach to apply for a job.

In my experience, these systems need care and feeding and for large companies a dedicated resource to make sure the data are accurate and someone who knows how to work the software— which can be tricky no matter what the salesperson told you. The last thing you want is to have your recruiters tied up and having to learn to be IT systems experts to keep your ATS churning. Therefore, I recommend the use of project coordinators to do this work so your recruiter is free to recruit.

Who has the most used and highest rated ATS?

Based on 2018 market share, as determined by Datanyze[215],

Oracle Taleo has the highest market share with 13.54 percent of the market, followed by iCIMS at 7.65 percent, JazzHR at 4.63 percent, NEOGOV Insight (which is for the public sector) at 4.31 percent, and Workable at 4.14 percent. Datanyze is a technographics provider for B2B technology companies to identify their best customers.

G2 Crowd provides ratings for applicant tracking systems. It is a peer-to-peer, business solutions review platform headquartered in Chicago, Illinois. The company was launched in May 2012 by former BigMachines employees, with a focus on aggregating user reviews for business software.[

According to G2 Crowd[216], the best applicant tracking system (ATS) software products are determined by customer satisfaction ratings (based on user reviews) and scale (based on market share, vendor size, and social impact) and placed into four categories on their Grid. Below is a summary of their grid from their website in May 2018.

- Products in the Leader quadrant are rated highly by G2 Crowd users and have substantial market presence scores. Leaders include Oracle Taleo, UltiPro, Workday HCM, Oracle PeopleSoft, Jobvite, iCIMS Recruit, ADP Workforce Now, Zoho Recruit, and Oracle HCM Cloud.
- High Performers are highly rated by their users but have not yet achieved the market share and scale of the companies in the Leader quadrant. High Performers include SmartRecruiters, ApplicantStack, Greenhouse, ClearCompany, Avature, Lever, and talentReef.
- Contenders have significant market presence and resources but have received below average user satisfaction ratings or have not yet received a sufficient number of reviews to validate the solution. Contenders include SAP SuccessFactors and Kronos Workforce Ready.
- Niche solutions do not have the market presence of the leaders. They may have been rated positively on customer satisfaction but have not yet received enough reviews to validate

them. Niche products include Cornerstone OnDemand, Kenexa, Lumesse, PeopleFluent, and SilkRoad Recruiting.

◆ In the small market segment, the companies in the Leader quadrant are Zoho Recruit, Lever, SmartRecruiters, BambooHR, and Bullhorn ATS.

◆ In the midmarket segment, the companies in the Leader quadrant are Lever, ApplicantStack, Greenhouse, SmartRecruiters, Newton ATS, iCIMS Recruit, BambooHR, UltiPro, Jobvite, ADP Workforce Now, Zoho Recruit, Bullhorn ATS, Google Hire, Kronos Workforce Ready, Paycom, and Paycor Perform.

◆ In the enterprise (large company) segment, in the Leader quadrant are UltiPro, iCIMS Recruit, Workday HCM, ADP Workforce Now, Jobvite, Oracle HCM Cloud, Oracle Taleo, Oracle PeopleSoft.

G2 Crowd ratings can be accessed online, including their rating grids for all companies, by small, mid, and enterprise categories at https://www.g2crowd.com/categories/applicant-tracking-system-ats?segment=enterprise.

There are other companies that rate ATSs. One is FinancesOnline, which can be found at https://financesonline.com/top-20-applicant-tracking-software-solutions/. Finances Online also provides a summary of capabilities for each of the ATSs they rate.

The Office of Federal Contract Compliance Programs (OFCCP), however, audits that federal contractors have affirmative action plans. The EEOC defines internet applicants, identifies electronic data collection methods, creates basic qualification standards, and establishes record-keeping requirements for compliance.

To follow the guidance of the EEOC and to pass an audit by the OFCCP, you will need to have an ATS that can store, track, and analyze hiring information, from the first applicant to an open position to the hiring decision, with a capability for large amounts of data. You do not want to have to maintain separate hard copy files or be forced to use Excel spreadsheets.

In Chapter 13, HR Legal Geek, I provide guidance on the list

of basic capabilities your ATS should have to support an AAP and the process flow to be compliant with EEOC guidance.

Best Job Boards

The best job board out there used to be Monster, which still makes the top ten list of most recruiting bloggers. It was relatively user friendly, and it provided recruiters with tons of candidates, many more than its competition at the time and from newspaper ads. And that became its problem. Too many candidates were not qualified for the position. Too much spam. One of my best recruiters in the 2000s, Nancy Schempf, commented that she hated it. "Monster gives me two hundred candidates for our positions who aren't qualified. It is a big waste of my time." She wasn't alone. Many of my other recruiters had the same concern. We shifted our job board recruiting strategies to rely more on a new platform at the time, LinkedIn, and specialty job boards such as BioSpace and Dice.

Today the field has changed. There are over ten thousand job boards out there, with most of them specializing in various professions and industries. Monster and LinkedIn are still major players, along with specialty job boards and what I call "recruiting dating services" (see my section "Online Dating Moves to Recruiting" later in this chapter). Technology is changing the landscape, with texting apps, chatbots, machine learning, artificial intelligence, and Blockchain.

I have researched ratings of job boards for this chapter. I tend to prefer information from surveys over one expert's opinion. But surveys on job boards are hard to come by. So I also turned to recruiting bloggers, job board websites for their claims, and my own opinions for this chapter. What they inform us is that Indeed and LinkedIn led the way, and then in the distance Glassdoor and CareerBuilder led the way for the quantity and quality of job candidates. Yes, Glassdoor, the internet site where you once visited only to read what former and current employees posted about the good and bad of a company's recruiting and management practices and its culture and CEO, has become a driving force for posting jobs. At the SmartRecruiters conference in February, 2019, they told me they are now the No. 2 job board.

The new entrant is Google for Jobs, which uses artificial intelligence to scroll for jobs on other job boards and anyone can use to search for a job on their Google web browser. It is now rather clumsy, but it will be a game changer, and I have dedicated the next two sections of this chapter to Google for Jobs and Hire by Google.

Here is my summary of the reviews. I encourage you to use these and other reviews to stay on top of this rapidly changing sector for recruiting. Remember, human resources and recruiting leaders and professionals need to be up on changing technology as much as they stay up-to-date on changes in the law, new economic and psychological research, organizational design and development, and sociodemographic changes.

Let's begin with SilkRoad and its Sources of Hire 2018 report.[217] Its report is based on a 2017 survey of one thousand participating companies with one hundred or more employers, including large enterprise organizations. Here is what they found.

Indeed is the most used job board, and Indeed's website claims that 200 million people visit its website every month. It scrolls job listings from thousands of websites, including company career sites, newspapers, and job boards. SilkRoad found that Indeed is the number-one external source for job posts for 50 percent of the one thousand companies covered in its survey, followed by LinkedIn, which was at 18 percent. Other job boards were at or below 6 percent, including Glassdoor and CareerBuilder, which barely held their ground against third-party search, campus recruiting, and company career pages. Based on SilkRoad research, Indeed provides six times more hires than any other job site.

Indeed uses artificial intelligence to scroll other job sites to list the openings on its site, and companies can also post jobs there. Indeed also uses text apps to ask job candidates basic job qualification questions so it can rank job candidates for recruiters. Companies can pay to promote their jobs on Indeed through sponsored jobs in order to find more qualified candidates faster. Sponsored jobs are the first jobs applicants see in Indeed search results, and they receive up to five times as many clicks, according to Indeed's website. Companies can also promote their company page on Indeed.

One other note for CareerBuilder: it might be described as the most efficient job board based on the applicants–to-hire ratio from the SilkRoad survey. Its ratio was 77:1 as compared to 106:1 for Glassdoor, 116:1 for Hire by Google, 130:1 for Indeed, and 148:1 for LinkedIn.

However, it is important to put this in perspective. Based on SilkRoad's research, the number one for hires and those interviewed are employee referrals. Employee referrals accounted for 54 percent of those hired by companies. Recruiter-sourced candidates were second at 15 percent, and Indeed was third at 12 percent. The rest, including third-party search, campus recruiting, company career sites, Glassdoor, and CareerBuilder were all at or below 6 percent.

This point is worth dwelling on even in a chapter on job boards. Your best source for high-caliber talent is from offline sources, and the number-one offline resource already works for you. They are your employees. Another great source is your former employees, either to rejoin your company or to make referrals. If you are struggling to find qualified job candidates, take a look at your referral program. It may be time to raise the incentive for successful referrals.

The best of these job boards, like Indeed, are rapidly expanding their investment in digital technology to screen candidates, often through text exchanges, before you see the résumés. Many of these job boards compete by providing career advice to the job seekers, such as advice on writing résumés or a software to help write and format the résumé, salary comparisons, and reports on trends.

Craigslist is still involved as one of the least expensive places to post open positions, but it also is rated as providing among the lowest number and quality of applicants.

Let's look at another survey on job boards, this one by Brian

Westfall and Software Advice, which can be found at https:// www.softwareadvice.com/resources/.

In Software Advice's 2013 Recruiting Channels Survey,[218] they found that traditional job boards delivered the highest volume of candidates to recruiters. Software Advice surveyed one hundred fifty recruiters with the help of the Recruitment Process Outsourcing Association, iCIMS, Jobvite, HRsmart, PCRecruiter, RPO Association, and the National Human Resources Association to identify the best job boards.

Here are their key findings.

1. LinkedIn and Indeed deliver the highest quality of applicants at an affordable price range. LinkedIn delivers by far the highest-quality applicants at a medium cost—as well as a high quantity of applicants, second only to Indeed (and not by much).
2. Craigslist is the least expensive but delivers lower quantity and quality of candidates than other job boards.

Software Advice asked recruiters to rate the quality level of the applicants they received through each job board. According to their survey, the majority (40 percent) of recruiters noted that LinkedIn delivers "high-quality" applicants. The runners-up, CareerBuilder and Indeed, were described as delivering "high-quality" job candidates by only 17 percent and 13 percent of recruiters, respectively. On the other end of the spectrum, Monster, Craigslist, and Glassdoor delivered the fewest "high-quality" candidates.

Craigslist was the least expensive option to use. LinkedIn's ratings on costs were all over, from as low as Craigslist to high costs, which may be due to the variety of plans LinkedIn offers recruiters, from $50 to $899 a month. On the other hand, Monster and CareerBuilder were the most likely to be rated as "high-cost" options.

The Software Advice survey also inquired about which job boards are best based on job levels. Indeed, CareerBuilder, and Craigslist were most effective for recruiting candidates for entry-level positions. Recruiters reported on the Software Advice survey that LinkedIn and Indeed were the most effective job boards when seeking candidates for mid- and senior-level positions. But while LinkedIn and Indeed were rated similarly in their effectiveness when recruiting for midlevel positions, when it came to senior-level positions, LinkedIn jumped ahead. According to the survey, 37 percent of respondents said LinkedIn was "very effective" for recruiting for senior-level positions, compared to just 11 percent rating Indeed as "very effective" for sourcing senior-level candidates. Meanwhile, recruiters noted that Craigslist was the least effective for recruiting candidates for positions at higher levels of responsibility.

There are several specialty job boards that I have used in the past. I have also rounded out this list by going to Google and typing in the profession, such as "clinical research" or "marketing" plus (+) "job search site" or "job website" and seeing what comes up. If you are looking for job boards outside of the United States, use the same technique but add the country name at the end of the phrase, like this: "marketing job websites in Australia."

Here is a short list of niche or specialty job websites to use.
Specialty Job Websites

Industry	Website	Comments
Biotech	BioSpace	I used successfully.
	CenterWatch	
	Medzilla	I used successfully.
Construction	Construction Jobs	
	Proven	
Engineering	Engineering	
	EngineerJobs	I used successfully.
	IEEE Job Site	I used successfully.
Executives	Nurole	
	The Ladders	I used successfully

	ExecuNet	
	Experteer	
Finance	eFinancialCareers	
High-level professionals	The Ladders	I used successfully
Marketing	MarketingHire	
	Talent Zoo	
Medical	HealthECareers.com	
Nonprofits	Idealists.com	
Programming	StackOverflow.com	
Restaurants	PoachedJobs.com	
Sales	Sales Gravy	
	SalesJobs.com	
Start-ups	Angel.co	
Tech	Dice	I used successfully.
	JustTechJobs	
	TechCareers	

Here are some other tips on working with websites. I advise you to open a dedicated email account for employment websites, so you avoid all the résumés and spam on your professional email account. You may also want to use free Google Voice phone numbers for applications.

Google for Jobs

Google for Jobs was launched in 2017. It is similar to Indeed. com, which pulls job listings from many different sources. The difference is that Google is pulling the job listings for the review of the job seeker, and Google's technology will power the search results. The purpose of Google for Jobs is to make job search easier for job candidates. Job candidates can go to Google and click "Google for Jobs," type in "software engineers in Minneapolis," and view job openings in a dedicated space at the top of the search results. Job candidates can use Google for Jobs to search for jobs using various filters, such as city, date posted, company name, and job category.

Google for Jobs is built on the Google Cloud Jobs API. It uses machine learning to understand how job titles and skills relate to one another and what job content, location, and seniority are the closest match to a job candidate's preferences. Google for Jobs combines the Cloud Jobs API with its powerful search engine features and puts it in the hands of job seekers. Google partnered with recruitment giants such as CareerBuilder, Monster, LinkedIn, and Glassdoor, to name a few.

One of the biggest obstacles for Google was the huge number of inconsistencies between industries and organizations in job titles and keywords used in job descriptions. The same job can have very different titles from company to company in the same industry and between industries. For example, the title "deputy program manager" in one company can have the title "program director" in another company in the same industry and location, with the same skill set and required years of experience. Google research found that you can search for a job like "truck driver" and find that the results obtained in FedEx, UPS, and other delivery services are totally different. They each use different words to describe that very job, so you must spend a lot of time searching each company's website to find the job you want. This same problem has given applicant tracking systems fits for years as their often-antiquated search algorithms were not able to bridge different job titles to identify qualified candidates.

Google, like all Artificial Intelligence platforms, used its taxonomy, search algorithms, and Google's Natural Language processing algorithms to read job descriptions and find out that "truck driver" and "delivery manager" are the same job across millions of jobs to train the algorithm over time. Their experimental work with early customers has been amazing: one client found that searches for "genetic engineering research" jobs barely surfaced a single job before using the Google technology; after using the Google search, the perfect job popped up in the first page.[219]

Google believes its machine learning will provide the job seeker all the relevant job postings despite this difference in titles because of the work of its machine learning to decipher the different titles by looking at the job description.

Job seekers can click to read job descriptions and apply to jobs right from Google for Jobs. Job candidates can share job postings with friends and read about companies and their employer brands.

For companies, it is designed to make it easier for job seekers to find your open positions and apply for your openings. The job candidates will also see your company's logo reviews, ratings, and job description.

How to Get Your Jobs Posted on Google for Jobs

Google for Jobs is not a job board. It is an Artificial Intelligence enhanced search tool. There is no way to actually post jobs on Google for Jobs. Instead, it scrapes and features job postings that are already published. When you post your job openings on job boards that have integrated with Google for Jobs, such as ZipRecruiter, Snagajob, Monster, Jibe, DirectEmployers, America's Job Exchange, Madgex, WayUp, myCNAjobs, Higher Education Recruitment Consortium, Jora, Jobing.com., Local Job Network, Care.com, Jobs. net, and Recruiting.com, the jobs automatically appear in Google for Jobs.[220]

Employers can also integrate directly with Google to have their jobs posted if you have a career page on your website. You do this by editing the HTML on your website's career page to post on Google for Jobs. Google provides a summary on how to do this at https:// developers.google.com/search/docs/data-types/job-posting.

As with anything that you want to be searchable on the internet, you need to optimize the posting, in this case your job opening, for search engines to rank your job higher in search results than the competition. Here are some search engine optimization (SEO) techniques to improve the Google rankings of your job listings.

How to improve the SEO of your job postings on Google for Jobs

- Use relevant keywords and phrases that pertain to your job description and job title.
- Avoid jargon and write clear job titles that candidates are likely to be searching for.
- Create a visual experience with photos and videos.
- Write brief job ads that include bulleted lists.

Hire by Google

Hire by Google is a service to enable recruiters to better use a company's existing candidate database, such as an applicant tracking system. Before the launch of Hire, Google launched Google for Jobs to help job seekers to use Google to find jobs. Now Google is turning to serve recruiters. According to TechCrunch,[221] to better mine this pool of past job applicants, the new so-called "candidate discovery" looks at the job description, title, and location of a job ad and matches that to a list of past candidates. Hire uses the company's search smarts to better understand the recruiter's intent. That means that the service can easily parse a job's location, for example, even if it isn't explicitly specified in a location field but only part of the text.

Hire by Google is also adding three new machine learning features to help reduce repetitive, time-consuming tasks, like scheduling interviews, into one-click interactions.[222] By using Google's machine learning, Hire now automatically suggests ideal time slots for interviews. If an interviewee cancels last minute, Hire will alert users, as well as recommend available replacement interviewers and send them an invite.

Hire will also now auto-highlight résumés by having its machine learning watch recruiters and hiring managers interact with its software. Google says it found that employers were constantly using "Ctrl+F" to search résumés and then highlight key phrases. Based on their machine learning, Google targets this as a repetitive, manual task that could easily be automated. Hire now uses its machine learning to analyze the terms in a job description or search query and auto-highlights them on résumés, including synonyms and acronyms. I am a little suspicious of this capability after having to correct inappropriate words in my email or texts that were inserted by machine learning as part of its spell-check. It isn't perfect.

Hire also now has a "click-to-call" functionality that automatically logs calls to keep track of candidate phone numbers and help recruiters know which candidates they have already spoken with.

Video Interviewing

Many companies have been using video interviewing as an alternative to the phone screen and even as the interview with the hiring manager before deciding to bring a candidate on campus for an interview. Now the best of these platforms offer scheduling and on-demand interviewing.

When I worked at Medtronic, we contracted with GreenJob Interview to conduct face-to-face interviews for remote candidates. We used video interviewing in place of the telephone screen by recruiters and as a first interview with the hiring manager and sometimes one other member of management. We found it a very helpful tool for screening candidates before making the costly decision to fly candidates to our location for a site visit and a day of interviewing. GreenJobInterview provides the option to record interviews, which can be handy when you are trying to recall some candidates' answers to a question or for using part of the video in reviews of top candidates.

The company also offers customized video introduction for interviews and a scheduling function and has an app to be used on smartphones. They also provide a technical screen using predetermined questions that the candidate answers on a prepared video interview, allowing all selected candidates to answer the same question and saving time for the interviewers. GreenJobInterview provides a prepopulated bank of questions to ask during an interview.

There are estimates that 60 percent of companies are using video interview, whether on systems like Skype and Zoom or by companies offering such services such as Jobvite. Other video screening companies include Wepow, Hire Value, and RIVS Digital Interviewing, which has applicant tracking system integration with Taleo, iCIMS, Kenexa, ADP, and AppliTrack.

There are a myriad of other job interviewing platforms available, such as RecRight, VideoBIO Recruiter, Spark Hire, and EasyHire to name a few.

Many of these companies, like Wepow, enable companies to share video content about their culture and work environment and to feature employee stories. The Wepow platform also allows the recruiter to personalize the invitation to specific job candidates and to allow job candidates to practice interviewing on camera. In addition, the interview can be recorded.

Video screening is not just for large companies. Small companies have found it helpful as well because of the time and money saved, which is handy with slim HR support.

Wepow co-founder and CEO Imo Udom is excited about how digital technology can solve problems. "HR leaders for a long time would come slowly to technology because they heard it was the thing to do," he told me in a recent interview. "Now, more of them use technology because they understand it makes them more efficient by reducing their costs and time-to-fill and improving the quality of their hires."

Video interviewing was originally used because the interviewer could see the job candidate and watch their reaction to questions and to save job candidates travel time and companies the cost of reimbursing candidates for air travel. Now, Imo explains, prerecorded or on-demand interviews are becoming more popular because they avoid the nightmare of scheduling—even with an app doing most of the scheduling.

Imo shared a key experience of Adidas, one of Wepow's first

customers, who now uses Wepow for over sixty different job openings. "Adidas had to conduct interviews in December 2011, a very busy month. They set up with us a prerecorded interview of five questions on Thursday and sent it to two hundred fifty job applicants. By Monday, Adidas had a staggering two hundred forty-seven responses, or 99 percent, of the targeted candidates complete their interview. Now Adidas has expanded its prerecorded video interviewing for much of its campus recruiting."

Another success Imo likes to talk about is how Gallaudet University, a school for the deaf and hearing impaired, began using Wepow to conduct interviews so they could see the job candidate sign. Previously, they had to use signing interpreters, which added cost and delays.

Imo cautions HR leaders about using technology to read facial expressions and to make judgments about authentic answers or judgments about a candidate's skills and capabilities. First, determining who is exaggerating the truth and who is telling the truth by reading facial expressions can be tricky and not reliable. Second, many artificial intelligence technologies perpetuate stereotypes because they are based on mostly white and male video libraries. He recommends HR leaders use technology in the *ironman* approach, not the *terminator* approach. That is, use technology as a tool to augment human decision-making, not in place of it.

Webow was acquired by Outmatch on Jan. 9, 2019.[223]

While video technology is growing in popularity, many job applicants are still warming up to it. The fault many job candidates make is failing to understand that this is a real job interview and should be treated as such. Many candidates make the mistake of not dressing for the virtual interview as if they were showing up in the company's offices. Other candidates (and even interviewers) have issues with personal hygiene, such as not combing their hair or even picking their nose while on camera. Another mistake is not having the proper lighting so there is no glare or shadows over the person's face. Finally, be aware of what people can see on your desk. Is it messy and gives a bad impression, or are sensitive documents sitting on your desk? Also, be mindful of what is behind you. A basket of dirty underwear behind you doesn't make for a good impression.

Companies rate videoconferencing software. The companies that rate video-conferencing software include g2 crowd, at g2crowd.com,/categories/video-conferencing, Capterra, at https://www.capterra.com/web-conferencing-software/, and FinancesOnline at https://communications-software.financesonline.com/c/video-conferencing-software.

When reviewing online reviews of whatever product, from hotel ratings to videoconferencing software, always ask how the company gets money to sustain its business and make a product. If you are getting a rating service for free, you are the product. More specifically, data from you and about you is the company's product to the vendors on its service. Always ask if the product or software is paying a service to the rating company, if the company is receiving a finder's fee if the vendor recommends the product to you or if the rating company has invested in the product or software. I also recommend you see how long the company has been in business and if it has any financial issues or ethical issues. You can do this by Googling the company, checking out the company on TechCrunch, and reading articles about the company on Yahoo Finance if it is publicly traded.

Capterra rates a wide range of software (over one hundred products) based on user reviews, which it validates, and also uses independent research to validate its reviews. It provides reviews for software from account-receiving software, applicant tracking software, big data software, bookkeeping software, clinical trial software, legal billing software, and so on.

Capterra was founded in 1999 and is based in Arlington, Virginia. For videoconferencing software, I set its online filter to companies with four reviews and up, over one thousand users, web-based deployment, and the following features: archiving, candidate portal, feedback management, invitations, one-on-one interviews, practice sessions, question bank, recording, scoring, and virtual/prerecorded interviews.

Capterra is a free product, meaning you are the product for them. Capterra says its website says they are free because of the following:

> Capterra is **free for users** because vendors pay us when they receive web traffic and sales opportunities. Capterra lists **all** vendors—not just those that pay us—so that you can make the best-informed purchase decision possible.
>
> We provide every vendor the opportunity to showcase their products and collect user reviews. Being the most comprehensive and helpful resource for software buyers has been our mission since we started in 1999. Our complete software lists, verified user reviews, sort and filter tools, and articles are all available to help in your task of finding the right solution for your needs.

Chatbots and Mobile Apps

The chatbots available today are amazing and will truly hack recruiting. Chatbots are another alternative to the phone screen or video interviewing, and they are also used to enable job candidates to better navigate career center websites, to schedule job interviews, and to begin the onboarding process.

A chatbot is a computer program that often uses human programming to recognize common questions about job openings and recruiting and then generates an automated response back to the job candidate. The second-generation chatbots have begun to use artificial intelligence with machine learning to simulate conversations with a human being, either using text or voice. When AI or machine learning is used, the software will actually learn the trends of questions and preferences by different job family openings, by recruiter, and by job candidate.

You or a friend have probably interacted with chatbots to place a pizza order by using Amazon's Alexa. Maybe you asked Apple's Siri to make a phone call or asked Siri a question, such as "Who is in the move *The Black Panther*?" Or asked for driving directions from Google (which has not named its chatbot) or of Microsoft's Cortana.

Chatbots are the new app. They are being used in business to help improve interactions with clients and customers and on websites. If you interact with an apartment website to find a new apartment it might not be a human being whom you are chatting with but a chatbot.

According to Jobvite, 43 percent of recruiters use texting to reach out to job candidates or current applicants, and 88 percent report positive feedback from the job seeker (and 4 percent negative feedback). But different generations have slightly different attitudes about receiving a text. Among Generation Z (who are now leaving college), 46 percent like it. Among millennials, 43 percent like it. Among baby boomers, 36 percent like it.[224] Frankly, I was surprised the positive feedback from baby boomers was that high.

Many job boards and applicant tracking systems frequently cite mobile activity from smartphones or tablets to their sites is 50 percent or more. Companies need to be sure their website career pages are smartphone and app friendly.

In fact, according to Indeed, nearly 80 percent of millennials and Generation X prefer using mobile phones and apps to find jobs. Baby boomers have gotten hip to this and now use their mobile phones 57 percent of the time to find jobs. However, not all professions search online equally. Engineers and architects are the lowest users of mobile job search but still at 50 percent. The United States does not lead the way with mobile job search.[225] That leadership goes to Asian countries, such as South Korea, Taiwan, and Japan, with over 80 percent mobile job searching.

This technology is now being applied to recruiting widely, especially with nonexempt roles and entry-level exempt roles. Many employers who are beginning to use the technology are using it as an app to text job candidates.

Companies are using chatbots to accelerate the recruiting process. Many employers use it as an app to text job candidates. Chatbots are reaching out to identified candidates to request a résumé, schedule an interview, ask candidates to respond to a short list of screening questions, make an offer, and even to begin the onboarding process with new hires.

TextRecruit and Olivia were the first to market chatbots for recruiting. They set up platforms that would send texts to job candidates who applied to jobs on a company's career site or to postings or purchased résumés from job boards, such as Indeed or CareerBuilder, and asked the job candidate if they were interested in a specific job. If the answer was yes, they would then set up an interview. They have expanded to include entry-level screening questions. Later the applicant tracking system iCIMS purchased TextRecruit, making their system more interactive with job candidates. TextRecruit now also provides candidates updates on their status in the recruiting process.

A more sophisticated chatbot for entry-level recruiting and more recent entrant to the chatbot market is AllyO. The company markets itself as a high-volume, end-to-end artificial intelligence recruiter that makes a company's recruiting more efficient by working with companies to set up end-to-end recruiting workflows and by automated conversations by text or web chat. AllyO's end-to-end definition is from "Hello" to a new job candidate all the way to a ninety-day new hire experience chat. The bot conversations screen applicants and collect personal contact information. AllyO enters the candidates' qualifications and contact information into the company's applicant tracking system without the candidate having to register. AllyO screens the candidates into qualification tiers, such as highly qualified, meets qualifications, or unqualified. AllyO's AI can also direct disqualified candidates to positions that may be a better job match.

AllyO uses AI to scrape the company's career site's job postings to identify job requirements and competencies. Recruiters also provide AllyO specifics on job requirements, such as years of experience. AllyO also collects and posts measures analytics on job applicants and the recruiting process.

AllyO provides a solution for overburdened recruiters by providing candidates with feedback and engagement throughout the recruiting process. In addition, AllyO reaches out to candidates as a recruiter would after an interview and asks, "How did it go?" AllyO can maintain communications through the offer, hiring, and onboarding process. Companies using AllyO have a candidate NPS (net promoter score) of 94 percent. It also can "chat" on conversation apps such as WhatsApp.

AllyO provided me a demonstration on a smartphone comparing a job candidate who went online to a career site with AllyO web chat and to one without an AllyO web chat. In the demonstration, the AllyO web chat greets the job searcher and asks which jobs he or she is looking for. It then directs the candidate to those postings and asks questions about the candidate's experience, education, which industries he or she has worked in, and if offered a position, when the candidate could start the new role. Depending on the answers to the questions, AllyO provides feedback, and if the candidate meets the minimal criteria, calendars an interview with the hiring manager.

According to David Bernstein, the head of partnerships for AllyO, the interface between recruiters and bots is becoming seamless. David noted that the platform's calendaring feature is more sophisticated than most and has the capability to schedule multiple interviews with a candidate in a continuous block of time, such as an afternoon. AllyO also offers a human feature during a web chat when the AI cannot figure out the candidate's question or provide a confident answer. AllyO's AI then involves a human recruiter to work through the discussion.

AllyO offers the following features:

- Their platform's conversational job matching can increase the capture and application rates on your career sites by two to six times.

- Their AI can screen and assess candidates for the best-fit roles and eliminate the drop-off rate from your career site to under 5 percent.
- They can automate interview scheduling for multi-interviews, not the simple scheduling of Calendly.
- They can automate offer extensions.
- They can automate post-hire check-ins and gather actionable insights to improve retention by 30 percent.

The company's website claims to have a 91 percent application completion rate with the use of their platform, a decrease in time to hire of 50 percent, and a decrease in cost to hire of 60 percent. The company states that 95 percent of job applicants complete the application with AllyO, compared to only 28 percent for a career center without AllyO. Company career centers with AllyO have a net promoter score (NPS) from job candidates of 94 percent.

AllyO has recently won some impressive industry awards, such as the 2018 Top HR Product Award from Human Resources Executive. Their clients in the restaurant industry include Chili's, Five Guys, Black Angus, Panda Express, and Arby's. Retail clients include Walmart and Michael's, industry clients Marathon Oil and Pitney Bowes, hospitality clients Hilton and Ocean Resort Casinos, and health care client Premise Health.

At IBM, Watson is used as a chatbot to assist job candidates who visit IBM's career site. Candidates who apply for jobs at IBM start an engagement with Watson, which walks them through the application process, including pulling in a candidate's LinkedIn profile. It then matches the profile to open IBM jobs (based on a Watson-developed success profile). Watson offers a personalized experience to candidates. It provides information to candidates about IBM's culture and environment.

According to Amber Grewal, vice president of IBM Global Talent Acquisition, who spoke at FPL Partners' "Automating Tomorrow's Workforce" panel on November 9, 2017, IBM learned that 86 percent of candidates use Watson over their own search of IBM jobs. Ninety-six percent looked at Watson's recommendations. The number of IBM job applicants has increased by 35 percent with the use of Watson. IBM has also seen an increase in the diversity of their applicants. Amber believes that Watson also has reduced unconscious bias. Watson is also used to answer new hire questions during onboarding.

For an illustrating example of a verbal conversational chatbot, I suggest you go to https://www.youtube.com/watch?v=D-5VN56jQMWM on YouTube and watch Google CEO Sundar Pichai demonstrate two examples of Google's new chatbot that uses a virtual assistant to mimic the sound and feel of a human voice—not a robotic voice. In the scenarios, the human-sounding chatbot interacts with a human being and can handle the nuances of the human conversations very smoothly. In the first example, the chatbot is scheduling a woman's haircut appointment at a salon. In the second example, the chatbot called to make reservations at a restaurant, only to learn that reservations are not taken on the day the client wanted for dinner. The chatbot processed the new information and then asked if the restaurant would be busy at the time of the appointment and the availability. The restaurant receptionist had a thick accent, but the chatbot could understand what she was saying. It is very impressive.

Are job candidates interested in using chatbots? My sense is that younger candidates may be interested in using chatbots for nonexempt and entry-level exempt positions.

Some chatbot providers loosely use the term *artificial intelligence* in talking about their capability. They are usually programmed by human beings and only now are beginning to have some artificial intelligence or machine learning capability. Chatbots usually recognize a few words and then ask questions based on that. For example, they may see the words "two bedrooms" on an apartment website and then ask, "Would you like to see our two-bedroom floor plans?" Chatbots usually interact with humans on a predetermined set of words or libraries to check for a set of patterns that they can respond to. This is pattern matching, not full-fledged artificial intelligence or machine learning. They are in essence only as good as the human programmers who created them.

However, machine learning is being applied more and more to chatbots and will increase their capability.

BI Intelligence reports that apps are now more widely used than social networks. In 2015 the biggest four messaging apps surpassed the big four social networking apps in usage. With the rise of messaging apps and chatbots, the way we are using social media to interact and share is changing. Studies consistently show that smartphone users have condensed their time into some of their favorite apps, often a browser, a couple of chats, social apps, and maybe a few games. With shrinking opportunities to make money from mobile apps, developers are looking forward to chatbots as a new path.[226] Chatbots are free to use, and we can chat with them by simply sending them a message as if they were a human user.

Is It Time to Let Artificial Intelligence Improve Recruiting?

Can human resources leaders use artificial intelligence (AI) platforms to manage recruiting in the same way marketing executives use customer relationship management (CRM) systems to find, nurture, and win over new clients?

We have heard the hype about AI. Now we are learning more about its capabilities to be a game changer in recruiting. Before turning to new AI platforms, let's look at recruiting today.

A 2017 study by Deloitte found that 33 percent of survey respondents already used some form of artificial intelligence in the hiring process to save time and reduce bias.[227] LinkedIn's Global Recruiting Trends for 2018 found that 56 percent of companies in their survey rated as very important the use of new interviewing tools, 50 percent rated the use data as very important, and 35 percent rated the use of artificial intelligence as very important.[228] However, only 8 percent of companies in the survey currently used AI, and only 18 percent currently used data and new interviewing tools in their recruiting processes. These data suggest we are in the middle of a major transition in how we go about recruiting—and that human resources leaders are resistant to using what will be inevitable: artificial intelligence in recruiting.

While the empirical evidence to demonstrate the effectiveness and return on investment of AI platforms may be years away, today there are AI platforms that can find and match external candidates to your jobs in seconds as opposed to a weeklong search on job boards and LinkedIn. Furthermore, these platforms claim to be much better at matching current candidates and employees to a company's open jobs than most applicant tracking systems. They may also help reduce unconscious bias while recruiting.

I have used AI in recruiting and was amazed at how quickly it was able to identify highly qualified job candidates. Well-researched and developed AI systems can save recruiters a lot of time. However, the process that comes next is the cold call. That is, contacting the desired passive job candidates from the AI list, who may not know your company or brand, and getting their attention and giving them a reason to consider your job and company. If your brand is subpar or little known, you will struggle to develop much of an interest. So even with AI and digitization, recruiting is still a process that requires building relationships and understanding the careers and aspirational needs of the job candidates. AI enables you to find the qualified job candidates for a strategic talent pool, but without building relationships, you won't build a dependable strategic talent pool.

A current pitfall of some of these AI-generated candidate lists is their contact information. Almost all of the candidates will have a LinkedIn or Facebook email, but personal emails and phone numbers can be as low as 20 percent of candidates. While LinkedIn is a good platform to reach out to most professionals, I and many recruiters prefer personal emails and phone numbers. I am sure this capability will improve over time. In the meantime, there are ways to research emails and phone numbers on Twitter or to use online platforms such as VoilaNorbert, Prophet (a Google Chrome plug-in), or Email Hunter https://hunter.io/to name a few. These platforms usually allow a certain number of searches for free, and then there is a fee.

How Recruiting Works at ThisWay Global

ThisWay Global Founder and CEO, Angela Hood, says that after three years of research, and a second round of funding, her firm, now has dozens of clients in nearly as many countries. ThisWay Global was launched from IdeaSpace, of the University of Cambridge, England.

After recruiters upload a job description into ThisWay Global's cloud-based web application, its AI immediately kicks in to suggest refinements to the job description based on their machine learning. After the job description is finalized and reviewed by the recruiter, the recruiter presses a button, and in less than one second, ThisWay Global reveals a ranked and scored list of qualified candidates. Recruiters can easily transfer this list into existing applicant tracking systems and CRM platforms without integration.

Recruiters can adjust the required competencies along the way, allowing them to create their own signature AI so the technology learns their specific way of sourcing and recruiting. Each company is provided a "passport" they use to track their jobs and the progress of candidates through the application process. As the interview process unfolds, the recruiter can ask questions and provide notes for greater and easier machine learning. ThisWay Global's system can also administer screening tests and assessments as requested by the recruiter or employer. The AI creates a personalized algorithm for each job and the recruiter to augment the recruiter's intelligence over time. This is known as "augmented intelligence."

Companies can also upload performance history by job classifications to allow ThisWay Global's AI to define the competencies of its most successful performers and include these competencies on the job. Angela also points out that most applicant tracking systems (ATS) are not capable of matching internal talent to new job opportunities in that company. ThisWay Global's capability unlocks extraordinary value for staffing agencies, Recruiting Professional

Organizations (RPOs), and recruiters at large organizations. This is an excellent use for AI.

ThisWay Global began engaging with "beta" customers in 2017. Angela says that recruiters can get started with a onetime job posting for as little as $399 and receive up to twenty-five qualified candidate matches. Start-ups and small firms with low-volume recruiting often use this feature. Most of their initial beta clients were filling about ten jobs a month. However, their new product release has attracted large-volume staffing, RPO, and recruiters that are filling more than fifteen hundred jobs per month. ThisWay Global has pricing packages for ten, twenty-five, and fifty jobs per month and Enterprise-level volume pricing specials for one hundred to five thousand jobs per month. While stories of anecdotal success and higher returns on investment exist from their beta clients, it will be a few years before they will be able to conduct empirical analysis on retention with longitudinal results.

Angela believes that AI will be able to improve upon the "the Big Five" personality texting architecture with better, current, and unbiased data to further improve predictions of job performance and success on the job.

Ideal is another artificial intelligence recruiting software that promises to relieve recruiters of tedious administrative tasks and enable them to be more of a strategic force in recruiting. Ideal's website claims that their AI can make recruiters three times more efficient. Furthermore, it will improve the candidate experience with timely feedback (a step many recruiters or their administrators simply do not have the time to provide) and keep them engaged. They also claim to improve the quality of your hire and reduce bias in hiring decisions.

Applicant tracking systems such as SmartRecruiters have integrated Ideal as their AI recruiting platform.

Ideal highlights on their website the experience of their client Indigo. Indigo is Canada's largest book, music, and book-related gift store, with over ninety stores under its main brand and 126 smaller stores under various brand names. It has over six thousand employees and is expanding in the United States.

Indigo receives over twenty-two hundred online job applications per week. Management's goals were to reduce the time and cost of searching through résumés while maintaining their high candidate experience and continuing to cultivate their award-winning culture.

Other complications for Indigo were that its applicants generally applied for one single job, and their ATS could not determine if the applicant was qualified for a different role or the same role at a different store. Their hiring, like that of most retailers, is seasonal, resulting in sharp spikes in hiring activity when the retailer was also busy with advertising and supply chain issues. They also needed to hire applicants with various languages. Finally, store managers do most of the hiring in a very decentralized system.

What attracted Indigo to Ideal, according to Sarah Wilson, director of talent at Indigo, was its seamless integration with its existing ATS system, SmartRecruiters. "We really didn't want to give our managers another tool to master," according to Wilson, "so the fact that Ideal could operate within our existing ATS was fantastic."[229]

Within four months after using Ideal, Indigo saw the following very impressive results:

- **Candidate experience**
  Candidate wait times dropped significantly; top candidates are quickly identified and contacted.

- **Time to hire**
  Ideal freed up precious time for store leaders that they now use for high-value tasks such as face-to-face interviewing and relationship building.

- **Screening costs and cost per hire**
  Screening costs plummeted 75 percent, and overall cost per hire is down 71 percent.

+ **Rediscovered candidates**
  Qualified candidates doubled (+196 percent) as the talent
  pool was optimized.

**Other platforms, such as Entelo, enable companies to au-
tomate the tedious and time-consuming tasks associated
with sourcing.** By using artificial analytics and predictive analytics,
Entelo's software platform, called Envoy, identifies the candidates
who are the best fit for a company's posted jobs, queries the candidates about their interest, and delivers the résumés of the interested candidates directly to the hiring manager's or recruiter's inbox.
Entelo claims their AI will save recruiters hours and free them up to
do more value-added screening work.

Entelo also uses its AI to predict the likelihood of when someone
on LinkedIn is interested in a move in ninety days. They do this in
part by calculating the turnover of the job candidate's company and
then comparing the candidate's tenure to the average turnover rate.
In this way, they predict when the job candidate may be ready to
make a move. Entelo predicts the cost of a job candidate by having
their algorithm calculate the candidate's years of experience for their
job family in their region and then averaging the salaries in that job
market for the same level of experience.[230]

However, having an algorithm doesn't mean its predictions will
be true. Job candidates can have very different expectations about
pay based on their performance, the feedback from their managers,
their relationships with peers, expectations about promotions, the
school they attended, and their confidence. Job candidates can
have very different ideas about when to leave a current company
based on their perceptions of their skills, their emotional state of
mind, and their feelings toward a company. These perceptions and
emotions are not measured by an algorithm looking at tenure and
average turnover.

Entelo, like ThisWay Global and other AI search tools, allow recruiters to hide the names, genders, and addresses of candidates
to protect against racial or gender bias. However, if any AI tool is

allowing the machine to learn as it goes, it may be building in the biases of its original human programmers, the recruiters and hiring managers who use it, or the job candidates or subsets of job candidates in its databases.

Solon Borocas is an assistant professor in Cornell's Information Science department who studies fairness in machine learning. His research has found that machine learning in hiring, much like its use in facial recognition, can result in unintentional discrimination. Algorithms can carry the implicit biases of their programmers. Or they can be skewed to favor certain qualities and skills that are overwhelmingly exhibited among a given data set. "If the examples you're using to train the system fail to include certain types of people, then the model you develop might be really bad at assessing those people," Borocas explained in an article for Bloomberg.[231]

Companies who use AI for recruiting, and frankly all companies, need to measure the decisions made about their job candidates and hires to be sure they are hiring candidates who are great performers and that there is no unconscious bias or discrimination built into their decision making.

Sandeep Purwar, the founder and CEO of artificial intelligence bootstrap start-up Bevov, is focusing his AI technology to automate the recruiting process so that hiring managers and recruiters spend more time interviewing job candidates, saving themselves lots of time and making better hiring decisions. Sandeep explains that he named his company Bevov to signal his customers that they will "be the evolution" with artificial intelligence in recruiting.

"For most organizations," Sandeep explains, "the recruiting process is a mess." In addition, many job boards can provide recruiters and hiring managers with hundreds of résumés, but they are a poor match for the job—and screening all those résumés takes time."

Bevov will source job candidates from social media and dozens of job sites like other AI recruiting platforms, but they screen hiring-qualified candidates so they fit the culture of the company, hiring manager, and team. They have put a focus on automating the recruiting function, which Bevov divides into five steps:

1. Single integration of job applicants who apply for a job opening.
2. Résumé screening based on the criteria of a well-thought-out and thorough job description.
3. Automatic testing of the job candidates based on an interactive online test developed for each job.
4. The use of machine learning to improve the process every time a hiring manager or recruiter uses the process.
5. Selecting the top five applicants for the role.

Bevov provides the recruiter with metrics throughout the process, including how many candidates have viewed the job opening, how many have applied, those who passed the application test, those who failed, and the top five applicants. Recruiters can use Bevov to generate emails to candidates telling them the résumé has been received and status on the test and to schedule interviews using Calendly.

Sandeep explains that AI today has not reached the ideal state where the technology can fully automate and hire great candidates without recruiter and hiring manager involvement. Their goal is to streamline the process, improve job qualification and culture matching, and save time.

What IBM Watson Has to Say

Amber Grewal, vice president of IBM Global Talent Acquisition, believes that the use of artificial intelligence will greatly improve recruiting, the predictive analytics for recruiting, and business outcomes, and reduce biased decision-making in hiring decisions. Amber spoke at FPL Partners' "Automating Tomorrow's Workforce" panel at Dolby Laboratories in San Francisco on November 9, 2017.

Amber explained that Watson learns, understands, reasons, and makes decisions to augment the professional it serves and to drive better outcomes. It is not intended to replace the professional. She maintains that 80 percent of the data that help companies is their internal data. External data is currently too poorly connected to be of much help. IBM uses Watson to fundamentally change how they recruit. It is no longer based on which department has an open requisition or how many. Watson analyzes recruiting outcomes to recommend recruiting priorities based on IBM business needs. Watson can recommend to an IBM business which jobs to fill first and where HR should prioritize recruiting activity. With Watson, Amber explained, IBM reduced recruiting cycle time from one hundred twenty-five to forty-five days.

IBM also saw an increase in the diversity of their clients. Amber believes that Watson also reduced unconscious bias.

Watson is also used to answer new hire questions during onboarding. IBM is also beginning to use Watson as part of its talent management strategy. Watson delivers talent alerts to managers about giving feedback or providing recognition to employees.

Amber believes that the power of AI's augmented intelligence will "up-skill" the HR and recruiting function and relieve recruiters of the many current tedious duties of job candidate search.

Robots Are Now Conducting Interviews

Raghav Singh, the director of analytics at Korn Ferry Futurestep, who frequently writes for www.ere.net, posted on September 25, 2018, "Meet the Robot Recruiters," on how robots are now conducting interviews face-to-face.[232] The chatbots I have written about above all use text or email interactions. These chatbots use voice components with a robotic image on the screen.

Matilda is a small toy like robot, developed by LaTrobe University in Australia. It was originally developed to help dementia patients. Matilda can read human emotions and respond to them. It is being tested for conducting interviews for sales jobs. The developers claim that the AI built into it can analyze people's reactions and determine if a candidate would be qualified for a job, while being free from biases and prejudices. Raghav notes in his blog that being interviewed by a toy like robot seems bizarre and notes it is a prototype. There are currently many autonomous devices, according to Raghav, that interact with humans and read their emotions, such as Jibo, ElliQ, and Pepper, but they are not in the recruiting space.

Raghav notes that there are two AI robots that are entering the face-to-face recruiting space. The other is Vera. Vera was created by a Russian start-up called Stafory and uses its AI to select the most appropriate job candidates, calls the candidates, and asks initial screening questions and makes video interviews with the candidates. The developers claim Vera can recognize job candidate emotions. Vera has also been covered by the *Economic Times*. Their report is on YouTube at https://www.youtube.com/watch?v=w9P-FVIHZ_AY. It feels a little cheeky to me, but these prototypes are just getting started.

Raghav also highlights apps that are chatbots, such as Replika and WoeBot, that can emote much like the chatbot in the movie *Her*. They are not visual but use a human voice to interact with people. These apps are not currently directed for recruiting, but Raghav notes that this type of functionality could well become more adept at screening candidates and drawing out details that humans may struggle to do consistently.

HireVue is a company that enables clients to set up pre-recorded video interviews and uses its AI to assess a job candidates answers and personality traits, tone of voice, body movements and vocabulary as it interviews job candidates. I first referenced HireVue in chapter 11, HR Geek: Additional Important Issues, under "How to Tell If a Job Candidate Is Lying to You."

During a November 14, 2018, webinar, Dr. Nathan Mondragon, HireVue's chief IO Psychologist, and Clemens Airchholzer, HireVue's SVP of game-based assessments, stated that HireVue's methodologies are based on a combination of cognitive testing, personality testing, communication skills, and job competency skills, and games—all in one experience for the job candidate—to look for the right candidates that who would perform as well as other recent hires. The officials claim that HireVue does not use facial recognition technology. However, in other posts on its website, which I will go through below, it says it uses expression technology and studies tone of voice, vocabulary and body movements to also make judgements on job candidates. The officials stated that HireVue has validated its tests with previous clients for four job families: retail clerks, sales, call centers, and software programmers. It did not, however, make public its validation results.

According to a November 14, 2018, white paper, "The Next Generation of Assessments," downloaded from its website, HireVue has used its AI and IO Psychology understanding to create on-demand, validated video interviews that are fifteen to thirty minutes long, much shorter than traditional assessments. The video interview assessments are based on the content of the job candidate's speech, the intonation, inflection, and other audio cues of how they say their words, and what they do while speaking. Specifically, the assessments examine the expressions a candidate portrays, particularly in relation to what is being said at the time. By using their ever-growing data, HireVue believes that it can detect adverse impact and remove it from consideration. Additionally, it can continue to refine its selection criteria as its AI continues to learn.

The advantage it gives its corporate customers is that its AI can conduct initial screens of job candidates faster than recruiters. HireVue says that its customers can remove steps like résumé resume reviews, phone screens, and traditional assessments from their recruiting processes, but does recommend that the next interviews be person-to-person. The company maintains that on-demand video interviewing allows candidates to schedule interviews when it is convenient for them.

HireVue uses structured interviewing with its AI, following best practices form Industrial Organizational Psychology, However, its analysis of facial expressions, tones of voice, vocabulary, and body movement is controversial, whether it is called facial recognition technology or something else, because many researchers believe these technologies, and even the more basic AI screening of resumes is biased. More on this controversy below.

HireVue's over seven hundred customers have completed close to one million assessments since the company started selling the service four years ago. In a promising development, HireVue maintains that its own customer base has become more diverse thanks to AI, but the company hasn't polled its entire user base to see if the same holds true across the board.

On HireVue's website is an interesting case study: "How an 'Interview First' Hiring Strategy Empowers Job Seekers and Promotes Diversity,"[233] which describes how its video interviewing technology "Introduce Yourself" is used by Children's Mercy Hospital (CMH) in Kansas City. Instead of requiring the job applicant to fill out a job application for specific jobs, CMH encourages job applicants to complete an "Introduce Yourself" video interview. Applicants who opt into the video interview are asked two questions:

1.   What are your skills and experience?
2.   What would you like to do for Children's Mercy?

Every morning two CMH staffers review the previous day's introductions and refer them to recruiters in the appropriate department. Those recruiters contact the job seeker and point them in the direction of the right application. Job seekers who are not a fit are sent a "Not a fit" response the next day. After the department recruiter reviews the résumé, the job applicant is told about a fit and is then directed where to apply (avoiding a long search of job listings) or is told "let's keep in touch." From there the process is rather standard. The blog states that with this approach, CMH increased its diverse hires by 58 percent, from 18 percent to 28 percent.

The advantages are that it helps job seekers find the jobs they are looking for and reduces the amount of time a job applicant is dedicating to filling out a job application.

HireVue maintains that its methodology improves the candidate experience and the net promoter score for its clients. As of 1.5 million candidates that who have gone through the HireVue experience, HireVue claims the following successes:

- Eighty percent enjoyed the experience and appreciated the opportunity to differentiate themselves.
- Eighty-five percent thought it reflected well on the employer's brand.
- Seventy percent rated the experience as 9 or 10 out of 10.
- Eighty-nine percent said it respected their time.

Face recognition technology, and I would add emotion recognition technology, is controversial. HireVue points to data they have collected and analyzed to make the claim that their AI will accurately assess candidates and is not discriminatory. I appreciate that HireVue compares the interviews of job candidates with the company's best employees, but I am curious as to whether HireVue researchers used control and experimental groups in making their claims, how large the samples were, and the statistical significance of the analysis. However, they are not releasing their information and analysis, which would be done if they had conducted an empirical, academic study. They are keeping it close to the vest. While they have good testimonials from clients such as Unilever, under US law a company is under great risk of being sued for discriminatory hiring practices if it does not use validated assessments. I would like HireVue to publicly publish its data and results in a white paper or to submit it them to an academic publication for peer- review and publication, like real science. Until that is done, we won't know for sure.

Does AI and Facial Recognition Technology Lead to Bias in Hiring?

According to Ifeoma Ajunwa, sociologist and law professor at Cornell University, the impact of a widely used algorithm in hiring among hundreds of employers is potentially more

damaging than a biased recruiter. In an interview with the *Wall Street Journal*, she cautions that microexpressions are still developing science, and there are no clear established patterns for what facial expression is needed for jobs. Applicants may be incorrectly rejected.[234]

Joy Buolamwini, a Rhodes scholar, Fulbright fellow, and researcher at the M.I.T. Media Lab has documented how some of the biases in the real world can seep into artificial intelligence, the computer systems that inform facial recognition.[235] She studied the performance of three leading face recognition systems—by using Microsoft, IBM, and Megvii of China—by classifying how well they could identify the gender of people with different skin tones. These companies were selected because they offered gender classification features in their facial analysis software — and their code was publicly available for testing. The results varied somewhat. Microsoft's error rate for darker-skinned women was 21 percent, while IBM's and Megvii's rates were nearly 35 percent. They all had error rates below 1 percent for light-skinned males.

Ms. Buolamwini shared the research results with each of the companies. IBM said in a statement to her that the company had steadily improved its facial analysis software and was "deeply committed" to "unbiased" and "transparent" services. The company said, it will roll out an improved service with a nearly 10-fold increase in accuracy on darker-skinned women.[236] Microsoft said that it had "already taken steps to improve the accuracy of our facial recognition technology" and that it was investing in research "to recognize, understand and remove bias."[237]

Even without facial or expression recognition technology, machine learning or AI software can be biased, towards men. According to Reuters, Amazon.com Inc's. machine learning specialists uncovered that its system was not rating candidates for software developer jobs and other technical posts in a gender-neutral way.[238] That is because Amazon's computer models were trained to vet applicants by observing patterns in resumes submitted to the company over a 10-year period. Most came from men, a reflection of male dominance across the tech industry. The company disbanded the system in 2017 because executives lost hope for the project, according to the people who spoke on the condition of anonymity. Amazon did not make hiring decisions solely on the systems recommendations.[239]

Companies are using AI to make judgments on personalities.

Deepsense.AI is an artificial intelligence company that builds AI solutions for real-time applications across a wide range of areas, such as market forecasting, cross selling, fraud detection, radical personalization, anomaly detection, and much more. It also uses artificial intelligence in recruiting. It scans social media and then makes work-related judgments about a candidate's personality and fitness for a role. The candidate may never know his or her Facebook, LinkedIn, and Twitter postings are being scanned. It is legal as the information is public. Its ethics are another question.

Deepsense.AI has its own personality test that it also uses to make judgments on what its AI reads on social media about people. Has it been validated for making hiring decisions? They aren't talking. It measures four traits: steadiness, dominance, compliance, and influence. According to Jason Bellini in his *Wall Street Journal* video story on Deepsense, his test results varied on two of these four traits: compliance and influence.[240] Two Fortune 500 companies are using Deepsense.AI. They did not release their data to Jason Bellini.

How Receptive Is Human Resources to AI?

Some surveys suggest that the human resources community is lukewarm to begin to use AI. In January 2018, LinkedIn completed its Global Recruiting Trends Report 2018, which surveyed nine thousand recruiters and hiring managers across the globe in 2017.[241]

One of the findings of the report was that only 35 percent of talent professionals and hiring managers said that AI was the top trend impacting how they hire. The LinkedIn survey asked recruiters to rate AI on different recruiting criteria and reported these results. Fifty-eight percent of recruiters said AI was helpful for sourcing candidates. Fifty-six percent said AI was most helpful screening candidates. Fifty-five percent said AI was helpful nurturing candidates.

On the downside, only 42 percent of the recruiters said AI was helpful scheduling candidate interviews. Only 24 percent said it was helpful with engaging candidates. And only 6 percent said AI was helpful interviewing candidates.

However, the results of surveys are mixed. Korn Ferry conducted a survey of 770 talent acquisition professionals from around the globe in November and December 2017.[242] The results, which were published in January 2018, showed that 63 percent of respondents said AI had changed the way recruiting was done in their organization, with 69 percent saying using AI as a sourcing tool garnered higher-quality candidates.

When asked to compare the quality of candidates today to five years ago, when AI was still in its infancy, 59 percent of the Korn Ferry survey respondents answered that candidates are more qualified today, and 51 percent said roles are filled in a timelier manner.

According to the Korn Ferry survey, talent acquisition professionals are welcoming AI as a tool. Nearly half (48 percent) said big data and AI were making their roles easier, with 40 percent saying the top way it helped was providing valuable insights, and 27 percent said it had freed up their time.

On the downside, 14 percent of the survey respondents said AI had made their jobs more difficult, with the majority saying they have too much data and they don't know what to do with it. Nine in ten recruiters did not believe that AI would replace their jobs.

Korn Ferry is a deep-rooted third-party search firm for the Fortune 500. Their clients are bigger and more sophisticated than those who depend on LinkedIn. While I am making no judgments here, it would not surprise me to learn that Korn Ferry's big corporate clients are more open to new, trendy technology and have the budgets to use them, than many other, smaller organizations with less-funded HR organizations.

What to make of AI for recruiting? My take is to use AI to find and screen candidates based on objective criteria from a well written job description. It can more efficiently conduct your ATS administration, track metrics, and provide you strategic information on talent and performance. With chatbot technology, AI can instantaneously communicate with job applicants and improve the job candidate experience. AI can identify your competitors in the labor market by finding their job posts on the internet. AI can assist you with understanding the real-time pay being offered for competitive positions. When it comes to reading facial expressions, tone of voice, and body movements, and to making decisions on who to advance for a face-to-face interview or to make a hiring decision–stick to humans who conduct structured interviews and uses validated assessments. I hold a high threshold for companies that claim that their facial recognition technologies—whatever they may call them--and machine learning can make substantive judgments on values, personality and leadership traits, and whether someone is lying. I would not use such a service unless the data from their research were made public and passed the statistical muster required for validation, or they published their results in an academic journal that required peer review. The higher the recruiting level, such as with executive recruiting, the more important it is to use human-driven processes, especially to get the candidate's attention, and use validated assessments with structured interviews.

Let's see in five years if AI can truly make accurate predictions on human personalities and expressions and improve our ability to recruit great talent without bias.

LinkedIn Recruiter and Its New TalentHub

For recruiters, LinkedIn has been a gold mine to find active but especially passive candidates with its Boolean search capability. But LinkedIn's Boolean search is not as fast or useful as artificial intelligence platforms. LinkedIn will need a makeover or acquisition, or it will lose out to stiff competition. It remains the largest professional social media site and the standard for learning about job candidates online. However, millennials prefer other social media.

LinkedIn has over 560 million global users, over 146 million US users, and on any given day over 10 million job postings. Over 60 million of LinkedIn users are in senior positions. About 40 percent of college students use LinkedIn, but only 13 percent of millennials use LinkedIn.[243] They, like other generations, now prefer mobile phone apps.[244]

LinkedIn uses gamification to instantaneously coach and prod job seekers to create their profiles and add pictures, endorsements, awards, and projects they are working on. It gives them a score on how good their job profile looks and prods them to act when they receive inquiries and when others, including recruiters, look at their profiles. This, in turn, helps the recruiter maintain relationships with passive candidates and to build a pool of candidates by occupation, which used to be done on spreadsheets.

These days LinkedIn is getting competition from new platforms such as Google for Jobs and the big job boards that are integrating platforms that are incorporating powerful machine learning and chatbots to improve their ability to search and interact with job candidates.

I know from experience that I can find passive job candidates using AI platforms faster than LinkedIn users who use its Boolean search technology—even when the passive job candidates are on LinkedIn. Moreover, there are platforms that use the online match-making algorithms that match job candidates to individual companies by specific industries.

For the fast-food business, there are Proven and RestaurantZone, hospitality Poached and Hcareers, and for software and other tech jobs WhiteTruffle and Underdog.io.

Online job boards such as ZIPRecruiter, Monster, and Indeed are helping recruiting departments in a way that LinkedIn is struggling to do. They are automating many of the tasks involved in listing open positions and communicating with job candidates, making administration easier.

LinkedIn is facing a lot of competition. On May 17, 2017, Google CEO Sundar Punchai announced the release of Google for Jobs, a service that will focus on all types of jobs from entry level to service industry to higher-end professional jobs. Google for Jobs will leverage Google technologies like machine learning and AI to better understand how jobs are classified. Job searchers can search Google for Jobs like they search Google, and applicants can use filters like job titles, location, and type of job among other categories. The service will also show the job applicant commute times for the job. Google is partnering with job boards such as CareerBuilder, Monster, and Glassdoor and with social media such as LinkedIn and Facebook.[245]

In the face of all its competition, LinkedIn is making upgrades. In late 2018 LinkedIn launched TalentHub, its new applicant tracking system for small- to midsize companies. According to LinkedIn's news feed, TalentHub allows companies to open requisitions and determine job targeting, source candidates via LinkedIn's recruiter search tools, manage the pipeline, schedule interviews, collect hiring team feedback, and extend offers to candidates. LinkedIn also claims Talent Hub will allow companies to use LinkedIn's data to get an accurate sense of available talent.[246]

Online Dating Moves to Recruiting

If you have used online dating services, you probably won't be surprised to know that this business model and technology have moved to recruiting, where closed communities of job seekers and hiring companies, which are screened, are matched by a combination of machine learning and interviews.

Below are a few examples.

WhiteTruffle is a job-matching software for engineers in San Francisco and New York that works a little like eHarmony. Founded in 2011, it is anonymous at first as candidates enter profiles and review company profiles. WhiteTruffle uses their AI algorithm to identify potential matches. The algorithm is based on work location, work history, skills, relocation availability, and other "unique data." Candidates are then told that an employer wants to "get to know them better," and if they agree to share their identity, WhiteTruffle shares the candidates identity with the prospective employer and they can arrange a meeting. For job candidates, it eliminates the "black hole" of résumé submissions and scouring job boards. For the high- tech firms, WhiteTruffle says they eliminate the need to source and cold call candidates.

Underdog.io started in 2014 with the goal of making it easier for job seekers to connect with top technology companies in San Francisco and New York. They, like WhiteTruffle, act like a marketplace (or dating service) that introduces growing technology companies to software engineers, designers, product managers, and businesspeople who have joined Underdog.io. Underdog.io claims to screen its companies to provide a better service to its member job candidates. Underdog.io companies are 95 percent privately held, venture-backed start-ups, and the rest are larger technology firms. Underdog.io states that only 50 percent of the companies that apply to join Underdog.io are approved for membership. They also maintain that they tightly screen job applicants. They provide full-time jobs and not gig work.

eHarmony, the online dating service that promotes itself as the place for long-lasting relationships, launched its own job-matching service, called Elevated Careers. Its career-matching service launched in 2014, and it begins with an assessment of a company's culture, employee engagement, and branding. Elevated Careers assesses the current situation by surveying employees, and it has a very thorough process. The survey provides a framework for employment branding to create messaging to attract the best workers. Elevated Careers has identified sixteen key factors that determine a candidate's capability to win a job in a company. They use their algorithms to source and match candidates who will match your culture to prevent you from having to search through candidates who are not a job match. They then look for a personality match. Early reviews of Elevated Careers say it takes too long to answer the over-130-question assessment in an era when most job applicants don't finish standard job applications, and it is expensive.[247]

Poachable. Many single readers out there know of Tinder, the anonymous dating site, or at least it is anonymous at first. Amorous individuals view a picture of a potential date, and if you like the picture, swipe to the right; if not, swipe to the left and move on to the next picture. Several online software have popped up with a similar idea of quickly and anonymously matching passive candidates, who have become restless with their current employers, to potential new employers. The first was Poachable, which works in a way similar to Tinder. Founded in 2014 and now with $1.5M in funding (according to TechCrunch), it is now commercially known as Anthology. Anonymous candidates can review abbreviated job postings of companies and swipe to the left if they are not interested and to the right if they are interested. As with Tinder, the software matches them up. Anthology members also can view anonymous information within their professions such as salaries and most desired locations, and compare skills.

Jobr is another technology platform that uses the Tinder swipe right or left approach to find jobs and job candidates. Jobr also sees job openings from other job boards, and if a job seeker is interested, it contacts the company to see if they are interested in the job seeker.

TalentBrew is a recruiting software that works off your applicant tracking system to distribute curated employer brand, news, employee stories, and job information directly to active and passive candidates, much like marketing organizations use technology to distribute product and service information to potential customers. Each piece of content is associated with specific job categories or locations, allowing for easy grouping with up-to-date, related job openings.

The content and specific job openings are then distributed to the company's career site and its social media and made available on both mobile and desktop through the TalentBrew platform.[248] The result is not only a content strategy aimed at both active and passive job seekers, but also new ways to measure the effects and expenditure of social strategies and content marketing by tying the efforts to candidate conversions such as applications, hires, and talent community growth and engagement.

TalentBrew clients include Fortune 200 companies such as Procter & Gamble, Nike, and Eli Lilly.

Gamification and Recruiting

Gamification is the application of typical elements of playing a game to other professional activities such as online marketing to engage potential clients to interact with a product or service. Typical in gamification is the use of point scoring, competition with others or competition of displaying your score against an average or best score, and of course well-understood rules.

If you or your children play video games, you know gamification. When there are signs that you are about to run out of time, there is often a pop-up that offers more time or points to enable play for an additional amount of money to your credit card or account. Friends of mine alerted me to this as their eight-year-old kept pestering them for their credit card for more money, and the time money buys, to continue playing his video game.

Gamification by design is addictive. It uses the principles of behaviorism: instant feedback, gratification, excitement, and competition. It gives instant gratification with results, usually encouragement, and compares your progress to that of others—adding the further addictive element of competition.

If you don't play video games, you can reflect on playing pinball. All the elements of gamification were in effect there, with the pinball rocketing from the levers controlled by your hand, the point totals, bells going off, and comparison of your score to the best on the machine. I am sure your pocket was loaded with quarters.

If you have created a profile on LinkedIn, you have experienced gamification at a professional level. As you complete your LinkedIn profile using gamification software, LinkedIn congratulates you on your progress and tells you what you need to do to finish.

The Domino's Pizza chain has used gamification as part of their marketing. Customers were invited to create and name their own digital pizza online. The customers were awarded with cash every time anyone purchased their created pizza.[249]

Now gamification is coming to recruiting. At first some thought of gamification as a tool to assess employee skills. Now that seems a little far-fetched in most applications.

With recruiting it has found a home in attracting job seekers and informing job seekers about the company's culture. It also can be used to attract college students to a particular industry.

A good example of this is the Plantsville online game by Siemens, which was published by Siemens in a 2014 case study.[250] In 2010, Siemens was struggling to recruit new professionals, build brand awareness, help employees understand the scope of manufacturing operations, and showcase their company. In the game, players were encouraged to maintain operation of their plant while improving productivity, efficiency, and facility health. Since it was launched on March 24, 2011, twenty-three thousand engineering professionals have spent approximately fourteen minutes with the game every time they visit the site. The players are from the following backgrounds.

- More than eleven thousand five hundred are employee prospects and customers.
- More than six hundred are engineering recruits from universities and colleges across the United States.
- Several are from government agencies.
- Several are from companies with more than thirty-five hundred employees.

Within seven months of its launch, the Plantsville facility saw the following increases on social media.

- Twenty-seven hundred friends on Facebook.
- Thirty thousand videos on YouTube.
- One hundred seventeen connections on LinkedIn.
- Even Pete, the Plantsville manager, had his own LinkedIn page.

It was considered a great success.

Another long-running recruiting game example is L'Oréal Brandstorm, which was started to engage and recruit millennials to the L'Oréal brand.[251] Brandstorm is a competition that gives teams of three undergraduate or graduate students eighteen years or older the chance to tackle a real business case and innovate new ideas for some of L'Oréal's twenty-four international brands. The only requirement to sign up is to be in school in the same country. Participants can also choose an academic mentor of their choice to help them with professional advice through the competition. According to its website, L'Oréal Brandstorm had over twenty-five thousand participants in 2017.

Notice in both examples, gamification is used to build brand awareness and to attract college students and others to careers in the respective industry and company. It is not used as a selection tool.

These seem like good examples for the scientific, technical, engineering, math, and medical fields to attract candidates to their professions. A Herculean effort was made in the 1960s to attract aeronautical engineers to the aerospace industries and to beat the Russians in the Cold War with President John F. Kennedy's challenge to put a man on the moon by the end of the 1960s. (It was accomplished by *Apollo 11* in 1969, when American astronaut Neil Armstrong put his foot on the surface of the moon.) Perhaps today it can be used to attract America's youth to STEMM professions.

Remember that for an assessment to be used as a tool to select employees from job candidates, the assessment must be validated to show that success on the assessment is a reliable and unbiased predictor of job success. Companies that use assessments or gamification to make hiring decisions without empirical validation put themselves at high risk of being sued if the results of the assessments turn out to be discriminatory against protected classes. That is just as bad as having an unvalidated assessment that does a poor job of predicting which candidates will do well on the job.

Whether gamification will ever be used for assessments is still to be determined, but I cannot recommend using them now. They do, however, offer great potential to attract college students and others to your brand through your career site and social media and as a training tool.

Blockchain

As a recruiter, wouldn't you like to receive 100 percent accurate and verifiable résumés and conduct instantaneous background checks? That technology is here and is being developed for HR. It is called blockchain.

Blockchain technology is a secure decentralized network of computers that verifies and automates the flow of information. However, the relative security of Blockchain networks is of ongoing concern. It now is more trustworthy (although blockchains for cryptocurrencies have been hacked and money and personal and security information stolen) and eliminates intermediaries. It is best known for use by cryptocurrencies such as Bitcoin, where it has a horrendous reputation because of estimates that as many as half of Bitcoin transactions (about $72 million) are with illegal activity.[252] Mainstream banking, however, is taking a significant interest in Blockchain technology to replace its aging infrastructure, gain efficiencies, compete with fintech start-ups, and create new business models.[253] In addition, companies such as Microsoft, Amazon, and IBM have made huge investments in the technology as part of their "cloud" business services.[254]

Blockchain will begin next year to disrupt human resources in the areas of recruiting, performance histories, employee background checks, I-9 verifications, and even payroll. Some technologists are predicting that it will replace the need for résumés as we think of them today and background checks. The careers of employees at other companies and their academic histories, graduation dates, degrees, and GPA may be pulled up from blockchain transactions.[255] In practice what this means is that as opposed to submitting a résumé, a candidate soon may submit a bio and then authorize the release of a full résumé to the ATS of an employer.

This future may have some hurdles, such as being complaint with EEO, Affirmative Action Plan OFCCP audits. For AAPs employers need to track all applicants, including their protected class status and the decisions made about each applicant and continue this tracking and decision-making until a hiring decision is made. If blockchain technology does not allow this tracking, that is a problem unless the regulations are changed.

The current lords of HR and ATS technology platforms, such as Workday, Oracle, SAP, Microsoft/LinkedIn, and Google, will want a piece of this futuristic pie. It will release a series of mergers and acquisitions, technology purchases, and an all-out battle for dominance, with economic winners and losers.

There is also the issue of standards and the technological underpinnings of blockchain. Currently, the protocols for transmitting and receiving data through the internet are the TCP/IP code that was developed in 1975 but did not become dominant until 1989, when AT&T put the TCP/IP code into UNIX for the public domain.[256] Prior to that, each computing product had its own proprietary data exchange. This gets to the issue of network externality.

The full implementation of blockchain is probably five years away. Why? Because for blockchain to be effective, it will require building a network externality of participating companies, job seekers, and academic institutions. For example, one widely anticipated application of blockchain for human resources is in immediately verifying academic credentials and work histories. For this to work, it would take a blockchain with participation from a majority of academic institutions, employers, and job candidates who give permission to release their personal data. A smartphone without a Verizon, ATT, or T-Mobile network, technology, and security is valueless. With the network, it is an incredible personal assistant, source of music and video entertainment, database, and telephone. Same with Blockchain. It needs a healthy participating network, safe with enabling technology.

Companies, including London-based start-up APPII Ltd., as reported in the *Wall Street Journal*, see blockchain as the future of the résumé. APPII is working with employers and universities to develop a product that first verifies the claims individuals make about their history and then issues them digital résumé listings of their data from multiple locations and institutions. The digital document can be shared with employers and updated as the owner's career progresses.

Jobeum is using blockchain to create a LinkedIn-like recruiting tool. According to its website, Jobeum is a blockchain-based professional network, a transparent system where users control who sees a specific part of the information in their profile. The profiles become their "digital twins" and earn "JobTokens" for them when other people ask them for certain information or an action (e.g., to open a part of their profile, show contact information, or confirm their skills).

According to Dave Zielinski, writing for SHRM, some start-up blockchain companies have begun operating in the recruiting space. Last year Recruit Technologies and Ascribe announced a partnership to develop a prototype blockchain résumé authentication service for job hunters. The service would enable the digital verification of official certificates and résumés previously done on paper. The two partner companies claim the effort of collecting multiple official certificates would be reduced for job hunters, and recruiters could handle confidential official certificates safely and without worry of fraud.[257]

A handful of educational institutions and technology companies are working on developing trustworthy, quickly verifiable digital diplomas and résumés. The Massachusetts Institute of Technology issued digital diplomas based on blockchain to all of its students who graduated in February 2018. The diplomas can be shared on social media or directly with employers.[258]

"There's a fair bit of effort required at the moment to determine the credentials that someone puts forward on their [résumé]," says Gary McKay, cofounder of the digital-identity start-up when interviewed by the *Wall Street Journal*. "That friction diminishes the ability for employers to find talent quickly and to have them sitting in a chair or taking on a role as quickly as they need."[259]

A digital diploma could allow organizations to check credentials without having to run background checks. Using a digital signature, for example, students could provide a copy of the diploma to employers, who could then upload the file onto a verification page to get confirmation that the degree is legitimate. The university doesn't need to be involved.

The Federation of State Medical Boards, which advocates for all the medical licensing boards in the United States, has issued sample verifications using the same Blockcerts system as MIT. Officials at the federation say they hope that its work will initiate a conversation at the state-boards level.

Resistance to change

Still, regulatory hurdles could slow wider adoption of blockchain verification. Mike Dugan, chief information officer of the Federation of State Medical Boards, says regulation at the state-level hasn't caught up with the technology. Only a handful of states have passed legislation to enable broader usage of blockchain technology. For example, in 2017, Arizona added a law to recognize blockchain-based digital signatures.

"Digital signatures have been around a lot longer than blockchain, and...there's still not a lot of widespread adoption" of those, Mr. Dugan says. "Some of this is skepticism, and [some is] people unwilling to change their processes."[260]

Members of the Blockchain in Transport Alliance, a global

freight-industry trade organization focused on commercialization and education, are experimenting with using blockchain technology as a form of driver identification.

The managing director of the alliance, Craig Fuller, says digital identity for drivers could help to protect companies from unnecessary litigation because whole work histories and skill sets could be on blockchain, easily accessible to companies when they hire.

"These big enterprise companies just can't afford to hire a driver that has any amount of risk," Mr. Fuller says. "[After an accident] you end up in court, and the attorneys suing you can prove you're making all this money and you're hiring drivers that are unsafe."[261]

Is Blockchain technology truly secure?

If the FBI, Defense Department, and White House can be hacked, so can any cloud platform, and that includes Blockchain. Both Bitcoin and another cryptocurrency, Ethereum, have been hacked several times. This should not be surprising, as many mainline commercial businesses have been hacked, such as Wells Fargo.

In the case of cryptocurrencies, *Fortune, Fast Company*, and the *Guardian*, as well as other publications, have published frightening stories of smart investors who invested in Bitcoin and Ethereum on money exchanges only to get an email warning that their digital wallet account was hacked. When they checked their accounts, they found that anonymous hackers had ripped them off for thousands of dollars.[262]

Like anything else, you must pick a blockchain technology that has a good track record for security and is serious about maintaining it.

Another issue for the success of blockchain exchanging résumés and background data is the permissions to provide it by employers or the employee. Employees may want more control on their "brand" and frankly not so much transparency. Gig workers on platforms such as Upwork may have a stronger interest in endorsing blockchain exchanges because of their need to convey their achievements, work histories, and technical competency.

As with any new technology, blockchain must catch on to be successful and become a network externality. That is, widely used to be successful. Only with wide use will it be successful.

CHAPTER 13: HR LEGAL GEEK: THE IMPACT OF LAWS AND REGULATIONS

There are many areas where the law impacts hiring. The areas include:

- validating job screening tests and assessments
- the questions interviews should not ask during an interview because they are discriminatory
- the use of negligent hiring, which can lead to lawsuits
- Ban the Box
- bans on asking questions about salary history
- the guidance of the US Equal Employment Opportunity Commission based on several US laws, to have hiring and people related decisions at work be non-discriminatory and free of harassment
- the requirement to have Affirmative Action Plans
- I-9 or E-Verify verification of having a legal right to work in the US

They will all be explained in this chapter.

Validating Job Screening Tests and Assessments

Employers need to be careful with any tests they use in the hiring or promotion processes. Job screening tests do not need to be validated under the EEOC's Uniform Guidelines on Employee

Selection Procedures. However, if the test results in "adverse Impact" on a group that is protected under Title VII, then the company can be sued for job discrimination by using the test. If the job test has been validated to predict the selection of successful job candidates, it may survive a legal challenge even if it can be shown to discriminate against women and minorities.

I encourage employers to validate their tests to be sure that they are using tests that select the best candidates for their jobs and do not accidentally discriminate. Protected class groups under Title VII, and subsequent extensions, include age, race, sex, color, national origin, ethnicity, religion, veteran status, including Vietnam era veterans, and in the past several years, sexual orientation. Other laws, such as the Americans with Disabilities Act, prohibit discrimination against employees (and job applicants) who have physical or mental impairments that substantially limit "major life activities." Major life activities include walking, sitting, reading, seeing, and communicating.

In August 2015, the EEOC settled a claim with Target over the retailer's former use of three employment assessments that the EEOC found disproportionately screened out applicants for entry-level professional positions based on race and sex.[263] Target agreed to pay $2.8 million and will perform a predictive validity study on assessments it expects to use in the future.

The EEOC said the tests were not sufficiently job-related and consistent with business necessity and violated Title VII of the Civil Rights Act of 1964. In addition, the EEOC found that one of the assessments violated the Americans with Disabilities Act. This assessment—performed by psychologists on behalf of Target—was a prohibited preemployment medical exam.

The EEOC is naturally suspicious of tests that measure soft skills such as personality fit and communications and tests that measure general intelligence in math, reading, and writing. The advice for employers is to use tests directly tied to the job, such as typing tests for secretaries. For more sophisticated testing, employers should validate their tests. Often the test supplier will provide advice on test validation or even do the validation study for the employer.

The Questions You Can't Ask during an Interview

Let's first cover what you can ask. You can ask candidates questions about why they left their past employers and why they want to leave their current employer and questions about their knowledge about the job they are applying for, their skills, credentials, qualifications, work experiences, and abilities to do the job, and how they overcame obstacles to achieve their goals. You can ask them questions to ascertain their level of consciousness and dedication, and questions to determine if they are aligned with the values, mission, and purpose of the organization.

What you can't ask them is a rather long list.

You cannot ask them questions about the same issues the United States and many state governments have outlawed as discriminatory. For example, you cannot ask candidates their age, race, sex, ethnicity, color of skin, national origin, religion, disability, marital status, or if they are pregnant. In many states it is also illegal to ask about sexual orientation.

Even if a woman appears to be obviously pregnant during an interview, it is illegal to ask her, "Are you pregnant?"

It is also illegal to ask many of the following questions.

1. Do you own a car? If there is a concern about transportation for all job applicants, you may ask, "Do you have a reliable means to get to work?"
2. Are you planning to have children?
3. How much longer do you want to work before you retire?
4. Do you have children?
5. Are you married or single?
6. How old are your children?

7. Are you a US citizen? Instead, ask, "Are you legally able to work in the United States?" This question should be on your application.
8. When did you graduate from high school or college? Asking this has been determined to be a form of age discrimination.
9. What does your spouse do?
10. Are you comfortable working with a member of the other sex?
11. Will you need time off for a religious holiday?
12. Are you comfortable working with black people, white people, Chinese, people younger than you, gays, straights, and so on?
13. Have had any serious illnesses or injuries in the past year?
14. Have you been a member of a labor union?

You may see a job candidate in a wheelchair. Rather than ask them, "Are you disabled?" which is illegal, wait for them to ask about a "reasonable accommodation" as covered under the Americans with Disabilities Act.

Negligent Hiring

Negligent hiring is a claim made by a party who was injured by an employee of a company against the company based on the legal theory that the company knew or should have known about the employee's background, which, if known, indicates a dangerous or untrustworthy character. Hiring someone with a criminal record or who has a pattern of past violence raises legitimate concerns about negligent hiring.

Roughly half of the states legally recognize that an employer is responsible for and can be held accountable for checking the background and references of any job applicant before placing that applicant in positions of high public contact. Employers have been found liable for negligent hiring or retention of dangerous or incompetent employees in most states, including Alaska, California, Illinois, Kansas, Maryland, New Mexico, and New York.

Because of concerns of safety in the workplace, hiring good employees, and not getting sued under negligent hiring, employers for years have been conducting reference checks and background checks to assure they are hiring employees who are who they claim to be and have the academic credentials, work histories, and achievements they claim to have on their résumés and while being interviewed.

Some of the professions that are most at risk for negligent hiring include real estate agents, rental apartment personnel, condominium personnel, delivery persons, service and maintenance persons, nursing and convalescent home workers, home health care aides, and utility personnel.[264]

Here are some additional professions where having a criminal record will make it difficult to get a job.

+ **Teaching**, particularly if job applicants were convicted of violent crimes or pedophilia
+ **Childcare**, just like teaching, if job applicants were convicted of violent crimes or pedophilia
+ **Health care**, with its exposure to access of all kinds of private data and information, as well as drugs and pharmaceuticals
+ **Law enforcement** requires a squeaky-clean record.
+ **Finance**, if one has been convicted of theft, fraud, or anything else that has to do with money
+ **Retail industries** that sell guns, alcohol, and pharmaceuticals can disqualify job candidates with criminal records.
+ **Government jobs** usually have tough screening criteria for felonies and other serious crimes.[265]

While negligent hiring is a legitimate legal issue to manage, a rapidly expanding trend, Ban the Box, is calling into question banning all formerly incarcerated individuals for roles that their crime does not prevent them from being hired. For example, those who have been incarcerated for drug offenses and have taken extraordinary steps to rehabilitate themselves can be considered for many roles. Research shows that they are more loyal than other workers, and often the number-one factor in preventing recidivism is getting a job quickly upon leaving prison. More on that to come.

Ban the Box

The Ban the Box movement encourages companies and public employers to eliminate blanket exclusions of people with criminal records until either after the first interview or after a conditional offer is made for a job.

Nationwide, over one hundred fifty cities and twenty-nine states have banned the criminal record questions in a movement called Ban the Box, at least at the time of editing this book. While most of these laws apply only to public sector employment, the policies extend to private sector employers in nine states and fifteen major cities.[266]

Born out of the group All of Us or None (a grassroots civil and human rights organization fighting for the rights of formerly and currently incarcerated people)**, this effort is to remove the conviction history question on the job application and delay the background check inquiry until later in the hiring process.**[267] The point is to have the candidate put his or her best foot forward and not automatically be eliminated from consideration due to a criminal record.

In the state of California, for example, on January 1, 2018, it became illegal for private sector employers to ask applicants about their criminal conviction histories on job applications. The California law prohibits most public sector and private employers with five or more employees from asking applicants about criminal convictions until after a conditional offer of employment has been made. Positions required by law to undergo employment screening for specified criminal convictions are exempt from the California law.

In order to be compliant with Ban the Box legislation in your city, county, or state, I encourage you to consult with your employment attorney or check the Resources and Tools section of the Society for Human Resource Management's website, found at https://www.shrm.org/resourcesandtools/tools-and-samples/exreq/pages/details.aspx?erid=1271.

Even in locations where employers may ban the box, employers are advised not to consider arrests, as they are not evidence of a conviction. Considering arrests can get employers into dangerous legal ground for discriminating against people of color. In addition, if you ask any one employee about his or her criminal history, make sure you are asking that question of every job candidate. Employers should only consider convictions and pending prosecutions that are relevant to the job in question. In addition, recruiters and hiring managers should also consider the number of years that have passed since a job-relevant conviction and evidence of rehabilitation.

Many applicant tracking systems have historically used a series of questions to determine if job candidates have criminal records or credit history issues (for certain financial professions) that would ban them from being considered for a role.

The Ban the Box movement has its critics, who fear the legislation will actually increase discrimination against people of color. Jennifer Doleac, an assistant professor of public policy and economics at the University of Virginia, who has conducted research in this area, said that without the box on the application, employers may be more likely to guess that black and Hispanic men have a criminal record.[268]

Many employers stopped Ban the Box questioning in 2012 after the US Equal Employment Opportunity Commission (EEOC) issued criminal record guidance.

Complicating matters is that Ban the Box laws in each city and state can be very different.

I advise employers to consider criminal records, especially for violations that are relevant to the job, such as securities fraud for finance roles, and past violent behavior and theft, later in the interviewing process and very discreetly—and to understand the Ban the Box laws in their cities, counties, and states.

The time has come, I believe, to offer second changes to America's over 70 million adults who were formerly incarcerated. Please see Chapter 14, Hiring Strategies during Full Employment.

Growing Bans on Salary History Questions

There is a growing trend to ban employers from asking job applicants questions about their current pay and salary histories. The purpose is to make a dent in the pay inequity between men and women and whites and people of color.

As of the time of this printing, the states of California, Delaware, Oregon, and Massachusetts, and New York City have salary history bans. Some noteworthy employers, such as Google and Facebook, have banned these questions from being asked even when the law does not require it.[269] I expect the trend to continue. Employers should prepare for the day when salary histories cannot be asked.

Penalties run the gamut as well. In New York City, infractions are a violation of the city's human rights law. That means employers could be required to pay damages and penalties of up to $250,000 and undergo mandatory training about the law. Delaware's legislation imposes civil penalties of up to $10,000 for each infraction.[270]

According to an article published by Pew Research in 2016, the median hourly earning gender pay gap for workers twenty-five or older and controlled for education remains stubbornly wide, but the gap is narrowing.[271] White women earn seventy-eight cents to a white man's dollar. The pay gap between white men and black men twenty-five or older and controlled for education is also seventy-eight cents to the dollar. For Hispanic men it is eighty-one cents to the dollar. Black women have a larger discrepancy to white men, at seventy-two cents to the dollar. Unlike women, black and Hispanic men have not made progress since 1980. Black women earn seventy-two cents to the white man's dollar and ninety-two cents to the white woman's dollar. Hispanic women earn sixty-eight cents to the white man's dollar and eighty-eight cents to the white woman's dollar. Asian men and women twenty-five and older, on the other hand, earn more money than white men and women respectively when controlled for education. Asian men earn $1.09 to the white man's dollar. Asian women earn $1.08 to the white woman's dollar. However, white men earn eighty-four cents to the Asian woman's dollar.[272]

A study released on November 28, 2018, by the Institute for Women's Policy Research (IWPR) found that the gender gap is worse than previously reported. It concludes that women earn forty-nine cents to every dollar men make. IWPR said earlier studies left out part-time workers and people who have taken time off from work, which is more common for women than men. When this is considered and taking a longer-term view, they learned the actual experience of women, who over a fifteen-year period are more likely to shoulder the demands of childcare than men.[273]

Why do these wage gaps persist? According to Eileen Patten, former employee of Pew Research, a majority of these gaps can be explained by differences in education, labor force experience, occupation or industry, and other measurable factors. However, the pay gap not explained by these factors is attributed in part to discrimination, risk aversion, or poor negotiations for wages.

> For example, NBER researchers Francine Blau and Lawrence Kahn found that education and workforce experience accounted for 8% of the total gender wage gap in 2010, while industry and occupation explained 51% of the difference. When it comes to race, sociologists Eric Grodsky and Devah Pager found that education and workforce experience accounted for 52% of the wage gap between black and white men working in the public sector in 1990, and that adding occupational differences explained approximately 20% of the wage gap. And NBER researcher Roland Fryer found that for one group of adults in

their 40s, controlling for standardized-test scores reduced the wage gap between black men and white
men in 2006 by roughly 70%.

The remaining gaps not explained by these con-
crete factors are often attributed, at least in part, to
discrimination. Blau and Kahn point out, however,
that there are both portions of this "unmeasured"
difference that could be due to factors other than
discrimination (e.g., gender differences in behaviors like risk aversion or negotiation) as well as portions of the "measured" difference that may in fact
be due to discrimination (e.g., a woman or minority
not entering a high-paying STEMM field because of
experiences that may be rooted in prejudice, such
as greater encouragement for men than women to
pursue these studies).[274]

Patten's article goes on to point out that the views on pay discrimination differ by race, with 60 percent of Americans saying
blacks and whites are treated equally, according to a 2016 pay research study. However, 64 percent of blacks say they are treated
less fairly than whites, while only 22 percent of whites say blacks
are treated less fairly and 38 percent Hispanics say they are treated
less fairly than whites. For their part, about a quarter of women (27
percent) say their gender has made it harder for them to succeed in
life, compared with just 7 percent of men.

In addition, a 2013 Pew Research Center survey found that about
one in five women (18 percent) say they have faced gender discrimination at work, including 12 percent who say they have earned less
than a man doing the same job because of their gender. By comparison, one in ten men say they have faced gender-based workplace
discrimination, including 3 percent who say their gender has been
a factor in earning lower wages.[275]

Sadly, other research shows that when women refuse to answer the pay history question, they are penalized by receiving a smaller offer. According to a PayScale study, a woman who is asked about her salary history and declines to disclose earns 1.8 percent less than a woman who discloses. If a man declines to disclose, he gets paid 1.2 percent more on average.

Sorry for all the numbers, but the differences of pay between men and women and whites and people of color and the starkly different perceptions about fair pay and discrimination at work reveal that this is a pressing issue that will not go away soon.

However, company policies can make significant differences in actual pay discrepancy and perception about fairness and discrimination. Based on my experience, when an employee begins their career or tenure at a company at very low wages for the position, many times the merit pay increases available do not allow them to catch up to true market pay. This is one reason that I implemented compensation structures that don't allow employees to be paid lower than 90 percent of market, rather than the more traditional 80 percent of market. The results of this three-year policy was that we eliminated pay gaps by gender and race, with the exception of differences by performance, degree, and experience or if someone was demoted and their pay was red-circled, meaning that they would not get a pay increase until the annual progression of pay for a job caught up to the pay they earned at the higher paying job.

I am a strong believer in pay for performance and in fairness and transparency. This issue can be overcome. The companies that overcome this issue often excel at innovation and outstanding financial performance and growth. If private industry doesn't narrow the pay gap, government regulations will enforce equity solutions that will reduce the use of pay for performance.

Equal Opportunity Employer

In the United States, federal laws prohibit workplace discrimination and are enforced by the Equal Employment Opportunity Commission, an office of the US Department of Labor. States (and comes cities) also have their own laws prohibiting workplace discrimination, often expanding the protections of federal laws. These states usually have their own enforcement agencies too. While this chapter focuses on US laws, the European Union, European countries, and Asian countries such as India have their own laws that prohibit workplace discrimination.

The US Equal Employment Opportunity Commission defines an equal opportunity employer as an employer who agrees not to discriminate against any employee or job applicant because of race, color, religion, national origin, sex, physical or mental disability, or age.

Below is a basic summary of federal laws that prohibit discrimination.

Title VII of the Civil Rights Act of 1964

Title VII of the Civil Rights Act of 1964 made it illegal to discriminate against people on the basis of race, color, religion, national origin, or sex. It passed after years of civil rights protests largely in the South and organized by Dr. Martin Luther King Jr., his followers, and supportive politicians like President John F. Kennedy and Minnesota Senator and Vice President Hubert H. Humphrey; the bill was signed by President Lyndon Johnson. This protection covers hiring and all employment decisions such as promotions, pay increases, training programs, reductions in force, and training programs that improve job skills or prepare employees for promotions and career advancement. The Civil Rights Act also applies to unions.

The law also makes it illegal to retaliate against a person who complained about discrimination, filed a charge of discrimination, or participated in an employment discrimination investigation or lawsuit. Title VII also requires that employers reasonably accommodate applicants' and employees' sincerely held religious practices, unless doing so would impose an undue hardship on the operation of the employer's business.

The administrative procedures set up to enforce the Civil Rights

Act and other successive laws to protect women and veterans led to the creation of the Equal Employment Opportunity Commission to enforce the act and to set up procedures to hear and adjudicate discrimination claims. Complaints filed need to occur within 180 days of the discrimination or harassment in most cases. Employees can have up to three hundred days if the complaint is also covered by state or local antidiscrimination laws.

The employee only needs to present enough evidence to make a prima facie case of discrimination. The real burden of proof is on the company to prove that discrimination *didn't* take place. Once the employee has met this burden of proof, the employer must present evidence of a legitimate, nondiscriminatory motive for the employment decision at issue. For example, if an employee claims she was discharged due to her age in favor of a younger male below the age of 40, the *employer* must present evidence that the reason for the discharge was due to poor performance or misconduct. The employee then has an opportunity to challenge the employer's evidence by showing that the reasons given for the decision were a pretext for discrimination.

In 1978, Title VII was amended to make it illegal to discriminate against women because of pregnancy, childbirth, or a medical condition related to pregnancy or childbirth.

Sections 102 and 103 of the Civil Rights Act of 1991. This law, among other things, amends Title VII and the ADA to permit jury trials and compensatory and punitive damage awards in intentional discrimination cases.

The Equal Pay Act of 1963

The Equal Pay Act of 1963 makes it illegal to pay different wages to men and women if they are on the same job requiring equal skill, effort, and responsibility and the jobs are performed under similar conditions. It was passed by Congress and signed by President John F. Kennedy. The law also makes it illegal to retaliate against a person because the person complained about discrimination. It is also illegal to retaliate against a person who filed a charge of discrimination or participated in an employment discrimination investigation or lawsuit.

The Age Discrimination in Employment Act of 1967 (ADEA)

The Age Discrimination in Employment Act of 1967 (ADEA) protects people who are forty or older from discrimination because of age. The law also makes it illegal to retaliate against a person who complains about age discrimination.

All employers with fifty or more employees are to provide equal opportunity for employment, promotions, and transfers and are to make hiring and work-related decisions without regard to age, race, sex, color, creed, religion, national origin, or veteran status, including Vietnam veteran status. These initial protections have been expanded to cover sexual orientation in many cities and states. The law also protects individuals who have filed a charge of discrimination or participated in an employment discrimination investigation or lawsuit.

Title 1 of the Americans with Disabilities Act of 1990 (ADA)

The Americans with Disabilities Act of 1990 (ADA) makes it illegal to discriminate against a qualified person with a disability in the private sector and in state and local governments who has physical or mental impairments that substantially limit "major life activities." Major life activities include walking, sitting, reading, seeing, and communicating.

An employer doesn't have to hire or retain someone simply because that person has a disability; the person must be qualified for the job. This means that the person must have the necessary degrees, licenses, experience, and so on for the job. It also means that the person must be able to perform the essential functions of the job with a reasonable accommodation, if necessary. The law also requires that employers reasonably accommodate the known physical or mental limitations of an otherwise qualified individual with a disability who is an applicant or employee, unless doing so would impose an undue hardship on the operation of the employer's business.

With the ADA Amendments Act of 2008, Congress made it clear that the ADA should be interpreted broadly to include many disabilities to offer protection to as many people as possible.

It was passed by Congress and signed by President George H. Bush. The ADA prohibits discrimination in all employment practices, including job application procedures, hiring, firing, advancement, compensation, training, and other terms, conditions, and privileges of employment. It applies to recruitment, advertising, tenure, layoff, leave, fringe benefits, and all other employment-related activities.

The ADA also makes it illegal to retaliate against a person because the person complained about discrimination, filed a charge of discrimination, or participated in an employment discrimination investigation or lawsuit.

The Genetic Information Nondiscrimination Act of 2008 (GINA)

The Genetic Information Nondiscrimination Act of 2008 (GINA) makes it illegal to discriminate against employees or applicants because of genetic information. Genetic information includes information about an individual's genetic tests and the genetic tests of an individual's family members, as well as information about any disease, disorder, or condition of an individual's family members (e.g., an individual's family medical history). The law also makes it illegal to retaliate against a person because the person complained about discrimination, filed a charge of discrimination, or participated in an employment discrimination investigation or lawsuit.

Data-Driven Recruiting That Is Fair; Also Called an Affirmative Action Plan (AAP)

The purpose of affirmative action plans are to collect and analyze data to determine if the employer's hiring and human resources practices are biased. In the private sector, they are not quota systems and should not be used as one. In fact, the law states that it is illegal to make a hiring decision based on age, race, gender, and other identified factors, even in the name of affirmative action—even in the name of diversity. In an era of big data, machine learning, and artificial intelligence, perhaps the AAP of the 1970s was simply ahead of its time.

All businesses of fifteen or more employees need to comply with Title VII and be equal employment opportunity employers, but not all businesses need to have an affirmative action plan. If you are a contractor with the US government and have fifty or more employees and a contract of $50,000 or more, you are required to have an affirmative action plan due to Executive Order 11246.

The affirmative action plan must be in place within 120 days from the commencement of the contract. In addition, section 503 of the Rehabilitation Act of 1973 requires contractors with contracts over $10,000 to take affirmative action with regard to qualified individuals with disabilities. The Vietnam Era Veterans' Readjustment Assistance Act of 1974 (VEVRAA), as amended by the 2002 Jobs for Veterans Act, requires contractors to take affirmative action to employ and advance in employment veterans with service-connected disabilities, recently separated veterans, and other protected veterans. The act applies to contractors with fifty or more employees and $50,000 in federal contracts, and it also requires a written affirmative action plan.

There are three other reasons that your company may be required to have an AAP. It may be required as a court order due to discrimination or harassment. An AAP is also required if your company has fifty or more employees and serves as a depository of government funds in any amount, or if your company is a financial institution that is an issuing and paying agent for US savings bonds and savings notes in any amount. If you are in the construction industry and have a federal construction contract or a subcontract of over $10,000, or several construction contracts or subcontracts that total over $10,000, an AAP is required.

The company CEO or chief operating officer is the signatory of the AAP and is accountable for the company's good faith efforts with equal employment and treatment of employees and for making sure all AAP goals and updates are made available to the organization. The CEO is also responsible to oversee HR's role as the administrator of the plan and that hiring managers are cooperative and compliant.

Human resources serves as the administrator of the AAP. HR needs to assure the plan is completed each year (usually the calendar year or the company's financial year) and that there is a hiring plan for each year and goals set to improve the utilization of underutilized job categories. Here are other duties of human resources with an AAP.[276]

- Ensure AAP notifications are being printed on purchase orders and check vouchers and are included in contract language.
- Ensure the company's EEO policy statement is signed and posted in a common area for all employees, with instructions on how to request a copy of the current year AAP, and post it with the other EEO/labor posters such as a five-in-one poster.
- Track all employees who take maternity leave.
- Maintain a list of all disabled employees and any accommodations that have been made for these employees.
- Invite all employees to self-identify their race, gender, ethnicity, and veteran status prehire.
- File EEO1 and Vets 100 reports annually and maintain copies of the current year plus two past years.
- Assist in providing interviewing skills training to hiring managers to ensure compliance with EEO and AAP regulations.

- Document community outreach activities.
- Monitor the employee relations environment.
- Track terminations by voluntary or involuntary status and the reason for the termination, such as "resignation," for example.
- Track all new hires, promotions, terminations, and transfers each plan year.
- Maintain complete job descriptions for each job title.
- Support the display of good faith efforts within all employment aspects.

Affirmative action plans are not filed with the Office of Federal Contract Compliance Programs (OFCCP). Instead, they are kept by the contractor and must be produced in case of an audit by the OFCCP. I have been audited several times during my career. They usually call to schedule an appointment but not with enough notice to generate a plan if you don't have one. It is best to have one, not just for legal compliance but also to generate analytics on your best sources for hiring different job families. I encourage using as much technology as you can afford, usually with your applicant tracking system, to generate and maintain an affirmative action plan (AAP).

Affirmative action plans are to see that federal contractors make employment decisions equally between white and male workers and protected class workers. In addition, they are to "affirmatively" recruit protected class classifications, especially if any classification is underrepresented in their workforce. (As stated above, protected class groups under Title VII and subsequent extensions include age, race, sex, color, national origin, ethnicity, religion, veteran status, including Vietnam era veterans, and in the past several years, sexual orientation.) In the private sector, affirmative action is not a "quota system." In fact, the law maintains that employers are to make employment decisions without regard to protected class status. The goal of affirmative recruiting is to improve the representation of protected class job applicants within the company, especially in protected class groups that are underrepresented at the company based on the availability of skilled and available labor.

Let me give you an interesting example. In the 1990s I worked in the Research Triangle Park area of North Carolina. There was an insurance company there then called North Carolina National Life Insurance Company. It was black owned, and 80 percent of its employees were black. The company was started after the Civil War during the Jim Crow years in the South. As a black-owned company, its mission was to sell insurance to black citizens who in this era were not able to buy insurance from white-owned companies in North Carolina. This occurred throughout the South. Its affirmative action plan, which it was required to manage since it had government contracts, required it to affirmatively recruit, train, and promote white workers and to see that they were equally paid. You may look at that as a strange irony of the Civil Rights movement, but it was, after all, the law.

I have managed several affirmative action plans, and I have never had a plan that achieved full utilization. That is where the availability of all protected class groups matches the availability of each group's skilled labor. The closest I achieved was 85 percent utilization across all the categories, with a workforce that was equally divided between blacks and whites, which frankly was pretty good. Even when you are audited by government auditors, they do not have an expectation that you will have full utilization. What they are looking for is the following.

1. a commitment to equal employment opportunity, affirmative action, and equal pay
2. a plan that the company has implemented and monitored
3. top management support
4. the company taking action based on the measures and metrics of their plan
5. processes and systems in place to make improvements
6. In addition, they love to see diversity and inclusion efforts.

The United States is not the only country to have affirmative action laws. Europe has affirmative action laws to promote female employment and representation among management and executives. India has affirmative action laws to promote employment and representation in management and executive rights across its many castes.

The federal government wants its contractors to track all applicants for each job, their protected class status, and why they are screened out from being hired at each decision in the hiring process. For example, if you receive one hundred applicants for a mechanical engineering role and if the recruiter screens out 95 percent of them, the government will want you to identify the category from which each of the ninety-five individuals were screened out. In short, the categories can be inexperience, documented insufficient performance, or lack of required degrees, training, or certification. The auditors want to see decision making based on the objective criteria of the job, such as not holding a required degree or only having one year of experience when three years are required. Listing a reason such as not a culture fit is considered to be a subjective and will raise concerns that the company is discriminating if the company is underutilized in the hiring of blacks, women or other protected classes..

Below is the list of the types of employment tests and selection procedures that the EEOC lists as examples of acceptable screening methods. They will want them all to be validated tools.

- Cognitive tests assess reasoning, memory, perceptual speed and accuracy, and skills in arithmetic and reading comprehension, as well as knowledge of a particular function or job;
- Physical ability tests measure the physical ability to perform a particular task or the strength of specific muscle groups, as well as strength and stamina in general;
- Sample job tasks (e.g., performance tests, simulations, work samples, and realistic job previews) assess performance and aptitude on particular tasks;

- Medical inquiries and physical examinations, including psychological tests, assess physical or mental health;
- Personality tests and integrity tests assess the degree to which a person has certain traits or dispositions (e.g., dependability, cooperativeness, safety) or aim to predict the likelihood that a person will engage in certain conduct (e.g., theft, absenteeism);
- Criminal background checks provide information on arrest and conviction history;
- Credit checks provide information on credit and financial history;
- Performance appraisals reflect a supervisor's assessment of an individual's performance; and
- English proficiency tests determine English fluency.[277]

After the recruiter screen often there is a screen of candidates by the hiring manager, and a final decision on who to hire. The government will want the AAP to record why each candidate was screened out by the hiring manager, who was the candidate to get the job, and why were the other two finalists screened out? Again, the government will want to see the use of objective measures and the selection tests and methods listed above.

If you hire two hundred employees in a year, the government will want to see these data for each job opening if they audit you. What they want you to also look for are discriminatory trends across the aggregate of jobs in each job classification and for the company.

A sample AAP for a company of one hundred fifty employees was developed by the US Department of Labor. It can be used as a guide for larger numbers of employees as well. You can access it in its PDF form at https://www.dol.gov/ofccp/regs/compliance/AAPs/Sample_AAP_final_JRF_QA_508c.pdf.

All AAPs need to be formulated according to OFCCP occupational categories. From there they are customized to reflect an employer's organizational structure, policies, practices, programs, and data. For large organizations, usually an AAP is required for each business unit or major location. A business may include multiple facilities if the sites are in the same labor market or recruiting area (for example, several sites in one city, such as Nashville, Tennessee). Below is the typical organization of an APP.

- Organizational Profile
- Job Group Analysis
- Utilization Analysis
  - Placement of Incumbents in Job Groups
  - Determining Availability
  - Comparing Incumbency to Availability
- Placement Goals
- Additional Required Elements
  - Designation of Responsibility for Implementation
  - Identification of Problem Areas
  - Action-Oriented Programs
  - Internal Audit and Reporting System
- Support Data
- General Requirements
- Guidelines on Discrimination because of Religion or National Origin

The PDF I cited above also provides sample forms to use in an AAP, such as Workforce Analysis, Job Group Analysis, Utilization Analysis forms, and Identification of Problem Areas.

No one should do AAPs manually. If you are a federal contractor, it is a necessity that your applicant tracking system provide you with the analytics to complete an AAP. At a minimum this will include the ability to track all job applicants to either a hire or reject decision, provide reasons for the decision, report on applicant flow, and collect self-identification data on race/ethnicity, gender, disability status, and protected veteran status. It will also need to assign disposition codes to job seekers and applicants and evaluate the effectiveness of your sourcing efforts in meeting AAP placement goals and hiring benchmarks. Paycor and HireCentric are two applicant tracking systems that claim to have these features for AAP reporting.

To follow the guidance of the EEOC and to pass an audit by the OFCCP, you will need to have an ATS that can store, track, and analyze hiring information, from the first applicant to an open position to the hiring decision, with a capability for large amounts of data. You do not want to have to maintain separate hard copy files or be forced to use Excel spreadsheets.

Below is a list of basic capabilities your ATS should have to support an AAP and the process flow to be compliant with EEOC guidance:.

1. Create well-written, standardized job descriptions with an attractive appearance. The postings should speak to your company's brand and employee value proposition, and the interesting work the employee will do to support the company's mission. In addition, the job description will need to list the minimum qualifications, and required knowledge, skills, competencies, and education and certification requirements. Using standardized job description templates will save you time and money and reduce hiring errors. Rewriting an application from scratch every time you post it opens too much margin for error, inconsistencies, and the potential for discrimination. All job descriptions should also include the Equal Opportunity Employer M/F/, D/F/ in the footer of the job description.

2. Track job requisition approvals throughout the chain of command in the ATS.

3. Track where the job ad was posted online or in physical locations and the timing of the postings. This may include online job boards, colleges, professional organizations, publications, associations representing diversity groups, job fairs, the Department of Labor website (which requires you post

all positions below the executive level on their sites), and professional networks.

4. Track referral sources.

5. List pay ranges. The EEOC has emphasized this guidance to assure female and people of color job candidates have full transparency on pay ranges, as an effort to reduce the gender and people of color pay gap.

6. Determine early in the process from each applicant for every job if they meet the minimum requirements. Minimum requirements could be a college degree in a certain degree field or a certification and years of experience-not a range of experience. All minimum qualification requirements must be applicable to the job and equally applied. If a candidate does not meet minimum qualification requirements, the US government does not require you to track them as an applicant. You want to select an ATS that allows you to automate this process. A good ATS will allow you to gather this information in an automated fashion from online Q&A, from a chatbot, or a pre-recorded video interview and store the data. The ATS should also then allow you to eliminate these candidates from your applicant flow logs automatically.

7. Collect from each applicant their equal employment opportunity information, which includes the date the application was received, name, position, race, gender, and veteran status. It also captures from the company the job group, reasons for non-selection, and date of hire.

8. Create applicant flow logs automatically for every job. It is required by the OFCCP and is used by them (and the company can do this analysis too) to determine adverse impact. That is, has there been some systematic discrimination against individuals because of protected class status? A Good ATS will allow companies to export applicant flow logs in the same form that the OFCCP will require of your company.

9. Have the capability of providing email correspondence directly from the ATS to the candidate. This way, all

communication to applicants is captured, easily retrievable, and consistent. It is important that each candidate be communicated to in a timely manner and with consistent verbiage.

10. Create hire/offer logs automatically. The OFCCP will require the company to record each hire or job offer made by your company during the reporting period being analyzed as a part of your AAP. It will require the same information as required in the applicant flow logs. These logs should be created with the click of a button and allow you to export the report to Excel.

11. Status codes should capture each candidate's status in the hiring process, such as rejected for not meeting education requirements. This allows the company to know how far each candidate progressed in the hiring process.

12. Disposition codes capture the reason why the company's recruiters or hiring managers have not chosen to hire someone and the date of the decision. This reason must be captured every time a decision is made in the hiring process, from who the recruiter selects for phone screens (or an initial screen) and who doesn't get selected for the phone screen, who the recruiter refers to the hiring manager, who the hiring manager selects for interviews, and who finally gets hired. Many legacy- based ATSs cannot capture this information. In addition, HR should keep all interview notes used to document interviews and hiring decisions for three years.

13. Continuously analyze this information in real- time. You will need to state in your AAP how often you audit your plan before the end of the plan year. For large companies that can be quarterly; for midsized companies, once at midyear, allowing enough time to adjust your recruiting strategies to reduce adverse impact against a protected class in a job group. Being proactive can allow you to avoid costly litigation. You want to select an ATS that allows you to generate dashboards and to signal alerts for adverse impact.

14. Create a report that can be used for compliance reporting. You want to be sure that the logs discussed above can be exported into reports that the OFCCP has formatted so they will not have to be formatted manually.
15. Prove confidentiality that no one outside of human resources has access to the disclosed ethnicity of any candidate before hiring decisions were made, and that no reports were run.

You also want a system that will display your EEO disclaimer and ask for voluntary EEO/AA information. In addition, you will want to require that all job applicants apply online through the ATS to ensure complete tracking.

The better the automation from your ATS to support tracking AAP-required data, the less manual work you will have to do. Today's technology has automated much of the work and has driven down the cost of tracking the required information. These systems can be set up in less than a week and can cost a few hundred dollars a month to operate—which is a lot cheaper than fighting off a discrimination lawsuit.

The federal government also requires that all federal contractors keep recruiting records for up to three years. This includes expressions of interest and résumés resumes for all applicants. Separate files are also to be stored for all applications and disability forms.

A final word on AAPs. They will help you gather the information to conduct the analytics to determine which recruiting sources are your best sources, the speed and effectiveness of your recruiting process, where the delays and shortcomings are in your process, and if your organization has systematic issues with attracting, hiring and equitably paying protected classes. With today's powerful Applicant Tracking and HRIS systems, and the advantage of having strategic talent data, having this data is critical.

I-9 Verification or E-Verify

The US government requires all US employers to verify that a worker has a legal right to work in the United States, whether the individual is a citizen or not a citizen. The process for doing this is the I-9 form and electronically E-Verification or E-Verify. Both employers and employees complete the form. The hired individual must present to the employer the documents to complete the form.

Employers may use the manual I-9 process unless they choose to use the E-Verify online process. If an employer is a federal contractor, and their state mandates E-Verify use, or a legal ruling requires it (such as past noncompliance), they are required to use E-Verify.

Applicant tracking systems that provide onboarding services should automatically collect and retain I-9 documents, and some do E-Verify. Check with your provider.

It is illegal to hire undocumented workers or to discriminate against individuals who have a legal right to work in the United Sates or to use the I-9 verification as a screening process. In addition, employers cannot specify which documents an employee must present to establish employment authorization and identity. Employers cannot refuse to hire or continue to employ an individual because the documentation presented has a future expiration date, which they usually do. Such a refusal may be constituted by the federal government as illegal discrimination. Individuals who use false documents may be imprisoned under federal law. Employers, however, are not to check for false documents.

The I-9 form, which is available from the website of the Department of Homeland Security, requires the employee to enter their personal information and US social security number. The individual must attest under penalty of perjury that they are a US citizen, a noncitizen of the United States, a lawful resident, or an alien authorized to work until the expiration date of their work authorization. A Spanish version of the form is also available.

The form requires documents from list A or a combination of documents on list B and list C. The form lists the acceptable documents. List A includes documents such as a US passport or US passport card or Permanent Resident or Alien Registration Card, and there are other less used documents that are also acceptable.

List B is also to identify the job applicant. Commonly used forms of documentation on list B include photo identifications that also have personal identification information, such as a state driver's license or ID card, federal, state, or local ID card, school ID card, voter registration card, US military card, or draft record. There are other acceptable options too that are listed on the I-9 form.

List C is to establish employment authorization in the United States. The most commonly provided forms are a social security card provided the card does not have restrictions on being used to validate employment. Also commonly used are birth certifications or an original or certified copy of a state birth record or US citizen card.

New hires are to present their documentation on the first day of work to a representative of the company. Employers are to verify employment of new hires within three days of hire unless the employee is to work three days a week or less. Then the form is to be completed no later than the first day the individual works for pay.

Employers must retain I-9 forms for three years after the date of hire or one year after the date the individual's employment is terminated, whichever is later.

There are monetary penalties for failing to collect and retain completed and signed I-9 forms. Monetary penalties for knowingly hiring and continuing to employ workers without following the I-9 process include violations ranging from $375 to $16,000 per violation, with repeat offenders receiving penalties at the higher end. Penalties for substantive violations, which includes failing to produce a Form I-9, range from $110 to $1,100 per violation.

E-Verify

The Department of Homeland Security has also created the E-Verify process to verify based on a web-based database if a new hire has legal authorization to work in the United States. E-Verify is voluntary. However, employers with federal contracts or subcontracts that contain the Federal Acquisition Regulation (FAR) E-Verify clause are required to enroll in E-Verify as a condition of federal contracting. Employers may also be required to participate in E-Verify if their states have legislation mandating the use of E-Verify, such as a condition of business licensing. Finally, in some instances, employers may be required to participate in E-Verify as a result of a legal ruling.

The E-Verify process begins with a completed Form I-9, Employment Eligibility Verification. Next, employers create a case in E-Verify, using the information from their employee's Form I-9, no later than the third business day after the employee starts work for pay. E-Verify checks information entered against records available to the Social Security Administration (SSA) and Department of Homeland Security (DHS).

If the employee presented a Permanent Resident Card (Form I-551), Employment Authorization Document (Form I-766), or US passport or passport card, E-Verify photo matching will prompt the employer to compare the photo on the employee's document with a photo displayed during creation of the E-Verify case. This helps ensure that the document the employee provided is genuine and relates to the employee.

E-Verify provides confirmation usually in seconds online, although some circumstances may require follow-up. The employer can close the case online once a final case result is determined.

CHAPTER 14: HIRING STRATEGIES DURING FULL EMPLOYMENT

The United States has benefited from a record recovery from the Great Recession of 2007 and 2008 thanks to a dramatic federal stimulus program and great recession management by the US Federal Reserve Bank chairmen Ben Bernanke and Janet Yellen. That is the good news.

Now employers are facing full employment and, with it, the challenges of recruiting in full employment. In February 2018, the US unemployment rate was 3.8 percent, with 6.2 million people unemployed. The lowest unemployment rate in record in the US was 3.7 percent which was achieved in June, 2018, and was equal to the lowest unemployment rate in 1969. The number of open jobs in the US is 7.6 million jobs, which is a record. This means there are more open jobs in the US than there are unemployed[278], and it has been that way for nine months, as of the printing of this book. It is virtually full employment. As a result, to attract new hires, you need to recruit passive job candidates who already have a job or new entrants such as graduates from technical programs or colleges.

It is time to switch from normal recruiting strategies to full employment recruiting strategies. Posting your jobs on your career sites and job boards won't cut it. Recruiting now is about being first to those new to the workforce and offering those who are employed and restless something better, building relationships, and acting with speed.

Eight tips to improve the speed of your recruiting and to build positive relationships with candidates.

1. **Improve your Glassdoor rating.** Many employers discount Glassdoor as a place that only the "gripers" go to register complaints. If that is the case, why do companies have Glassdoor ratings above 4.0? Nearly 80 percent of job applicants go to websites like Glassdoor to review the ratings and the employee reviews of the company's culture, interview process, and even the CEO. What they say about your company is important—too important to discount as the expression of "gripers."

   How do you improve Glassdoor ratings? Here are a couple of suggestions. When employees give a compliment to their manager or to human resources, thank them, ask them more about it, and then ask them to tell others about it on Glassdoor. Also, ask them to make a hiring referral to their friends. When employees make a hiring referral, thank them and ask them to tell the world on Glassdoor what they like about working at your company.

   When there is a criticism of your company on Glassdoor, respond to it and thank them for their views, and if possible, correct any facts that are wrong.

2. **Improve processes and respond quickly.** According to Deloitte, more than 45 percent of candidates never hear back from the companies to which they've applied, and a startling 83 percent of candidates rate their job search experience as poor.[279] It is time to get your internal recruiting processes in order so that those who apply for your jobs and get interviewed have a great experience. Every job candidate is

a valuable employment prospect. If you do not act quickly, you will lose the candidate to your competition.

Have clear daily processes and standards for reviewing résumés, initiating phone screens, inviting candidates for an on-site interview, and generating job offers. Make sure you are keeping job candidates up-to-date on their status through the recruiting process. Among your recruiters and hiring managers, make sure everyone knows their part and does it in a timely fashion. Have your interview questions for each role prepared and allow only trained managers to interview job candidates. Make sure when the candidates are on-site that you give them a tour of the facility, show them whatever you have that is new and leading in the marketplace, and allow them to interact with workers. You want them leaving impressed. And if *you* are impressed with them, give them a conditional offer at the end of the day or within twenty-four hours.

Implement a net promoter score for job candidates.

3. **Show off your employer brand.** Does your career site talk about your company's value and purpose? The cool work your employees do? Better yet, are there testimonials and podcasts from your employees talking about their mean-ingful work, their careers and why they like working for you? Do you discuss the medical, 401(k), paid leave, and wellness programs you offer? Do you summarize the coaching, men-toring, training, and career development you provide? Many employer career sites I see discuss the employer's products and services but never take these steps to explain the value of working for the company from the employee's point of view and the employer's brand. In an economy of full em-ployment, that decision is a big mistake. Job candidates have choices. If you want them to choose you, then you need to

explicitly tell them the impressive attributes of your company in a compelling way.

4. **Use metrics.** You can't have streamlined processes without metrics to make sure your processes are working. Many recruiting departments track time to fill or average days open for requisitions, and costs per hire. But these metrics are only a start, especially if you have high-volume recruiting. Also, monitor the days it takes to screen applications, the response rate to inquiries, time to generate offers, candidate dropout rates throughout the process, and six-month and first-year retention rates. In addition, you should track applications and hires by sources such as the job boards you use, referrals, LinkedIn, social media sites, and your career site. Don't just admire your metrics. Use them to manage your process. What gets measured gets done. Implement a net promoter score for job candidates.

5. **Make sure you have enough employee referrals.** If your referral rate is not 33 percent of your hires in retail or 50 percent in manufacturing, then something is wrong. Is it poor pay and benefits, mean supervisors, or a bad culture? Or is the problem that you're not encouraging employees to make referrals or you don't have an easy process for doing so? Consider doubling your current referral bonus and make sure the process for making a referral is easy and easily understood. Referrals with bonuses are often the cheapest and most reliable hiring strategy.

6. **Make friends with the employees who resigned or were laid off.** Some companies have a strange animosity for employees who resign and go to work for a competitor or in another industry. I can understand the concerns if someone is taking with them the valuable training and even worse Intellectual Property off to a competitor. But in a competitive labor economy, it is important to realize that not every career move works out. Some of those employees may have discovered that the company they moved to wasn't as good

as they thought. They may even be willing to move back, especially if they are employees early in their careers. In times of tight employment, it is time to be open to such moves and even to regularly reach out to the employees that you may have laid off and also to those who resigned from your jobs.

7. **Update your technology to what marketing is using.** Recruiting technology has changed dramatically in the past two years. I am not talking about social media recruiting on Facebook or Instagram. That has become standard. I am talking about augmenting your legacy applicant tracking system (which is often clunky and requires an hour to complete an application—ugh!) with automatic scheduling, text recruiting, and machine learning. With these technologies, you can contact a passive job candidate with a text and invitation to submit a résumé and schedule a phone screen. TextRecruit is powered by IBM Watson and IBM claims a 37 percent response rate within twelve minutes of the text. You can use various scheduling technologies such as Acuity to make the scheduling process easier.

For more sophisticated screening, consider using chatbots such as AllyO.

There is also video interviewing technology, which has been around for ten years but is getting much more sophisticated. Wepow technology, for example, allows you to have live or prerecorded interviews to move the process along. According to Wepow CEO and Cofounder Imo Udom, one of Wepow's first customers was Adidas. Imo told me in a recent interview that Adidas had to conduct interviews in December 2011, a hectic month. "They set up with us a prerecorded interview of five questions on Thursday and sent it to one hundred fifty job applicants. By Monday, Adidas had a staggering 147 responses, or 99% of the targeted candidates, complete their interview." Now Adidas has expanded its prerecorded video interviewing for much of its campus recruiting and uses Wepow for numerous job openings across the globe.

8. **Use artificial intelligence to identify and build relationships with a strategic talent pool**. Don't count alone on post and pray with job boards during full employment. If you are like many recruiters, you are finding that the number of applicants per job posting is sharply decreasing. Instead, find and directly contact the job candidates. Today, there are new and reliable artificial intelligence (AI) technologies that have been in development for more than three years before their commercial release. They are easy to use. After developing a detailed job description, these platforms (which have online, global databases of more than 300 million candidates) will find and highlight the qualifications and employment histories of job candidates—and even rate the candidates who best match your job requirements.

These AI technologies are not old-fashioned lists. They are current online real-time inquiries that comb tens of current job boards, social media, and LinkedIn to find your ideal candidates and provide you with contact information. With demonstrations I have provided using ThisWay Global's AI technology, clients have found candidates in seconds that they could not find on big-name job boards and LinkedIn. With AI, your strategy goes from post and pray to proactively and quickly contacting candidates and beginning a dialogue with them. It also enables you to build a strategic talent pool with the candidates who are not now ready to make a career move.

AI can also be used to target new entrants in the workforce, such as college graduates from your preferred universities and military personnel beginning their civilian careers. It also can be used proactively to improve diversity recruiting. It is very flattering when a company calls the candidate as opposed to waiting for the candidate to make the first move. In addition, AI platforms can tell you how many competing job postings exist in a regional labor market, at what companies, the average pay being offered, and the average days open. It can be used as a data analytics tool to shape your recruiting strategies.

Artificial intelligence can be economical too. Because of the volume of qualified candidates AI identifies for many jobs, you can spend your money on AI and less money on ineffective job boards.

However, to be effective with AI, you need to develop strategies to reach out to passive job candidates and get them to respond to your texts or emails, and for strategic positions, to your phone calls. With entry-level roles, it is good to offer entry into a raffle for responding to your text.

Once you have a candidate on the phone or responding to your text, you need to build a relationship with them. Start by learning what they are currently doing, why they are interested in leaving their current company, and what specific characteristics they are looking for in new opportunities. If they are not ready to leave now, ask them to tell you about a time they might consider a new job. After their project is over? After the next performance review and pay cycle? After they receive their bonus? Tell them you see them as a valuable resource for your company and that you will follow up with them at a specific time.

You will also want to add them to whatever social media list you have for job candidates or make sure your ATS tells them when a job opening occurs that meets their criteria. If they are strategic candidates, it is still best to call them.

If this feels like sales, that is because it is like sales.

If your company has a problem with oppressive or bullying management or a toxic work culture, you will need to begin by addressing those issues. Start now. Employees today have choices.

In addition to the steps I have outlined above and working to have an inclusive work culture that attracts and retains the best workers without regard to demographic factors or gender orientation, which I have discussed at length in this book, I also recommend that you consider expanding or getting serious about one or more of the strategies I will elaborate on in the five sections below. They are

1. The long-term unemployed and the disabled
2. Veterans (There are about 240,000 vets entering the labor market each year.)
3. The formerly incarcerated (who number over seventy million)!
4. Immigrants who can work legally in the United States
5. People over age fifty-five

You will need to take up strategies that fit within the purpose, culture, and values of your organization and have the support of executive management. The company's talent strategies will need to be revised to identify and recruit these different categories of US workers. It is probably best to prioritize where you put your focus depending on the skill sets you need and your accessibility to this talent. For example, in Phoenix it might be wise to increase your emphasis to hire those over age fifty-five, veterans, and immigrants because of the high concentration of these workers there.

During times of full employment, successful companies will devise strategies to recruit and train the workforce they need to be successful.

The Long-Term Unemployed and the Disabled

In 1990, the US unemployment rate was 5.6 percent, and I needed manufacturing workers for an aerospace business located in the Raleigh-Durham-Research Triangle Park area of North Carolina. Our manufacturing jobs did not require technician training, and this was before digitization. We needed workers who followed directions, were great team players, and had good manual dexterity.

I employed two strategies. The first was to hire workers who came out of job employment programs sponsored by the local government and funded by the federal government. The program was known as Private Industry Councils. Local government would recruit workers who had struggled to find jobs. They assessed the workers' needs and provided training to round out their skill sets. If workers did not have a high school diploma, they enrolled them in GED programs. They also provided them with work readiness and socialization skills.

We hired a handful of workers in this program after interviewing them and having them take the general aptitude test battery, the GATB. They were very appreciative of the opportunity, did well at work, and were dependable.

The second strategy was to dedicate a manufacturing line with both hearing-impaired and hearing-enabled workers. We already had the hearing-enabled workers. I reached out to a local organization that provided job readiness and basic skill training to the hearing impaired. My suggestion was that we would train the factory supervisors and any current hearing-enabled workers who volunteered to learn sign language. We would then contact agencies that worked to find jobs for the hearing impaired and ask for referrals. I briefed these agencies on the products we made, the type of work we did, and the skills we were looking for and asked the agencies to refer qualified workers to us. They enthusiastically agreed.

With the support of top management of the facility, I reached out to our manufacturing management and asked them to identify a manufacturing manager and team they thought would be ideal for this type of work. They identified two lines. The managers and at least three assemblers per line were trained on signing. We hired three hearing-impaired employees. They worked out well and were very thankful for the work. The employees whom we trained to sign also volunteered to sign for the employees when they attended employee meetings or briefings on open enrollment benefit changes. One of the most rewarding outcomes of this effort was to see how the hearing-enabled assemblers, particularly the ones who learned to sign, coached and looked after the hearing-impaired employees. As one of our long-term assemblers told me, "We kind of became their workplace mothers."

Six Strategies to Recruit a Veteran Workforce of 240,000

I was pleasantly surprised to learn that the unemployment rate for veterans in October 2018 was lower than the US unemployment rate—2.9 percent versus 3.7 percent. Hiring veterans is a useful recruiting strategy during full employment because two hundred forty thousand veterans leave active duty and enter the US workforce every year, and two-thirds of veterans have completed transitional services to work in the economy at large. Moreover, 80 percent of military training has a direct transition to the civilian workforce, and 20 percent of veterans have college degrees.[280] The US military is fully integrated, so veterans have training and experience to work in a diverse workforce successfully.

Many employers may resist veteran recruiting due to concerns about how successfully veterans may transition to civilian work life, and disabilities such as post-traumatic stress disorder. There are, however, many successful strategies to overcome issues of transition and PTSD.

Veterans represent a ready workforce eager to begin careers outside of the military.

Here are six strategies to improve your ability to attract and hire veterans.

1. **Promote on your career site that your organization values the service that veterans and their family members have given to our country and state that you support the hiring of returning service members and military spouses.** You can use terms such as: *If you are a veteran or wounded warrior and would like assistance with the employment process at XYZ Company, please contact us at xyz@ yourcompany.com.* It is essential to provide all new hires, regardless of disability or perceived need, information outlining the process for requesting accommodations at every point in the employment process.

2. **Know where to find veterans.** Websites such as Military. com, HireVetsFirst.gov, and HelmetstoHardhats.org are great resources for recruiting top veteran applicants. What's more, most of these resources will let you post open positions at no cost. Ask your current veterans to help you with recruiting by referring their unit friends for open positions in your company.

3. **Target your search.** Just as with typical recruiting practices that mention required degrees, certifications, job competencies, and experience, consider using military language in your outreach and job descriptions. You can target specific military occupational specialty codes that relate to civilian positions by using O*NET OnLine.

4. **Create a culturally sensitive new hire orientation plan that provides insights to veterans on the more ambiguous reporting and authority structures in corporations.** Companies need to understand that the military has a very clear hierarchical structure. Rank is worn, literally, on your uniform (and understood by *all*). There is no misunderstanding as to who's in charge, who gives the orders, and who follows them. Furthermore, career growth and promotion

opportunities are clear and distinct. The civilian workforce tends to be more ambiguous. Thorough onboarding programs that also provide new hires with a mentor or coach can help veterans transition to the new work environment. This approach can also clarify how work gets done, how they will be trained, how decisions are made, and ultimately how the mission is achieved.

5. **Promote a veteran-friendly workplace.** Just as many companies recognize and celebrate black history during the month of February or breast cancer awareness during the month of October, so too should service members and the families of service members be recognized for their service and the ultimate sacrifice on Veterans Day and Memorial Day. If you are a large employer, start an affinity group for veterans like you may have for women, Hispanics, blacks, Asians, Native Americans, the disabled, and LGBTQI members of your workforce.

6. **Make available resources to deal with post-traumatic stress disorder (PTSD).** Post-traumatic stress disorder is a trauma- and stress-related disability that may develop after exposure to an event or ordeal in which death, severe physical harm, or violence occurred or was threatened. Traumatic events that may trigger PTSD include violent personal assaults, natural or unnatural disasters, accidents, or military combat. PTSD affects about 8 million American adults and can occur at any age, including childhood. Women are more likely to develop PTSD than men. Depending on where they served, the percentage of veterans with PTSD is expected to be roughly 10 percent for the Gulf War, 12 percent for the Afghanistan War, and 30 percent for the Vietnam War. PTSD is frequently accompanied by depression, substance abuse, or anxiety disorders.[281] There are many successful treatments for PTSD.

What can employers do to help workers overcome PTSD?

The workplace is not a treatment setting, and organizations should not try to replicate the role of mental health providers. However, by providing an environment of awareness, support, and tolerance, and health plans that cover mental health, companies can help ensure workers living with PTSD succeed in attaining healthy and productive lives. Workplace Mental Health has easy–to-implement strategies to help people with PTSD better manage any physical, cognitive, or emotional limitations they may be experiencing.

Is your organization actively recruiting and integrating veterans in your work environment? With roughly two hundred forty thousand veterans entering the workforce every year, they are too large a source of trained labor to ignore. [282]

Hire People with Criminal Records for Targeted Roles

I presented at DisruptHR at Domenico Winery in San Carlos, California, on May 31, 2018. DisruptHR is a forum where ten speakers are given five minutes each, twenty slides that automatically change every fifteen seconds to present a disruptive idea to improve HR, culture, and leadership. My presentation was "It Is Time to Face the Truth about Employee Engagement."

The truth I presented was that the $74 billion employee engagement industry is an outdated idea that isn't moving the needle much on improving employee engagement or business performance. Rather than employee engagement, more time and energy should be spent on culture development and training. The crowd loved it.

The crowd, however, preferred the first speaker of the evening. She was Shelley Winner. Shelley is a lovely, tall, slender, young, white woman who had the air of confidence and invincibility I find among many young women in Silicon Valley.

Shelley had an extraordinary and courageous story to tell about herself in her five minutes of disruption. Shelley told us that she was incarcerated for selling drugs. She publicly thanked a multinational high-tech firm for giving her a second chance at life and asked her two managers to stand so she could introduce them to the audience and thank them. They stood and received a rousing ovation from the audience.

In Silicon Valley, many of the DisruptHR presentations are about new technology, topics like how IBM Watson and artificial intelligence will disrupt recruiting. The need for more big data analytics. The latest platform for performance management, delivering rewards, and employee engagement, yadda, yadda, yadda.

Shelley reminded us all about caring and forgiveness in society. Shelley reminded us all what human resources can be about.

As a father of three adult children, including two daughters, Shelley's story tugged on my heart—made a little cynical over thirty years of business cycles, legal and employee relations issues, organizational politics, and HR. You could have heard a mouse scurry across the floor during her presentation.

It should not have been that disruptive a story, but it was.

After my presentation, Bernadette Jones, the head of Visionova, an HR Consulting firm in the Bay Area, got up to present at DisruptHR and began with a slide that said, "One-third of working adults have a criminal record."

One-third! Astounding. It made me ask the question, with more open jobs in the United States than unemployed, is it time to more seriously consider formerly incarcerated adults for our entry-level job openings?

Listening to Bernadette, I recalled a program started in the mid-1980s by my mentor at Honeywell, the vice president of Minneapolis labor relations, Mike Lynch, to give what were then called "ex-cons," a term that is no longer preferred, jobs in Honeywell's Minneapolis factories. It was approved through Honeywell's CEO. It worked well. The formerly incarcerated employees were overall good and loyal employees. Then one day disaster struck. One of the formerly incarcerated employees murdered another employee during nonworking hours at a private party. Although the incident did not occur at work, word spread, and the program was ended.

Is it time to try this again? Both Shelley and Bernadette gave compelling reasons for a yes answer.

A few weeks after DisruptHR, I met Bernadette Jones in her office in Emeryville, across the Bay Bridge from San Francisco. "How did you get an interest in hiring the formerly incarcerated?" I asked.

"It goes back to the late 1990s," she began. "My husband and I have been entrepreneurs for some time. We had just won a contract and had to hire fifteen field technicians almost overnight. It was low unemployment. We started group interviews to tell the job candidates about the job, working conditions, and pay and that we would do background checks. We then asked anyone who was interested to stay. Several people left. Three of the people who stayed were formerly incarcerated. They told us their stories, and we decided to hire them after waiting on the background check.

Two of them lasted about a year as field technicians. They were good employees, nothing extraordinary. However, the third one worked for us for five years. He rose to be a lead field tech and interacted with our customers. He was arrested at age nineteen for a public disturbance issue. When the police arrived, he resisted arrest and was arrested and incarcerated for twelve yers."

Bernadette explained that his performance at first wasn't very good. "We could tell that he lacked basic life skills with teamwork and feeling comfortable asking for help. We gave him one-on-one training for these skills. It worked. He eventually left us for more pay at a larger company. He and his wife were able to build their first home when he left us to work for the larger company.

"Ever since then, I have been an advocate of hiring the formerly incarcerated, banning the box—which means doing the background check after making a conditional offer—and the Fair Chance Movement."

I began to further research the question.

Citing the "around 70 million" Americans who have some sort of a criminal record, President Barack Obama in November

2015 asked business and educational institutions to take the Fair Chance Pledge. The pledge is outlined in the box insert on this page. According to President Obama, "Millions of Americans who have criminal records have difficulty even getting their foot in the door to try to get a job, much less actually hang on to that job. That's bad for not only those individuals, it's bad for our economy. It's bad for the communities that desperately need more role models who are gainfully employed. So we've got to make sure Americans who've paid their debt to society can earn their second chance."[283]

A total of thirty states have adopted Fair Chance Policies at least for public-sector hiring. Over 70 percent of the US population now lives in one of those thirty states or the more than one hundred fifty cities and counties that have banned the box.[284]

> ### Fair Chance Pledge
> **Promote Fair Chance Hiring Practices:**
>
> The most important contribution businesses can make to this effort is to give a fair chance to all applicants to ensure that information regarding an applicant's criminal record is considered in proper context, and to engage in hiring practices that do not unnecessarily place jobs out of reach for those with criminal records. Specifically, you can commit to:
>
> Banning the Box by delaying criminal history questions until later in the hiring process;
>
> Training human resources staff on making fair decisions regarding applicants with criminal records;
>
> Ensuring internships and job training are available to individuals with criminal records;
>
> Using reliable background check providers to help ensure accuracy;
>
> Hosting a Fair Chance and Opportunity Job Fair; and
>
> Taking Action in Your Local Community.
>
> While the focus is on fair chance opportunity, there are other important ways for businesses to contribute to this effort, such as:
>
> Supplying tools for success (business clothing, cell phones, internet service, transit cards, or child care services);
>
> Offering support to regional reentry facilities; and
>
> Providing mentors to children of incarcerated parents.
>
> We encourage you to share best practices and success stories with other employers.
>
> From the President Obama Whitehouse Archives.

According to the National Employment Law Project, Fair Chance hiring reforms were embraced in both red and blue states across the country in 2017. The governors of Kentucky, Indiana, Pennsylvania, and Arizona issued executive orders delaying conviction and arrest inquiries for hiring in the state executive branch. Nevada and Utah enacted legislation to delay background checks and record-related inquiries in state or local government hiring. California enacted legislation requiring public- and private-sector employers to delay inquiries and background checks until after selecting a candidate and making a conditional job offer.[285]

According to the Brennan Center for Justice at New York University Law School, the number of Americans with a criminal history has risen sharply over the past three decades. Today, nearly one-third of the adult working-age population has a criminal record. As Bernadette Jones said, that is 70 million adults. In fact, so many Americans have a criminal record that counting them all is nearly impossible. The Brennan Center puts 70 million adult working-age people in perspective.

- America now houses roughly the same number of people with criminal records as it does four-year college graduates.
- Nearly half of black males and almost 40 percent of white males are arrested by the age of twenty-three.
- If all arrested Americans were a nation, they would be the world's eighteenth largest nation. Larger than Canada. Larger than France. More than three times the size of Australia.
- The number of Americans with criminal records today is larger than the entire US population in 1900.
- Holding hands, Americans with arrest records could circle the earth three times.[286]

These are alarming numbers.

Many adults with a criminal record served time for using illegal drugs. Some for selling illegal drugs. About two-thirds of the nation's 2.3 million inmates are addicted to drugs or alcohol, compared to 9 percent of the general population, according to a study by the National Center on Addiction and Substance Abuse at Columbia University. Yet only 11 percent of addicted inmates receive any treatment.[287] Studies have found that more than half of them go back to using drugs within two weeks of being released. Their risk of over-dose is highest during this time. [288]

The American Civil Liberties Union (ACLU) published a definitive 2017 report on hiring the formerly incarcerated. It is called *Back to Business: How Hiring Formerly Incarcerated Job Seekers Benefits Your Company.*[289]

Their report begins with an eye-popping factual observation. More than six hundred forty thousand people are released from prisons each year. But because of the stigma associated with a criminal record, nearly 75 percent of formerly incarcerated individuals are still unemployed a year after release.[290] Research has found that lack of stable employment increases the likelihood that an individual will return to jail or prison, and joblessness is the single most important predictor of recidivism.[291] For blacks, the adverse effect of a criminal record on getting a job interview is 40 percent greater than for whites with similar histories.[292]

The next factoid the ACLU presented was also eye-popping for me. The consequences of unemployment for this population can be ruinous. At the national level, economists estimate that the gross national product is reduced between $78 and $87 billion dollars as a result of excluding formerly incarcerated job seekers from the workforce.[293] The ACLU reports that corporations like Total Wine & More, Starbucks, Home Depot, American Airlines, Koch Industries, and Under Armour have begun hiring people with criminal records. Smaller companies are also tapping into this pool of job seekers, including Butterball Farms, Dave's Killer Bread, and Haley House Bakery. [294]

Economists confirm that hiring people with criminal records is smart business. Retention rates are higher, turnover is lower, and employees with criminal records are more loyal. At Total Wine & More, human resources managers found that annual turnover was on average 12.2 percent lower for employees with criminal records.[295] Electronic Recyclers International (ERI) saw a similar outcome: by adopting a program to recruit employees with criminal histories, it reduced turnover from 25 percent to just 11 percent.[296]

That brings us back to Shelley Winner and her story of awakening and courage. And her struggle for rehabilitation, redemption, and to earn a fair chance at getting a job on the "outside" with a multinational technology company.

I invited Shelley to lunch in San Francisco in late June 2018 to learn more about her experience getting work after being incarcerated—not an easy endeavor. Shelley suggested Café du Soleil on Third Street, an excellent and unassuming French café with croissants, lobster bisque, sandwiches and salads, and sidewalk seating. I asked her to tell me her story, beginning with the influences on her that led to crime, her arrest, and what were the factors that prevented her from returning to her old habits and landing a good job that pays a living wage with benefits. I sat back and listened for two and a half hours.

"My father left my mother and me when I was two months old," she said, politely munching on a prosciutto and brie sandwich on hard-crust ciabatta bread. Her mother met her stepfather when Shelley was a toddler. He would serve as her father figure. Although kind to her, Shelley's stepdad had a severe problem with serious addictive drugs. He was frequently in and out of prison for using and selling drugs. Shelley remembers her mother taking her and her brother to a park in Sacramento, California, where they lived, to tell them that Dad was arrested for drugs and would not be coming home for some time because he was in jail. "It was devastating as a child," Shelley said. "After a long period in jail, he was released, and my mother helped him get an apartment."

After he managed to stay out of jail for a while, Shelley decided to move in with him when she was a freshman in high school. She discovered that her dad was selling drugs, and his house was one party after another late into the night. "He got me drunk for the first time when I was eleven," she said. "All of the drug use at the house did not sit well with me. His rules of the house were, 'If you have drugs, you have to share them with me.' I dabbled with drugs then, more like a recreational user, but not too heavy. And I never did drugs with my dad. That was too creepy."

But in her twenties, she began to use methamphetamines. "It got so I had to use them to start my day." She augmented them with narco (an opiate pain medication that is a combination of opiates and acetaminophen) and other prescription drugs to allow her to sleep.

She ran into her high school sweetheart, who was also using drugs. She suggested to him that they leave Sacramento to find a better life. He excelled at construction. She created a résumé for him and helped him apply for construction jobs. He was hired by a firm in Louisiana, which paid to relocate them. "We packed up my little Honda and moved to Louisiana. We cleaned up our act and didn't do drugs. He did well at construction and was moving up in the company," she said. "I thought I would be living the rest of my life with him." But with success, he began to cheat on her. Feeling betrayed and without friends or family in Louisiana, she decided to leave. On a tip from a friend, Shelley applied for a bartending job in North Dakota at the height of the shale oil boom. She was interviewed over the phone and hired. The week she was hired, she drove alone to North Dakota "in my little Honda."

On her first night on the job at the bar, a coworker offered her some meth. "I will do it this one time," she thought. Unfortunately, the one time became a habit. Shelley quickly learned that meth, which sold for $30 a gram in Sacramento, was a scarce commodity in North Dakota and would sell for way more than that, $300 a gram, in the booming shale economy. Shelley purchased an ounce of meth from friends in California with the intent of selling it. With twenty-eight grams in an ounce of meth, if she sold most of it, she could pay off her car loan, she figured. "At $300 a gram, I could make $8,400," she said. "I stopped working at the bar and just sold meth."

Her business was good. "I did it for eight or nine months until I was caught. In a small town, word gets around fast. The cops knew who I was and that I sold it. They told the feds, who knew I was getting it from across state lines. They set up a sting."

They arrested one of her customers. "The feds found out that this woman wanted, more than anything, to be reunited with her baby son, who was taken away from her for her being unfit to raise the boy." They told her she would not serve jail time, but they would help reunite her with her baby son if she would help them catch her supplier, who was Shelley. "A sting was set up in a parking lot, where the woman was wearing a wire and a camera, so the whole purchase of two ounces of meth from me was recorded."

Shelley's arrest occurred at four o'clock in the morning a few days after the sting. The federal agents took their case to a grand jury, which authorized Shelley's arrest. "I was up for two or three days (on meth) and was finally sleeping when I heard the federal agents knocking on the door. It was so surreal. I heard them saying, 'Shelley Winner, open up this door. We are federal agents,' and I knew it was over. They sat me down in a chair and arrested me. I knew the minimum sentence for selling meth was ten years because of the minimum sentencing guidelines. They took me to jail, where I was in a cell with ten girls. It was overcrowded. We had to sleep on boat mattresses on the floor. I was also going through withdrawal. It was awful.

"In about five days, I was brought before a judge, who told me I was in a lot of trouble. He asked me if I understood the charge. I told him I did."

While awaiting trial and sentencing, Shelley was sent to a federal halfway house. She was still withdrawing from meth. The halfway house was very strict. No cell phones. Set hours for everything. But Shelley was allowed to work and found a job waitressing, which was her emotional release.

During this period and while still getting nauseous from her withdrawal, Shelley found out she was pregnant. "That was the turning point for me. I needed to make real changes for my unborn son and me. I decided to enroll in treatment. I enrolled in Teen Challenge, a faith-based addiction and recovery program."

Teen Challenge was started by Dean Wilkerson in New York and, after its success with teens, was expanded to adults. More can be learned about Adult & Teen Challenge at https://www.teenchallengeusa.com/.

"When I started at Teen Challenge in North Dakota, I was a mess. I was pregnant, hormonal, and angry. Of the ten girls there, I only liked two of them. I caused a lot of trouble and was on the verge of getting kicked out. Thankfully, Teen Challenge called my probation officer." The probation officer told Shelley that if she blew this opportunity to turn her life around, she would go to jail for ten years and lose her son.

"I wanted to keep my son. I wanted to change my life, but I didn't know how. Every day I prayed to God to take away my anger and to purify me. Every day, I prayed for that. I started to change. The other women saw it. I kept praying to God to work with me." Shelley built strong bonds with all the ten women in the program. They began to build trust in each other. "My last meal there was a real special night. I will never forget that last meal with those women.

"I was frightened by the thought of ten years in jail, which was the minimum jail sentence for my crime. The night before my court date and sentencing, I kept praying to God to help me prepare to go to prison. The federal judge was really cool. He told me that he was only going to give me four years, but if I was a model prisoner and completed rehabilitation, I could get one year off and one year in a halfway house. That became my plan."

Before entering prison, Shelley gave birth to her son (who is now being raised by Shelley's mother). She asked to go to Federal Correctional Institution for female prisoners in Dublin, California, across the Bay from San Francisco, to be near to her mother and son in Sacramento and to have visits from them. Dublin is a low-security prison and is known as *Club Fed* for women. At Dublin, she went to church, joined Bible study and the choir, and learned to sing and play the guitar. Shelley completed many programs, including an anger management program and a forgiveness program.

Shelley enrolled in a drug treatment program called Residential Drug Abuse Program (RDAP) that gave her new tools for dealing with stress and anger. She was taught the rational self awareness (RSA) technique. "It works like this," Shelley began. "When something makes you really mad, you write on the left side of a page of paper the incident that angered you. Then you write down how you feel, what you want to do about it, and the outcome of that action." Shelley went on to explain that on the right side of the paper next to "what you want to do," you write a new alternative action and its better outcome.

"Getting busted and becoming pregnant were wake-up calls for me. Teen Challenge gave me faith. God gave me strength and wisdom to make better choices. Techniques like rational self awareness gave me new tools to deal with the everyday stressors of life. Hey, everybody has stress and gets angry in life. The key is how you handle it. It really isn't that big a deal. Doing RSA's every day trained me to be more rational."

Just before Shelley's sentence was to end, she heard about Defy Ventures (see inset box)**, a program to teach the formerly incarcerated how to become entrepreneurs.** Over one hundred women in prison signed up for it. Shelley was one of the first to sign up. The program started while the women were still in prison. They had to create a business idea and plan, then pitch their idea in front of a group of CEOs, VCs, and Google executives in a

---

Defy Ventures

Defy's vision, according to its website, is to end mass incarceration and cycles of recidivism by using entrepreneurship as a tool to transform legacies and human potential.

Defy Ventures is an employment, entrepreneurship, and personal development training program that supports the incarcerated and formerly incarcerated to become successful, legal entrepreneurs and employees. They "transform the hustle" and maximize the potential of Entrepreneurs-in-Training (EITs) impacted by the criminal justice system by building redemptive communities that pursue entrepreneurship and personal growth.

Defy serves EITs through its affiliate regions of Nebraska, Northern California, Southern California, Colorado, and the Tri-State region (New York, New Jersey, and Connecticut).

"Shark Tank"-style competition. "None of us spoke publicly before," Shelley explained. "The night before the shark tank competition, I was so nauseous, I thought for sure I was going to mess up. I kept thinking, 'What if I forget and make a mistake?' I won the competition, and it was one of the greatest accomplishments of my life. It taught me to trust the strength in me."

From the Defy Ventures experience, Shelley met DeeDee Towery, the owner of ProActive Business Solutions, located in Oakland, California. Shelley knew she would need guidance when she got out of prison, and DeeDee offered to mentor her. "I called Deedee when I got out of prison and was living in the halfway house. She asked me what I needed, and I said, 'I really need a job.' She hired me on a part-time basis as I went to school.

"In Dublin, I saw a TV program about Code Tenderloin [see inset box] in San Francisco. They advertised a way for people who were formerly incarcerated or homeless to get into tech jobs. I signed up. They provided job readiness training. They helped us with résumés and provided mock interviews. Code Tenderloin also took us on tours of high-tech companies in San Francisco, such as Twitter and LinkedIn."

A manager at one of the high-tech firms Shelley toured with Code Tenderloin advised her to apply for a job at the company. An advisor at Code Tenderloin told Shelley she should apply for the job. "I decided to go for it. Code Tenderloin prepped me to apply for the position. I practiced interviewing so much, the real interview was not that scary. I applied and was surprised when one of their recruiters called me. I got an interview with the hiring manager, who loved me. She told me that she wanted to

Code Tenderloin, San Francisco, California

Code Tenderloin is a five-year-old project started by Del Seymour, a thirty-year resident of the neighborhood. It is sponsored by Independent Arts and Media, a 501(c)(3) organization.

Code Tenderloin provides dignity and opportunity through an intense job readiness and workforce development program.

It removes barriers that keep people from securing long-term employment. It helps people overcome barriers from finances, legal issues, soft skills, technical skills, child care, transportation, and education.

For more information, to donate, or to become a partner, go to http://www.codetenderloin.com/.

hire me and that she did not need to interview anyone else. I told her I was fresh out of prison and of my criminal record for selling narcotics. She said that was no problem but to be honest on the application. I completed the application and was totally honest."

During this whole process, the company sent Shelley some information about San Francisco's Fair Chance Ordinance. The ordinance states that the formerly incarcerated cannot be discriminated against in employment if their crime has nothing to do with the job. Shelley had applied for a sales role with the company. If she had been convicted of theft, that would have been a reason for the company not to hire her for the open position. The company requested that Shelley send them a letter outlining her crime, conviction, and the steps she took to be rehabilitated.

"I wrote the letter, and in it, I admitted I was wrong. I outlined what I did to be rehabilitated. I had several people review it before I mailed it back to the company." Three weeks went by, and Shelley's optimism for the job, once so high immediately after the interview, was sinking fast. "I was lying on my bed in the halfway house when another girl came in and said that I had a package at the front desk. My heart was pounding in my chest when I opened it. The company decided not to hire me due to my criminal record. I was crushed and began crying. I called my mom. She asked me, 'Who is in charge of this situation?' I told her God was. She told me 'to put it in God's hands.'"

"I had to fight this," Shelley stated. She called the San Francisco Fair Chance Ordinance, Office of Labor Standards Enforcement, and spoke with Donna Mandel. Shelley told Donna about being rejected for her criminal record, even though her crime was not related to the job. Donna asked her to email the letter. "Donna told me this is the worst form of discrimination." Donna offered to call the company and reassured Shelley that she had a 95 percent success rate in getting the formerly incarcerated job offers when connecting with companies to explain San Francisco's law and discussing options with the company.

It turns out that Shelley was rejected for the role by the human resources department at corporate headquarters, which was in a different city in a different state, and they had no idea about San Francisco's Fair Chance Ordinance. Donna explained San Francisco's ordinance to them and told them that based on her understanding, they violated the ordinance by rejecting Shelley for that role. The company told Donna that the position had been filled, but Shelley could apply for another opening with the same hiring supervisor. Three other candidates were being considered for the role, however.

"Thank God, I didn't give up," Shelley exclaimed. "I prepared for the interview really hard. When I went to interview with the same hiring manager, the mood was totally different. Not happy. At the end of the interview, I asked her if there was any reason she would not hire me. The manager said, 'I don't see any sales experience, but we can train you.'

"When I went home to the halfway house, I was so emotionally drained, I went straight to bed. Two days later, the company called and offered me the job. The hiring manager and the recruiter were both very happy for me. It was one of the happiest days of my life, to get a job like this with a living wage, benefits, and with this wonderful company. I told everyone at the halfway house, my mom, all the people that had helped me. I was so thankful for everyone who had helped me in my life. I got this job because I didn't give up."

After two months on the job, Shelley was voted the MVP. After six months she was promoted. She was invited to the company's headquarters as an honor, where she met the human resources manager who initially decided not to hire her. "She said to me, "Holy shit, girl! You made MVP in two months and was promoted in six months. I am so proud of you.'" The manager told Shelley that her example meant the company was going to be considering other formerly incarcerated people and not just in San Francisco and California.

Shelley asked her if she would be welcome to apply for other positions outside the Bay Area. The HR manager told her, "Yes. I am on your side now!"

Reflecting on the fight to get her job, Shelley said, "God opened the door for me with the Fair Chance program in San Francisco, and I had the courage and determination to walk through it. He put the will in me to fight and not give up. I felt like I had to fight for this job for every formerly incarcerated person in the United States. My perspective on life has changed so much since when I was busted. I am no longer the person who was incarcerated."

Since the interview Shelley has begun publicly speaking about her experiences at various recruiting fairs in the United States and Europe.

The website 70millionjobs.com provides advice and a job board for companies that want to tap this underutilized workforce during a time of full employment. It was started by Richard Bronson, who is the cofounder and CEO of 70MillionJobs. He has a criminal record and an incredible story to share about his days on Wall Street and a world of white-collar crime and securities fraud—which will be shared in his own words below.

70MillionJobs connects companies to adult Americans with some type of criminal record. Companies gain nationwide access to a pipeline of ignored talent—at scale. The website states that for large employers that need to hire hourly wage workers, it delivers applicants nationwide on demand. Their clients include ADP, Thor Industries, Airstream, Checkr, BNSF Railway, and Perdue. Richard himself has been interviewed by *Fortune, Forbes, Fast Company*, and *Quartz*.

Richard Bronson's story is fascinating. He lived the life portrayed in the Academy Award-nominated movie *The Wolf of Wall Street*, starring Leonardo DiCaprio, Margot Robbie, Jonah Hill, and Matthew McConaughey. Like Shelley Winner, he has owned his crime, made restitution for it, and is very thankful for the support of Defy Ventures.

The 70MillionJobs website provides an excellent summary of empirical evidence that outlines the benefits of hiring people with a criminal record.

- ◆ Studies show that employees with a criminal record perform better for you than those without a criminal record.[297]
- ◆ Retention rates can be higher, and employees with criminal records are often more loyal.[298]
- ◆ Individuals with criminal records are more motivated to perform at work because they have fewer employment options.[299]
- ◆ Employers who hire workers with criminal records can reduce their federal income tax by as much as $2,400 per employee through the Work Opportunity Tax Credit. In addition, the US Department of Labor offers bonding for the formerly incarcerated employees through the Federal Bonding Program to help employers mitigate any risk to other employees from hiring them.
- ◆ Enlistees with a felony conviction are 33 percent more likely to be promoted to sergeant in the US military than their peers with no criminal conviction.[300]

The website also emphasizes the social good of hiring formerly incarcerated people. Nearly 80 percent of those released from jail or prison will be rearrested within five years. Almost all of them will be unemployed at the time of rearrest. People with jobs, on the other hand, almost never recidivate.

"In the 1980s," he told me in an interview in June 2018 at Bravado, a café on King Street in San Francisco, "I decided to make a lot of money. The way to do that back then for a New Yorker was to work on Wall Street. I began working for Shearson Lehman/American Express, then Lehman Brothers, and then went to Bear Stearns. The last two companies collapsed in the 2008 financial crisis. Back then, it was an amoral culture at these companies. A culture characterized by Gordon Gekko, who said: 'Greed, for lack of a better word, is good.'" (Gordon Gekko was played by Michael Douglas in the 1987 movie *Wall Street*. It is debated whether Ivan Boesky, the real-life Wall Street insider stock trading criminal the character was based on, said, "Greed...is good," but his actions depicted greed.)

"I did okay at Lehman Brothers but left it to pursue other interests when friends of mine told me about a company on Long Island, Stratton Oakmont [the company depicted in *The Wolf of Wall Street*]. They told me I could make a lot of easy money there. I checked it out, and my friends were correct.

"The people there were not like the Ivy League types at Shearson Lehman/American Express, Lehman's, and Bear Stearns. They were often from Brooklyn, not that clever or gifted. Some of them could barely complete a sentence. But they were well trained in phone sales and were motivated to work hard and make a lot of money. I started there and quickly become a partner. I was able to incorporate the practices of the more established Wall Street firms. Stratton Oakmont specialized in new small cap companies that were going public. We filed and managed their initial public offerings (IPO).

"Our strategy was to file a new IPO every two months. We made money by selling large allocations of lucrative IPO shares provided the buyer would also buy a large number of aftermarket shares. They made money on the IPO shares but lost money on the more expensive post-IPO shares. Sometimes losing much more than their original gain. Stratton Oakmont manipulated the market by purchasing large numbers of the IPO shares, driving up the price, and then sold our shares short or long to make money afterward.

"I made a lot of money, traveled on private jets, had women, gambled big-time, and met famous people. I left Stratton Oakmont to start my own company with a partner in Miami, Biltmore Securities. Within a year, I hired five hundred people and had annual revenues of $100 million. However, the life caught up with me. Regulators were closing the loopholes. Lawsuits were being filed against us, and we were making settlements. In 1997 after making millions of dollars, I had enough. I was sick to my stomach realizing how much money people had lost. I left the company and set up a fund, which I publicly advertised, to repay people who claimed they lost money dealing with Biltmore Securities. The rest of the money I gave to charity.

"Then one day two federal agents knocked on my door and told me they were going to indict me on securities and exchange fraud. They wanted me to wear a wire and help them catch and arrest others. I told them I would not do that. I couldn't ruin other people's lives, but I would tell them all about what I did. Because I returned money to those who lost money, I received a light sentence and served twenty-two months at 'Club Fed' on Eglin Air Force Base in Florida. It was the original 'Club Fed,' where the Watergate prisoners served time. If you are going to serve time, it is a good place to do it. I have never been a good sleeper. Always struggled with insomnia. But in prison I slept well every night because lawyers were no longer calling me, I wasn't accountable for anything, and finally my conscience was clear. I felt like a human being. The prison took care of everything. It gave me time to read, play the guitar, and get my head screwed on straight.

"When I got out, I was fifty-one years old, and I needed to get my confidence back. I went back to New York and tried working for small companies with younger people, but it didn't work. I was the old guy with a record. I wasted years doing that. I finally got a job working for a nonprofit, Defy Ventures. They work to transform the lives of those formerly incarcerated by training them to be entrepreneurs.

"While working at Defy Ventures, the CEO of the business gave me great advice: 'Own your past.' She told me to be forthcoming about my past. After all, the internet has no secrets. In being forthcoming, it is kind of strange, but you tell the truth about your criminal past, and you give people an opportunity to feel good about forgiving you. It became uplifting for me not to lie. I give this advice to other formerly incarcerated people. I tell them this is a wonderful time to reinvent themselves and move away from their criminal past. Don't be lured by the drugs and women waiting for them in their neighborhoods. Figure out what you really want to do. Get an entry-level job. Get your foot in the door. I have always tried to swing for the fences and hit home runs. I tell them to be patient. Let nature take its course.

"The pace of nonprofits is slow and thoughtful. It didn't fit me.

I am a neurotic New York Jewish type who is never satisfied. So I left Defy Ventures to start my own for-profit business to help the formerly incarcerated get jobs. I launched 70 Million Jobs in New York. The city of Los Angeles found out about it and asked me to work with the city to place the formerly incarcerated. I then was chosen to participate in the Y Combinator Summer 2017 batch program [an incubator in Silicon Valley]. I was in there with these young Stanford grads. I was three times older than them and the least technical person there. When it ended, I received VC funding, and I stayed in San Francisco to grow my business. At 70 Million Jobs, we seek double-digit revenue and profit growth, do societal good, and reduce recidivism. I have a staff of six—two were formerly incarcerated—and hope to be profitable in a couple of months. The companies we call are generally open to the mission and employing those formerly incarcerated.

"The formerly incarcerated are not *eager beavers*. They did not have role models that worked regular jobs. We must market these entry-level jobs to the formerly incarcerated. However, once they start jobs, the research shows they are very loyal and hardworking. They appreciate the opportunity."

Richard told me that his business does not offer any mentoring or coaching to the formerly incarcerated. It is a job board that allows the formerly incarcerated to post for jobs with companies. He also does not have a way of tracking the employment rate and retention rate of those who get jobs through his job board.

You might be thinking, "Not so fast. If I hire a felon who served time for a violent crime or murder, and then they assault or kill an employee or customer, my company will be sued." I have lived through this scenario in the 1980s, as described above with Honeywell in Minneapolis, Minnesota. With full employment in the United States and more open jobs than unemployed (as of June 2018), I think it is time to try again.

There are of course legal limits on hiring the formerly incarcerated based on the crime, usually for industries and professions where a certification is required. For example, Richard Bronson, cannot work in securities because of his conviction for securities fraud. The US Securities and Exchange Commission (SEC) has a bad-actor disqualification for those convicted of certain crimes or who have restraining orders from being investment managers and principals of pooled investment fund issuers, promoters, compensated solicitors, executive officers, and 20 percent beneficial owners of the issuer. Disqualifying events include, among other things, certain criminal convictions, court injunctions and restraining orders, SEC disciplinary orders and cease and desist orders, and US Postal Service false representation orders. More can be learned by going to the US Securities and Exchange Commission website at https:// www.sec.gov/info/smallbus/secg/bad-actor-small-entity-complianc e-guide.htm.

Employers have a right to see an individual's criminal record before hiring them (if they are in compliance with Ban the Box regulations in their state or locality). However, that right has several key limitations, as we have discussed above. The decision not to hire someone who was previously incarcerated must be related to the job, meaning the criminal record indicated that the person could be a liability in that position. It makes sense to me that in retail, health care, childcare, and elderly care, you would not hire anyone who has recently finished serving sentences of theft. Certainly it is legal and not wise to hire convicted pedophiles in positions dealing with minors. Employers reasonably want to avoid negligent hiring lawsuits by not hiring someone who would be dangerous or unfit for some positions.

How do employers discern this? Here are some straightforward steps.

1.   First, follow Ban the Box provisions in your state and locality. Your labor attorney and organizations such as the Society for Human Resource Management (SHRM) have up-to-date listings of states and localities that have Ban the Box provisions.
2.   Run all applicants through your hiring process, which I hope uses structured interviews and validated assessments to

identify which candidates have the highest probability of success on the job. You may find that a formerly incarcerated job applicant has the experience and skills you need for your open positions; or if you are hiring entry-level individuals, is someone who will be a loyal and conscientious employee you need.

3. When you do find you have made a provisional offer to a job candidate who after the background check has a criminal record, if the crime is not job-related or legally disqualifies the formerly incarcerated person from being an employee, consider them. Look for actions and behaviors that show that the individual has learned from his or her mistakes, has gone through treatment for drug abuse, stress, and anger management, and has learned new tools to deal with the stressors of life.

Reflect on the cases of Shelley Winner and Richard Bronson above. What makes Shelley's and Richard's history instructive is that they both acknowledge their mistakes, are remorseful, and are committed to be better. It shows up in the actions they have taken since their crimes. Shelley enrolled herself in rehabilitation programs to learn new tools to alleviate her anger, to be forgiving, and to make better decisions when upset. She went through job readiness training and learned new job skills and how to write a résumé and participate in an interview. Shelley was also very determined to find and earn employment. Both Shelley and Richard enrolled in Defy Ventures to learn how to take their criminally risky entrepreneurial skills and apply them to legal ventures. They have both not fallen into recidivism. Shelley has been out of prison for two years, Richard for eight years.

Reflect back on Bernadette Jones's story of the formerly incarcerated individual she hired who worked for her company for five years and was promoted. He needed life skills coaching to take feedback, ask for help, and be a better team player. She and her husband provided that coaching to him, and he improved and thrived.

When you are looking to hire someone who was formerly incarcerated, look for these traits.

Hire Immigrants Lawfully and Lobby Politicians for Sanity

When I was hiring six hundred fifty employees over eighteen months at Medtronic's businesses in Santa Rosa, California, in the mid-2000s, our recruiting team would not have been successful with legally hiring immigrants both in low-skilled positions and for the highly skilled roles of statisticians, regulatory affairs professionals, some engineering fields, and scientists.

We hired many of these needed skilled workers as graduates from America's best national and regional universities, such as Johns Hopkins, San Diego State University, and California Polytechnic State University and MBAs from our top MBA universities, such as Harvard, Stanford, Wharton, and Kellogg. Most of the students we hired were born overseas, earned student visas to come to the United States, were accepted in our best universities, and had outstanding academic achievement, complemented with fantastic internships. We hired them using an H-1B visa, and many times we sponsored their US citizenships. We hired them because we could not find enough US citizens for our openings.

At the time, we executives talked about this as the *Brain Drain*, the draining of the best minds from China, Europe, the Middle East, and Southeast Asia, who preferred to work in the United States because of our civil liberties, civil rights, and relatively low levels of corruption over their home countries despite the ties with their families and indigenous cultures. This was importing the highly skilled to America, hardworking, savvy young people who would earn more money and pay more taxes than average Americans. The success of Medtronic's Santa Rosa businesses would not have succeeded without them.

Immigration has become politically charged in the world during 2016 and thereafter. The Syrian Civil War in 2011–2018 led to 5.6

million immigrants streaming across Turkey, Jordan, and North Africa trying to find asylum and a way to Europe to avoid the atrocities of war.[301] The arrival of these Syrian (and other North African) asylum seekers in Europe has given rise to nationalism and destabilized the political order of many countries and of the European Union, as evidenced by Brexit.

During the 2016 and 2018 US political seasons, immigration from Mexico, Muslim countries, and South America was a hot topic and was regularly blamed for causing unemployment among native-born US citizens, raising crime rates, and holding down real gains in wages, despite little empirical evidence to establish these claims. Based on research conducted by the Cato Institute using data from the state of Texas in 2015, there were 50 percent fewer criminal convictions of illegal immigrants than of native-born Americans in Texas. In addition, the criminal conviction rate for legal immigrants was about 66 percent below the native-born rate.[302] Even support for passing laws supporting the Dreamers (the children of illegal immigrants who were born in the United States) was not discussed much during the campaigns despite the support of 75 percent of Americans for such legislation.[303]

Now the United States is facing the *Reverse Brain Drain*, and it will hurt our economy as US-trained university graduates return to their countries of origin or migrate to Canada due to a lack of US work visas and also because the economies in their home countries are getting better. It is hurting the ability of US companies in the United States to hire STEMM workers.

I know from earning a BS in history from Saint John's University in Minnesota that the United States has always been the "land of opportunity," and each successful American generation has had its own wave of immigrants in varying degrees. In the colonial era, it began with the English, French, and Spanish who were escaping political persecution or looking for opportunity, the capture and enslavement of Africans brought to the United States, and the conquering and subjugation of native people.

In the 1840s there was a major shift due to the Irish escaping the potato famine and the Chinese arriving on the United States' western shores to work the railroads or California's gold mines. In the 1870s, the influx of southern and central Europeans, Mediterraneans, came to escape severe economic recession and extreme poverty, and with World War II came an influx of refugees and survivors of the Holocaust.

With World War II, there was a need for labor due to US men fighting overseas and limits to what Rosie the Riveter could do, and many people preferred higher-paying jobs in the defense industry over agriculture or lower-paying factory work. President Franklin Delano Roosevelt enacted the Bracero (which means *work with arms* in Spanish) Program with Mexico to enable American farms and factories to remain staffed and productive during the war. Despite the racial and wage discrimination and poor housing for the 4.6 million Mexican workers in the program and the occasional strikes for better pay and working conditions, it was a success and continued until the presidency of Lyndon Johnson. The program did accelerate the automation of farm and factory work and give rise to the United Farm Workers, headed by Cesar Chavez.

In 1965, a significant change occurred. Congress passed the Immigration and Nationality Act, which eliminated the nationality quota system of the Immigration Act of 1924. That act set a 2 percent limit on the total number of people of each nationality in America based on the 1890 national census. This system favored immigrants from Western Europe and prohibited immigrants from Asia.

With the change in 1965, Americans could now sponsor relatives from their country of origin. It led to a shift in immigration patterns away from Europe and opened doors to immigrants from Asia, once again, and increasingly from Mexico and Latin America.

In 1970s, immigration to the US accelerated. It accelerated further in the 1980s, after Congress passed the Refugee Act of 1980 and allowed for special treatment for Cuban immigrants.[304] The Refugee act of 1980 was passed due to President Jimmy Carter and Congress' concern for hundreds of thousands of Vietnamese and Cambodian refugees fleeing their homelands. It raised the annual refugee ceiling from 17,400 to 50,000.[305]

Currently, 43.7 million people in the United States are foreign born, which is 13.6 percent of the population. It is about a 50 percent of the ratio of immigrants to citizens for other industrialized countries, but triple the percentage of immigrants in 1970. Luxembourg, Switzerland, and Australia lead the list of having the most immigrant residents, with over 26% of their respective populations being immigrants.[306] About 11 million of the United States' immigrant population is estimated to be illegal, largely from Mexico and South America, which is about 25 percent of US immigrants. Beginning with the Great Recession in 2007, the number of illegal immigrants has decreased about 1 million, with largely Mexican immigrants returning to their homeland. This decrease was partly offset by the rise of unauthorized immigrants from Central America, sub-Saharan Africa, and Asia. Most US immigrants today come from Mexico, China, and India and live in California, Texas, and New York.[307]

Immigrants are good for the United States, and they always have been good for the United States in the long term, even though the process for immigrants and their children to find their place in US society (after the colonial period) usually takes two generations. Until that integration occurs, the immigrant generation and the first generation born in the United States tend to observe the culture of their country of origin, eat its foods, speak its language, and live and marry others of their culture. The exception to this is among African Americans, whose ancestors were brought to the United States as slaves in the colonial period and the Antebellum South, and with the Native Americans, who were conquered and moved to reservations, some to the point of extinction.

Today, some Americans point to Mexican, South American, Sub-Saharan African, Muslim, and Asian immigrants for their differences from America's dominant white culture and are concerned about how their presence will negatively impact American culture and drain the budgets of local social services and school districts. Today, most Americans would not consider people of Irish, Polish, and Italian ancestry to be a scourge, but that was not the case in the mid-1800s and even up to the election of America's first Catholic president, John F. Kennedy, in 1960, when these immigrant generations arrived in the United States. As with other immigrants and today's immigrants, they melted into America's melting pot and rose to success in American culture, as is evidenced by outstanding individuals whose parents immigrated from these countries, such as the Kennedys, A. P. Giannini, who founded the Bank of America, Frank Sinatra, and Apple founder Steve Jobs, whose biological father Abdulfattah "John" Jandali was a Syrian immigrant.

Today, immigrants make up 36 percent of the students pursuing STEMM degrees and over half of the PhD students pursuing mathematics, engineering, and computer science degrees in US universities.[308] Immigrants make up an extraordinary number of our entrepreneurs. In Silicon Valley the percentage of immigrants who are key founders of companies is 44 percent. Between 2006 and 2012, 24 percent of companies across the United States had at least one key founder who was foreign born.[309]

Immigrants improve the age distribution of the United States, according to the US Census Bureau, and can help generate the taxes required to reduce America's long-term debt, which largely goes to paying for Medicare, Medicaid, and Social Security obligations.[310] Finally, unskilled foreign-born workers make up 71 percent of US farm laborers. We wouldn't have most of our crops at affordable prices without them.[311]

Contrary to what some would say, repeated economic studies show that immigrants have no effect to at most a small effect on the wages of native-born workers.[312]

IT outsourcing firms have historically petitioned for many H-1B visas and have been widely suspected of abusing the system, but the number of their petitions has dropped, leading to an overall decline in petitions. However, the number of H-1B visa petitions from large high-tech giants such as Amazon, Microsoft, Intel, Alphabet, Facebook, and Apple jumped in 2017. In addition, fewer foreign students are applying to US colleges, and more foreign tech workers are headed to Canada, where there is an open door for skilled immigrant labor.[313]

The buzz in the San Francisco Bay Area is that high-tech firms are simply moving their high-tech jobs to Canada, Mexico, and overseas, where they can find the skilled labor. The buzz in Arizona, where I also have clients, much smaller than the big Silicon Valley giants, is the same. In order to get the skills needed, small and midsize firms there are hiring workers in foreign countries such as Canada and Mexico and overseas in Europe and Asia. This is, to be clear, outsourcing high-paying jobs and the income taxes on the salaries of those jobs out of the United States.

The United States currently needs skilled and unskilled immigrant labor. There simply are not enough native-born US citizens and even legal and illegal immigrants to meet our needs. I know this because I have this discussion with employers every week, and I have reported throughout this book the numbers that show that the United States has more open jobs than unemployed workers. I have had desperate business leaders tell me that they don't even bother with verifying the legal status of their unskilled workers (despite my urging that they do so) because without these workers, they don't have businesses, and the fines if they are caught are a cost of business. Native-born US citizens simply don't want to toil in their working conditions. While automation will continue to reduce the need for unskilled labor and will automate administrative roles, it won't happen at the pace required to make up for the low numbers of immigrants.

Congress set the number of annual H-1B petitions at sixty-five thousand and the master's cap at twenty thousand in 2005. However, after the 2016 US election, it was found that H-1B petitions and challenges, known as "requests for evidence," increased significantly in the third quarter of 2017 as the Trump administration changed how H-1B visas are administered and cracked down on abuse. Abuse, certainly, should not be tolerated.

As with hiring the disabled, veterans, and the formerly incarcerated, the decision to step up hiring of legal immigrants needs to fit within your strategies and have the support of top management. (Remember, you cannot discriminate against immigrants who have a legal right to work in the United States.) However, it is now more difficult to get visas. Hiring the unskilled will require job skill training and often making available English as a second language or having bilingual managers. Be compliant with I-9 requirements to verify that your workers can work in the United States legally.

This strategy also will require making your voice as a business leader heard to end the hypocrisy of our current political debate on immigration and to allow for sane immigration and work visas as well as control of US borders. It will also require, in my view, the assuaging of the fear of native-born working-class Americans. Businesses and business groups need to support government-sponsored or subsidized job training programs to enable native-born Americans displaced by economic downturns or in dying industries to be trained in the growing STEMM professions.

Hire Those over Age Fifty-Five

If you are fifty-five and over, you are now in the hottest labor group in America, with an unemployment rate of 2.7 percent[314] (October 2018 according to the US Bureau of Labor Statistics). In 2014, 40 percent of those fifty-five or over are employed or looking for work; a that number is expected to grow.[315] A decade ago, that would have been less than 33 percent. The hot labor market is luring older workers and the retired back into the labor market. Why work? They are healthier than past generations at their age, living longer, and worried that they haven't saved enough for retirement. Many companies are figuring out how to make it work.

At Tufts Health Plan in Massachusetts, older workers make up 34 percent of the company's workforce in positions such as physicians, clinical care managers, and administrators. According to Tufts CHRO Lydia Greene, "They bring so much experience to the table. They're very stable and very reliable and help us develop and mentor our younger workers."[316]

Even Wall Street is getting into the act. Goldman Sachs created a "Returnship Program" (I love the name) that provides mature workers with a ten-week skill training and mentoring program for those who have talent after a career break of more than two years. Of the three hundred fifty participants, roughly half returned to work for Goldman Sachs.[317]

Massachusetts General Hospital allows snowbird retirees returning to Boston to work again through a temporary agency the hospital established. A retiree medical plan allows eligible employees a more affordable way of paying the cost of medical coverage after retirement. The company provides a small financial subsidy and access to a private Medicare exchange, which has brokers who work individually with employees to find the most affordable Medicare plan that meets their medical needs.[318]

Despite the empirical evidence that age is not a predictor for job success, age discrimination is rampant, especially in some industries such as high-tech, even when job performance improves with age in high tech.[319] The US EEOC received 18,736 age discrimination complaints in 2017. That is nearly 22 percent of all types of complaints filed with the EEOC and fifth from the top after retaliation (49 percent), race (34 percent), disability (32 percent), and gender (30 percent) complaints.[320]

Many managers and recruiters are afraid to hire older workers for fear of their skills being out-of-date, being shown up by them, generational differences in socialization and communication patterns, that they will demand too much pay, and they will drive up the cost of their health plans because of their age.

Still, the examples above have shown how companies have figured out how to make it work with special training programs, temporary employment, and specialized health care programs. The use of flexible work arrangements would also enable older workers to avoid stressful commutes.

Can you imagine using older workers as part of your talent strategy?

Most companies cannot successfully integrate all five of these hiring strategies during times of full employment. The question is which ones of these five will improve your ability to recruit and retain great employees and be a great fit for your company's culture and purpose during labor scarcity?

Chapter 15: Call to Action

It is easy to be anxious and overwhelmed with all the rapid changes going on in recruiting. The landscape seems to change every month with something new in digital technology for recruiting or the acquisition of a new recruiting technology start-up by a current big player such as Indeed or Microsoft. Frankly, there are many technology companies out there making claims they cannot or will not support with disclosing or publishing their empirical data for all to see and analyze.

But the times have never been better to Hack Recruiting. Let's start with the basics.

Your company has a purpose and a brand to your customers and investors, a business model, strategies, products, and services that are competitive in the marketplace, integrated operating mechanisms across the company's functions, and digital technologies to improve operational efficiencies and help the company come up with disruptive innovation.

As with your company brand to your customers and investors, your employer brand will need its own model and integrated strategies across all human resources functions to lead and involve the workforce. HR will need to aggressively and wisely incorporate digital technologies to make HR and recruiting more effective and to appeal to millennials and Generation Z, who expect digital communications and platforms.

Recruiting is a high-volume, repeatable process and should be managed just as rigorously as an engineering design or

manufacturing process. Your recruiting process will need to operate efficiently and, in this era of competitive talent strategies, move
with digital speed. It will need to be agile to respond to changing
demands in volume. Everyone in the recruiting process will need
to understand their role, understand how their role interfaces with
digital technology, and be trained for their role, with ongoing feedback, coaching, and measures.

HR should strategically lead the recruiting effort and know
which sources of labor are best for the company based on its strategic workforce needs, financial resources, and global and flexible
workforce capabilities, all within the legal and regulatory environment around the world. That might be the use of contingent workers through technology platforms such as Upwork, contractors,
or temporary employees. Some companies are creating their own
temporary workforce platforms because the technology is easily
developed, and it allows them to save costs. For employees who
see the need for strong cultures and have long product and service
development cycles, they will probably need to recruit and nurture
a talented and dedicated workforce that is aligned to the purpose
of the company and the benefits it brings to humanity.

Long standing empirical research shows the best methods for
selecting job candidates. This is the work done by industrial/orga-
nizational psychologists. They study human behavior in organizations and the workplace and create scientifically developed tests
or assessments to predict who will be high-performing employees
at work. IO psychologists also scientifically measure which knowledge, skills, and abilities are most important for success in various
professions and determine how to measure performance and other
critical abilities at work.

Their body of research has consistently shown that the following, and a combination of the following, are the best methods for
selecting great performers on your job.

- **Work Sample Test,** which is a hands-on simulation of part or all of the job and can be used to select the best among *experienced* workers.
- **General Mental Aptitude Test,** which is a preemployment assessment test for IQ and other tests of general mental ability, special relationships, and reading, writing, and mathematics needed on a job. The more complex the job, the more important is IQ as a predictor of job success. They work if they are validated for the job family and do not adversely exclude otherwise qualified job candidates based on demographic factors.
- **Emotional Intelligence**, however, is just as important for job success as is IQ for positions which require empathy, self-awareness and self-discipline such as with executives, leaders, sales and customer facing workers. If you are not measuring the emotional intelligence of your candidates to move into leadership, executive or sales, or customer facing roles, you should be!
- **Structured Interviews,** which are preplanned interviews that go into detailed fact gathering on the person's work history and look for matches to the required job competencies, teamwork skills, and alignment to the company's purpose, values, and culture.
- **Peer Ratings,** which have high reliability compared to other methods, but they are hard to get during an interview process with external job candidates.
- **Job Knowledge Tests,** which are assessment tests, for example, for Microsoft Office and project management skills for project coordinators or software coding for software engineers.
- **Training and Education Behavioral Consistency Method,** which is hiring people whose training, education, skills, and previous experiences align with the job. It requires a structured interview or assessments to discern who is or is not a job fit.

- **Job Tryout Procedures,** usually a thirty- to ninety-day period for unskilled workers; works best with heavy doses of training and coaching.
- **Assessment Centers** are rated low for most jobs but do well for leadership and sales roles.

Here is what doesn't work based on the empirical evidence of I/O psychologists.

- **Age,** the only factor with a negative correlation—old or young, it isn't a predictor.
- **Graphology,** which is handwriting analysis and is almost as bad as age.
- **Interests.** Many start-ups and call centers love to select for interest, but if you don't also select for job skills, collaboration skills, conscientiousness, and integrity, you are depending on luck.
- **Years of Education**. A bachelor's degree, and to a lesser extent a master's degree, is essential for many professions such as finance, human resources, science fields, and many engineering, medical, and leadership disciplines because of the need to learn the theories, models, body of knowledge, legal framework, professional skills, and strategic thinking skills required and as an indicator of perseverance. However, higher years of education does not correlate well with job success.
- **Training and Education Point Method.** This is typical civil service methodology to earn points for job hiring preference or to get a promotion. It is objective and can help guard against political cronyism.
- **Job Experience Measured by Years.** The problem with job experience is that there is no correlation with performance after five years on a job.
- **Biographical Measures.** These include life experiences and also gender, age, race, color, and so on, all of which

are outlawed in the United States and other countries as a screening criterion.

Technology is hacking recruiting whether you like it or not. It is best to get in front of the power curve and determine which technologies will best improve your company's ability to recruit without busting your budget. Even more critical is to successfully integrate the technology with your work processes, which will mean changes in the roles of your recruiters, hiring managers, and administrators. It will reduce the need for repetitive administrative tasks, and the role of the recruiter will go from being the person who finds talent to the person who reaches out to, builds a relationship with, and builds a strategic talent pool.

Armed with vast databases, video interviewing, machine learning, digital communications, robotics, and measures, recruiting will become more data driven and strategic. Artificial intelligence will make previously unknown discoveries of who and where the talent resides and how much to pay them, and will identify your talent competitors. Human resources and recruiting leaders now can tell their executives the best talent strategies and even shape business strategies to match new locations to where the talent, best universities, and business environments reside. While artificial intelligence won't end the need for job boards overnight or even in the next five years, networking, finding, and assessing talent will significantly change in the years ahead.

The promise of AI is that it can improve I/O psychology's understanding of the best knowledge, skills, and abilities for job families and how to access them without adverse impact based on demographics and sexual orientation. That will require digital start-ups in this space to be transparent and to cut the high-tech marketing bullshit. They will need to share their data, methods, statistical analysis, and findings just like academics have for decades and let others examine their results and determine if they have value. HR and IT leaders will also need to become discerning on new technology to be able to pick out what new platforms are helpful and which ones are just flash. There is too much at stake not to have transparency with recruiting technologies.

The future arrival of blockchain networks will also quicken the speed of learning the backgrounds of job candidates and improve the integrity of the recruiting process, but it will take years to build these networks and assure they are secure and accurate.

During this time of labor scarcity in the United States, and frankly around the world, companies need to adapt their talent strategies. Certainly speed is of the essence. The early birds do get the worms when they know where to look. Improving your processes, training, and digital technologies will help you move with speed. You also need to treat job candidates like valued customers. Remember, they rate your hiring process and your employees rate your company like you rate a restaurant or service on Yelp. Job candidates have choices, and if you treat them poorly, they will accept someone else's offer. If their experience on the job during the first three months is bad, they will jump ship—and that costs you thousands of dollars of turnover, depending on the job family.

For too long, companies have ignored or given lip service to hiring the disabled, long-term unemployed, veterans, the formerly incarcerated, and those over age fifty-five. These groups represent vast swaths of workers. It is time to get serious about attracting, screening, and hiring them. The formerly incarcerated alone number 70 million. There are two hundred forty thousand veterans entering the workforce every year. These strategies will require work train-ing. Finally, lobby our government to create sane immigration and border security policies and stop the politically charged hypocrisy. America needs skilled and unskilled labor for the roles native-born US citizens either don't want to do or (for whatever reason) have not chosen to pursue in our universities. Immigration has always driven American renewal, innovation, invention, and entrepreneurism and is a source of our strength.

If you are a CEO, you should hold your human resources depart-ment accountable to knowing and implementing digitization in its recruiting practices in the same way you would hold your chief technology, marketing, operations, and IT officers accountable for using effective digitization. You should also hold them accountable for the effective implementation of technology and to track their progress and results just as you would other departments.

If you are a recruiter or HR leader, significant changes are here and accelerating. The days of HR staying safe in the payroll and benefits administration box and posting jobs on your favorite job board and LinkedIn and handing the screening off to the hiring manager are at an end. Machine learning and robotics will do those roles better.

HR and recruiting leaders need to expertly use the power of the databases and technology that are now available to them. With that knowledge they can guide the business on the best sourcing and talent strategies, how long it will take, what it will cost, what the candidates can do for them, and its return on investment. This is powerful, and when explained in the context of business strategies and the threat of competition, and in financial terms, it will shape strategy.

Back to you CEOs. It will be wise of you to listen to these strategic HR leaders, the ones who have awakened. They will be great partners to grow your business profitably.

Start hacking.

ABOUT THE AUTHOR

Victor Assad is the CEO of Victor Assad Strategic Human Resources Consulting and managing partner of InnovationOne. With over thirty years of experience, Victor has been an active member of executive business teams and leader of human resources organizations in fast-growth, high-technology, global businesses, such as Honeywell and Medtronic.

He is known for his business acumen, developing innovative cultures, leaders, and teams, excellence with integrated talent strategies, and innovative solutions to business challenges.

Victor now consults with small and large companies in various industries, including biotech, health care, real estate development, and management, retail, software, and semiconductors.

Victor blogs weekly and is publishing a second book *Brand It! Build It!*, which explores how agile, collaborative, and transparent cultures of innovation drive ongoing transformation and profitable growth and the talent strategies required to develop and nurture cultures of innovation, to be published in 2020.

Victor holds a master of arts degree in human resources and industrial relations from the Carlson School of Management at the University of Minnesota. He has executive certifications from Harvard and Kellogg.

ENDNOTES

1   Gallup, "Gallup State of the American Workplace Report," (2017);https://www.
    gallup.com/workplace/238085/state-american-workplace-report-2017.aspx
2   "Bersin by Deloitte: U.S. Spending on Recruitment Rises, Driven by Increased
    Competition for Critical Talent: Dramatic Shift in Recruitment Spending to
    Professional Networks from Agencies, Accelerates," (April 23, 2015, 08:29
    ET); https://www.prnewswire.com/news-releases/bersin-by-deloitte-u
    s-spending-on-recruitment-rises-driven-by-increased-competition-for-critical
    -talent-300070986.html.
3   Ibid.
4   Roy Maurer, "US Unemployment Drops to Lowest Rate in 50 Years: Wages
    Rise 2.8 Percent Year-over-Year," Society for Human Resource Management
    (October 5, 2018); https://www.shrm.org/resourcesandtools/hr-topics/
    talent-acquisition/pages/us-unemployment-drops-lowest-50-years-bls-jobs.
    aspx.
5   Eric Morath, "American Job Openings Now Outnumber the Jobless," *Wall Street
    Journal,* (June 5, 2018, 3:28 PM ET); https://www.wsj.com/articles/american-job
    s-outnumber-the-jobless-1528212776.
6   Roy Maurer, "US Unemployment Drops to Lowest Rate in 50 Years: Wages
    Rise 2.8 Percent Year-over-Year," Society for Human Resource Management
    (October 5, 2018); https://www.shrm.org/resourcesandtools/hr-topics/
    talent-acquisition/pages/us-unemployment-drops-lowest-50-years-bls-jobs.
    aspx.
7   Talent Board, "2017 Talent Board North American Candidate
    Experience Research Report"; http://3cmsd11vskgf1d8i-
    r311irgt.wpengine.netdna-cdn.com/wp-content/up-
    loads/2018/01/2017_Talent_Board_NAM_Research_Report_FINAL_180130.pdf.
8   Ibid..
9   Stacey Clark (Jan. 9, 2018), "Global Recruiting Trends 2018: The 4 Ideas
    Changing How You Hire," LinkedIn Talent Solutions.
10 Eric Schmidt and Jonathan Rosenberg, *How Google Works* (New York: Grand
    Central Publishing, 2014).
11 Vivian Hunt, Sara Prince, Sundiatu Dixon-Fyle, and Lareina Yee, "Delivering
    through Diversity," McKinsey and Company (January 2018).

And Thomas Barta, Markus Kleiner, and Tilo Neumann, "Is There a Payoff from Top-Team Diversity?," *McKinsey Quarterly*, McKinsey and Company (April 2012); http://www.mckinsey.com/insights/organization/is_there_a_payoff_from_top-team_diversity. And Rachel Emma Silverman, "Men and Women at Work: Unhappy, But Productive," *Wall Street Journal* (December 15, 2014); http://blogs.wsj.com/atwork/2014/12/15/men-and-women-at-work-unhappy-but-productive/?mod=WSJ_Management_At_Work&mod=wsj_valettop.

12   Chad Brooks, "Get Your Facts Straight: The Truth About Background Checks," Business News Daily (March 26, 2017, 8:16 AM EST); https://www.businessnews-daily.com/9834-background-check-myths.html.

13   Eric Morath, "American Job Openings Now Outnumber the Jobless," *Wall Street Journal* (June 5, 2018, 3:28 PM ET); https://www.wsj.com/articles/american-job s-outnumber-the-jobless-1528212776.

14   Brian Westfall, (2014) :How Job Seekers Use Glassdoor Reviews," Software Advice. https://www.softwareadvice.com/resources/job-seekers-use-glassdoor-reviews/.

15   Susan Adams, "How Companies Are Coping with the Rise of Employee-Review Site Glassdoor," *Forbes* (February 24, 2016, 3:49 PM); https://www.forbes.com/sites/susanadams/2016/02/24/how-companies-are-coping-with-the-rise-of-employee-review-site-glassdoor/#79e8f2716263.

16   "Salary and Benefits Are Most Important for US Workers and Job Seekers Looking at Job Ads, according to Glassdoor Survey," Glassdoor Press Center/Press Release (July 25, 2018); https://www.glassdoor.com/press/job-seeker-preferences/.

17   Ibid.

18   Mario Nunez, "Does Money Buy Happiness? The Link between Salary and Employee Satisfaction," Glassdoor Economic Research Blog (June 18, 2015); https://www.glassdoor.com/research/does-money-buy-happiness-the-link-between-salary-and-employee-satisfaction/.

19   Ibid.

20   Frederick Herzberg, "One More Time: How Do You Motivate Employees?," *Harvard Business Review* 46 (1) (January–February 1968): 53–62, OCLC 219963337.

21   Kerry Jones, "The Most Desirable Employee Benefits," *Harvard Business Review* (February 15, 2017); https://hbr.org/2017/02/the-most-desirable-employee-benefits.

22   Henry J Kaiser Family Foundation, "2018 Employer Health Benefits Survey," (Oct. 3, 2018), https://www.kff.org/report-section/2018-employer-health-benef its-survey-section-1-cost-of-health-insurance/.

23   Rachel Emma Silverman, "The Price of Unused Vacation Time: $224 Billion," *Wall Street Journal* (March 4, 2015, 1:41 PM ET); https://blogs.wsj.com/atwork/2015/03/04/the-cost-of-unused-vacation-time-224-billion/.

24   "The Pros and Cons of Unlimited PTO: Fear and Loathing or Unbridled Joy?" Glassdoor (June 8, 2017); https://www.glassdoor.com/employers/blog/the-pro s-cons-of-unlimited-pto-fear-and-loathing-or-unbridled-joy/.

25 "We Offered Unlimited Vacation for One Year: Here's What We Learned," *Fast Company* (November 02, 2015); https://www.fastcompany.com/3052926/we-offered-unlimited-vacation-for-one-year-heres-what-we-learned.

26 David P. Costanza, Jessica M. Badger, Rebecca L. Frazer, Jamie B. Severt, and Paul A. Grade, "Generational Differences in Work-Related Attitudes: A Meta-Analysis," *Journal of Business and Psychology* 27, no.4 (December 2012): 375–394.

27 Christy Hopkins, "Study: Millennials in the Workplace—Which Stereotypes are True?" (April 11, 2017), Fit Small Business. https://fitsmallbusiness.com/study-millennials-in-the-workplace/.

28 David P. Costanza, Jessica M. Badger, Rebecca L. Frazer, Jamie B. Severt, and Paul A. Grade, "Generational Differences in Work-Related Attitudes: A Meta-analysis," Journal of Business and Psychology, Vol 27, No.4 (December 2012), pp. 375-394.

29 Dr. Andrew Chamberlain, and Morgan Smart, "Why Do Workers Quit? The Factors That Predict Employee Turnover," Glassdoor. https://www.glassdoor.com/research/studies/why-do-workers-quit/.

30 "Employee Retention: What Makes Employees Stay or Leave," Paychex (August 19, 2016); https://www.paychex.com/articles/human-resources/employee-retention-what-makes-employees-stay-leave.

31 "Reinforcing the Performance Review: The 5 Forces that Are Changing Employee Performance Reviews," Namely; http://cdn1.hubspot.com/hub/228948/Namely_White_Paper_Performance_Review.pdf.

32 David Stillman and Jonah Stillman, *Gen Z at Work*: *How the Next Generation Is Transforming the Workplace* (New York, NY, Harper Publishing, 2017).

33 Janet Adamy, "Gen Z Is Coming to Your Office: Get Ready to Adapt," *Wall Street Journal* (September 6, 2019, 10:30 AM ET).

34 Ibid.

35 Ibid.

36 Ibid.

37 Ibid.

38 David Stillman and Jonah Stillman, Gen Z at Work: How the Next Generation Is Transforming the Workplace (New York, NY, Harper Publishing, 2017).

39 Jacob Passey, "Move over millennials, members of Generation Z are ready to work," MarketWatch. July 10th, 2017, 7:19 AM ET), Found at http://www.marketwatch.com/story/move-over-millennials-members-of-generation-z-are-ready-to-work-2017-07-07.

40 HR Drive, "Salary History Bans: A running list of states and localities that have outlawed pay history questions," (Feb. 20, 2019), https://www.hrdive.com/news/salary-history-ban-states-list/516662/.

41 Jodi Kantor and Megan Twohey, "Harvey Weinstein Paid Off Sexual Harassment Accusers for Decades," *The New York Times*. (Oct. 5, 2017), https://www.nytimes.com/2017/10/05/us/harvey-weinstein-harassment-allegations.html.

42 "Salary and Benefits Are Most Important for US Workers and Job Seekers Looking at Job Ads, according to Glassdoor Survey," Glassdoor Press

Center/Press Release (July 25, 2018); https://www.glassdoor.com/press/job-seeker-preferences/.

43 Kerry Jones, "The Most Desirable Employee Benefits," *Harvard Business Review* (February 15, 2017); https://hbr.org/2017/02/the-most-desirable-employee-benefits.

44 Frederick Herzberg, . "One More Time: How Do You Motivate Employees?," *Harvard Business Review*. 46 (1) (January–February 1968): 53–62; OCLC 219963337.

45 Herzberg, F. (1959). Work and motivation. Behaviour science concepts and management application: Studies in personnel policy, 216.

46 Nigel Bassett-Jones and Geoffrey C. Lloyd, "Does Herzberg's Motivation Theory Have Staying Power?" *Journal of Management Development* 24, no. 10: 929–943. Copyright Emerald Group Publishing Limited, 2005.

47 Nigel Bassett-Jones and Geoffrey C. Lloyd, "Does Herzberg's Motivation Theory Have Staying Power?" *Journal of Management Development* 24, no. 10: 929–943. Copyright Emerald Group Publishing Limited, 2005.

48 Ibid.

49 Ibid.

50 Vincent S. Flowers and Charles L. Hughes, "Why Employees Stay," *Harvard Business Review* (July 1973); https://hbr.org/1973/07/why-employees-stay.

51 Jessica Rohman, "Perks Are Great—But They Won't Make Employees Stay," *Fortune* (March 14, 2016); http://fortune.com/2016/03/14/3-reasons-to-stay-at-your-job/.

52 Pat Didomenico, "What Do Millennials Want from a Benefits Package?" The H R Soapbox, Business Management Daily (March 14, 2016, 12:23 PM); http://www.businessmanagementdaily.com/45868/what-do-millennials-want-from-a-benefits-package. And the Employee Benefits Research Institute, https://www.ebri.org/.

53 "Breaking Boredom: What's Really Driving Job Seekers in 2018?" Korn Ferry Institute (January 8, 2018); https://www.kornferry.com/institute/job-hunting-2018-boredom.

54 Vincent S. Flowers and Charles L. Hughes, "Why Employees Stay," *Harvard Business Review* (July 1973); https://hbr.org/1973/07/why-employees-stay.

55 Dr. Andrew Chamberlain and Morgan Smart, "Why Do Workers Quit? The Factors That Predict Employee Turnover," Glassdoor (February 15, 2017); https://www.glassdoor.com/research/studies/why-do-workers-quit/.

56 Jessica Rohman, "Perks Are Great—But They Won't Make Employees Stay," *Fortune* (March 14, 2016); http://fortune.com/2016/03/14/3-reasons-to-stay-at-your-job/.

57 Dr. Andrew Chamberlain and Morgan Smart, "Why Do Workers Quit? The Factors That Predict Employee Turnover," Glassdoor (February 15, 2017); https://www.glassdoor.com/research/studies/why-do-workers-quit/.

58 Vincent S. Flowers and Charles L. Hughes, "Why Employees Stay," *Harvard Business Review* (July 1973); https://hbr.org/1973/07/why-employees-stay.

59 Kate Lister, Global Workplace Analytics; www.globalworkplaceanalytics.com.

60   Lydia Saad, "The '40-Hour' Workweek Is Actually Longer—by Seven Hours: Full-Time U.S. Workers, on Average, Report Working 47 Hours Weekly," (August 29, 2014); http://www.gallup.com/poll/175286/hour-workweek-actually-longer-seven-hours.aspx.

61   John Simons, "IBM, a Pioneer of Remote Work, Calls Workers Back to the Office: Big Blue Says Move Will Improve Collaboration and Accelerate the Pace of Work," *Wall Street Journal* (May 18, 2017 8:00 am, ET); https://www.wsj.com/articles/ibm-a-pioneer-of-remote-work-calls-workers-back-to-the-office-1495108802?shareToken=stb788572d03694bdd8ce33e425b09c-be7&reflink=article_email_share.

62   Julia Kollewe, "VW Profits Down 20% after Diesel Emissions Scandal. *Guardian* (May 31, 2016); https://www.theguardian.com/business/2016/may/31/vw-volkswagen-profits-down-20-diesel-emissions-scandal.

63   Alison Griswold, "Lyft Is Capitalizing on Uber's Woes with a Half Billion Dollars in New Funding," *Quartz* (April 6, 2017); https://qz.com/952257/lyft-is-capitalizing-on-ubers-woes-with-a-half-billion-dollars-in-new-funding/.

64   Laura Keller, "Wells Fargo New Accounts Drop 31% as Scandal Impact Drags On," *Bloomberg Markets* (February 17, 2017); www.bloomberg.com/news/articles/2017-02-17/wells-fargo-new-accounts-decline-31-as-scandal-impact-drags-on.

65   Matthew Harper, "From $4.5 Billion to Nothing: Forbes Revises Estimated Net Worth of Theranos Founder Elizabeth Holmes," *Forbes* (June 1, 2016); https://www.forbes.com/sites/matthewherper/2016/06/01/from-4-5-billion-to-nothing-forbes-revises-estimated-net-worth-of-theranos-founder-elizabeth-holmes/#242602373633.

66   Rich McKay, Reuters, "Harvey Weinstein's Film Studio to File for Bankruptcy following #MeToo Allegations," *Business Insider* (February 26, 2018, 3:22 AM); http://www.businessinsider.com/harvey-weinsteins-film-studio-to-file-for-bankruptcy-2018-2.

67   "Employees Prefer Ethical Company to Higher Pay," *Workspan, The Magazine of World at Work* (March 2007); https://www.worldatwork.org/workspan/Pubs/News_and_Notes-Employees_Prefer_Ethical_Company_to_Higher_Pay.pdf.

68   "Millennials at Work: Reshaping the Workplace," PwC (2012); https://www.pwc.com/m1/en/services/consulting/documents/millennials-at-work.pdf.

69   Matthew Jenkins, "Millennials Want to Work for Employees Committed to Values and Ethics," *Guardian* (May 2015); https://www.theguardian.com/sustainable-business/2015/may/05/millennials-employment-employers-values-ethics-jobs.

70   "Three Reasons Job Seekers Prefer Sustainable Companies," Network for Business Sustainability (June 7, 2013); http://nbs.net/knowledge/three-reasons-job-seekers-prefer-sustainable-companies/.

71   Vincent S. Flowers and Charles L. Hughes, "Why Employees Stay," *Harvard Business Review* (July 1973); https://hbr.org/1973/07/why-employees-stay.

72   Lazlo Bock, *Work Rules! Insights from Inside Google that Will Transform How You Live and Lead* (New York: Twelve Hachette Book Group, 2015).

73 Ibid.

74 Carol R. Miaskoff, "Title VII and ADA: Hiring/Job Requirements/Job Descriptions," Office of Legal Counsel, the US Equal Employment Opportunity Commission (June 21, 2005); https://www.eeoc.gov/eeoc/foia/letters/2005/titlevii_ada_job_requirements_descriptions.html.

75 Chuck Hutchcraft, "Hooters Case Won't Get a Second Look," *Chicago Tribune* (May 2, 1996); https://www.chicagotribune.com/news/ct-xpm-1996-05-02-9605020273-story.html.

76 "Supreme Court Rules in Favor of EEOC in Abercrombie Religious Discrimination Case: Employers Cannot Refuse to Hire Applicants Based on Religious Belief or Practice, Even If Not Specifically Asked for an Accommodation," US Equal Employment Opportunity Commission Press Release (June 1, 2015); https://www.eeoc.gov/eeoc/newsroom/release/6-1-15.cfm.

77 "Accommodations, Office of Disability Employment Policy," Department of Labor; https://www.dol.gov/odep/topics/Accommodations.htm.

78 "Salary and Benefits Are Most Important for US Workers and Job Seekers Looking at Job Ads, according to Glassdoor Survey," Glassdoor Press Center/Press Release (July 25, 2018); https://www.glassdoor.com/press/job-seeker-preferences/.

79 Ibid.

80 Ronen Shetelbolm and Weljen Hsu, "2018 Recruiting Benchmark Report: How to Optimize Your Recruiting Performance," Jobvite; www.Jobvite.com.

81 Bernard J. Luskin, Ed.D., LMFT, "MRIs Reveal Unconscious Bias in the Brain: Shining a Light on an Elephant in the Room," *Psychology Today* (April 7, 2016); https://www.psychologytoday.com/us/blog/the-media-psychology-effect/201604/mris-reveal-unconscious-bias-in-the-brain.

82 Ibid.

83 R. L. Dipoye, H. L. Fromkin, and K. Wiback, "Relative Importance of Applicant's Sex, Attractiveness, and Scholastic Standing in Evaluation of Job Applicant Resumes," *Journal of Applied Psychology* 60 (1975): 39–43.

84 B. M. Springbett, "Series Effects in the Employment Interview," unpublished doctoral dissertation, McGill University (1954). Discussed in Wayne Casio, *Applied Psychology in Personal Management* (Reston, VA: Reston Publishing Company, 1978).

85 B. I. Bolster and B. M. Springbett, "The Reaction of Interviewers to Favorable and Unfavorable Information," *Journal of Applied Psychology*, 45 (1961): 97–103.

86 A. S. Imada and B. W. Hamstra, "Influence of Nonverbal Communication and Rater Proximity on Impressions and Decisions in Simulated Employment Interviews," *Journal of Applied Psychology* 62 (1972): 295–300.

87 J. T. Pricket, N. Gada-Jain, and F. J. Bernieri, "The Importance of First Impressions in a Job Interview," paper presented at the annual meeting of the Midwestern Psychological Association, Chicago, Illinois (2000). Discovered in Lazlo Bock, *Work Rules! Insights from Inside Google that Will Transform How You Live and Lead* (New York, Hatchet Book Group, 2015).

88 M. R. Barrick, B. W. Swider, and G. L. Stewart, "Initial Evaluations in the Interview: Relationships with Subsequent Interviewer Evaluations and Employment Offers," *Journal of Applied Psychology* 95 (2010): 1163–1172. a Berkley S. (1984).

89 Ibid.

90 Lauren A. Rivers, "Hiring as Cultural Matching: The Case of Elite Professional Service Firms," *American Sociological Review* (November 28, 2012); http://journals.sagepub.com/doi/abs/10.1177/0003122412463213.

91 Iris Bohnet, Alexandra van Green, and Max Bazerman, "When Performance Trumps Gender Bias: Joint vs. Separate Evaluation," *PubsOnLine* (September 29, 2015); https://pubsonline.informs.org/doi/abs/10.1287/mnsc.2015.2186?journalCode=mnsc.

92 Alison Wolf, *The XX Factor: How the Rise of Working Women Has Created a Far Less Equal World*, 2013, Crown Publishers of Random House, Inc. New York.

93 Jeanna Smialek, "Millennial Women Are Winning the Jobs Recovery as Men Struggle, Bloomberg Businessweek, (January 13, 2019, 10:00 PM MST). https://www.bloomberg.com/news/articles/2019-01-13/millennial-women-are-pouring-into-jobs-fueling-u-s-labor-gains.

94 Stephen J. Rose, Ph.D., and Heidi I. Hartmann, Ph.D., (Nov. 28, 2018). "Still a Man's Labor Market: The Slowly Narrowing Gender Wage Gap," Institute for Women's Policy Research (November 28, 2018).;. https://iwpr.org/wp-content/uploads/2018/11/C474_IWPR-Still-a-Mans-Labor-Market-update-2018-1.pdf. .

95 Ibid.

96 Ibid.

97 "Women 80% More Likely to be Impoverished in Retirement," *National Institute on Retirement Security* (March 2016); https://www.nirsonline.org/.

98 Iris Bohnet, "How to Take the Bias Out of Interviews," *Harvard Business Review* (April 18, 2016); https://hbr.org/2016/04/how-to-take-the-bias-out-of-interviews?referral=03759&cm_vc=rr_item_page.bottom.

99 Iris Bohnet, Alexandra van Green, and Max Bazerman, "When Performance Trumps Gender Bias: Joint vs. Separate Evaluation," *PubsOnLine* (September 29, 2015); https://pubsonline.informs.org/doi/abs/10.1287/mnsc.2015.2186?journalCode=mnsc.

100 Marianne Bertrand and Sendhil Mullainathan, "Are Emily and Greg More Employable than Lakisha and Jamal? A Field Experiment on Labor Market Discrimination," *American Economic Review*, 94(4) (2004): 991–1013; DOI: 10.1257/0002828042002561. https://www.aeaweb.org/articles.php?doi=10.1257/0002828042002561.

101 Nancy Ditomaso, "How Social Networks Drive Black Unemployment," *New York Times* (May 5, 2013); http://opinionator.blogs.nytimes.com/2013/05/05/how-social-networks-drive-black-unemployment/?_r=0.

102 Miguel A. Quinones, "Getting More Hispanics to the Top," *Forbes* (August 23, 2010, 2:28PM); http://www.forbes.com/2010/08/23/hispanic-cox-school-leadership-citizenship-training.html.

103 Ibid.

104 John Bateson, Jochen Wirtz, Eugene Burke, and Carly Vaughan, "When Hiring, First Test, and Then Interview," *Harvard Business Review* (November 2013); https://hbr.org/2013/11/when-hiring-first-test-and-then-interview.

105 Laszlo Bock, *Work Rules! Insights from Inside Google that Will Transform How You Live and Lead.* (New York: Twelve Hachette Book Group, 2015).

106 I cite three references here for the importance of trust and team success. Anita Wolley, Thomas W. Mallone, and Christopher Chabris, "Why Some Teams Are Smarter than Others," *New York Times Sunday Review* (January 18, 2015): 5. And Alex "Sandy" Pentland, "The New Science of Building Great Teams," *Harvard Business Review* (April 2012). And Julia Rozovky, "The Five Keys to a Successful Google Team," Google (November 17, 2015); https://rework.withgoogle.com/blog/five-keys-to-a-successful-google-team/.

107 Talent Board, "2017 Talent Board North American Candidate Experience Research Report"; http://3cmsd11vskgf1d8i-r311irgt.wpengine.netdna-cdn.com/wp-content/up-loads/2018/01/2017_Talent_Board_NAM_Research_Report_FINAL_180130.pdf.

108 Jobvite, "2018 Recruiting Benchmark Report: How to Optimize Your Recruiting Performance," (2018). http://web.jobvite.com/Q118_Website_2018Benchmarks_LP.html

109 Sources of Hire 2018: Where the Candidate Journey Begins," SilkRoad; https://zerista.s3.amazonaws.com/item_files/ab2f/attachments/458970/original/source_of_hire_2018_pdf.

110 J. T. O'Donnell, "How Your Company's Lame Hiring Process Is Losing You Customers," *Fast Company* (April 15, 2016); https://www.fastcompany.com/3058571/how-your-companys-lame-hiring-process-is-losing-you-customers.

111 Wade Burgess, "Research Shows Exactly How Much Having a Bad Employer Brand Will Cost You," *LinkedIn Talent Blog* (March 30, 2016); https://business.linkedin.com/talent-solutions/blog/employer-brand/2016/research-shows-exactly-how-much-having-a-bad-employer-brand-will-cost-you.

112 Heather Boushey and Sarah Jane Glynn, "There Are Significant Business Costs to Replacing Employees," Center for American Progress (November 16, 2012); www.americanprogress.org/issues/labor/report/2012/11/16/44464/there-are-significant-business-costs-to-replacing-employee/.

113 Leigh Branham, *The 7 Hidden Reasons Employees Leave* (New York: AMACOM, a Division of the American Management Association, 2005).

114 Richard J. Reibstein, "New GAO Report on Contingent Workforce Shows 85% of Independent Contractors Are Contingent with Their Employment Type," *JDSUPRA Business Advisor* (May 26, 2015); http://www.jdsupra.com/legalnews/new-gao-report-on-contingent-workforce-10541/.

115 Lawrence F. Katz and Alan B. Krueger, "The Rise and Nature of Alternative Work Arrangements in the United States, 1995–2015," Princeton (March 29, 2016); https://krueger.princeton.edu/sites/default/files/akrueger/files/katz_krueger_cws_-_march_29_20165.pdf.

116 "Freelancers Predicted to Become the U.S. Workforce Majority within a Decade, with Nearly 50% of Millennial Workers Already Freelancing, Annual 'Freelancing in America' Study Finds," Upwork press release (October 17, 2017); https://www.upwork.com/press/2017/10/17/freelancing-in-america-2017/.

117 "Contingent and Alternative Employment Arrangements—May 2017," Bureau of Labor Statistics, US Department of Labor (10:00 AM June 7, 2018); https://www.bls.gov/news.release/pdf/conemp.pdf.

118 "Freelancers Predicted to Become the U.S. Workforce Majority within a Decade, with Nearly 50% of Millennial Workers Already Freelancing, Annual 'Freelancing in America' Study Finds," Upwork press release (October 17, 2017); https://www.upwork.com/press/2017/10/17/freelancing-in-america-2017/.

119 Katia Dmitrieva, "There Are Probably More Gig Workers Than Counted in the US Survey," *Bloomberg* (June 7, 2018); https://www.bloomberg.com/news/articles/2018-06-07/there-are-probably-more-gig-workers-than-counted-in-u-s-survey.

120 Ibid.

121 Stephen Greenhouse, "Technology: Temp Workers at Microsoft Win Lawsuit," *New York Times* (December 13, 2000); https://www.nytimes.com/2000/12/13/business/technology-temp-workers-at-microsoft-win-lawsuit.html.

122 Ashton Riley, ©Fisher Phillips, "California Supreme Court Adopts Broad New Misclassification Tests," Society of Human Resources Management, https://www.shrm.org/ResourcesAndTools/legal-and-compliance/state-and-local-updates/Pages/California-Supreme-Court-Adopts-Broad-New-Misclassification-Test.aspx?utm_source=SHRM%20Wednesday%20-%20PublishThis_HRDaily_TEMPLATE%20(03.19.18%20DO%20NOT%20DELETE)%20(4)&utm_medium=email&utm_content=May%2002,%202018&SPMID=00164061&SPJD=07/01/1988&SPED=07/31/2019&SPSEG=Career+Builder&SPCERT=&spMailingID=34122107&spUserID=ODM1OTIzODg2ODUS1&spJo-bID=1280212943&spReportId=MTI4MDIxMjk0MwS2.

123 Stephen Greenhouse, "Technology: Temp Workers at Microsoft Win Lawsuit," *New York Times* (December 13, 2000); https://www.nytimes.com/2000/12/13/business/technology-temp-workers-at-microsoft-win-lawsuit.html.

124 Patrick Chu, "Why FedEx's $228 Million Settlement May Dent Uber, Lyft and Postmates, Homejoy and Caviar," *San Francisco Business Times* (June 16, 2015, 7:26 AM PDT).

125 Patrick Chu, "Meet the Ex-Uber Driver in San Francisco Who Won a Labor Case against the Ride-App Giant," *San Francisco Business Times* (June 17, 2015, 5:50 PM PDT).

126 "Definition of Validity Generalization," *Criteria Pre-Employment Testing*; https://www.criteriacorp.com/resources/glossary_validity_generalization.php.

127 "Employment Testing and Selection Procedures" (September 23, 2010); https://www.eeoc.gov/policy/docs/factemployment_procedures.html.

128 Malcolm Gladwell, *Outliners, The Story of Success*, Little, Brown and Company, 2008.

129 Thorndike, E. L. (1920), "A Constant Error in Psychological ratings," *Journal of Applied Psychology,* 4(1), 25-29. https://psycnet.apa.org/doiLanding?doi=10.1037%2Fh0071663.

130 Frank L. Schmidt and John E. Hunter, "The Validity and Utility of Selection Methods in Personnel Psychology: Practical and Theoretical Implications of 85 Years of Research Findings," *Psychological Bulletin*, 124, no. 2 (1988): 262–274. Copyright 1998 by the American Psychological Association, Inc. 0033-2909/98/.

131 Ibid.

132 Ibid.

133 Frank L. Schmidt and John E. Hunter, "The Validity and Utility of Selection Methods in Personnel Psychology: Practical and Theoretical Implications of 85 Years of Research Findings," *Psychological Bulletin*, 124, no. 2 (1988): 272. Copyright 1998 by the American Psychological Association, Inc. 0033-2909/98/.

134 John B. Hunter and F. L. Schmidt, "Validity and Utility of Alternative Predictors of Job Performance," *Psychological Bulletin* 96 (1984).

135 "Cognitive Ability Tests"; https://psychology.iresearchnet.com/industrial-organizational-psychology/individual-differences/cognitive-ability-tests/.

136 Cristina Bertua, Neil Anderson, and Jesus F. Salgado, "The Predictive Validity of Cognitive Ability Tests: A UK Meta-Analysis," *Journal of Occupational and Organizational Psychology* (January 11, 2011); https://onlinelibrary.wiley.com/doi/abs/10.1348/096317905X26994.

137 "Cognitive Ability Tests"; https://psychology.iresearchnet.com/industrial-organizational-psychology/individual-differences/cognitive-ability-tests/.

138 John B. Hunter and F. L. Schmidt, "Validity and Utility of Alternative Predictors of Job Performance," *Psychological Bulletin* 96 (1984).

139 David C. McClelland, "Testing for Competence Rather than Intelligence," *American Psychologist* 46 (1973).

140 C. Steele, "A Threat in the Air: How Stereotypes Shape Intellectual Identity and Performance," *American Psychologist* 52 (1997): 613–629.

141 John Manning, "General Mental Ability," [GET LINK AND UNIVERSITY].

142 Several studies have concluded that GMATs are not culturally biased. "Cognitive Ability Tests"; https://psychology.iresearchnet.com/industrial-organizational-psychology/individual-differences/cognitive-ability-tests/. And K. R. Murphy, B. E. Cronin, and A. P. Tam, "Controversy and Consensus Regarding the Use of Cognitive Ability Testing in Organizations," *Journal of Applied Psychology* 88(4) (2003): 660–671; http://psycnet.apa.org/doi/10.1037/0021-9010.88.4.660. And Arthur R. Jensen, *Bias in Mental Testing* (New York: The Free Press, 1980).

143 "Cognitive Ability Tests"; https://psychology.iresearchnet.com/industrial-organizational-psychology/individual-differences/cognitive-ability-tests/. And J. F. Salgado, N. Anderson, S. Moscoso, C. Bertua, and F. De Fruyt, "International Validity Generalization of GMA and Cognitive Abilities: A European Community Meta-Analysis, *Personnel Psychology* 56 (2003): 573–605.

144 Frank L. Schmidt and John E. Hunter, "The Validity and Utility of Selection Methods in Personnel Psychology: Practical and Theoretical Implications of

85 Years of Research Findings," *Psychological Bulletin*, 124, no. 2 (1988): 272. Copyright 1998 by the American Psychological Association, Inc. 0033-2909/98/.

145 Hunter and Schmidt, "Quantifying the Effects of Psychological Interventions on Employee Job Performance and Work-Force Productivity," *American Psychologists* 38 (1982): 473–474.

146 M. A. McDaniel, D. L. Whetzel, F. L. Schmidt, and S. D. Maurer, "The Validity of Employment Interviews: A Comprehensive Review and Meta-Analysis," *Journal of Applied Psychology* 79 (1994): 599–616.

147 Julia Levashina, Christopher J. Hartwell, Frederick P. Morgeson, and Michael A. Campion, "The Structured Employment Interview: Narrative and Quantitative Review of the Research Literature," *Personnel Psychology* 67 (2014): 241–293).

148 Frank L. Schmidt and John E. Hunter "The Validity and Utility of Selection Methods in Personnel Psychology: Practical and Theoretical Implications of 85 Years of Research Findings," *Psychological Bulletin*, 124, no. 2 (1988): 262–274. Copyright 1998 by the American Psychological Association, Inc. 0033-2909/98/.

149 Willi H. Wiesner and Steven F. Cronshaw, "A Meta-Analytic Investigation of the Impact of Interview Format and Degree of Structure on the Validity of the Employment Interview," *Journal of Occupational Psychology* 61 (1988): 275–290. Printed in Great Britain. Copyright 1988 The British Psychological Society.

150 Ibid.

151 D. A. Terpstra, A. A. Mohamed, and R. B. Kethley, "An analysis of federal court cases involving nine selection devices," *International Journal of Selection and Assessment*, Vol. 7(1), (1999): 26-34.

152 Frank L. Schmidt and John E. Hunter "The Validity and Utility of Selection Methods in Personnel Psychology: Practical and Theoretical Implications of 85 Years of Research Findings," *Psychological Bulletin*, 124, no. 2 (1988): 262–274. Copyright 1998 by the American Psychological Association, Inc. 0033-2909/98/.

153 J. M. Conway, R. A. Jako, and D. F Goodman, "A Meta-Analysis of Interrater and Internal Consistency Reliability of Selection Interviews," *Journal of Applied Psychology*, 80 (1995): 565–579.

154 A. I. Huffcutt and D. J. Woehr, "Further Analysis of Employment Interview Validity: A Quantitative Evaluation of Interviewer-Related Structuring Methods," *Journal of Organizational Behavior* 20 (1999): 549–560.

155 Frank L. Schmidt and John E. Hunter, "The Validity and Utility of Selection Methods in Personnel Psychology: Practical and Theoretical Implications of 85 Years of Research Findings," *Psychological Bulletin*, 124, no. 2 (1988): 272. Copyright 1998 by the American Psychological Association, Inc. 0033-2909/98/.

156 David C. McClelland, "Testin for Competence Rather Than for "Intelligence", *Harvard University*, (1973). https://www.therapiebreve.be/documents/mcclelland-1973.pdf

157 Daniel Goleman, *Working with Emotional Intellgience*, October, 2006, page 16, Bantam Books, New York.

158 Charles Huckabee, "Another Academic Physician's Ties to Industry Come under Senator's Scrutiny," *Chronicle of Higher Education* (July 28, 2009); https://www.chronicle.com/article/Another-Academic-Physicians/47484.

159 Frank L. Schmidt and John E. Hunter, "The Validity and Utility of Selection Methods in Personnel Psychology: Practical and Theoretical Implications of 85 Years of Research Findings," *Psychological Bulletin*, 124, no. 2 (1988): 272. Copyright 1998 by the American Psychological Association, Inc. 0033-2909/98/.

160 Eran Hermelin, Filip Lievens, and Ivan T. Robertson, "The Validity of Assessment Centres for the Prediction of Supervisory Performance Ratings: A Meta-Analysis," *International Journal of Selection and Assessment*, 15, no. 4 (December 2007); https://www.research-gate.net/publication/237831139_The_Validity_of_Assessment_Centres_for_the_Prediction_of_Supervisory_Performance_Ratings.

161 George C. Thornton III and Alyssa M. Gibbons, "Validity of Assessment Centers for Personnel Selection," *Human Resources Management Review* 19 (2009): 169–187.

162 Frank L. Schmidt and John E. Hunter, "The Validity and Utility of Selection Methods in Personnel Psychology: Practical and Theoretical Implications of 85 Years of Research Findings," *Psychological Bulletin*, 124, no. 2 (1988): 272. Copyright 1998 by the American Psychological Association, Inc. 0033-2909/98/.

163 Ibid.

164 Ibid.

165 Career Builder, "More Than Half of Employers Have Found Content on Social Media That Caused Them NOT to Hire a Candidte, According to Recent Career Builder Survey," (August 9, 2018). http://press.career-builder.com/2018-08-09-More-Than-Half-of-Employers-Have-Found-Content-on-Social-Media-That-Caused-Them-NOT-to-Hire-a-Candidate-According-to-Recent-CareerBuilder-Survey.

166 Ibid.

167 Ibid.

168 Frank L. Schmidt and John E. Hunter, "The Validity and Utility of Selection Methods in Personnel Psychology: Practical and Theoretical Implications of 85 Years of Research Findings," Psychological Bulletin, 124, no. 2 (1988): 272. Copyright 1998 by the American Psychological Association, Inc. 0033-2909/98/.

169 Meredith Lepore, "This is How Many People Are Lying on Their Resume," LEVO (August 18, 2017); https://www.levo.com/posts/this-is-how-many-people-are-lying-on-their-resume.

170 "2017 Employment Screening Benchmark Report," HireRight; https://www.hire-right.com/benchmarking.

171 Mark Murphy, "Study, Words that Cost You The Job Interview," Leadership IQ: A Mark Murphy Company (2017). https://www.leadershipiq.com/blogs/leadershipiq/study-words-that-cost-you-the-job-interview.

172 Frank L. Schmidt and John E. Hunter, "The Validity and Utility of Selection Methods in Personnel Psychology: Practical and Theoretical Implications of 85 Years of Research Findings," *Psychological Bulletin* 124, no. 2 (1988): 262–274. Copyright 1998 by the American Psychological Association, Inc. 0033-2909/98/.

173 Lazlo Bock, *Work Rules! Insights from Inside Google that Will Transform How You Live and Lead* (New York: Twelve Hachette Book Group, 2015).

174 "New Interview Technique Could Help Police Spot Deception," Economic and Social Research Council *Science Daily* (June 8, 2007); https://www.sciencedaily.com/releases/2007/06/070607062917.htm.

175 Monica Torres, "New App Scans Your Face and Tells Companies Whether You're Worth Hiring," Ladders (August 25, 2017); https://www.theladders.com/career-advice/ai-screen-candidates-hirevue.

176 Steve Lohr, "Facial Recognition Is Accurate, If You're a White Guy," *New York Times* (February 9, 2018); https://www.nytimes.com/2018/02/09/technology/facial-recognition-race-artificial-intelligence.html.

177 "Survey Finds Employment Background Checks Nearly Universal Today," *GlobalHR Research Blog*; https://www.ghrr.com/survey-finds-employment-background-checks-nearly-universal-today/.

178 Chad Brooks, "Get Your Facts Straight: The Truth About Background Checks," *Business News Daily* (March 26, 2017, 8:16 AM EST); https://www.businessnews-daily.com/9834-background-check-myths.html.

179 Kathy Gurchiek, "Uptick in Hiring Highlights Importance of Background Screening," *Society for Human Resource Management* (April 9, 2015); www.shrm.org/hrdisciplines/staffingmanagement/articles/pages/hiring-background-screening.aspx.

180 Trusted Employees, "Results of NAPBS Background Check Survey of HR Pros," (March 23, 2018). https://www.trustedemployees.com/learning-center/articles-news/results-napbs-background-check-survey-hr-pros/.

181 Ibid.

182 "Back to Business: How Hiring Formerly Incarcerated Job Seekers Benefits Your Company," American Civil Liberties Union, New York, 2017.

183 "Nationwide Trends," National Institute on Drug Abuse (June 2015); https://www.drugabuse.gov/publications/drugfacts/nationwide-trends.

184 Jennifer Warner, "U.S. Leads the World in Illegal Drug Use," WebMD, LLC (July 1, 2008, 11:30 AM); www.cbsnews.com/news/us-leads-the-world-in-illegal-drug-use/.

185 "Overdose Death Rates," National Institute on Drug Abuse (August 2018); https://www.drugabuse.gov/related-topics/trends-statistics/overdose-death-rates.

186 Roy Mauer, "Nearly 8 in 10 Employers Screen for Alcohol, Drugs," *SHRM* (May 31, 2013); https://www.shrm.org/resourcesandtools/hr-topics/risk-management/pages/employers-screen-alcohol-drugs.aspx.

187 "Pre-Employment Drug Testing Statistics"; https://www.statisticbrain.com/pre-employment-job-drug-testing-statistics/.

188 "Drug War Facts"; http://www.drugwarfacts.org/chapter/drugtesting_employment.

189 Chad Brooks, "Employee Drug Use Continues to Rise," *Business News Daily* (May 19, 2017; 7:27 AM EST); https://www.businessnewsdaily.com/7121-drug-use-rising.html.

190 Roy Maurer, "Drug Test Your Workforce Lawfully, Effectively," Society for Human Resource Management (February 3, 2015); www.shrm.org/hrdisci-plines/safetysecurity/articles/pages/drug-test-workforce-lawfull.aspx.

191 Joanne Deschenaux, "Colorado High Court: Employer Can Fire Employee for Off-Duty Medical Marijuana Use," Legal Issues, Society for Human Resource Management (June 15, 2015); http://www.shrm.org/legalissues/stateandlocal-resources/pages/colorado-marijuana.aspx.

192 Ibid.

193 Joe Pinsker, "Pointlessness of the Workplace Drug Test: Cup-Peeing and Mouth-Swabbing Are Reagan-Era Relics that Frequently Do Little More than Boosting the Revenues of Companies that Analyze Samples," *Atlantic* (June 4, 2015); https://www.theatlantic.com/business/archive/2015/06/drug-testing-effectiveness/394850/.

194 Roy Maurer, "Onboarding Key to Retaining, Engaging Talent," MySHRM, Society of Human Resources Management, (April 16, 2016). https://www.shrm.org/re-sourcesandtools/hr-topics/talent-acquisition/pages/onboarding-key-retainin g-engaging-talent.aspx.

195 Jerry Useem, "Why It Pays to Be a Jerk," *Atlantic* (June 2015): 49–58.

196 Toegel G, Barsoux JL (2012). "How to become a better leader". MIT Sloan Management Review. 53 (3): 51–60.

197 User S. "TechnoFunc - Five-Factor Personality Model of Leadership". www.tech-nofunc.com; and "The Five Factor Theory of Personality". Mind Forums. 5 April 2009. Archived from the original on 8 May 2009

198 Judge TA, Bono JE, Ilies R, Gerhardt MW (August 2002). "Personality and leader-ship: a qualitative and quantitative review". The Journal of Applied Psychology. 87 (4): 765–80. doi:10.1037/0021-9010.87.4.765. PMID 12184579.

199 "The Big Five Personality Traits," Wikipedia; https://en.wikipedia.org/wiki/Big_Five_personality_traits.

200 Frank L. Schmidt and John E. Hunter, "The Validity and Utility of Selection Methods in Personnel Psychology: Practical and Theoretical Implications of 85 Years of Research Findings," *Psychological Bulletin* 124, no. 2 (1988): 276–274. Copyright 1998 by the American Psychological Association, Inc. 0033-2909/98/.

201 Robert M. Guion and Richard F. Gottier, "Validity of Personality Measures in Personnel Selection," *Personnel Psychology* 18 135 (1965): 159–160.

202 Peter Salovey and John Mayer, *Emotional Intelligence* (1990); http://www.unh.edu/emotional_intelligence/EIAssets/EmotionalIntelligenceProper/EI1990%20 Emotional%20Intelligence.pdf.

203 Daniel Goleman, *Working with Emotional Intelligence* (New York: Bantam Dell, division of Random House, Inc., 1998); Reissued in October 2006.

204 Ernest H. O'Boyle Jr. et al., "The Relation between Emotional Intelligence and Job Performance: A Meta-Analysis," *The Journal of Organizational Behavior* 32 (2011): 788–818.

205 The Ruth Jacobs and Wei Chen study is cited in Daniel Goleman, (1998) Working with Emotional Intelligence, page 319, (New York: Bantam Dell, divi-sion of Random House, Inc. New York, 1998).; Reissued in October, 2006..

206 Amy L. Kristof-Drown, Ryan D. Zimmerman, and Erin C. Johnson, "Consequences of Individuals' Fit at Work: A Meta-Analysis of Person-Job, Person-Organization, Person-Group, and Person-Supervisor Fit," *Personal Psychology* 58 (2005): 281–342; http://nreilly.asp.radford.edu/kristof-brown%20et%20al.pdf.

207 There are several studies that shows that diversity leads to higher productivity and innovation: Pierpaolo Parrotta, Dario Pozzoli, and Mariola Pytlikova, (2010) "Does Labor Diversity Affect Firm Productivity?" Department of Economics, Aarhus School of Business, University of Aarhus. ISBN 9788778824615 (online); and Andrea Garnero, Francois Rycs (2013) "The heterogeneous effects of work-force diversity on productivity, wages and profits." Found at https://www.iza.org/conference_files/SUMS_2013/garnero_a8067.pdf; and Deborah Gladstein Ancona, Sloan School of Management, MIY and David F Caldwell, Leavey School of Business, Santa Clara University, (Aug 1, 1992) "Demography and Design, Predictors of New Product Team Performance," Organizational Science. Found at http://pubsonline.informs.org/doi/abs/10.1287/orsc.3.3.321.

208 Several studies are referenced here. Marianne Bertrand and Sendhil Mullainathan, "Are Emily and Greg More Employable than Lakisha and Jamal? A Field Experiment on Labor Market Discrimination," *American Economic Review*, 94(4) (2004): 991–1013, DOI: 10.1257/0002828042002561; https://www.aea-web.org/articles.php?doi=10.1257/0002828042002561. And Nancy Ditomaso, "How Social Networks Drive Black Unemployment," *New York Times* (May 5, 2013); http://opinionator.blogs.nytimes.com/2013/05/05/how-social-networks-drive-black-unemployment/?_r=0. And Miguel A. Quinones, "Getting More Hispanics to the Top," *Forbes* (August 23, 2010, 2:28PM); http://www.forbes.com/2010/08/23/hispanic-cox-school-leadership-citizenship-training.html.

209 "Is Culture Fit a Qualification for Hiring or a Disguise for Bias?" *Knowledge @ Wharton* (July 16, 2015); http://knowledge.wharton.upenn.edu/article/cultural-fit-a-qualification-for-hiring-or-a-disguise-for-bias/.

210 Lauren A. Rivera, "Guess Who Doesn't Fit In at Work?" *New York Times* (May 30, 2015); http://www.nytimes.com/2015/05/31/opinion/sunday/guess-who-doesnt-fit-in-at-work.html.

211 Frank L. Schmidt and John E. Hunter, "The Validity and Utility of Selection Methods in Personnel Psychology: Practical and Theoretical Implications of 85 Years of Research Findings," *Psychological Bulletin*, 124, no. 2 (1988): 262–274. Copyright 1998 by the American Psychological Association, Inc. 0033-2909/98/.

212 Deloitte University Press, 2017 Deloitte Global Human Capital Trends: Rewriting the rules for the digital age. (2017). https://www2.deloitte.com/content/dam/Deloitte/global/Documents/About-Deloitte/central-europe/ce-global-human-capital-trends.pdf.

213 Talent Board, "2017 Talent Board North American Candidate Experience Research Report"; http://3cmsd11vskgf1d8i-r311irgt.wpengine.netdna-cdn.com/wp-content/up-loads/2018/01/2017_Talent_Board_NAM_Research_Report_FINAL_180130.pdf.

214 Stephan van Calker, "The 5 Things Driving Online Applicants the Most Crazy," ERE Recruiting Intelligence (May 31, 2018); https://www.ere.net/the-5-things-driving-online-applicants-the-most-crazy/?utm_source=Marketo&utm_medium=Email&utm_campaign=ERE%20Daily%20Digest-2018-06-01T06:30:00.000-07:00&mkt_tok=eyJpIjoiWldWaFpqSm1OVGN6TXpJeSIsInQiOiJKRldURkxkeWx2SDNxcjJyVGczOFh3K1h6XC9mdmJVTWRFYWsrdndcL1JPYm9NV2Z5elhKUktpZTJnM2NVYWMzZlJsV2RZMStqMTdyN0RGMkdvejhMdzN5TTdGUTM0dkk2Z2JNckZtS2dFYmVTSE9jjN2xZY0NGdWN6NHM1RGZ0WkxYIn0%3D.

215 Datanyze, A Zoom Info Company, Applicant Tracking Systems (2018). https://www.datanyze.com/market-share/ats.

216 G2 Crowd, "Best Applicant tracking System (ATS) Software," (2018), https://www.g2crowd.com/categories/applicant-tracking-system-ats?segment=enterprise.

217 "Sources of Hire 2018: Where the Candidate Journey Begins," SilkRoad; https://zerista.s3.amazonaws.com/item_files/ab2f/attachments/458970/original/source_of_hire_2018_pdf.pdf.

218 Brian Westfall, "The Best Job Boards for Your Recruiting Dollar," Software Advice (2014); https://www.softwareadvice.com/resources/hr-best-job-boards-2014/.

219 Josh Bersin, "Google for Jobs: Potential to Disrupt the $200 Billion Recruiting Industry," *Forbes* (May 26, 2017, 10:25 AM); https://www.forbes.com/sites/joshbersin/2017/05/26/google-for-jobs-potential-to-disrupt-the-200-billion-recruiting-industry/2/#ac9fbad4e473.

220 Rohma Abbas, "How to Post Jobs Listings on the 'Google for Jobs' Search Engine," Workable; https://resources.workable.com/tutorial/google-for-jobs.

221 Frederic Lardinois, "Hire by Google Makes It Easier to Find the Right Job Candidates," *TechCrunch* (March 28, 2018); https://techcrunch.com/2018/03/28/hire-by-google-makes-it-easier-to-find-the-right-job-candidates/.

222 Joel Cheesman, "Google Introduces 3 New AI Features to Hire, Focused on Reducing Monotonous Tasks," ERE Recruiting Intelligence (June 19, 2018); https://www.ere.net/google-hire-introduces-new-features/?utm_source=Marketo&utm_medium=Email&utm_campaign=ERE%20Daily%20Digest-2018-06-21T06:30:00.000-07:00&mkt_tok=eyJpIjoiWTJNME5qTm1Zakk0TTJSaCIsInQiOi-JsKz BlS3IwaXZcL1E0UHISQWhSWHZoemJhTmt5b3BWNjZ5a2NmZUJoZ0hMaGtYWFczOEh3Mk8zbVhLdWZCM2JudTVxZXo0UHdjWWxaKzRcL2JTZlFIUVExOXkwdUVQZ3JXdENtVlwvMW5DeXQrbHRzRlZYMFIRcFVXYUlsVDdjV1FqZyJ9.

223 Crunchbase. https://www.crunchbase.com/organization/wepow#section-overview.

224 "2018 Recruiter Nation Survey: The Tipping Point. The Next Chapter in Recruiting," Jobvite (2018), PDF.

225 "The Unstoppable Rise of Mobile Job Search: What Employers Need to Know," *Indeed Blog* (July 27, 2017); http://blog.indeed.com/2017/07/27/the-unstoppable-rise-of-mobile-job-search/.

226 Maruti Techlabs, "Here's All That You Need to Know about Chatbots"; https://www.marutitech.com/heres-need-know-chatbots/.

227 Deloitte University Press, *2017 Deloitte Global Human Capital Trends: Rewriting the rules for the digital age.* (2017). https://www2.deloitte.com/content/dam/Deloitte/global/Documents/About-Deloitte/central-europe/ce-global-human-capital-trends.pdf.

228 LinkedIn Talent Solutions, *Global Recruiting Trends 2018, The 4 ideas Changing How You Hire*, (2018). https://business.linkedin.com/content/dam/me/business/en-us/talent-solutions/resources/pdfs/linkedin-global-recruiting-trends-2018-en-us.pdf.

229 Sarah Wilson, Indigo Talent Acquisition Director; https://ideal.com/customer/indigo-books-music/.

230 Rebecca Koening, "Your Next Recruiter Could Be an Algorithm," *US News and World Report* (August 22, 2018: 3:23 PM); https://money.usnews.com/careers/applying-for-a-job/articles/2018-08-22/your-next-recruiter-could-be-an-algorithm.

231 Rebecca Greenfield and Riley Griffin, "Artificial Intelligence Is Coming for Hiring, and It Might Not Be That Bad: Even with All of Its Problems, AI is a Step Up from the Notoriously Biased Recruiting Process," *Bloomberg* (August 8, 2018, 2:00 AM PDT; Updated on August 8, 2018, 6:56 AM PDT); https://www.bloomberg.com/news/articles/2018-08-08/artificial-intelligence-is-coming-for-hiring-and-it-might-not-be-that-bad.

232 Raghav Singh, "Meet the Robot Recruiters" (September 25, 2018); https://www.ere.net/meet-the-robot-recruiters/?utm_source=Marketo&utm_medium=E-mail&utm_campaign=ERE%20Daily%20Digest-2018-09-26T06:30:00.000-.07:00&mkt_tok=eyJpIjoiWlRSaFltRTRZamM1TnpKKb
CIsInQiOiJCTTAxcWNxXC9Ob3F1YU5CY2U2dlFuY0o3
Vk9CbHdSXC9GVEUzYjNlODlKcDg4cXlFcFF6c1YyWHF
rM2Mzc3pBa3BHQU9LZzVmM1RKR2NDYndkWng2Rlph
K0JoOG93cjBTNHI4NWttZnNQU0NXSUtQN0RQaVFte
EpBbXlPQW9keThoIn0%3D.

233 Jon-Mark Sabel, "How an 'Interview First' Hiring Strategy Empowers Job Seekers and Promotes Diversity," (September 20, 2017); https://www.hire-vue.com/blog/how-an-interview-first-hiring-strategy-empowers-job-seekers-and-promotes-diversity?utm_source=hs_automation&utm_medium=email&utm_content=66113974&_hsenc=p2ANqtz-9dVg34rZqEmnD-OvR78LrClUx0Kijeb8XxFHAnqqhPeAqU_8qLxWwxNJ7PXBrsbgRbA
sXrWJSAiPjGJ6k1NqGh0j7Qrag&_hsmi=66113974.

234 Hilke Schellmann and Jason Bellini, "Artificial Intelligence: The Robots Are Now Hiring—Moving Upstream: How New Data-Science Tools Are Determining Who Gets Hired," *Wall Street Journal* (September 20, 2018, 2:29 PM); https://www.wsj.com/video/series/moving-upstream/artificial-intelligence-the-robots-are-now-hiring-moving-upstream/2790C6B9-4E47-4544-9331-36DB418366CF?mod=djem10point.

235 Steve Lohr, "Facial Recognition Is Accurate, if You're a White Guy," (Feb. 9, 2018), *The New York Times*. https://www.nytimes.com/2018/02/09/technology/facia l-recognition-race-artificial-intelligence.html.

236 Ibid.

237 Ibid.

238 Jeffrey Dastin, "Amazon scraps secret AI recruiting tool that showed bias against women," (Oct. 9, 2018/8:12 PM) Reuters. https://www.reuters.com/ article/us-amazon-com-jobs-automation-insight/amazon-scraps-secret-ai-rec ruiting-tool-that-showed-bias-against-women-idUSKCN1MK08G.

239 Ibid.

240 Hilke Schellmann and Jason Bellini, "Artificial Intelligence: The Robots Are Now Hiring—Moving Upstream: How New Data-Science Tools Are Determining Who Gets Hired." *Wall Street Journal* (September 20, 2018, 2:29 PM); https:// www.wsj.com/video/series/moving-upstream/artificial-intelligence-th e-robots-are-now-hiring-moving-upstream/2790C6B9-4E47-4544-9331 -36DB418366CF?mod=djem10point.

241 Maria Ignatova and Kate Reilly, "The 4 Trends Changing How You Hire in 2018 and Beyond," *LinkedIn Talent Blog* (January 10, 2018); https://business. linkedin.com/talent-solutions/blog/trends-and-research/2018/4-trends-sh aping-the-future-of-hiring.

242 "Korn Ferry Global Survey: Artificial Intelligence (AI) Reshaping the Role of the Recruiter," Korn Ferry (January 18, 2018); https://www.kornferry.com/ press/korn-ferry-global-survey-artificial-intelligence-reshaping-the-role- of-the-recruiter/.

243 Salman Aslam, "LinkedIn by the Numbers: Stats, Demographics and Fun Facts," *Omnicore* (September 18, 2018); https://www.omnicoreagency.com/ linkedin-statistics/.

244 "Mobile Fact Sheet," *Indeed Blog* (July 27, 2017); http://blog.indeed. com/2017/07/27/the-unstoppable-rise-of-mobile-job-search/.

245 Sarah Perez, "Google to Launch Jobs Search Engine in the US," *TechCrunch* (May 17, 2017); https://techcrunch.com/2017/05/17/google-to-launch-a-job s-search-engine-in-the-u-s/.

246 Sarah-Beth Anders, "LinkedIn's Talent Hub Brings Together the Entire Hiring Process in One Place," *LinkedIn Talent Blog* (October 10, 2018); https:// business.linkedin.com/talent-solutions/blog/product-updates/2018/ linkedin-talent-hub.

247 Michelle V. Rafter, "Why Robots Won't Take Over HR Recruiting Anytime Soon: eHarmony Is the Latest Predictive Analytics-Based Service to Match People with Jobs, But Predictive Analytics as a Tech Is Still in Its Infancy," *PCMag* (April 20, 2016); https://www.pcmag.com/article/343627/why-robots-wont-take-ove r-hr-recruiting-any-time-soon.

248 Talent Brew. http://www.marketwired.com/press-release/talentbrew-platfor m-becomes-first-to-tie-content-marketing-for-talent-acquisition-1827318.htm.

249 "Gamification in Recruiting," Recruiter Box; https://recruiterbox.com/blog/ gamification-in-recruiting.

250 "Plantsville: Case Study of Gamification in Industrial Automation Industry: Siemens Initiative" (November 12, 2014); http://prasenjitdasgupta1975.blog-spot.com/2014/11/plantsville-case-study-of.html.

251 Dave Zielinski, "The Gamification of Recruitment: Virtual games are scoring points for companies' talent acquisition strategies," (November 1, 2015), *MySHRM*, Society of Human Resources Management. https://www.shrm.org/hr-today/news/hr-magazine/pages/1115-gamification-recruitment.aspx.

252 Sean Foley, Jonathan R. Karlsen, and Talis J. Putnins, "Sex, Drugs, and Bitcoin: How Much Illegal Activity Is Financed through Cryptocurrencies?" *SSRN* (January 15, 2018); https://papers.ssrn.com/sol3/papers.cfm?abstract_id=3102645.

253 Andrew Meola, "How Banks and Financial Institutions Are Implementing Blockchain Technology," *Business Insider* (September 20, 2017, 4:44PM); http://www.businessinsider.com/blockchain-technology-banking-finance-2017-9.

254 Diva Joshi, "IBM, Amazon & Microsoft Are Offering Their Blockchain Technology as a Service," *Business Insider* (October 24, 2017, 1:06 PM); http://www.businessinsider.com/ibm-azure-aws-blockchain-service-2017-10.

255 Ashik Ahmed, "How Blockchain Will change HR Forever," *Forbes* (March 14, 2018, 11:21 AM); https://www.forbes.com/sites/ashikahmed/2018/03/14/how-blockchain-will-change-hr-forever/#649add8e727c.

256 Rebecca Campbell, "Drawing Parallels between TCP-IP-and the Blockchain," *Blockchain Works* (November 21, 2017); https://blockchain.works-hub.com/learn/Drawing-Parralels-between-TCP-IP-and-the-Blockchain.

257 Dave Zielinski, "Is HR Ready for Blockchain Technology?" MySHRM Society for Human Resource Management (November 21, 2017); https://www.shrm.org/resourcesandtools/hr-topics/technology/pages/is-hr-ready-for-blockchain-technology.aspx.

258 Henry Williams, "Blockchain May Offer a Resume You Can Trust: Colleges and Tech Companies Are Using Digital Ledger to Develop Easily Verifiable Diplomas and Employment Records," *Wall Street Journal* (March 11, 2018, 10:02 PM ET); https://www.wsj.com/articles/blockchain-may-offer-a-resume-you-can-trust-1520820121.

259 Ibid.

260 Ibid.

261 Ibid.

262 Jen Wieczner, "Hacking Coinbase: The Great Bitcoin Bank Robbery," *Ledger* (August 22, 2017); http://fortune.com/2017/08/22/bitcoin-coinbase-hack/. And Steven Melendez, "Bitcoin Heist Adds $77 Million to Total Hacked Hauls of $15 Billion," *Fast Company*; https://www.fastcompany.com/40505199/bitcoin-heist-adds-77-million-to-hacked-hauls-of-15-billion.

263 Allen Smith, "Target Will Pay $2.8M over Employment Tests," *SHRM Workplace Compliance News*, Society for Human Resource Management (August 25, 2015); http://www.shrm.org/legalissues/federalresources/pages/target-employment-tests.aspx?utm.

264 "Negligent Hiring Law and Legal Definition," *US Legal*; https://definitions.usle-gal.com/n/negligent-hiring/.

265 Sam Becker, "7 Jobs You Can Never Get with a Criminal Record," *Money and Career Cheatsheet* (October 19, 2017); https://www.cheatsheet.com/money-career/jobs-criminal-record.html/?a=viewall.

266 Michele Natividad Rodrigues and Beth Avery, "Ban the Box: US Cities, Counties, and States Adopt Fair Hiring Policies," National Employment Law Project (October 1, 2016); http://www.nelp.org/publication/ban-the-box-fair-chance-hiring-state-andlocal-guide/.

267 Beth Avery and Phil Hernandez, "Ban the Box: US Cities, Counties and States Adopt Fair Hiring Policies," National Employment Law Project (August 1, 2017); http://www.nelp.org/publication/ban-the-box-fair-chance-hiring-state-and-local-guide/.

268 Lisa Nagele-Piazza, "Do Ban-the-Box Laws Work? More Cities and States Are Limiting Criminal History Inquiries in the Hiring Process," *SHRM* (January 12, 2017); https://www.shrm.org/resourcesandtools/legal-and-compliance/state-and-local-updates/pages/do-ban-the-box-laws-work.aspx.

269 Jessica Lutz, "Salary Question Ban Benefits Women and Millennials," *Forbes* (January 31, 2018, 8:27 PM); https://www.forbes.com/sites/jessicalutz/2018/01/31/salary-question-ban-benefits-women-and-millennials/#5179333c5a8c.

270 Susan Milligan, "Salary History Ban Could Reshape Pay Negotiations," *SHRM* (February 16, 2018); https://www.shrm.org/hr-today/news/hr-magazine/0318/pages/salary-history-bans-could-reshape-pay-negotiations.aspx.

271 Eileen Patten, "Racial, Gender Wage Gaps Persist in U.S. Despite Some Progress," Pew Research Center (July 1, 2016); http://www.pewre-search.org/fact-tank/2016/07/01/racial-gender-wage-gaps-persist-in-u-s-despite-some-progress/.

272 Ibid

273 Stephen J. Rose, Ph.D., and Heidi I. Hartmann, Ph.D., "Still a Man's Labor Market: The Slowly Narrowing Gender Wage Gap," Institute for Women's Policy Research (November 28, 2018); https://iwpr.org/wp-content/uploads/2018/11/C474_IWPR-Still-a-Mans-Labor-Market-update-2018-1.pdf.

274 Eileen Patten, "Racial, Gender Wage Gaps Persist in U.S. Despite Some Progress," Pew Research Center (July 1, 2016); http://www.pewre-search.org/fact-tank/2016/07/01/racial-gender-wage-gaps-persist-in-u-s-despite-some-progress/.

275 Ibid.

276 Parts of this list were taken from the article written by Connie Maniscalco, "Best Ways to Display Good Faith Efforts in Affirmative Action Compliance," *Helios HR* (February 2014); https://www.helioshr.com/2014/02/best-ways-to-display-good-faith-efforts-in-affirmative-action-compliance-2/.

277 "Employment Tests and Selection Procedures," The US Equal Employment Commission (September 23, 2010); https://www.eeoc.gov/policy/docs/factemployment_procedures.html.

278 Economic News Release, "Joe Openings and Labor Turnover Summary-January 2019, (March 15, 2019, 10:00 AM), Bureau of Labor Statistics, US Department of Labor. https://www.bls.gov/news.release/jolts.nr0.htm.

279 Deloitte University Press, 2017 Deloitte Global Human Capital Trends: Rewriting the rules for the digital age. (2017). https://www2.deloitte.com/content/dam/Deloitte/global/Documents/About-Deloitte/central-europe/ce-global-human-capital-trends.pdf.

280 "Latest Unemployment Numbers," United States Department of Labor; https://www.dol.gov/vets/latest-numbers/#.

281 "Post-Traumatic Stress Disorder," *Psychology Today*; https://www.psychologytoday.com/us/conditions/post-traumatic-stress-disorder.

282 Ibid.

283 "Take the Fair Chance Pledge," Obama White House Archives; https://obamawhitehouse.archives.gov/issues/criminal-justice/fair-chance-pledge.

284 Beth Avery, "Seven States Adopted Fair Chance Policies in 2017," *National Employment Law Project* (January 19, 2018); https://www.nelp.org/blog/seven-states-adopted-fair-chance-policies-in-2017/.

285 Ibid.

26 "Just Facts: As Many Americans Have Criminal Records As College Diplomas," Brennan Center for Justice at New York University Law School; https://www.brennancenter.org/blog/just-facts-many-americans-have-criminal-records-college-diplomas.

287 "Ending the Opioid Crisis: A Practical Guide for State Policymakers," National Center on Addiction and Substance Abuse at Columbia University (October 2017); https://www.centeronaddiction.org/addiction-research/reports/ending-opioid-crisis-practical-guide-state-policymakers.

288 Ibid.

289 American Civil Liberty Union Foundation, "Back to Basics: How Hiring Formerly Incarcerated Job Seekers Benefits Your Company," (2017) https://www.aclu.org/sites/default/files/field_document/060917-trone-reportweb_0.pdf.

290 Associated Press, "Ex-Cons Face Tough Path Back into the Work Force: Advocates Hope Federal Program Will Encourage Employers to Take a Chance" (July 30, 2009); http://www.nbcnews.com/id/32208419/ns/business-careers/t/ex-cons-face-tough-pathback-work-force/#.V_V1dY8rJhE.

291 Justice Center, National Reentry Resource Center, "What Works in Reentry Clearinghouse: Employment," The Council of State Governments, n.d.; https://whatworks.csgjusticecenter.org/.

292 Devah Pager, "The Mark of a Criminal Record," *American Journal of Sociology* 108, no. 5 (2003): 937–75; http://scholar.harvard.edu/files/pager/files/pager_ajs.pdf.

293 Cherrie Bucknor and Alan Barber, Center for Economic and Policy Research, "The Price We Pay: Economic Costs of Barriers to Employment for Former Incarcerated Individuals and People Convicted of Felonies" (2016); http://cepr.net/images/stories/reports/employment-prisoners-felonies-2016-06.pdf.

294 American Civil Liberty Union Foundation, "Back to Basics: How Hiring Formerly Incarcerated Job Seekers Benefits Your Company," (2017) https://www.aclu.org/sites/default/files/field_document/060917-trone-reportweb_0.pdf.

295 Data collected by Total Wine & More, processed March 22, 2017.

296 Matt Krumrie, "Why You Should Give Candidates with a Criminal Background a Second Chance" (October 4, 2016); https://www.ziprecruiter.com/blog/why-you-should-give-candidates-with-a-criminal-background-a-second-chance/.

297 Dylan Minor, Nicola Persico, and Deborah M. Weiss, "Criminal Background and Job Performance," Working Paper (October 30, 2016); File://Users/test/Downloads/SSRM-id2851951%20(1).pdf.

298 Daryl Atkinson, "The Benefits of Ban the Box," The Southern Coalition for Social Justice (2014); http://www.southerncoalition.org/wp-content/uploads/2014/10/BantheBox_WhitePaper-2.pdf. And Dylan Minor, Nicola Persico, and Deborah M. Weiss, "Criminal Background and Job Performance," Working Paper (October 30, 2016); file:///Users/test/Downloads/SSRN-id2851951%20(1).pdf.

299 Jennifer Lundquist, Devah Pager, and Eiko Strader, "Does a Criminal Past Predict Worker Performance? Evidence from America's Largest Employer," Working Paper (2016); file:///Users/test/ Downloads/ASRDraft01222016.pdf.

300 Ibid.

301 "Syrian Refugee Crisis: Facts, FAQs, and How to Help," World Vision (November 19, 2018); https://www.worldvision.org/refugees-news-stories/syrian-refugee-crisis-facts.

302 Alex Nowrasteh, "Criminal Immigrants in Texas: Illegal Immigrant Conviction and Arrest Rates for Homicide, Sex Crimes, Larceny, and Other Crimes," Cato Institute (February 26, 2018); https://www.cato.org/publications/immigration-research-policy-brief/criminal-immigrants-texas-illegal-immigrant.

303 Chris Nichols, "Do Three-Quarters of Americans Support the DREAM Act? Nancy Pelosi Says So," PolitiFact California (September 19, 2017, 5:36 PM); https://www.politifact.com/california/statements/2017/sep/19/nancy-pelosi/nancy-pelosi-claims-three-quarters-americans-suppo/.

304 Jie Zong, Jeanne Batalova, and Micayla Burrows, "Frequently Requested Statistics on Immigrants and Immigration in the United States, (March 14, 2019), Migration Policy Institute. https://www.migrationpolicy.org/article/frequently-requested-statistics-immigrants-and-immigration-united-states.

305 National Archives Foundation, "Refugee Act of 1980," https://www.archives-foundation.org/documents/refugee-act-1980/.

306 Dr. Patricia Buckley, "How immigration is shaping the United States: Issues by the Numbers, May 2013." Deloitte Insights (2013https://www2.deloitte.com/insights/us/en/economy/issues-by-the-numbers/how-immigration-is-shaping-the-united-states.html

307 Gustavo Lopez, Kristen Bialik, and Jynnah Radford, "Key Findings about US Immigrants," *Pew Research Center* (September 14, 2018); http://www.pewresearch.org/fact-tank/2018/09/14/key-findings-about-u-s-immigrants/.

308 "Who Earns a Doctorate?", National Science Foundation, Doctorate Recipients from U.S. Universities: 2011; http://nsf.gov/statistics/sed/digest/2011/theme1.cfm#2.

309 Vivek Wadhwa, AnnaLee Saxenian, and F. Daniel Siciliano, *America's New Immigrant Entrepreneurs: Then and Now*, The Kauffman Foundation (October 2012); http://www.kauffman.org/uploadedFiles/Then_and_now_americas_new_immigrant_entrepreneurs.pdf.

310 Dr. Patricia Buckley (2018), "How immigration is shaping the United States: Issues by the Numbers, May 2013.," Deloitte Insights (20138);. Found at https://www2.deloitte.com/insights/us/en/legal/terms-of-use.html. https://www2.deloitte.com/insights/us/en/economy/issues-by-the-numbers/how-immigration-is-shaping-the-united-states.html.

311 Ibid.

312 Noah Smith, "Immigrants Haven't Hurt Pay for Americans: Wages Actually Rose Faster When More Foreign Laborers Were Entering the U.S.," *Bloomberg Opinion* (February 14, 2018, 2:00 AM PST); https://www.bloomberg.com/opinion/articles/2018-02-14/immigrants-haven-t-hurt-pay-for-americans. And Alan de Brauw, "Does Immigration Reduce Wages?" Cato Institute (Fall 2017); https://www.cato.org/cato-journal/fall-2017/does-immigration-reduce-wages.

313 Deborah Dsouza, "The Impact of Trump's H-1B Visa Crackdown in 5 Charts," Investopedia (August 1, 2018, 10:33 AM EDT); https://www.investopedia.com/news/impact-trumps-h1b-visa-crackdown-5-charts/.

314 Bureau of Labor Statistics, United States Department of Labor, (Feb. 2019). https://www.bls.gov/web/empsit/cpseea10.htm.

315 Mitra Toosi and Elka Torpey, "Older workers: labor force trends and career options," *Career Outlook*, (May 2017) Bureau of Labor Statistics, United States Department of Labor. https://www.bls.gov/careeroutlook/2017/article/older-workers.htm.

316 Julia Halpert, "The Suddenly Hot Job Market for Workers over 50," CNBC (March 20, 2018, 9:50 AM EDT); https://www.cnbc.com/2018/03/20/the-suddenly-hot-job-market-for-workers-over-50.html.

317 bid.

318 Ibid

319 Wolf Richter, Wolf Street, "Tech workers get better with age-but that's not stopping 'systematic' discrimination," (Oct. 2, 107, 6:44 PM),

320 United States Equal Employment Opportunity Commission, Charge Statistics (Charges filed with EEOC) FY1997 Through FY2017. https://www.eeoc.gov/eeoc/statistics/enforcement/charges.cfm.

CPSIA information can be obtained
at www.ICGtesting.com
Printed in the USA
LVHW090903300719
R15007400001B/R150074PG625367LVX1B/1/P